THE PAPERS OF
BENJAMIN FRANKLIN

SPONSORED BY

The American Philosophical Society
and Yale University

Benjamin Franklin: a miniature by C. Dixon

THE PAPERS OF

Benjamin Franklin

VOLUME 7 *October 1, 1756, through March 31, 1758*

LEONARD W. LABAREE, *Editor*

RALPH L. KETCHAM, *Associate Editor*

Helen C. Boatfield and Helene H. Fineman, Assistant Editors

New Haven and London YALE UNIVERSITY PRESS, 1963

Designed by Alvin Eisenman and Walter Howe, and printed in the United States of America at The Lakeside Press, R. R. Donnelley & Sons Company, Chicago, Illinois, and Crawfordsville, Indiana.

Library of Congress catalogue number: 59–12697

William E. Lingelbach: In Memoriam

Since the planning a decade ago of the publication of this edition of *The Papers of Benjamin Franklin*, an Administrative Board has been associated with the work. For these ten years the membership of this group has been continuous and unbroken, even its attendance record has been well nigh perfect. Now it is a melancholy duty to announce the first break in our ranks. Dr. William E. Lingelbach, sometime Professor of History and Dean of the College of the University of Pennsylvania, and long time member of the American Philosophical Society, took leave of this life on November 24, 1962, in his ninety-second year.

After retiring from the University he had made the study of Franklin a second career. As member and chairman of the Library Committee of the American Philosophical Society, as one of its secretaries and vice presidents, and latterly as its librarian, he had been indefatigable in collecting Frankliniana for the Society and in promoting a definitive edition of the Philosopher's work. Upon occasion, he contributed to the pages of the Society's publications the fruits of his study of Franklin's efforts in the "promotion of useful knowledge."

Those of us who were closely associated with him will never forget his interest and his infectious enthusiasm, his zeal for the project and his encouragement of its progress. His activity and vitality up unto the very end were remarkable. Rarely do men over ninety come so regularly to meetings which require travel and contribute such interest and knowledge to these deliberations. We can but record our loss and invite those who seek Franklin's wisdom to pause and think for a moment about one who shared so much of it.

Roy Franklin Nichols
Chairman of the Administrative Board

LR 08 h
4E

Contents

List of Illustrations

Miniature on ivory painted in October 1757 by C. Dixon, an artist of whom very little is known. "Franklin here wears a reddish purple banyan or dressing gown beneath which one sees his yellow waistcoat and white shirt, and on his head is the turbanlike cap which a gentleman wore in the privacy of his home, as a comfortable substitute for the wig. . . . It is reasonable to suppose that the picture shows Franklin as Dixon must have found him that autumn, ailing and confined." Charles C. Sellers, *Benjamin Franklin in Portraiture* (New Haven, 1962), pp. 47–50, 236–9, esp. 49–50. Franklin's "Account of Expences" shows that he paid Dixon six guineas for the miniature. He sent it to Deborah, Jan. 21, 1758, asking her to forward it to his sister Jane Mecom (see below, p. 365). One of her descendants presented it in 1899 to the Museum of Fine Arts in Boston, and it is here reproduced through the courtesy of the Museum.

Mezzotint engraving, 1755, by John Faber, Junior (1695?–1756), after an oil painting, 1747, by Allan Ramsay (1713–1784). Ramsay, official portrait painter to George III and also active as a political writer, had spent much of his time during his earlier years as an artist in his native city of Edinburgh, where among his closest friends were David Hume, Sir Alexander Dick, and others whom Franklin later also knew well. To Faber, who learned the art of mezzotint engraving from his father, "posterity owes the preservation of the school of portraiture which was in vogue between the days of Sir Godfrey Kneller . . . and those of Reynolds and Gainsborough." Ramsay's oil painting is in the possession of the Dowager Marchioness of Bute at Dumfries House, Cumnock, Ayershire; the Faber engraving is in the Scottish National Portrait Gallery, by whose courtesy it is here reproduced.

Franklin's drawing to illustrate his experiment showing that under identical conditions lead and wood have very different capacities for conducting heat. His original letter to Dr. John Lining, April 14, 1757, which contained this sketch has not been found, but he redrew

Contributors to Volume 7

The ownership of each manuscript, or the location of the particular copy used by the editors of each contemporary pamphlet or similar printed work, is indicated where the document appears in the text. The sponsors and editors are deeply grateful to the following institutions for permission to print in the present volume manuscripts or other materials which they own:

INSTITUTIONS

American Philosophical Society
Archives of the Moravian Church, Bethlehem
Franklin Institute, Philadelphia
Free Library of Philadelphia
Friends Library of the Society of Friends, London
Harvard College Library
Historical Society of Pennsylvania
Henry E. Huntington Library and Art Gallery
Library Company of Philadelphia
Library of Congress
Pierpont Morgan Library
Morristown National Historical Park, Morristown, New Jersey
Nantucket Atheneum
New-York Historical Society
New York Public Library
Pennsylvania Historical and Museum Commission
Princeton University Library
Public Record Office, London
Rosenbach Foundation
The Royal Society
Salem County Historical Society, Salem, New Jersey
Suffolk County Registry of Probate, Boston
Horace Howard Furness Memorial Library of the University of Pennsylavania
Trustees of the University of Pennsylvania
University of Pittsburgh Library
Yale University Library

Method of Textual Reproduction

An extended statement of the principles of selection, arrangement, form of presentation, and method of textual reproduction observed in this edition appears in the Introduction to the first volume, pp. xxxiv–xlvii. A condensation and revision of the portion relating to the method of reproducing the texts follows here.

Printed Material:

In general Franklin's writings printed under his direction should be regarded as his ultimate intention and should therefore be reproduced without change, except as modern typography requires. In fact, however, newspapers and pamphlets were often set by two or more journeymen with different notions of spelling, capitalization, and punctuation. Although the resulting inconsistencies and errors did not represent Franklin's intentions, they are not eliminated by the editors. Again, in cases where Franklin's writings were printed by another, they were sometimes carelessly or willfully revised without his consent. He once complained, for example, that an English printer had so corrected and excised one of his papers "that it can neither scratch nor bite. It seems only to paw and mumble."[1] What was thus printed was obviously not what Franklin wrote, but, in the absence of his manuscript, the editors have no alternative but to reprint it as it stands. Still other Franklin letters are known only in nineteenth-century printings, vigorously edited by William Temple Franklin, Duane, or Sparks. Here, too, the editors follow the texts as printed, only noting obvious misreadings.

In reproducing printed materials, the following general rules are observed:

1. The place and date of composition of letters are set at the top, regardless of their location in the original printing.

2. Proper nouns, including personal names, which were often printed in italics, are set in roman, except when the original was italicized for emphasis.

1. BF to William Franklin, Jan. 9, 1768.

3. Prefaces and other long passages, though italicized in the original, are set in roman. Long italicized quotations are set in roman within quotation marks.

4. Words in full capitals are set in small capitals, with initial letters in full capitals if required by Franklin's normal usage.

5. All signatures are set in capitals and small capitals.

6. Obvious typographical errors are silently corrected. An omitted parenthesis or quotation mark, for example, is inserted when the other of the pair was printed.

7. Every sentence is closed with a period or other appropriate mark of punctuation (usually a question mark).

8. Longhand insertions in the blanks of printed forms are set in italics, with space before and after.

Manuscript Material:

a. *Letters* are presented in the following form:

1. The place and date of composition are set at the top, regardless of their location in the original.

2. The complimentary close is set continuously with the text.

3. Addresses, endorsements, and docketing are so labeled and printed at the end of the letter.

b. *Spelling* of the original is retained. When, however, it is so abnormal as to obscure meaning, the correct form is supplied in brackets or footnote, as: "yf[wife]."

c. *Capitalization* has been retained as written, except that every sentence is made to begin with a capital. When there is doubt whether a letter is a capital, it is printed as like letters are in the same manuscript, or, that guide failing, as modern usage directs.

d. Words underlined once in the manuscript are printed in *italics;* words underlined twice or written in large letters or full capitals are printed in SMALL CAPITALS.

e. *Punctuation* has been retained as in the original, except:

1. Every sentence ends with a period or other appropriate mark (usually a question mark), unless it is not clear where the sentence ends, when the original punctuation (or lack of it) is preserved.

2. Dashes used in place of commas, semicolons, colons, or periods are replaced by the appropriate marks; and when a sentence ends with both a dash and a period, the dash is omitted.

3. Commas scattered meaninglessly through a manuscript are eliminated.

4. When a mark of punctuation is not clear or can be read as one of two marks, modern usage is followed.[2]

5. Some documents, especially those of a legal character, lack all punctuation. This is supplied with restraint, and the fact indicated in a footnote. In some other, inadequately punctuated documents, it is silently added when needed for clarity, as in a long series of names.

f. *Contractions and abbreviations* in general are expanded except in proper names. The ampersand is rendered as "and," except in the names of business firms, in the form "&c.," and in a few other cases. Letters represented by the thorn or tilde are printed. The tailed "p" is spelled out as per, pre, or pro. Symbols of weights, measures, and monetary values follow modern usage, as: £34. Superscript letters are lowered. Abbreviations in current use are retained, as: Col., Dr., N.Y., i.e.

g. *Omitted or illegible words or letters* are treated as follows:

1. If not more than four letters are missing, they are silently supplied when there is no doubt what they should be.

2. The omission of more than four letters or one or more words is supplied conjecturally within brackets. The addition of a question mark within the brackets indicates uncertainty as to the conjecture.

3. Other omissions are shown as follows: [*illegible*], [*torn*], [*remainder missing*], or the like.

4. Missing or illegible digits are indicated by suspension points in brackets, the number of points corresponding to the estimated number of missing figures.

5. Blank spaces are left as blanks.

2. The typescripts from which these papers are printed have been made from photocopies of the manuscripts, and marks of punctuation are sometimes blurred or lost in photography. It has often been impossible to consult the originals in these cases.

h. *Author's additions and corrections.*

1. Interlineations and brief marginal notes are brought into the text without comment. Longer notes are brought into the text with the notation [*in the margin*].

2. Author's footnotes are printed at the bottom of the appropriate pages between the text and any editorial footnotes.

3. Canceled words and phrases are in general omitted without notice; if significant, they are printed in footnotes. The canceled passages of important documents, such as drafts of treaties, are brought into the text enclosed in angle brackets *before* the words substituted.

4. When alternative words and phrases have been inserted in a manuscript but the original remains uncanceled, the alternatives are given in brackets, preceded by explanatory words in italics, as: "it is [*written above:* may be] true."

5. Variant readings of several versions are noted if important.

Abbreviations and Short Titles

ADS	Autograph document signed.[1]
ALS	Autograph letter signed.
APS	American Philosophical Society.
BF	Benjamin Franklin.
Bigelow, *Works*	John Bigelow, ed., *The Complete Works of Benjamin Franklin* . . . (10 vols., N.Y., 1887–88.)
Cohen, *BF's Experiments*	I. Bernard Cohen, ed., *Benjamin Franklin's Experiments. A New Edition of Franklin's Experiments and Observations on Electricity* (Cambridge, Mass., 1941).
Colden Paps.	*The Letters and Papers of Cadwallader Colden.* New-York Historical Society *Collections* for 1917–23, 1934, 1935.
DAB	*Dictionary of American Biography.*
DNB	*Dictionary of National Biography.*
DS	Document signed.
Darlington, *Memorials*	William Darlington, *Memorials of John Bartram and Humphry Marshall* (Phila., 1849).
Dexter, *Biog. Sketches*	Franklin B. Dexter, *Biographical Sketches of the Graduates of Yale College* . . . (6 vols., N.Y. and New Haven, 1885–1912).
DF	Deborah Franklin
Duane, *Works*	William Duane, ed., *The Works of Dr. Benjamin Franklin* . . . (6 vols., Phila., 1808–18). Title varies in the several volumes.
Eddy, *Ledger "D"*	George Simpson Eddy, *Account Books Kept by Benjamin Franklin* [Volume II]. *Ledger "D," 1739–1747* (N.Y., 1929).
Evans	Charles Evans, *American Bibliography* (14 vols., Chicago and Worcester,

1. For definitions of this and other kinds of manuscripts, see above, I, xliv–xlvii.

	Mass., 1903–59). Surviving imprints are reproduced in full in microprint in Clifford K. Shipton, ed., *Early American Imprints, 1639–1800* (microprint, Worcester, Mass.).
Exper. and Obser.	*Experiments and Observations on Electricity, made at Philadelphia in America, by Mr. Benjamin Franklin, ...* (London, 1751). Revised and enlarged editions were published in 1754, 1760, 1769, and 1774 with slightly varying titles. In each case the edition cited will be indicated, e.g., *Exper. and Obser.*, 1751 edit.
Gipson, *British Empire*	Lawrence H. Gipson, *The British Empire before the American Revolution* 10 vols. to date: Volumes 1–3, Caldwell, Idaho, 1936; Volumes 4–10, N.Y., 1939–61; Volumes 1–3, revised edit., N.Y., 1958–60.
Hunter, *Forts*	William A. Hunter, *Forts on the Pennsylvania Frontier, 1753–1758* (Harrisburg, 1960).
Lib. Co. Phila.	Library Company of Philadelphia.
LS	Letter signed.
MS, MSS	Manuscript, manuscripts.
Montgomery, *Hist. Univ. Pa.*	Thomas H. Montgomery, *A History of the University of Pennsylvania from its Foundation to A.D. 1770* (Phila., 1900).
N.J. Arch.	William A. Whitehead and others, eds., *Archives of the State of New Jersey* (2 series, Newark and elsewhere, 1880–). Editors, subtitles, and places of publication vary.
PMHB	*Pennsylvania Magazine of History and Biography.*
Pa. Arch.	Samuel Hazard and others, eds., *Pennsylvania Archives* (9 series, Phila. and Harrisburg, 1852–1935).
Pa. Col. Recs.	*Minutes of the Provincial Council of Pennsylvania* ... (16 vols., Phila.,

	1838–53). Title changes with Volume 11 to *Supreme Executive Council.*
Pa. Gaz.	*The Pennsylvania Gazette.*
Pa. Jour.	*The Pennsylvania Journal.*
Pargellis, *Lord Loudoun*	Stanley M. Pargellis, *Lord Loudoun in North America* (New Haven, 1933).
Pargellis, *Military Affairs*	Stanley Pargellis, *Military Affairs in North America 1748–1765* (New York, 1936).
Par. Text edit.	Max Farrand, ed., *Benjamin Franklin's Memoirs. Parallel Text Edition . . .* (Berkeley and Los Angeles, 1949).
Phil. Trans.	The Royal Society, *Philosophical Transactions.*
Sibley's Harvard Graduates	John L. Sibley, *Biographical Sketches of Graduates of Harvard University* (Cambridge, Mass. 1873–). Continued from Volume 4 by Clifford K. Shipton.
Smyth, *Writings*	Albert H. Smyth, ed., *The Writings of Benjamin Franklin . . .* (10 vols., N.Y., 1905–07).
Sparks, *Works*	Jared Sparks, ed., *The Works of Benjamin Franklin . . .* (10 vols., Boston, 1836–40).
Van Doren, *Franklin*	Carl Van Doren, *Benjamin Franklin* (N.Y., 1938).
Van Doren, *Franklin-Mecom*	Carl Van Doren, ed., *The Letters of Benjamin Franklin & Jane Mecom* (Memoirs of the American Philosophical Society, XXVII, Princeton, 1950).
Votes	*Votes and Proceedings of the House of Representatives of the Province of Pennsylvania, Met at Philadelphia . . . 1750, and continued by Adjournments* (Phila., 1751–).
WTF, *Memoirs*	William Temple Franklin, ed., *Memoirs of the Life and Writings of Benjamin Franklin, LL.D., F.R.S. &c. . . .* (3 vols., 4to, London, 1817–18).
WF	William Franklin

Genealogical references. An editorial reference to one of Franklin's relatives may be accompanied by a citation of the symbol assigned to that person in the genealogical tables and charts in volume I of this work, pp. xlix-lxxvii, as, for example: Thomas Franklin (A.5.2.1), Benjamin Mecom (C.17.3), or Benjamin Franklin Bache (D.3.1).

Chronology

October 1, 1756, through March 31, 1758

1756

October 2–14: BF accompanies Governor Denny on inspection trip to Susquehanna Valley.

October 15: Disallowance of Militia Act announced in Philadelphia, voiding BF's commission as colonel.

November 5–18: BF attends Indian conference at Easton.

December 26: BF and Col. Henry Bouquet settle quartering dispute.

1757

February 3: BF appointed Pennsylvania Assembly agent in England.

March 14–27: Lord Loudoun in Philadelphia for council of war; confers with BF and Denny on local political disputes.

March 23: Denny accepts £100,000 supply bill on Loudoun's advice.

April 4: BF and WF leave Philadelphia for New York to embark.

April 8–June 5: BF in New York and vicinity awaiting passage to England (for detailed chronology see below, p. 174).

June 5–20: BF on board packet *General Wall,* at anchor off Sandy Hook with vessels of Louisbourg expedition.

June 20–July 17: BF and WF on voyage to Falmouth, England.

July 7: BF finishes writing preface for *Poor Richard improved* for 1758: "Father Abraham's Speech," later known in shortened form as "The Way to Wealth."

July 17–26: BF and WF travel from Falmouth to London.

July 30: BF and WF take lodgings at No. 7 Craven Street, with Mrs. Margaret Stevenson.

August 13–20: BF has first conferences with Thomas and Richard Penn; submits Heads of Complaint.

September 7: BF attends meeting of the Society of Arts for the first time.

September–October: BF seriously ill; attended by Dr. John Fothergill.

November 14: BF resumes conferences with Thomas Penn.

November 24: BF attends meeting of the Royal Society, signs obligation, and is formally admitted as a fellow.

December 21: BF appears before the Board of Trade for the first time.

1758

January 6: Pennsylvania Assembly commits Rev. William Smith to jail for contempt; recommits him after hearing on January 25; BF learns of these events at least by late March.

January 12: BF confers with Proprietors on Indian trade bill and acquires a "cordial and thorough Contempt" for Thomas Penn.

January 27: BF confers with Proprietors on new supply bill.

THE PAPERS OF BENJAMIN FRANKLIN

VOLUME 7

October 1, 1756, through March 31, 1758

Provincial Commissioners:[1] Orders for Payment

DS: Historical Society of Pennsylvania

The last orders for payments under the £60,000 act of Nov. 27, 1755, were signed by the provincial commissioners July 22, before Franklin's return from New York.[2] They were unable to issue any more orders until early October, when funds provided by the £30,000 act of September 21 became available. The thirty-eight orders signed between October 4 and November 5, when a majority of the commissioners prepared to accompany Governor Denny to the Easton conference with the Indians, are listed below in the same form as those signed earlier (see above, VI, 392–5). The first order, dated at Lancaster, in Franklin's hand and signed also by Governor Denny, and the second order, were both drawn during Franklin's western journey with the governor (see below, p. 9 n). The orders which Franklin did not sign are indicated by an asterisk (*).

Date	*Payee*	*Purpose*	*Amount* £	*s.*	*d.*
October					
4	Capt. Hugh Mercer	Pay for himself, July 1 to Oct. 1	46	0	0
12	James Young	To pay troops; delivered to Thomas Apty	5000	0	0
16*	Benjamin Franklin	Advances; expenses in Cumberland Co.	801	3	5
16*	Conrad Weiser	Victualling Capt. Busse's co., June 17 to Oct. 6	233	4	0
16*	Conrad Weiser	Indian expenses	36	8	3
22	Thomas Apty	Riding expresses for the government	26	1	5
22	James Ennis	Riding several expresses	60	9	0
22	Joseph Fox	To discharge sundry accounts	100	0	0
22	John Hughes	Rum and paper sent to frontiers; advances to Edw. Croston[3]	114	15	6

1. The £30,000 supply act passed Sept. 21, 1756 (above, VI, 515 n), provided for expenditure of the money by commissioners named in the act, as had the £60,000 act of Nov. 27, 1755. Those appointed were: from the Assembly, Speaker Isaac Norris, BF, Joseph Fox, John Hughes, and William Masters; from the Council, Lynford Lardner and John Mifflin. Masters and Lardner replaced Evan Morgan and James Hamilton, respectively, who had been commissioners under the previous measure. When BF went to England in 1757, his place as commissioner was taken by Joseph Galloway.

2. See above, VI, 470 n, 472, on BF's trip to New York from about June 20 to July 28, 1756.

3. See above, VI, facing p. 392, for a facsimile of an earlier order to pay Edward Croston.

Date	*Payee*	*Purpose*	*Amount* £	s.	d.
22	Capt. Samuel Mifflin	Bounties for 31 seamen sent to join Commodore Spry, and their maintenance and passage to Halifax	242	15	6
22	Capt. John Welsh	Pay drawn by James Young, Oct. 17	60	0	0
23	Barnabas Hughes	Accounts settled by Commrs. of Provisions	259	8	2
25	William Buchanan	Furnishing garrisons west of Susquehanna, incl. £156 for Wm. West and £200 for John Smith	428	6	6¾
25	Dr. Thomas Graeme	Medicines for Indians, Mar. 3 to July 15	37	13	6
25	William Griffitts	Duffels, shoes and stockings for troops	411	4	3
25	Adam Hoops	Provisions, and payment to Saml. Neave	1152	0	7½
25	Andrew Meacomson	Maintenance of French Neutrals on Province Island	14	7	0
25	Wharton & Story	Sundries	53	8	5
26	Joseph Fox	To be paid for public service	100	0	0
27	Lt. Col. John Armstrong	Pay	40	0	0
27	Capt. Joseph Inslee	Account settled as of Sept. 11	189	6	2
27	Samuel Neave	Goods furnished for July treaty at Easton	63	7	0
27	Conrad Weiser	Maintaining his co. at Reading; expresses	153	1	6
29	Lt. Col. John Armstrong	Horse-hire and loss, pilots in Kittanning expedition[4]	349	13	0
29	Peter Bard or his wife	Salary as commissary general of stores and provisions	46	10	0
29	Adam Deshler	Provisions furnished forces in Northampton Co.	259	18	7
29	James Young	To pay provincial forces [only received £1900]	6000	0	0
30	Lt. Col. John Armstrong	Scalps and prisoners from Kittanning	271	17	6
30	Allen & Turner	408 muskets, etc. and 15 months' interest	1074	12	0

4. Armstrong scored a limited victory by an attack on the Indian settlements at Kittanning on the Allegheny River, Aug. 30–Sept. 14, 1756. William A Hunter, "Victory at Kittanning," *Pa. Hist.*, XXIII (1956), 376–407; Hunter, *Forts*, pp. 405–10.

Date	Payee	Purpose	Amount		
November			£	s.	d.
1	Richard Peters	Expresses and Indian expense	238	9	7
1	Jonas Seely	Victualling Capt. Morgan's co., paid to Daniel Harvey	378	19	0
4	Sebastian Levan	Per Jacob Levan's provisioning Capt. Andrew Engel's co.	227	14	0
4	John Moore's widow	Service of husband as wagoner	19	0	0
4	Isaac Norris	Expenses of gov.'s trip to Easton; presents to Indians; signed over to Joseph Fox	500	0	0
4	Capt. John Van Etten	Account, Sept. 16, for service of his co.	477	4	0
4	Capt. John Van Etten	Balance for co. to Nov. 1	83	9	2
5	Capt. Edward Croston	Provisions for provincial forces	1500	0	0
5	David Edwards	Attendance on commissioners	10	0	0

Pennsylvania Assembly: Reply to the Governor

Printed in *Votes and Proceedings of the House of Representatives*, 1756–1757 (Philadelphia, 1757), pp. 23–4.

When the newly elected Assembly met to organize on October 14, Governor Denny informed it that "several weighty Affairs" required their immediate attention: viz., an embargo on food, clothing, and warlike stores to possessions of France; provision for transporting and quartering British troops which might be stationed in the province; the need for new defense appropriations in view of rumors of enemy aggression; a new militia law to replace the one recently disallowed by the King; and a plan to deal with the Indians expected to appear in the province for a conference.[1] Though it made no formal reply, the Assembly discussed the message during the next two weeks and took several steps in pursuance of its requests. A committee appointed the 20th brought in an embargo bill the next day, but no further action was taken on it. On the 21st Franklin and others were asked to bring in a bill regulating transportation for the King's troops, the next day he and still others were appointed to draw a quartering bill, and on the 23d the provincial commissioners were asked to pay the Indian expenses. Following a message from Denny telling of more Indian attacks, Franklin and others were appointed to confer with him on "the most proper Manner of disposing of"

1. Message of Oct. 19, 1756, and accompanying papers, *Votes*, 1756–57, pp. 6–13.

the Indians who had come to Philadelphia. The same day the Assembly requested an estimate of defense costs for the coming year and resumed its consideration of a new militia law. On October 28 Franklin brought in "a Bill for regulating the Forces in the Pay of this Province," delivered (as its president) the annual report of the Pennsylvania Hospital, and was appointed to a committee to draft a new militia law. The next day Denny told the House that Teedyuscung and over 100 threatening Indians were near Fort Allen expecting to meet the governor in treaty as had been planned at Easton the previous July. Since such a treaty would violate Lord Loudoun's most explicit orders,[2] Denny asked the Assembly for its advice. Franklin and others were appointed to draft a reply (printed here), which was done in half an hour, then amended, approved, and promptly delivered to Denny.[3]

May it please your HONOUR, [October 29, 1756]

We have considered your Honour's Message of this Day, with Lord Loudoun's Letter, laid before us at the Beginning of the Session. And since you are pleased to ask our Opinion and Advice on this important Occasion, we shall give it with all dutiful Freedom and Sincerity.

We are truly thankful to our gracious Sovereign for the late wise Regulation of putting Indian Affairs, especially those that relate to War or Peace with them, under a more general Direction than they have heretofore been, as we think the British Interest will now have more Weight with the Indians, than if separate Treaties of Peace might be made by separate Colonies for themselves, without consulting the Interest or Safety of their Neighbours. We cannot therefore desire, however burdensome the present War with the Indians may be to this Province, that such a separate Treaty should be concluded on our Behalf. We are, however, of Opinion, that the Treaty begun by the late Governor (before Sir William Johnson's Powers were made known)[4] in Pursuance of which the

2. Contained in his letter to Denny, Sept. 22, 1756, of which the governor had sent a copy to the Assembly, *ibid.*, p. 12.

3. *Ibid.*, pp. 14–24.

4. Governor Morris had agreed at the Easton treaty, July 28–31, 1756, to meet again with the Indians in two or three months time. He hoped that by then they would have further organized their councils and might make conclusive agreements to aid the English. Carl Van Doren and Julian P. Boyd, eds., *Indian Treaties Printed by Benjamin Franklin* (Phila., 1938), pp. lxxvi–lxxviii. Morris did, however, know of Johnson's commission as sole Indian agent before he met the Indians at Easton. *Pa. Col. Recs.*, VII, 192–4.

Indians are now come down, should not be wholly discontinued on our Part, lest the Indians be disgusted, and the Opportunity of bringing them to a general Peace with all the British Colonies be lost. We rather think it adviseable, that your Honour would give them an Interview, make them the customary Presents, in Behalf of this Government, to relieve their Necessities, and assure them of our sincere Inclination to take them again into Friendship, forgive their Offences, and make a firm Peace with them; but at the same time to let them know, that the Government of this Province cannot agree to make a Peace with them for itself, and leave them at Liberty to continue the War with our Brethren of the neighbouring Colonies: That we are all Subjects of one great King, and must, for the future, be all at Peace or all at War with other Nations at the same Time: That our King has appointed Sir William Johnson to manage these general Treaties for all the Governments in this Part of America, and to him we must therefore refer the Indians for a final Conclusion and Ratification of this Treaty; promising also to write to him, acquaint him with the good Dispositions the Indians have shown at these Conferences, and recommend it to him to make the Agreement firm and lasting for all Parties. An Interview of this Kind with the Indians, we apprehend, may at this Time be greatly for His Majesty's Service, and for the Advantage not only of this, but of all the neighbouring Colonies, and not inconsistent with the Intention of Lord Loudoun's Letter: Which we nevertheless submit to your Honour's prudent Consideration.[5]

5. Denny and the Assembly each hoped and assumed that the negotiations would be held in Philadelphia, but the Indians refused to come down; Denny and his advisors went to Easton to meet them in mid-November. See below, pp. 15–23. Richard Peters and other proprietary officials resented the order excluding them from Indian negotiations long in their charge and were determined to preserve their influence one way or another. Peters wrote Thomas Penn, Oct. 2, 1756, that "all our friendly Indians will soon turn against us and we shall have a most lamentable winter" if Loudoun's order were obeyed. Peters abhorred the order all the more because he thought it "dictated by Mr. Pownal who ... is the Councellor and Preparer of Letters of Business with Lord Loudoun and is in close confederacy with Mr. Franklin." *PMHB,* XXXI (1907), 247. But see above, VI, 487, for BF's own disgust at Johnson's Indian policy.

Mutiny Act

Reprinted (in part only) from *The Statutes at Large of Pennsylvania from 1682 to 1801*, v (Wm. Stanley Ray, State Printer of Pennsylvania, 1898), 266–8.

The Mutiny Act passed on April 15, 1756 (see above, VI, 434–7), expired by its own limitation on October 30. Two days before that event Franklin brought in a bill, by leave of the House, to renew the law for a short term. With nearly a minimum of debate in the Assembly and discussion with the governor the bill was enacted on November 4.[6] Except for the substitution of Denny's name for that of Morris in the enacting clause, the law was identical with the one it succeeded down to the final sentence of the first act, which specified its terminal date. That sentence was omitted and the paragraphs printed below were substituted. The identical portion is not reprinted here.

[November 4, 1756]

* * * * *

And in order to prevent all doubts that may arise in relation to punishing of crimes and offenses committed against a former act of assembly of this province, entitled "An act for regulating the officers and soldiers commissionated and raised by the governor for the defense of this province":

Be it declared and enacted by the authority aforesaid, That all crimes and offenses which have been committed against the said former act shall and may during the continuance of this present act be inquired of, heard, tried, determined, adjudged and punished before and by the like courts, persons, powers, authorities, ways, means and methods as the like crimes and offenses committed against this present act may be inquired of, heard, tried, determined, adjudged and punished.

This act to continue and to be in force until the twenty-fifth day of March next and no longer.[7]

6. *Votes*, 1756–57, pp. 17, 25, 26–7. The governor suggested that the number of officers required to constitute a general court martial might well be reduced from the thirteen required by the British Mutiny Act, because of the difficulty of getting so many together in Pennsylvania, but the House replied that the bill was only to be in effect for a short time and, since Denny was in a hurry to get away for an Indian conference at Easton and any change would take time, the proposed alteration should be postponed. Denny acquiesced.

7. On December 14 the Assembly appointed a committee, which did not include BF, to bring in a new bill for regulating the troops raised by the

To Peter Collinson

ALS: Pierpont Morgan Library; also extract: The Royal Society[8]

Dear Friend Nov. 5. 1756

The above is a Copy of my last, and I now send the two second Bills of Steevens and Ludwell.[9] I wrote then in great Hurry, being just setting out for the Frontiers, to visit some of the Forts with the Governor; a long Journey.[1] Since our Return, I have scarce had a Moment's Time to write to my Friends, the Assembly sitting twice a day, and twice a Day the Commissioners for laying out the last given £30,000 besides continually, when at home, hearing People who have Business to lay before the Assembly or Commissioners. And now I am just ordered by the House to attend the Governor at Easton in Northampton County, on a Treaty with the Delaware Indians:[2] We set out immediately, so must entreat your Excuse if I do not write fully.

I have before me your several Favours of May 27. June 3. June 4. and 30. and July 9.[3] The Quakers have now pretty generally declined their Seats in Assembly, very few remaining. We shall soon see if Matters will be better managed by a Majority of different

---

governor. The measure was reported Jan. 6, 1757, and passed the House six days later. The governor proposed an amendment to make the number of officers necessary for a general court martial not less than seven nor more than thirteen, but did not adhere to it over the Assembly's objection. He signed the measure on January 18. The act repeated the main text of its predecessors virtually without change and made its terms applicable to military offenses committed against those acts; it was to remain in force until March 25, 1758. BF was not directly concerned in its drafting nor, except as a voting member of the Assembly, in its passage. *Votes*, 1756–57, pp. 47, 64, 66, 68–70; *Pa. Col. Recs.*, VII, 390–2; *Stat. at Large of Pa.*, V, 281–3.

8. The extract, in Collinson's hand, is of the first three sentences of the third paragraph.

9. See above, VI, 532.

1. BF, James Hamilton, Governor Denny, and military engineer Elias Meyer, visited Carlisle, Harris's Ferry, and York, October 2–14, though they apparently did not go to Fort Augusta, the main post on the frontier. *Pa. Gaz.*, Oct. 7 and 21, 1756; 1 *Pa. Arch.*, III, 8–10. Denny told his Council that they had "found the Frontiers in a deplo[rable] Condition; . . . the People dispirited . . . [and] . . . earnest for a Militia." *Pa. Col. Recs.*, VII, 278.

2. See the documents immediately following.

3. None of these letters have been found.

religious Persuasions.[4] The Governor tells me, that you recommended me to him very warmly,[5] for which accept my grateful Acknowledgments. We have, I think, a very good Understanding with each other. He was pleased to offer me any Service in his Power. My Answer was, that I had at present no Favour to ask, that I was nevertheless oblig'd to him for his frank Offers of Friendship; would always be ready to do him any honest Service, requesting only in Return his Good Will and Good Opinion.[6]

4. See above, VI, 456 n, for the first resignation of Quaker Assemblymen. Three more Quakers who had voted against defense measures were not reelected in October 1756, and four others resigned on the 16th, two days after the new Assembly's first meeting. This left but six of the seventeen members (mostly Quakers) who had voted against the Mutiny Act still in the Assembly. Anglicans predominated among those who replaced the Quakers. According to *Pa. Gaz.*, Oct. 7, 1756, sixteen Quakers were elected to the new Assembly, only twelve of whom remained after the resignations later in the month. The October 1st election had been conducted under conflicting stresses of war news and political alignments. Early in September Richard Peters reported that BF would have his own way since William Allen and James Hamilton refused to exert themselves, but alarmed by the loss of Oswego, they and Benjamin Chew conferred with BF and decided upon a slate for Philadelphia Co. which included two proprietary men. The Quakers refused to back them, and in their places secured the election of Joseph Galloway and John Baynton, both "bitter on the side of the Party." Thus, though the strict Quakers had pledged to retire from the Assembly, Peters felt the Quaker electioneering had been "assiduous," and that their political influence was as strong as ever. The result was deplorable: "A weaker Assembly never was in the world; it looks, as if the Quakers in a passion of resentment, had chosen the most ignorant and headstrong wretches they could pick up" to be guided at every step by "two ill-disposed Persons [BF and Isaac Norris]." Peters to Penn, Sept. 4, 16, and 22, Oct. 2 and 30, Dec. 11, 1756; Robert Hunter Morris to William Alexander, Oct. 10, 1756, Penn Papers, Hist. Soc. Pa.; *Votes*, 1755–56, pp. 15, 31, 54, 74, 101; *Votes*, 1756–57, pp. 3–5.

5. At dinner with Collinson about June 1, just before he sailed for America, Denny had expressed his determination "if possible to heal all differences." Collinson found Denny "a mild, moderate man," and doubtless recommended BF to him as an ally in his peacable intentions. Darlington, *Memorials*, p. 208.

6. See above, VI, 489 n, for other comments, including BF's, about Governor Denny. His offer of friendship made at an entertainment shortly after his arrival, was recalled more fully by BF in his autobiography: "After Dinner, when the Company as was customary at that time, were engag'd in Drinking, he took me aside into another Room, and acquainted me that he had been advis'd by his Friends in England to cultivate a Friendship with me, as one who was capable of giving him the best Advice, and of contributing most

Your Information of my being chosen a Member of the Royal Society, was extreamly agreable, and the more, as I had not the least Expectation of ever arriving at that Honour. The Diploma you mention, is not yet come to hand. I must request the Favour of you to present my humble Thanks to the Society, whose truly noble Designs I wish I may be able in any Degree to promote. Please to pay for me the yearly and other Charges that arise on such Occasions, out of any Money of mine in your Hands.[7] Of late I have said nothing to you on Philosophical Subjects, for I fear I overdos'd you with my last Pacquet from Boston.[8] I had lately a

effectually to the making his Administration easy. That he therefore desired of all things to have a good Understanding with me; and he begg'd me to be assur'd of his Readiness on all Occasions to render me every Service that might be in his Power. He said much to me also of the Proprietor's good Dispositions towards the Province, and of the Advantage it might be to us all, and to me in particular, if the Opposition that had been so long continu'd to his Measures, were dropt, and Harmony restor'd between him and the People, in effecting which it was thought no one could be more serviceable than my self, and I might depend on adequate Acknowledgements and Recompences, &c. &c. The Drinkers finding we did not return immediately to the Table, sent us a Decanter of Madeira, which the Governor made liberal Use of, and in proportion became more profuse of his Solicitations and Promises. My Answers were to this purpose, that my Circumstances, Thanks to God, were such as to make Proprietary Favours unnecessary to me; and that being a Member of the Assembly I could not possibly accept of any; that however I had no personal Enmity to the Proprietary, and that whenever the public Measures he propos'd should appear to be for the Good of the People, no one should espouse and forward them more zealously than my self, my past Opposition having been founded on this, that the Measures which had been urg'd were evidently intended to serve the Proprietary Interest with great Prejudice to that of the People. That I was much obliged to him (the Governor) for his Professions of Regard to me, and that he might rely on every thing in my Power to make his Administration as easy to him as possible, hoping at the same time that he had not brought with him the same unfortunate Instructions his Predecessor had been hamper'd with." Par. Text edit., pp. 388–90.

7. See above, VI, 375–6. Collinson read the first three sentences of this paragraph at a meeting of the Society, Feb. 24, 1757. Royal Society Archives. The Society had already voted, July 15, 1756, to waive the charges mentioned. Raymond P. Stearns, "Colonial Fellows of the Royal Society of London, 1661–1788," 3 *Wm. and Mary Quar.*, III (1946), 244–6.

8. BF had apologized to Collinson, Dec. 29, 1754, from Boston, for not sending him the scientific writings finally conveyed on June 26, 1755. See above, V, 453, and VI, 83–4.

Letter from Paullus Frisi of St. Alexander's College at Milan,[9] who writes to me as if I liv'd in London, and desires me to mention a Matter to Mr. Short,[1] which I can only do, by transcribing that Part of the Letter, and desiring you to show it to that Gentleman, viz. "Optarem etiam, ut Cl. Short reverentiam meam, et gratum animum testeris, quodque occasione data animadversiones meas circa controversum illum Newtoni errorem judicio ipsius submittam."[2]

I deliver'd the Letter inclos'd in yours of June 3. to Smith. But your former Letter relating to his Freemason Sermon[3] he never had as I suppose; for I receiv'd it when abroad, and lost it with some other Papers, that I hoped to recover, but have not. And he and I not being on speaking Terms, I have said nothing to him about it. He has scribbled himself into universal Dislike here: The Proprietary Faction alone countenance him a little; but the Academy dwindles, and will come to nothing if he is continued.[4]

9. Paolo Frisi (1728–1784), Italian astronomer and mathematician, author of many works on scientific subjects, and member of nearly every learned society in Europe, probably saw BF in London, 1766, and for nearly 30 years they were associated from time to time in the international brotherhood of science. Antonio Pace, *Benjamin Franklin and Italy* (Phila., 1958), pp. 34–5. The letter from him has not been found.

1. James Short (1710–1768), optician of London and Edinburgh; F.R.S., 1737; recognized as the foremost maker of glass specula of his day. *DNB*.

2. Letters of John Dolland and Leonhard Euler differing on some Newtonian propositions on aberration in refracting telescopes were presented to the Royal Society by Short in 1752, but there is no record of any contribution by Frisi to the controversy. *Phil. Trans.*, XLVIII, 287–96.

3. William Smith, *A Sermon preached in Christ-Church, Philadelphia; before the provincial grand master, and general communication of Free and Accepted Masons. On Tuesday the 24th of June, 1755* ... Printed by Franklin and Hall, [1755] (Evans 7571).

4. See above, VI, 420–2 n, 457 n, for Smith's political writings, and below, p. 50, for the Academy's enrollment. BF's replacement as president of the Academy's Board of Trustees by Richard Peters, May 11, 1756, doubtless increased the fears of many non-Anglicans that the Academy, contrary to the intent of its founders, was fast becoming sectarian, a circumstance responsible for the withdrawal of both students and financial support. In the midst of the controversy over Smith's "politicking," however, both the students and Trustees had expressed their confidence in him. Montgomery, *Hist. Univ. Pa.*, pp. 227, 273. BF wrote Ebenezer Kinnersley, July 28, 1759: "Before I left Philadelphia, everything to be done at the Academy was privately preconcerted in a Cabal without my Knowledge or Participation."

I am sorry we have no good News in this Part of the World to ballance your Loss of Minorca. Oswego is taken, and a fine New England Army, collected at Lake George, is, thro' Inaction, wasted by Sickness and Desertion, so as to be at present of little Strength or Value; and I am afraid those Governments will be unable to produce such another for the next Campaign. These Northern Colonies have a vast Frontier to defend, and the Expence is excessive, much less Money would defray an Expedition by Sea against Quebec: That, in my Opinion, will be our most effectual Defence, and much the cheapest.

Runkin is not yet arriv'd, on board whome you have put the Air Pump, &c.[5] The Invoice I have receiv'd per last Ship.

You write that "you hear I ride about with a Party of Men with drawn Swords, which gives great Offence to some Folks." I wonder who could think it worth their While to send such trifling News to England,[6] or how it has been represented so as to give Offence. I must tell you the Matter as it was. The People happen to love me. Perhaps that's my Fault. When I was on the Frontier last Winter, a great Number of the Citizens, as I was told, intended to come out and meet me at my Return, to express their thankful Sense of my (small) Services. To prevent this, I made a forc'd March, and got to Town in the Night, by which they were disappointed, and some a little chagrined. But as I could not fully conceal the Time of my setting out for Virginia, 20 Officers of my Regiment with about 30 Grenadiers, presented themselves on Horseback at my Door just as I was going to mount, to accompany me to the Ferry about 3 Miles from Town. Till we got to the End of the Street, which is about 200 Yards, the Grenadiers took it in their Heads to ride with their Swords drawn, but there they put them up peace-

5. See below, pp. 23, 50.

6. Richard Peters made such a report to Thomas Penn, June 1, 1756; see below, pp. 72–3. Collinson had other sources of criticism for BF's conduct, however; Cadwallader Colden had written him, April 23, 1756, of Pennsylvania's "infatuated" persistence in "the greatest civil confusions" during the Indian attacks, and added that "Mr. Franklin's conduct is the most surprising to me of any thing. I can no way account for it, so as to give my mind satisfaction consistently with the esteem I had of him." Collinson replied that he was "really a Stranger to Mr. Franklin's conduct. I wish you had been more explicite on that Head." Maggs Bros. Catalogue No. 320 (Jan.–Feb. 1914), pp. 37–8; *Colden Paps.*, V, 104.

ably into their Scabboards, without hurting or even terrifying Man, Woman or Child; and from the Ferry where we took Leave and parted, they all returned as quietly to their Homes. This was the only Instance of the kind: For tho' a greater Number met me at my Return, they did not ride with drawn Swords, having been told that Ceremony was improper, unless to compliment some Person of great Distinction. I, who am totally ignorant of military Ceremonies, and above all things averse to making Show and Parade, or doing any useless Thing that can serve only to excite Envy or provoke Malice, suffer'd at the Time much more Pain than I enjoy'd Pleasure, and have never since given an Opportunity for anything of the Sort.[7]

The Proprietors, you write me word, are greatly incensed at some Parts of my late Conduct. I am not much concern'd at that, because if I have offended them *by acting right,* I can, whenever I please, remove their Displeasure, *by acting wrong*. Tho' at present I have not the least Inclination to be in their good Graces on those Terms. I have some natural Dislike to Persons who so far *Love Money,* as to be *unjust* for its sake: I despise their *Meanness,* (as it appears to me) in several late Instances, most cordially, and am thankful that I never had any Connection with them, or Occasion to ask or receive a Favour at their hands.[8] For now I am persuaded that I do not oppose their Views from Pique, Disappointment, or personal Resentment, but, as I think, from a Regard to the Publick Good. I may be mistaken in what is that Publick Good; but at least I mean well. And whenever they appear to me to have the Publick Good in View, I think I would as readily serve them as if they were my best Friends. I am sometimes asham'd for them, when I see them differing with their People for Trifles, and instead of being ador'd, as they might be, like Demi Gods, become the Objects of universal Hatred and Contempt. How must they have managed, when, with all the Power their Charter, the Laws and their Wealth give them, a private Person (forgive your Friend a little Vanity, as it's only between ourselves) can do more Good in their Country

7. See above, VI, 425 n, for another account of this incident.

8. Over a year earlier (July 3, 1755), Thomas Penn had written otherwise to Peters of a "favour" to BF: "I think it no small Act of Friendship that I have recommended him to Sir Everard Falkoner," BF's superior in the Post Office Department. Penn Papers, Hist. Soc. Pa.

than they, because he has the Affections and Confidence of their People, and of course some Command of the Peoples Purses. You are ready now to tell me, that Popular Favour is a most uncertain Thing. You are right. I blush at having valued myself so much upon it. I have done. Adieu, my dear Friend, and enjoy forever the Esteem of all the Good and Worthy, as well as the sincere Affection of Your obliged humble Servant B FRANKLIN

Inclos'd is a little Memorandum for some Musick and Harpsicord Wire, which I want for a Friend. If not too much out of your Way please to send it.

I did not think I should write so long a Letter. There is too much in it about my self. I must mend that Fault in my next, for I cannot now correct it in this.

[*In the margin in Collinson's hand:*] Mr Jacksons Bank sent Him Coldens papers

Peter Collinson Esq

Draft of a Speech for William Denny

AD: Pennsylvania Historical and Museum Commission

At the Council meeting following receipt of the Assembly message urging him to meet the Indians in spite of Lord Loudoun's orders not to,[9] Denny was distressed to learn that the Indians insisted the conference be held in Easton. He agreed unwillingly to go, declaring it "rediculous" to leave the comforts of Philadelphia "to humour the Indians," and asked the Assembly to appoint some members to go with him. On November 4, Speaker Isaac Norris, Joseph Fox, John Hughes, Franklin, and William Masters, all provincial commissioners,[1] were duly appointed, and they all, except Norris, left the 5th. Stopping overnight at Samuel Dean's inn on Tohicon Creek, Bucks Co., they reached Bethlehem the next day where they heard alarming reports of Indians in the woods. They arrived in Easton the afternoon of the 7th.[2]

During the first two days of the conference, November 8 and 9, the participants exchanged the usual expressions of good will and elaborate

9. See above, pp. 6–7.

1. See above, p. 3 n.

2. *Pa. Col. Recs.*, VII, 308–14; *Votes*, 1756–57, p. 27; *PMHB*, XXX (1906), 418.

invocations to open their "Eyes and Ears." After a Council meeting on the 10th, Denny and the commissioners discussed their approach to the central question: did the Indians have any grievances "in Land Affairs" for which retribution might now be made? The governor agreed to add to his next speech "a Paragraph putting the Question in plain Terms." The speech printed below from the draft in Franklin's hand, perhaps prepared with the help of the other commissioners and probably submitted to Denny at this meeting, is, with the additions indicated, substantially the same as Denny's speech of November 12 printed in the official record of the conference.[3]

Brother Tediuskung[4] [November 12, 1756]

What I am now going to say to you should have been mentiond sometime ago I now desire your strict attention [?] to it.[5]

You was pleased to tell me the other Day that the League of Friendship made by our Forefathers was as yet fresh in your Memory. You said it was made so strong that a small Thing could not easily break it. As we are now met together at our Council Fire,

3. *Minutes of Conferences, held with the Indians, at Easton, In the Months of July and November, 1756 . . .* Phila., Franklin and Hall, 1757, pp. 16–19; cited in this and the following documents relating to the conference as *Minutes*, and reproduced in facsimile in Carl Van Doren and Julian P. Boyd, eds., *Indian Treaties Printed by Benjamin Franklin, 1736–1762* (Phila., 1938), 135–66. See above, V, 84–107, for the full record of the Indian treaty at Carlisle in which BF participated.

4. Teedyuscung (*c.* 1700–1763), "One Who Makes the Earth Tremble," Delaware Indian leader; born in New Jersey; resided near Easton and later in the Wyoming region, 1730–50; baptized "Gideon" by the Moravians, 1750, and lived for a time at Gnadenhütten; in 1754 he turned his back on white civilization and resumed traditional Indian ways. He led some of the murderous attacks against which BF contended in Northampton Co., but after mid-1756 he seems generally to have sought accord with the English as a means of maintaining Delaware independence from their Iroquois overlords and from the French. Though often the tool of Quakers anxious to convict proprietary agents of Indian land frauds, he was also often a shrewd and able negotiator for the Indians of whom he dubiously claimed to be "King." Vain, pompous, sometimes eloquent but more often merely loquacious, and usually drunk, he was a colorful, dominant figure on the Pennsylvania frontier during the French and Indian War. He burned to death in a drunken stupor when his Wyoming house was set on fire, probably by a vengeful Iroquois. *DAB;* Anthony F. C. Wallace, *King of the Delawares: Teedyuscung, 1700–1763* (Phila., 1949).

5. This short paragraph in Richard Peters' hand; probably added at the Council meeting on the morning of the 12th when final "Alterations" were made in Denny's speeches. *Minutes*, p. 19.

kindled by us both, and have promised on both Sides to be free and open to one another, I must ask you how that League of Friendship came to be broken? Have we, the Governor or People of Pensilvania done you any kind of Injury? If you think we have, you should be honest and tell us your Hearts; you should have made Complaint before you struck us; for so it was agreed in our ancient League: However, now the Great Spirit has thus happily brought us once more together, speak your Mind plainly on this Head, and tell us if you have any just Cause of Complaint, what it is? That I may obtain a full Answer to this Point, I give this Belt.[6]

Give a Belt.

To Deborah Franklin

MS not found; reprinted from William Duane, ed., *The Works of Dr. Benjamin Franklin,* VI (Philadelphia, 1817), 14.

My Dear Child, Easton, Saturday Morning, Nov. 13, 1756.

I wrote to you a few days since, by a special messenger, and inclosed letters, for all our wives and sweethearts;[7] expecting to hear from you by his return, and to have the northern newspapers and English letters, per the packet; but he is just now returned without a scrap for poor us. So I had a good mind not to write to you by this opportunity; but I never can be ill-natured enough, even when there is the most occasion. The messenger, says he left the letters at your house, and saw you afterwards at Mr. Dentie's and told you when he would go, and that he lodged at Honey's,[8] next door to you, and yet you did not write; so let Goody Smith,[9] give one more just judgment, and say what should be done to you; I

6. The document continues with Peters' notes on two more speeches; Teedyuscung's request for time to consider the inquiry, and Denny's polite concurrence which closed the conference for the day. *Minutes,* pp. 20–1. Apparently BF gave this draft to Denny, who gave it to Peters, and the secretary recorded the minutes for the rest of the session on it.

7. Not found.

8. "Dentie" may be a misreading for Duché. George Honey was a tavern-keeper on Market St.

9. Sarah Franklin wrote BF, March 23, 1766, of the death of "our dear Friend" Mrs. Mary Smith the day before, adding that their mutual friend Mrs. Duffield "and poor Mama are in great distress, it must be hard to lose a Friend of 50 Years standing." APS.

think I wont tell you that we are well, nor that we expect to return about the middle of the week, nor will I send you a word of news; that's poz. My duty to mother, love to the children, and to Miss Betsey and Gracey, &c. &c.[1] I am, Your *loving* husband,

B. FRANKLIN

PS. I have *scratched out the loving words,* being writ in haste by mistake, when I *forgot I was angry.*

Draft of a Speech for William Denny

Copy[2]: Pennsylvania Historical and Museum Commission

Teedyuscung, responding to Denny's "Question in plain Terms" about land fraud[3] on November 13, said that French influence with the young braves was the principal cause of the Indian attacks in Pennsylvania. Then, being pressed on the land question, he made the dramatic accusation the anti-proprietary interest, and especially the Quakers, had so long sought to publicize:[4] "This very Ground, that is under me (striking

1. "Gracey," though mentioned frequently by BF in his letters home, has not been identified; "Miss Betsey" may have been Elizabeth Ross of Elizabethtown, N.J., who was soon to marry Benjamin Mecom. Van Doren, *Franklin-Mecom,* pp. 58–9.

2. In BF's hand; apparently a fair copy rather than a draft. Peters' endorsement on it may indicate BF furnished this copy to Peters after the conference; in any case, it is virtually identical with the official printed version (*Minutes,* pp. 26–7), and almost certainly is the part of Denny's speech particularly representing the views of BF and the commissioners.

3. See above, p. 17.

4. See above, VI, 253–5, for proprietary and Quaker differences on Indian policy. Armed with substantial funds and a zeal to uphold Indian rights, Israel Pemberton and other Quakers organized the "Friendly Association for Regaining and Preserving Peace with the Indians by Pacific Measures," and appeared more and more at conferences as their counsellors. Convinced that the Indians had been cheated and aware of the advantage to themselves that publication of such fraud would bring, the Quakers doubtless encouraged the Indians to recall and magnify forgotten or fancied grievances. Hence, at this and other Indian treaties, both sides of the dialogue bore Quaker marks: through the provincial commissioners they saw to it that questions on land frauds were asked, and then they put the desired answers into Teedyuscung's mouth. This string-pulling, of course, infuriated the official negotiators who felt that the Quakers were acting treasonably in emboldening the Indians, and undercutting efforts to control them. Theodore Thayer, *Israel Pemberton King of the Quakers* (Phila., 1943), pp. 123–31, relates the Quaker role at Easton.

it with his Foot) was my Land and Inheritance, and it is taken from me, by Fraud." When urged to say what he meant by fraud, he charged that "when I had agreed to sell the Land, to the old Proprietary, by the Course of the River, the young Proprietaries came, and got it run, by a straight Course, by the Compass, and, by that Means, took in double the Quantity intended to be sold."[5] At a Council meeting the next day, Secretary Richard Peters and Conrad Weiser, the interpreter, both long charged with negotiations for proprietary land purchases, denied that any injustice had been done and proposed that the matter be looked into upon the governor's return to Philadelphia, where the records were.[6] Denny decided to promise the Indians a full investigation but first called on Franklin and the other commissioners for advice. They pointed out that promised investigations had so often been used as excuses for inaction that the Indians would have no faith in another such promise. They urged, therefore, that the presents provided by the government and the Quakers be distributed to the Indians regardless of the justice of the charges, since only thus could they be persuaded to cease their attacks. Denny concurred, and an "Answer to their [the Indians] Complaints was framed accordingly." The portions of Denny's speech printed below, probably agreed upon at this time though perhaps drawn up by Franklin and the commissioners earlier, were delivered on the 15th following some brief, friendly comments on other matters Teedyuscung had mentioned two days before.[7]

5. The terms of the famous "Walking Purchase" of 1737 provided for sale of as much land north and west of a point in Bucks Co. as could be covered in a walk of a day and one half. The Indians expected the walk would be a normal one: along a crooked path in the woods with leisurely stops for meals and rest. Instead the proprietary agents cleared a straight path and hired strong woodsmen to make a non-stop walk, thus permitting a claim for far more than the Indians intended to sell, including the lands at the forks of the Delaware where the treaty was held. The alleged fraud of this purchase played a prominent role in the protests against proprietary rule in Pennsylvania which were soon to send BF to London. Charles Thomson, *An Enquiry into the Causes of the Alienation of the Delaware and Shawanese Indians from the British Interest* (London, 1759), published with BF's assistance, details the Quaker side of the argument. Teedyuscung's doubtful assertion that *he* had been cheated in the Walking Purchase, and his pointed reference to the venality of the new Proprietors, Thomas and Richard Penn, as compared to the goodness of their father, William Penn, are probably examples of Quaker promptings in his speeches.

6. *Ibid.*, p. 101; Paul A. W. Wallace, *Conrad Weiser* (Phila., 1945), pp. 459–65; *Minutes*, p. 24.

7. *Ibid.*, pp. 24–7.

Brethren [November 15, 1756]

You have opened your Heart and shown us the Reasons you thought you had for differing with us. You have done well in speaking so plainly on that Head. But you should have made your Complaint to us before you lifted your Hand to strike, and that might have prevented the Mischief. When the great Creator made Man, he gave him a Tongue to complain of Wrongs, two Ears to hear a Brother's Complaints, and two Hands to do him Justice by removing the Cause; all these were made before the Hatchet, and should be first used. Had the Man, in your Comparison, whose Pipe was taken from him, said, Brother, you took my Pipe from me at such a Time, and I must have Satisfaction; his Brother might have answered, I did not think you valued a Pipe so much; don't let us differ about a small Matter; here Brother, take two of mine. That this Method, agreable to our ancient Treaties, may be remembred, and Complaints always made by you to us, or by us to you, in a publick Manner, and Justice demanded before we strike, I give you this Belt [String].[8]

Give a Belt [String]

Brethren

I am but lately come among you; the Grievances you mention are of old Date. If former Indian Kings have, as you say, sometimes sold more Land than they had a right to sell, in so doing they injured us, and we, as well as you, have Cause to complain of them. But sometimes, tho' they sold no more than their own, sold it fairly, and it was honestly paid for by the English, yet, when the Indian Children grow up, they may forget that their Fathers sold the Lands and divided the Goods; and some evil Spirit or bad Man that loves to make Mischief, may tell them, The Land is still yours, your Fathers never sold it, the Writings are false. Moreover, many People both English and Indians concern'd in former Purchases of Lands are now dead; and as you do not understand Writings and Records it may be hard for me to satisfy you of the Truth, tho' my Predecessors dealt ever so uprightly; Therefore, to show our sincere Desire to heal the present Differences, and live in eternal Peace with you our Brethren, tell me what will satisfy you for the Injustice

8. Changed to "String" by another hand, probably Peters', in the MS and so printed in the official minutes.

you suppose has been done you in the Purchase of Lands in this Province; and, if it be in my Power, you shall have immediate Satisfaction, whether it be justly due to you or not. The good People of this Province are willing and ready to open their Hands[9] and help me by contributing freely to this good Work. Or, if you are not impowered to receive such Satisfaction at this Time, or have not Convenience to carry away the Goods that may be given you on that Account; then I will lodge the Goods in such Hands as you shall appoint, till you bring to our next Meeting your old Men of the several Nations who may have a Right to a Share in the Division of those Goods, where they shall be ready to be delivered to them and you. This may be done at a Council Fire to be rekindled at Philadelphia for you and us, or here, as you shall chuse; when we expect and insist that you bring down all the Captives that still remain in your Country.

And as you mention Grievances from the neighbouring Governments,[1] I make no doubt but on proper Application you will have the utmost Justice done you; and if I can be of any Service to you in making the Application, it will give me great Pleasure. In Testimony whereof, I give you this Belt.[2]

A Belt

Endorsed [*in Richard Peters' hand*]: Mr. Franklin Minute at Easton Novr. 1756

9. The assemblymen present at the conference had made this offer to help out in a critical situation, but because the matter was not settled at once (see next document), they reported, Jan. 29, 1757, that the responsibility should be left with the Proprietors, where it belonged.

1. Teedyuscung had spoken of injustices to the Indians in New Jersey, and on November 16 he explained that he wanted to see "some of my Brethren and Relations" who were confined there. *Minutes*, pp. 22, 29.

2. Denny concluded the day's negotiations by reminding the Indians that since Sir William Johnson now had final authority in Indian treaties, Teedyuscung should go to "a general Council-Fire at his House on the Mohochs River . . . to obtain Confirmation, and take Advice as to your future Conduct," and then announced that £400 worth of blankets, clothing, utensils, ammunition, and trinkets provided by the government and the Quakers would be distributed. *Ibid.*, p. 27.

Draft for a Speech by William Denny

Draft: Pennsylvania Historical and Museum Commission

On November 16, Teedyuscung replied to Denny's speech of the day before, emphasizing again that the delusion of the young braves by the French was "the first and principal Cause" of the Indian attacks in Pennsylvania, though the land frauds he had mentioned reluctantly made "the Blow fall quicker and heavier." He then explained that he could not specify what would satisfy the Indians since the question had not been fully explored nor were all the persons concerned present at the conference. The next day the commissioners advised Denny to "fix . . . the Sum to be given in full Satisfaction of all Injuries done to the Indians, and offer it to them now." Franklin probably submitted the draft printed below for the governor to use in informing Teedyuscung of his decision. But when the Indian again told Weiser that he could not settle the matter then, it was dropped and the speech was never delivered. After brief closing remarks by Denny and Teedyuscung the latter "shewed great Pleasure in his Countenance, and took a kind Leave of the Governor and all present."[3]

Brother [November 17, 1757]

I desired you to mention the Value of the Damages you complained that the Delawares had suffered in the Purchases of Lands; you have declin'd to make any Valuation, but left it to me,[4] and now I tell you I have considered the Matter and find that the People of this Province have suffered greatly by the late unhappy bad stormy Weather. The Clouds were black and dark, spread over the Country and prevented the Sun's shining on their Lands, so that they did not bring forth so much Fruit; besides the Lightning came out of the Clouds, struck down and burnt their Houses and Barns, and kill'd their Servants and Cattle; so that they have suffered much more than you have done in the Purchases of Lands you mention, and therefore are not so able to give much as they were in former times when the Weather was good [and] all things prospered with

3. *Minutes*, pp. 28–30.

4. There is no such proposal in the official minutes; perhaps BF had heard informally that the Indians were willing to let Denny make the evaluation. Teedyuscung had generally been severe about the damages, though, having earlier spoken of "Interest . . . to be added," and told Weiser he could not settle "tho' the Governor should offer him never so much." *Ibid.*, pp. 29, 30.

them. However, they are willing to give you Goods to the Value of Pounds in full Satisfaction of all Damages you complain of. They will lodge it in my hands. When you come down in the Spring, bring all the Delaware People that sprang out of this Ground to receive and divide the Goods, and I will deliver them to you and those People; provided the Prisoners are all faithfully delivered up to me on or before that Time.[5]

To Peter Collinson

Duplicate: Pierpont Morgan Library; also extract: The Royal Society[6]

Dear Friend Philada. Nov. 22. 1756

Since mine of the 5th Instant, a long one, per Capt. Snead, I have receiv'd the Air Pump and Apparatus per Rankin.[7] There is some Breakage, of which shall send an Account per next Ship, to have the Glasses renew'd. We are exceedingly oblig'd to you for your Care in the Affair, and return you cordial Thanks.

I am just return'd from the Forks of Delaware, where I with some others attended the Governor, at a Conference with the Indians. They complain of Injuries from the Proprietors. I hope he will give timely Orders to redress them when they come down next Spring. It is said by many here, that the Delawares were grosly abus'd in the Walking Purchase; that they have frequently complain'd, and their Complaints were suppress'd or conceal'd, and the 6 Nations set on their Backs to make them quiet. That they

5. Denny had repeatedly sought Teedyuscung's agreement to release white prisoners held by the Indians; on November 16 the Delaware leader had stated he had only two in his power and would need assistance to free those held by others. He agreed, however, to "gather and scoop in as many as I can." *Ibid.*, p. 29.

6. The original ALS not found; the duplicate is one of three prefacing BF's letter to Collinson, Jan. 31, 1757. He has marked it "Copy." The extract, in Collinson's hand, consists of the sentence about Canton and the errata in *New Exper. and Obser.*, followed by Collinson's notation: "This I have Given Dr. Birch."

7. *Pa. Gaz.*, Nov. 4, 1756, reported the ship *Betty Sally*, Capt. Edward Snead, as cleared for London. The brig *Otter*, Capt. George Rankin, arrived in Philadelphia before Nov. 11, 1756; *Pa. Gaz.*, that date. See below, p. 50, for the air pump and apparatus.

have remember'd these Things, and now, by the Connivance of the 6 Nations, as 'tis thought, and supported by the French, they have taken Revenge.[8] Much has the Province suffer'd by this War; some Hundreds of Lives lost, many Farms destroy'd, and near £100,000 spent, yet the Proprietor refuses to be taxed, except for a trifling Part of his Estate; the Quit Rents, located unimprov'd Lands, Money at Interest, &c. &c. being exempted by Instructions to the Governor: Which is the harder, if by his Ill-Treatment of the Indians the War has in any Degree been occasioned.[9]

The 49th Vol. of the Transactions and other Books for the Library, sent in the Care of Neate and Neave,[1] are come to hand in good Order. In my Paper of Experiments in the Transactions are the following Errata, viz.

Page 301 line 12. for, *elastic,* read *electric.*

line 18. for, *but nigh enough,* read, *but not nigh enough.*

as they hurt the Sense, I mention them; some smaller of little moment I omit. I should be glad to know if the very ingenious Mr. Canton has repeated those Experiments, and what are his Observations.[2]

I thank Dr. Wright for his Piece on Thunder.[3]

Mr. Eeles's Experiments do not succeed with me.[4]

8. See above, pp. 15–23, for BF's attendance at the Easton conference, and especially p. 19 n for the Walking Purchase. BF's summary of the conference suggests a possible connection with the informal Quaker (anti-proprietary) consultations there.

9. See above, VI, 515–31, on the proprietary instructions.

1. On the London and Philadelphia mercantile firms of these names, see above, IV, 115 n.

2. For BF's experiments in pursuance of those made by John Canton, see above, V, 516, where the lines appear correctly. Canton continued to perform ingenious electrical experiments until his death in 1772; subsequent volumes of this work will record BF's collaboration with him in London.

3. Edward Wright (d. 1761), physician, F.R.S., microscopist, and author of *Conjecture on the Course of Thunder* (Paris, 1756). *Gent. Mag.*, XXXI (1761), 431; *Phil. Trans.*, XLIX, 553–8, 670–82; *The Extraordinary Library of Hon. Samuel W. Pennypacker . . . Dec. 14, 1905,* Stan V. Henkels, Cat. 943, Part I, p. 67.

4. A letter from Henry Eeles of Lismore, Ireland, March 31, 1755, describing experiments to determine the effect of smoke, steam, and other "vapours" on charged bodies, appeared in *Phil. Trans.*, XLIX, 151–4.

I wish you had sent me Dr. Hoadly's and Mr. Wilson's Experiments on the Leyden Bottle. I see such a Piece advertis'd, but it is not come over.[5] I am, my dear Friend, Yours affectionately BF.

Mr. Collinson

Provincial Commissioners: Orders for Payment

DS: Historical Society of Pennsylvania

After the return of the provincial commissioners from the Easton Indian conference they resumed their regular sessions and began again to issue orders for money payments on November 23. By December 28 the end of their available funds was once more in sight and on that day and the next they authorized a few large payments, including one which turned over to Charles Norris the remaining balance. Although commissioners under later acts issued hundreds of orders for payments, Franklin dropped from the group because of his impending journey to England as agent for the Assembly, and he did not resume this sort of activity until after his return to Philadelphia in 1762. The seventy-four orders issued during the last five weeks of his responsibility in 1756 are listed below in the same form as those signed earlier (see above, VI, 392–5). The orders which he did not sign are indicated by an asterisk (*).

Date	*Payee*	*Purpose*	*Amount* £	*s.*	*d.*
November					
23	William Bramson	Hand grenades, grape shot, cannon balls	48	0	3
23	James Hamilton	Cash advanced to Edward Croston	150	0	0
23	John Hughes	Payment to John Van Etten, Sept. 24	150	0	0
23*	Capt. Frederick Smith	Pay for self and co. per Sgt. Peter Shaver	150	0	0
24*	Jacob Cantzon	Medicines and attendance on soldiers at Ft. Hunter	9	1	0
24*	Stephen Carpenter	Board, shoes, stockings for 2 Indian boys	17	9	0

5. Benjamin Hoadly (1706–1757), physician and playwright (*DNB*), and Benjamin Wilson (above, IV, 391 n) published *Observations on a Series of Electrical Experiments* (London, 1756), which had been advertised in *Gent. Mag.*, XXVI (August, 1756), 406, though nothing is said about the work dealing with Leyden jars. A copy of the Hoadly and Wilson *Observations*, bearing paragraph numbers in BF's hand, is in Yale Univ. Lib. He sent his comments on the work to Wilson, Jan. 28, 1759.

Date	Payee	Purpose	Amount £	s.	d.
24*	Nathaniel Grubb	Maintenance of French Neutrals, Chester Co.	5	14	2½
24*	Abraham Kintzey	Part pay, hiring team to province	75	0	0
24*	Jesse Maris	Maintenance of French Neutrals, Springfield, Chester Co.	11	12	6½
24*	Samuel Neave	Goods for Easton Indian treaty	404	6	11½
24*	Thomas Nuzen [?]	Maintenance of French Neutrals, Ridley and Providence Twps., Chester Co.	3	4	11
24*	Christopher Sower, Jr.	Maintenance of French Neutrals, Germantown	20	7	4
24*	Francis Smedley	Maintenance of French Neutrals, Wells and Goshen Twps., Chester Co.	12	4	6¼
24*	Samuel Smith	Executor of William Grant: tin kettles, flints, nails, certified justly due	10	19	11
24*	Thomas Wharton	2 casks nails, for use at Ft. at Shamokin	13	8	0
26	Capt. Christian Busse	Part pay of co.	400	0	0
26	William Edmonds	Brethren's account for maintaining Indians	144	15	5¼
26	Timothy Horsfield	Sundries for Indians and Geo. Claus's account	21	4	0
26	Samuel Neave	For order of John Harris, Oct. 24	20	0	0
27*	Jeremiah Warder	Sundries and victualling Wetterhold's co.	409	13	3
29*	Joseph Armstrong	Keeping guard, Hamilton Twp., Cumberland Co.	74	16	0
29*	Dr. William Chancellor	Medicine for forces in Carlisle	4	9	0
29*	Doughty Jones	Lodging, dieting and nursing Capt. Newcastle and wife	8	1	6
29*	Jacob Levan	Provisions for Capt. Reynolds's co.	203	8	9
29*	Jacob Orndt	Pay for self and co. to Dec. 4	801	1	6
29*	John Pumpshire	Service as Indian interpreter	20	0	0
29*	Capt. George Reynolds	Pay for self and co. to Dec. 1	722	7	0
29*	Capt. Edward Ward	Part pay for co.	100	0	0
29*	Conrad Weiser	Part pay of his co. at Reading	400	0	0
30	Joseph Fox	Balance for accounts examined and settled	234	2	11½

Date	Payee	Purpose	Amount £	s.	d.
December					
1	John Baldwin	50 pr. shoes for forces	18	15	0
2*	Robert Owen	Book-keeper for Commissioners	20	0	0
3	Anthony Benezet	Maintenance of Neutral French to Nov. 29	27	19	9
3	William Galbreath	Pay as commissary of stores at Hunter's Mills	98	16	5
3	William Moore of Lancaster	Carrying 10 bbls. rum, 18 spades, 19 shovels, 50 hatchets for Clapham's use to Ft. Hunter	7	0	0
4	William Clinton	6 spades and 2 shovels	3	4	0
4	John Abraham Denormandie	In part, maintenance of Neutral French in Bucks Co.	100	0	0
4	Ens. William Johnston	To pay men absent when mustermaster paid	84	5	6
4	Ens. William Johnston	Pay for garrison at Hunter's Fort	388	8	6
4	Matthew Rea	Maintenance of Neutral French and purchase of wool "to employ said French in working"	12	1	5½
4	Capt. Elisha Salter	Part pay for self and co.	100	0	0
5	William Henry of Lancaster Co.	Work done at Harris's and Shamokin	43	17	6
5	Capt. Thomas McKee	Expense of journeys; service as interpreter; allowance for trouble and time; paid in full	61	8	6
6	Joseph Fox	Disbursements for gov. and commrs. at Easton	112	9	2
6	Lynford Lardner	Sundry small accounts	100	0	0
6	Capt. Frederick Smith	Part pay for self and co.	569	17	6
6	Moses Tattamay	Attending Indians to Fort Allen, and other services	10	0	0
13*	Hughes & Jones	Sundries furnished province	240	6	9
13	Philip Syng	Work and materials to alter workhouse to guardhouse for King's troops	95	11	3
16	Robert Armstrong	Timer and boards delivered to Clapham	25	6	6¼
16	Rev. Charles Beatty	Chaplain to Col. Clapham's regt., 111 days at *6s. 8d.*	37	0	0
16*	Benjamin Franklin	For David Barclay of London, for arms	1365	11	2¼
16	Johan Leidig	Medicines and attendance on Esther Clear	17	8	0

Date	Payee	Purpose	Amount £	s.	d.
16	Capt. James Patterson	Advance pay for his co. of rangers	20	0	0
16	Richard Peters	Express to Col. Clapham; expenses of Denny and Logan at Easton	12	5	0
17*	John Baker and Abraham Wayne	Shipwrights; work for province	47	2	6
17*	Capt. Thomas Lloyd	James Young drafts on Michael Teass and Lloyd	250	0	0
17*	Capt. John Van Etten	Pay and subsistence of his co., per James Hyndshaw	308	2	6
18	Capt. Edward Croston	Advance, victualling Shamokin forces	200	0	0
18	Joseph Fox	Avance, to pay sundry small accounts	100	0	0
22	Samuel Hunter	Pasturage, victuals and rum furnished forces at Shamokin	28	13	6½
24	Charles Coyle	For mare lost on Kittanning expedition	9	0	0
24	Nathaniel Miles	Diet furnished sundry soldiers	7	0	6
24	Charles Osborne	Medicines for Armstrong's battalion	19	14	7½
27*	David Edwards	Maintenance of Indians at State House	134	14	19½
27	Michael McGuire	Carpenter's work at Shamokin	17	14	6
28	Hannah Boyte (Boyd)	Maintenance of sundry Indians, Dec. 3	25	8	0
28	Thomas James	Services on Indian affairs	2	15	2
28*	Henry Keppele	Maintaining Hambright's men before May 30	40	1	0
28	Capt. George Noarth or Benjamin Loxley	Disbursements for use of city artillery	39	6	5
28	Charles Norris	Residue of £30,000 funds	1420	19	5¾
29	William Buchanan	Contract to supply troops west of Susquehanna	1500	0	0
29	John Hughes	Rugs, blankets, bedding, pots, kettles, utensils used by King's troops in city	500	0	0
29	Conrad Weiser	Pay, self and co.; victualling Capt. Busse's co., 25 pr. shoes for Geo. Gabriel; saddle, bridle, and rifle for Indian; and in full Wolfganhager the gunsmith's account	457	17	3

Pennsylvania Assembly: Message to the Governor

Printed in *Votes and Proceedings of the House of Representatives, 1756–1757* (Philadelphia, 1757), pp. 32–3.

After renewing the Mutiny Act and appointing members to attend the Easton conference on November 4, the Assembly had adjourned to the 22nd. On November 23, Franklin and Joseph Galloway[6] were appointed to draft a message requesting copies of such proprietary instructions "as relate to Matters of Legislation" and of the minutes of the recent Easton Indian conference. The message printed here was brought in, agreed to, and sent to Denny the next day.[7]

May it please your HONOUR, [November 24, 1756]

You were pleased by your Message, at the Beginning of this Session,[8] to represent to us the Expediency of framing sundry Laws that are necessary for the Defence and Utility of the Province; and

6. Joseph Galloway (*c.*1731–1803), son of a Maryland landowner; moved to Philadelphia as a youth and was admitted to practice before the Supreme Court of Pennsylvania in 1749. Already related to the Shippens and Pembertons, he added to his profitable connections when, in Christ Church, 1753, he married Grace, daughter of former Assembly speaker and councilor Lawrence Growdon. Marked as "a young rising Quaker lawyer" though no longer a member of any Friends' Meeting, he entered the Assembly in October 1756 as a member for Philadelphia Co., where he gained immediate prominence as BF's ally, and succeeded to most of his assignments and the leadership of the antiproprietary interest in the Assembly when BF went to England the following year. A trusted correspondent and co-worker during the missions to England, Galloway's political pre-eminence in Pennsylvania was marked by his reelection to the Assembly every year but one until 1776, and by his service as speaker, 1766–75. At the approach of the Revolution, he performed his last important act as a colonial leader when he drafted a loyalist imperial plan of union rejected by the First Continental Congress. Having little use for the plan of union, BF tried to overcome Galloway's loyalist sentiments after returning to America in 1775, but he was unsuccessful and their political connection came to an end. Their personal relationship remained close enough, however, for BF to deposit all his papers in Galloway's Bucks Co. house, Trevose, in October 1776 before sailing for France. In December of that year Galloway fled to New York and joined General Howe. He served the British as civil administrator during the occupation of Philadelphia, 1777–78, and then went to England, where he was an industrious lobbyist and writer for the Loyalists until his death. *DAB;* Julian P. Boyd, *Anglo-American Union, Joseph Galloway's Plans to Preserve the British Empire, 1774–1788* (Phila., 1941), esp. pp. 15–27; Oliver C. Kuntzleman, *Joseph Galloway, Loyalist* (Phila., 1941).

7. *Votes*, 1756–57, pp. 30, 33.

8. I.e., Denny's speech of October 19; see above, p. 5.

we think many others, not recommended to us by your Honour, may likewise be for the Benefit of the People, which we are determined at this Time to take into our serious Consideration, and pay that Regard and Attention to them that their Importance deserves: But as many Bills, prepared at a burthensome Expence to the Publick by antecedent Assemblies for the Defence of the Province, in Compliance with His Majesty's Orders, and other salutary Purposes, after much Time, and great Pains had been spent in framing them, have been rejected by your Honour's Predecessors, because not consistent with certain Instructions that they had received from the Proprietaries, as directory to them in Matters of Legislation; which Instructions, notwithstanding, were unreasonably concealed from the Representatives of the People; we are, in Justice to ourselves, and in Duty to those we represent, obliged humbly to request that your Honour would be pleased to lay before us full Copies of all such of your Instructions that are of a publick Nature, and in anywise relate to Matters of Legislation, that we may, as we are sincerely inclined, avoid all unnecessary Delays at this critical Juncture, in Matters of real Importance, and yield a chearful Obedience to His Majesty's most gracious Orders for our Defence.

When we reflect on a late Instance of your Honour's Candour on the like Occasion,[9] and the evident Proof you gave a former Assembly, of a sincere Inclination to facilitate and expedite Matters,[1] in which the publick Welfare was concerned, we have no Room to doubt your Honour will favour us in complying with this reasonable and necessary Request.[2]

We also further request, that your Honour would be pleased to lay before us the Minutes taken at the last Conference held at Easton with Teedyuscung and other Indian Chiefs, that the Representatives of the People may be acquainted with Matters which so intimately relate to the publick Weal and the Peace of the Province.[3]

9. See above, VI, 515–16.

1. BF and Galloway probably referred to Denny's willingness to override Council advice and approve a ten-year excise bill. See above, VI, 515 n.

2. On November 26 Denny forwarded a copy of an instruction urging him to "take the first favourable Opportunity to settle a regular and useful Militia" in Pennsylvania.

3. Denny complied on the 30th. On Jan. 29, 1757, BF and the other commissioners reported that the minutes were inaccurate in important particulars. See below, pp. 111–14.

Timothy Horsfield to the Provincial Commissioners

ALS: American Philosophical Society

Gentlemen Bethm. Novr. 29. 56

I Received the Cash £21 4*s*. for the Account per Mr. Edmonds[4] for which I Return my harty thanks. Would now Inform you that when the Indians returnd from the Treaty they came thro Bethlehem and One of them Named John Smaling[5] Was taken Sick. We Lodgd him and Wife in a Shed Made of Boards &cr. having no Better place to put them. I Visited him and found he was Broke Out with the Small Pox, I then Went to one of Our Neighbours G. Clows and prevaild on him to take him and Wife into his House where he could Lay Near a fire and Desired Clows to provide him With Fire wood &cr. and one of the Brethren goes Every day to carrey him Such Necessary's as is Needfull. Since he has been there another Indian and Wife Relations to Smaling are come to them with 2 Horses which makes Much trouble and Charge. Clows has been with me Makeing heavy Complaint and has Since Wrote me a Letter In German Which I here Inclose with an Inglish Translation.[6] The Indians over the Watter Namly Nickodames, and Nathaniel's[7] Familey's with Some others Amounts to 16 in

4. On Nov. 26, 1756, William Edmonds was paid £341 3*s*. 7¼*d*. "for Indian maintenance at Bethlehem," including £21 4*s*. "for T. Horsefield, Esq;" *Votes*, 1755–56, p. 171.

5. John Smalling, said to be Teedyuscung's grandson, had attended the July 1756 conference at Easton, and apparently the November one as well. Conrad Weiser escorted the Indians from Easton to Bethlehem, where they arrived "after Dark" on November 18, and departed for Fort Allen the next morning. *Pa. Col. Recs.*, VII, 220; 1 *Pa. Arch.*, III, 66.

6. Moravian accounts for the winter of 1756–57 record frequent payments for food, clothing, and sundries to Smalling and his wife, and for one George Hayes, said to be a Delaware follower of Teedyuscung, and his wife. Smalling died of smallpox before Jan. 18, 1757, when Horsfield charged £2 10*s*. 9*d*. for "visits and medicines . . . and for incisions and dressing of above 10 impostunes," as well as £1 9*s*. 6*d*. for a shroud, coffin, and burial expenses for him. William C. Reichel, ed., *Memorials of the Moravian Church* (Phila., 1870), I, 283–5. No letter from George Clouse has been found, but on Aug. 19, 1757, he received £7 9*s*. 4*d*. for "Sundries supplied the Indians at Bethlehem." *Votes*, 1757–58, p. 120.

7. Nicodemus, half-brother of Teedyuscung, baptized in 1749, had deserted the Moravian mission at Gnadenhütten in 1754, and probably participated in the attacks of 1755–56. He and six members of his "family" were frequently

Number and I hear More Intends to come and if They do I Dont Know What we Shall do with them, for the House Where they are is Small and they are now Much Crouded. I have Endavourd all I cou'd to perswaid these to Go to Easton Philadelphia or to the Proprietors Tract Near Bristoll. But Invain. They Answer No We Will Stay in Bethlehem. They have 4 Horses amongst them which makes Much trouble. I went over to Spoke with them and tould they could Not Expect the Goverment would pay for their Horses Keeping and urged them to Sell them, But I Much Question there doing it. In Short they Behave as if they thought the White People was now obligd to do Every thing for them they require, and Indeed it is too Much so. I do assure you, Gentlemen, I cannot Explain to you the trouble and Vexation the Brethren and My Self have with these Savage Wretches and if more Comes I dont Know what we Shall do.[8]

I Shall be Exceedingly obliged to you and very thankfull if you could send some Discreet Person who understands to manage Indians, for I must own my Inability to reside here or At Some Other plase where you could provide for the Indians. I had almost forgot to Mention that a Boy and Guirl Children of the Indians that Fled from Gnadenhutten Broke out with the Small Pox Some time Since and are Near recovered. As very few of them has had it, and they was very much in fear of the Distemper, the Brethren Was obliged to Send a Man and [h]is Wife to a House 1/2 a Mile of[f] to take care of them. I hope Gentlemen you will take these things into consideration, and Grant us Such Advice and Releif as you, in your Wisdome think Best Which Will be thankfully Acknowledged by the Brethren and My self Who am Gentlemen your Most Obedient Humble Servant

T H

Messrs. Franklin Fox &cr.

---

noted in Horsfield's accounts of Indian expenses, and he himself attended most of the Indian conferences held in Pennsylvania in 1756–58. Nathaniel, a Delaware baptized in 1749, seems to have been with Nicodemus most of the time. Reichel, *Memorials*, I, 238, 264, 267–83 *passim.* The Indians were spoken of as "over the Watter" because they were cared for in the "Indian House" and the new log house built for refugees in the summer of 1756 across the Manakasy Creek from the village of Bethlehem. *Ibid.*, I, 230–1.

8. Horsfield was anxious to be rid of the wandering Indians not only because they were an expense, but because the Moravians feared their bad influence on the converted Indians.

From Augustus Gottlieb Spangenberg

Copy: Archives of the Moravian Church, Bethlehem

Sir, Bethl. 29. Nov. 56.

To wait on you at Bethlehem, on your Return from Easton to Philadelphia, would have been a great Satisfaction to many of us, who have the Honour of your Acquaintance. I flatter myself with the Opinion, that you would not have pass'd by, had your Affairs permitted any longer stay in the Country.[9] And now I take this Opportunity of letting you Know by some Lines, how it goes with us here; believing, that you have a particular Care for this part of our Province, which you have seen yourself in the greatest Distress by the Injury of Times, and which has been an Object of your tender Concern. We do live at present, Thanks to God, pretty quiet; but We are careful, how to trust people, who have no God but the Devil. We are on our Guard, as much as We can; tho' We must own, it is the Lord, and He alone, that Keeps us.

Some people at allmangel, Neighbours of that unhappy Family, which fell but lately into the cruel Hands of the Sauvages, have brought their Wives and Children to Bethlehem, to be shelterd there; and we have about Fourty of them received into our Houses here and at Nazareth, whose resp[ective] Husbands and parents are returnd to their resp[ective] Habitations, viz. to Allmangel.[1]

Our Indians, who just a year ago came to Bethlehem from Gnadenhütten, when they could not exspect any Thing else, but what they would be destroyed with us, have hitherto behaved quiet and inoffensive to every One, thankful for the good protection, which they have had hitherto in this Government. But I am sorry that I

9. "Governor Denny and his suite" had spent the night of November 17 in Bethlehem on their way back to Philadelphia from the Easton conference. William C. Reichel, ed., *Memorials of the Moravian Church* (Phila., 1870), I, 274 n. BF apparently was not with them; by hurrying he could have arrived home the 18th, a day before the governor's party reached the city. *Pa. Gaz.*, Nov. 25, 1756.

1. The captured family were the wife and four children of Johannes Adam Busz, taken in Albany Township, Berks Co. (Allemängel), on November 6. Busz, who was away from home, a daughter "being in a turnip Patch," and a baby in a cradle had been spared. Those who had "returnd" were greeted with fresh attacks on the 28th by supposedly friendly Iroquois returning from the Easton conference. Hunter, *Forts*, p. 296; *Pa. Gaz.*, Nov. 18, 1756.

must mention to you, that a white Man, but last Week, fired at One of the said Indians of Bethlehem, when he was a Mile or Two of[f] in the Woods; and I do fear, that such a Thing as that, may create great Confusion among all the Indians, if not prevented.[2]

The greatest Hardship We meet with now, is the coming of the Sauvages from the Susquehanna to Bethlehem, and their Obstinacy, to stay here with us.[3] We have no Houses nor no Room for them and must needs build Winter-Houses for them, if more should come; as We hear they intend to do, by those that are come. I fear also, we shall be oblig'd to keep watching about them Day and Night, not so much to prevent Mischief, which they might be doing, but to hinder others from hurting them, which very likely might be the Case, as people are very bitter against them. Pray, be so Kind, to consider of these Things. For us there is no Proclamation gone out, (as far as I Know) to prevent such evil Things:[4] it may prove very bad to this province, if such a Thing should happen.

To have your Advice or Ordres, and to Know what to do, will oblige very much Sir your humble Servant SPGBG

Endorsed: Indian. Wandern beym Wildenkriege

Pennsylvania Assembly Committee: Report on Precedents in the House of Commons

Printed in *Votes and Proceedings of the House of Representatives*, 1756–1757 (Philadelphia, 1757), pp. 36–7.

In its zeal to present strong candidates for the October 1756 Assembly election, the proprietary party nominated and elected Chief Justice Wil-

2. Timothy Horsfield reported the same attack to Denny, Nov. 29, 1756. 1 *Pa. Arch.*, III, 76–7. Pennsylvania authorities were well aware of this problem; at the Easton conference they had warned Teedyuscung to tell his people "not to straggle about" lest they be mistaken for hostile Indians. *Pa. Col. Recs.*, VII, 337–8.

3. See the preceding document; even Teedyuscung's wife wanted to stay in Bethlehem, because of her husband's "debauched way of Living," but Conrad Weiser finally persuaded her to leave. 1 *Pa. Arch.*, III, 66.

4. The Moravians were worried that the successive monthly suspensions of hostilities against the Indians east of the Susquehanna (*Pa. Col. Recs.*, VII, 144, 192, 247) might have expired, thus again legalizing the murder of Indians for scalp bounties.

liam Allen in both Cumberland and Northampton Counties. When Allen chose to represent Cumberland, a new election was ordered for October 25 to fill the vacated Northampton seat. The sheriff's certification that proprietary stalwart William Plumsted had defeated Moravian William Edmonds, presented to the House on the 30th, was accompanied by a petition alleging that multiple balloting frauds had voided the election. The next day Plumsted was denied his seat, and on November 4 the hearings on the case were postponed until the 23d, when the dispute was referred to the Committee of Grievances, of which Franklin was a member. The whole Assembly resumed consideration of the case on December 1, and the next day a motion to "determine how the Costs arising upon the Hearing of the Merits of the late Election of a Representative for the County of Northampton, and the Charges of the Evidences who are summoned to attend the same are to be paid," was followed by appointment of a committee "to inspect the Journals of the House of Commons for Precedents relating to the Payment of such Costs and Charges as attend controverted Elections."[5]

December 3. 1756.

In Obedience to the Order of the House, we have examined the Votes of the House of Commons, and do find the following Precedents relating to the Charges and Expences arising in Cases of Complaint enquired into by the House.

In the Parliament of the Twenty-first of JAMES I. the Mayor of Arundel having misbehaved himself in the Election of a Burgess for that Town, was sent for, and ordered to pay the Charges of the Witnesses, to be assessed by three Members.

In the Eighteenth and Nineteenth of the same Reign, a Constable of York was sent for up, and accused of Misdemeanors; but being acquitted, he had Five Pounds ordered him for his Charges. Also one Napper being committed to the Serjeant for serving a Subpoena on Mr. Brereton, was dismissed, after paying Costs to Mr. Brereton, and due Fees to the Officers of the House.

In the Fourth of CHARLES I. the Sheriff and one of the Aldermen of York, having conducted an Election illegally, to the Prejudice of Alderman Hoy, a Candidate, were ordered to pay all the Charges of the Witnesses of the said Hoy, to be assessed by four of the Committee.

In 1699, March 9. Thomas Hawksly, and Roger Hunt, Overseers of the Poor for Nottingham, being summoned to attend the

5. *Votes*, 1756–57, pp. 5, 24–7, 29, 35–7.

Committee of Privileges and Elections, by George Gregory, Esq; Petitioner against Robert Sacheverell, Esq; prayed that they might be relieved for their Charges in coming to Town, Expences in Town, and returning home. And it was ordered, that the said Gregory do pay the Petitioners their reasonable Charges, to be assessed by the Chairman of the Committee.

In 1711, the 22d of March, a Complaint being made to the House, that John Cunningham was summoned in Behalf of Major General Hamilton, to attend the Committee of Privileges and Elections, to testify his Knowledge touching the late Election of a Member to serve in Parliament; and that Major General Hamilton refuses to pay him his reasonable Charges for his Journey and Attendance; it was ordered that the said John Cunningham have his reasonable Charges for his Journey and Attendance on the Committee, to be ascertained by the Chairman.

In 1715, September 8. Ann Cater, John Burton, James Coot, and Stephen Norman, praying that they may be relieved for their Charges in coming up and staying in Town, being summoned as Witnesses by John Hervey, Esq; to attend the Hearing of the Merits of the Election for the County of Bedford; and the said Hervey having refused to give them reasonable Satisfaction, it was ordered that the said Mr. Hervey do pay the Petitioners their reasonable Charges, to be settled by Mr. Speaker.

In 1717, June 18. Thomas Prowse, Steward of the Manor of Minehead, complained, that he was required, by a Warrant from Mr. Speaker, to permit George Speke, Esq; or his Agents, to inspect the Rolls of the said Manor, and to take Notes or Copies therefrom, and to attend the House with the said Rolls; and that he did appear accordingly, and was examined; but that Mr. Speke's Agent refused him reasonable Satisfaction for the same; and praying Relief, it was ordered, that the said Prowse be paid his reasonable Charges, to be settled by Mr. Speaker.

In 1695, December 21. It was resolved, that Sir George Meggot, having preferred to the House a groundless and vexatious Petition, relating to the Election of Members to serve in Parliament for Southwark, do make Satisfaction to the Members he petitioned against for the Costs and Expences they have been put to by Reason of such Petitions.

In the same Year, March 4. It was resolved, that Sir Richard Gipps, having preferred to the House a frivolous, vexatious and groundless Petition, relating to the Election of Members for Totness, be taken into Custody of the Serjeant, and make Satisfaction to the Members he petitioned against, for the Costs and Expences they have been put unto by reason of such Petition.

The Votes of Parliament being voluminous, and mostly without Indexes, these are all the Precedents that the Committee, in so short a Time, have been able to find relating to the Payment of Witnesses Charges. Many there are in which no Application appears for the Payment of such Charges, nor any Determination who should pay them; but whether there are any Determinations different or contrary in like Cases, we cannot say. These, without presuming to make any Remarks upon them, are humbly submitted to the Consideration of the House,[6] by

JOHN BAYNTON,[7]	JAMES WRIGHT,
BENJAMIN FRANKLIN,	JOHN WRIGHT,
JOHN ABRAHAM DENORMANDIE,[7]	WILLIAM ALLEN,
GEORGE ASHBRIDGE,	THOMAS YORKE.

6. The Assembly then resolved that "it is the undoubted Right of this House . . . to assess and ascertain the reasonable Costs and Expences of such Witnesses and others, summoned to attend the House, and order Payment . . . to be made by such Persons as it shall appear to the House ought in Justice to pay the same." *Ibid.*, p. 37. After ten days of acrimonious debate on the merits of the election the Assembly only managed to defer consideration indefinitely. On March 3 it was insinuated that Rev. William Smith had interfered improperly in the election, and on April 7 the Assembly resolved to resume consideration of it at its next session, to begin on Aug. 8, 1757. At that sitting, William Parsons was accused of improper conduct at the election, and following his unannounced departure from Philadelphia, "a great Majority of the Members" ruled the election illegal on Sept. 23, 1757, seven days before the Assembly rose. The long dispute, of course, barred Plumsted from his seat for a year; he was re-elected in October 1757 and seated without question when the new Assembly met. *Ibid.*, pp. 37–46, 97–8, 108, 143–4, 153–4; *Votes*, 1757–58, p. 3.

7. John Baynton (1726–1773), merchant, and member for Philadelphia Co., and John Abraham Denormandie (1713?–1757), physician, landowner, ironmaster, member for Bucks Co., were elected in October 1756 to replace pacifist Quakers who had withdrawn from the Assembly. *Votes*, 1756–57, pp. 3, 17; *PMHB*, VI (1882), 17–18; [Thomas Balch], *Letters and Papers Relating Chiefly to the Provincial History of Pennsylvania* (Phila., 1855), p. 64; Lancaster Co. Hist. Soc. *Papers*, XIX (1915), 311–14.

Pennsylvania Assembly: Reply to the Governor

Printed in *Votes and Proceedings of the House of Representatives*, 1756–1757 (Philadelphia, 1757), p. 41.

Franklin and John Baynton were appointed on Dec. 8, 1756, to reply to Governor Denny's message of that date on quartering the British troops momentarily expected in Philadelphia. Submitted the same morning, the reply was approved and sent to Denny at once.[8] Since it is quoted in full in the message of December 19 (below, p. 43), it is not separately printed here.

Pennsylvania Assembly: Message to the Governor

Printed in *Votes and Proceedings of the House of Representatives*, 1756–1757 (Philadelphia, 1757), pp. 48–9.

Franklin and others were appointed on Dec. 16, 1756, to "prepare a Draught of a Message to the Governor, concerning the Report now prevailing in the City of the Governor's having given Orders for Quartering of Soldiers upon private Houses." It was brought in, approved, and sent to Denny the next day.[9] Since it is quoted in full in the message of December 19 (below, pp. 46–7), it is not separately printed here.

Pennsylvania Assembly: Message to the Governor

Printed in *Votes and Proceedings of the House of Representatives*, 1756–1757 (Philadelphia, 1757), pp. 50–3.

After Pennsylvania became a theater of war in 1755, it was apparent that the province would soon have to provide quarters for British troops. When the remnants of Braddock's army passed through Philadelphia that summer, the Assembly hastily extended what it considered were the relevant portions of the British quartering act to Pennsylvania.[1] Since the troops were not billeted on the city, the law had little effect, but its disallowance, July 7, 1756, foreshadowed difficulties to come. Attorney General William Murray (later Lord Mansfield) advised its rejection because the act wrongly assumed that "propositions true in the mother country and rightly asserted in the reigns of Charles the 1st and Charles the 2nd in times of peace and when soldiers were kept up without con-

8. *Votes*, 1756–57, p. 41.
9. *Votes*, 1756–57, pp. 48–9.
1. *Votes*, 1754–55, p. 138.

sent of Parliament" were applicable "to a colony in time of war in the case of troops raised for their protection."[2] That is, the Pennsylvanians were not to be granted the sweeping immunities from forced quartering of soldiers in private homes which had been part of English law since Stuart days. Moreover, the matter was confused by one law for England under which troops were to be quartered on the numerous, large public houses, and another law for Scotland permitting soldiers to be quartered on private houses. Further, it was uncertain how war and invasion altered these privileges and obligations. When Parliament failed to pass clarifying legislation, the Duke of Cumberland dumped the confusion into Lord Loudoun's lap by ordering that "Quarters must be taken in the plantations as they are in Britain in time of war."[3] Obviously, Loudoun was expected to requisition such quarters as he needed, but he had nothing beyond general military authority upon which to base his actions. Thus, the scene was set for a contest which led eventually to a clause in the Declaration of Independence and to the third amendment to the Constitution: could soldiers be forced upon private homes, even to the expulsion of their inhabitants, without the sanction of law? In December 1756, the passage of another quartering law, several exchanges between Governor Denny and the Assembly, and the arrival of over 500 troops in Philadelphia, produced a crisis, and the Assembly summarized its case in the following message, reported by Franklin and others on the 18th and ordered to be sent to Denny on Sunday morning, the 19th.[4]

May it please your HONOUR, [December 19, 1756]

To prevent, if possible, any Misunderstanding between your Honour and this House, we beg Leave to recapitulate what has passed on the Article of Quarters, during the present Session.

On the 19th of October last, your Honour was pleased to communicate to us a Letter from Lord Loudoun to yourself, dated September 22, 1756, in which Quarters, and the Necessaries allowed in Quarters by Act of Parliament, were demanded of this Province: The Building of Barracks came first under our Consideration, but if the House had been disposed to build them, the

2. *The Statutes at Large of Pennsylvania* ([Harrisburg,] 1898), v, 194–5, 537. This opinion was incorporated into the Board of Trade recommendation of disallowance which was submitted to the Assembly on Oct. 19, 1756. *Votes*, 1756–57, p. 10.

3. See Pargellis, *Lord Loudoun*, pp. 187–92, for these difficulties and pp. 187–210, for a full discussion of the quartering problem.

4. *Votes*, 1756–57, pp. 49–50, 53.

Season was too far advanced, and the Dimensions could not be judged of, as the Number of Forces to be quartered here was not expressed.[5]

The House then endeavoured to procure the last Act of Parliament that was made for the Quartering of Soldiers in England, to be their Guide in making the necessary Provision here; your Honour was applied to for a Sight of that Act, which you were so kind as to promise to procure for us, but some Time passed before we obtained it.[6]

On the 24th of November your Honour was pleased to lay before us another Letter from Lord Loudoun, dated October 28, 1756, in which the Demand for Quarters was repeated, and one Battalion of the Royal Americans was mentioned to be provided for in Philadelphia, but the Number of which that Battalion should consist was not mentioned. His Lordship is not particular as to Quartering, or the Necessaries to be furnished in Quarters, as he is pleased to say, "he is writing to one who is so thoroughly acquainted with the Quartering in England in Time of Peace, and what Things are furnished in Quarters for the Officers and Soldiers, and how much further Quartering extends in Time of War, and even must do so from the Nature of Things."[7]

5. Loudoun had written, "I must expect, that in the Article of Lodging, and such other Necessaries as are furnished in Quarters in Great-Britain in Time of War, your Province will . . . chearfully make full and sufficient Provision." BF and others were appointed, Oct. 22, 1756, to bring in a quartering bill. *Votes*, 1756–57, pp. 13, 16.

6. On November 26, the Assembly clerk was ordered to secure from Secretary Peters a copy of the British Mutiny Act (which contained articles relating to quartering in England and Scotland), "which the Governor had been pleased to say he would send to the House," to assist the committee preparing a quartering bill for Pennsylvania. *Ibid.*, p. 34. Denny's failure to forward a copy of the British act, however, was hardly responsible for the nearly six weeks' delay between the appointment of a committee to draw a bill and its report to the Assembly on December 2. The Assembly was adjourned during most of November, and does not seem to have resumed work on the quartering bill until after receipt of Loudoun's letter mentioned below made its enactment urgent.

7. *Ibid.*, p. 31. This was disingenuous on Loudoun's part, to say the least. As already pointed out, the British Mutiny Act dealt with quartering only in time of peace, and there had been no clear precedents for quartering in the British Isles in time of invasion since the Mutiny Act was first framed, not even during the rebellions of 1715 and 1745. Loudoun had tried to get definite

Your Honour has never been explicit on these Points with the Assembly. We know nothing of them but what is to be learnt from the Act of Parliament you were so good as to furnish us with. We presented to your Honour a Bill so exactly conformable to that Act, that it brings over the very Clauses, by which Troops are quartered in England.[8] After this Bill had lain four Days in your Honour's Hands, the House hearing the Soldiers were expected in Town the next Day, sent up to know your Result upon it. You were then pleased in a Message to object to the Preamble of one of those Clauses; we immediately agreed to strike it out, and had no Reason to expect any farther Objections.[9]

However, before the Bill passed, and after the Amendment was agreed to, your Honour did indeed send us down the following written Message, viz.

---

guidance on wartime quartering from the Duke of Cumberland before leaving England, but had failed. Pargellis, *Lord Loudoun*, pp. 192–3. He could hardly expect Denny to know, when neither he nor the home authorities did, "how much further Quartering extends in Time of War."

8. The Assembly had shrewdly taken advantage of the British statutes on quartering to make the troop burden in Pennsylvania as light as possible: it promulgated the cherished right that quartering must be under law, and then repeated the English legal provisions on quartering in public houses even though, in contrast to England, the public houses in Pennsylvania were ill-equipped to handle the soldiers. Thus, for the only time in "the whole history of the British army in America," an extension of English practices was *not* what the King's commanders sought. *Ibid.*, p. 187.

9. The bill providing for the quartering of troops in the public houses passed the House on Friday, December 3, and the next day Denny ordered an inspection to find out how many quarters the local public houses could provide. On Sunday the 5th he noted that the objectionable preamble to the bill of the previous year had been "artfully included" in the body of the new bill giving it "the very same" effect as the disallowed act. Denny therefore sent the bill back to the House on the 7th stating this objection. *Votes*, 1756–57, pp. 38, 40; *Pa. Col. Recs.*, VII, 346–7. While quarreling with the Assembly, Denny also sought quarters for the expected soldiers at the new Pennsylvania Hospital which could accommodate 500 men, but "all of a sudden the Application miscarried." Denny then tried to find "Gentlemen" in town willing to accommodate the officers, but this failed too, since there was "an ill-humour spreading itself everywhere." Richard Peters to Thomas Penn, Dec. 11 and 26, 1756, Penn Papers, Hist. Soc. Pa. The "sudden" action of the hospital managers and the "ill-humour" in town probably had the same underlying cause—arrival of news that smallpox raged among the soldiers. 1 *Pa. Arch.*, III, 82.

"GENTLEMEN, December 8. 1756.

"Since your Message of Yesterday Evening, I am well informed, from the strictest Enquiry, that the Quarters demanded by my Lord Loudoun for the Officers and Soldiers that are every Moment expected here, cannot be had in the Publick-houses of this City.[1] The Bill now before me therefore being insufficient to answer the End proposed by it, and the great Inconveniences that may arise if proper Quarters are not provided for the Reception of His Majesty's Troops being evident, I must, in the warmest Terms, recommend it to you, to make immediate Provision for that Service. WILLIAM DENNY."

With the above written Message your Honour was pleased farther to send us a verbal One in these Words, viz.

"SIR,

"The Governor commands me to acquaint the House, that if they do not think proper to make any further Provision than what is expressed in the Bill, the Governor agrees to the Alteration, and is ready to pass it as it now stands."[2]

As the House had been informed that the Number for which Quarters were demanded, did not exceed 600 Men, Officers included, and were of Opinion that the Publick-houses of Philadelphia were sufficient to provide Quarters for that Number, they acquainted your Honour with their Sentiments in the following respectful Message.[3]

1. The constables' returns, according to the governor, showed accommodations for 400 men, but "on examining the Constables [who had surveyed the public houses], it appeared that the publick Housekeepers had offered abundantly more quarters than their Houses wou'd allow of, from a mistaken notion that they were to be paid a Shilling a day for every head, in the same manner that they had been paid for the lodging and dieting Recruits, and that the returns cou'd not be depended upon." *Pa. Col. Recs.*, VII, 349. The Pennsylvania act provided a basic rate of *4d. per diem* for quartering foot soldiers. *Pa. Stat. at Large*, V, 275.

2. Denny agreed to the bill since it "was good as far as it would go, and besides established quartering of Troops by Law throughout the Province." To the Proprietors, April 9, 1757, 1 *Pa. Arch.*, III, 110. The Council agreed that, since the troops were near the city, it was best to accept this "immediate provision for the greatest part of them" and then seek a supplementary bill to make up the deficiency. *Pa. Col. Recs.*, VII, 350.

3. The reply which here follows is the first one cited above, p. 38.

"May it please your HONOUR, December 8. 1756.

"On examining the Lists of recommended and licenced Publick-houses, we find there are no less than One Hundred and Seventeen in this City only, exclusive of the Suburbs. We hope therefore your Honour will be of Opinion with us, that the Number of Soldiers for which Quarters are required may very well be disposed of among them in the Manner directed by the Act of Parliament now to be extended hither; especially as it is not necessary the Soldiers should all be lodged in the Publick-houses, but those who keep such Houses may provide lodging for the Men in other Houses, if they find it more convenient so to do.[4] Signed, by Order of the House, ISAAC NORRIS, Speaker."

Your Honour made no Reply to this Message, but passed the Bill the same Day; and therefore we had Reason to believe you were satisfied with it.

The Bill passed on the Eighth Instant: On the 13th, the Mayor and Aldermen of Philadelphia presented to the House the following Remonstrance, and withal laid before us the annexed Paper, expressing the Number for which Quarters were demanded.[5]

4. The discrepancy between Denny's calculation and the Assembly's, even after the inaccuracies of the constables' returns were corrected, rested upon two assumptions by the Assembly: that public-house keepers could disperse troops assigned to them among neighboring dwellings, and (as came out in later discussions) that quartering in suburban public houses, as well as those in the city itself, would be satisfactory. Both proposals would have made more beds available but would also have weakened training and discipline.

5. Between December 8 and 13, the troops arrived and brought matters to a crisis, but the Assembly's whole concern now was the disputed Northampton Co. election (see above, pp. 34–5), and the Council did not meet. Denny later told the Proprietors that after he had been denied use of the Pennsylvania Hospital and the City Corporation had refused to rent vacant houses for quartering, "a very deep Snow fell, succeeded by a sharp Frost," during which the troops arrived, and, crowded into public houses, they "suffered extreme Hardships," and caught the smallpox in large numbers. 1 *Pa. Arch.*, III, 111. At its meeting of December 9, the Philadelphia Common Council noted that the Quartering Act was insufficient since the officers especially would be dissatisfied with "Lodging and Entertainment" at the public houses, but, dominated by the proprietary party, it refused to do anything, resolving instead to refer all complaints to the Assembly. *Minutes of the Common Council of the City of Philadelphia, 1704 to 1776* (Phila., 1847), pp. 601–2.

"City of Philadelphia, Dec. 11. 1756.

"To the Honourable the REPRESENTATIVES of the Freemen of the Province of Pennsylvania, now sitting in Assembly,

The REMONSTRANCE of the Mayor, Recorder, and Aldermen of the City of Philadelphia, sheweth,

"That your Remonstrants have prepared Billets on the Publick-houses of this City, according to the Directions of a late Act in such Case made and provided, for such of His Majesty's Forces as Lord Loudoun hath been pleased to order into Winter Quarters here; but we find, on the strictest Enquiry into the Circumstances of the Keepers of such Publick-houses, that many of them are so poor and indigent, that they are neither of Ability to support the Burden of providing for so great a Number of Troops, or have proper Houses and Accommodations suitable for their comfortable Reception. We further beg Leave to remonstrate, that the Commanding-Officer hath demanded a Hospital, with Bedding, Fire, and other Necessaries, to be provided for a Number of Sick; but as no publick Building hath been erected in this City for that Purpose,[6] your Remonstrants, though willing and desirous to do every Thing in their Power to demonstrate their Loyalty to His Majesty, and to promote the Good of his Service, are sorry to find themselves incapable of complying with this Demand, without the Aid and Assistance of the Legislature of this Province: We therefore thought it our Duty to lay the Premises before you our Representatives, that such Regulations and Provision may be made therein as you in your Wisdom shall judge most expedient.

ATTWOOD SHUTE, Mayor,[7]
BENJAMIN CHEW, Recorder,
WILLIAM PLUMSTED,
ROBERT STRETTELL,
JOHN MIFFLIN,
JOHN STAMPER,
THOMAS LAWRENCE,
ALEXANDER STEDMAN."

6. See below, pp. 63–6, for hospital quartering.

7. Attwood Shute (d.1759), an Association Company officer in 1748, organizer of St. Peter's Church, and overseer of the poor in Philadelphia, had been elected mayor of that city in October 1756. Above, III, 309; *Pa. Gaz.*, Oct. 7, 1756, March 29, 1759; *PMHB*, XLVII (1923), 349; XXXI (1907), 199. The only other signers of this remonstrance not yet identified in these volumes are John Stamper (d. 1782), merchant, and to be mayor of Philadelphia in 1759; *ibid.*, I (1877), 419; XLVII (1923), 339; LXI (1937), 286–8; and Alexander Stedman (1703–1794), vestryman of St. Peter's Church, and with his brother Charles a merchant and later part owner of an iron furnace in Lancaster Co.;

"Captain TULLEKEN'S[8] Demand of Quarters, &c.

"December 13. 1756.

"In Obedience to Orders received from his Excellency the Earl of Loudoun, Colonel Stanwix[9] has thought proper to send Captain Tulleken to Philadelphia to demand Quarters for the First Battalion of His Majesty's Sixty-second, or Royal American, Regiment.

"Captain Tulleken demands Quarters as follows.

"Quarters for 500 Men; and Hospital for the Sick; a Storehouse; a Guard-room for an Officer, and Men.

"Billetts for the Officers.

"Colonel one; Lieutenant-Colonel one; Majors one; Captains eight; Subalterns thirty; Staff-Officers six. Total Forty-seven.

"N. B. There must be Fire and Candles for the Guard-room, and for the Hospital.[1]

"Besides the above, Captain Gate's Company of Independents, Forty-seven Men, four Officers.[2]

"The whole have Billets delivered them on the Publick-houses.

ATTWOOD SHUTE, Mayor."

The House, how desirous soever that the King's Troops might have good and suitable Quarters, could not proceed to make

---

he returned to Great Britain in 1776. *DNB* (under Charles Stedman, 1753–1812); *PMHB*, I (1877), 67, 69; XLVIII (1924), 41.

8. John Tulliken, a capable officer of the Royal American Regiment, came to Philadelphia in early December to arrange for troop quarters. He also served in South Carolina, and Western Pennsylvania, and was wounded at the battle of Ticonderoga, July 9, 1758. Pargellis, *Military Affairs*, pp. 349, 421; *PMHB*, LXXI (1947), 347.

9. John Stanwix (1690?–1766), at this time colonel-commandant of the first battalion of the Royal American Regiment; elected to the Pa. Assembly from Cumberland Co., 1757; later served at Pittsburgh and on the New York frontier before returning to England in 1760. *DNB*. Because of the death of his infant son, Stanwix did not come to Philadelphia at this time; a circumstance the more regretted by Richard Peters since, in his opinion, Stanwix was one officer who could have dealt harshly and summarily with BF and the other obstructing commissioners. Peters to Thomas Penn, Dec. 26, 1756, Penn Papers, Hist. Soc. Pa.

1. See the next document for these details of quartering.

2. Capt. Horatio Gates (1728–1806), wounded in Braddock's campaign and later major general in the American Revolutionary army. *DAB*. He and his company had arrived in Philadelphia for winter quarters on Dec. 5, 1756. *Pa. Gaz.*, Dec. 9, 1756.

further Provision by a Supplementary Act, without being well informed of the present State of the Quartering, that they might know what was deficient, and what was necessary to be supplied; they therefore immediately required the Mayor to lay before the House a List of the Names of the Publick House-keepers, with the Number of Officers and Soldiers billeted on each House (which he accordingly undertook to do by the next Morning) that we might be able to judge whether they could, or could not, be comfortably quartered by those Publick House-keepers.

This Order of the House, though of some Days standing, not being complied with,[3] and the House being sincerely desirous that the King's Troops should be well provided for, took Occasion, from the Report that your Honour had issued Orders for Quartering on private Houses, to send up their Message of Yesterday, in the following Words, viz.[4]

"May it please your HONOUR, December 17. 1756.

"A Report having Yesterday prevailed in Town, that your Honour had given Orders to the Sheriff to quarter the Soldiers on private Houses, which greatly surprized the Inhabitants,[5] the House

3. Mayor Shute's promise to deliver the list was severely qualified: "as several of the Tavern-keepers had already resigned, and he expected that many more would do the same before Night," it was virtually impossible to determine the status of troop quarters. *Votes*, 1756–57, p. 47. Public-house keepers failing to provide a billet as required by law for any soldier quartered on them were subject to a fine of £5. *Pa. Stat. at Large*, v, 277. Thus, keepers who lost money if paid but 4*d. per diem* for quartering a soldier, and who could be fined £5 per soldier if they refused quarters, were in a difficult position, and obviously preferred not to be inn-keepers under such circumstances. Moreover, since the Assembly had long felt the Proprietors licensed too many bad taverns, it was not upset to see the keepers penalized in the settlement of the troublesome quartering business. William S. Hanna, "Benjamin Franklin and Pennsylvania Politics, 1750–1766," unpublished Ph. D. dissertation, Univ. of California, 1958–59, pp. 62–3. See the Assembly's message of Feb. 9, 1757, for further legislation on quartering in public houses.

4. The message which here follows is the second one cited above, p. 38.

5. The possibility of forcible quartering arose when Denny told his Council on December 15 that, in spite of repeated pleas for assistance from the Assembly, the commissioners, and the magistrates, made by himself and by Colonel Bouquet, commander of the troops, "the King's Forces still remained in a most miserable Condition, ... the Weather grew more pinching, and the small Pox was encreasing among the Soldiers to such a Degree

(though they do not believe it possible your Honour could be prevailed with to issue Orders so diametrically opposite to an express Law passed by yourself but a few Days before) think it necessary on this Occasion humbly to request, that your Honour would be pleased to direct the Magistrates and Officers of the City and Liberties, who have billeted the Soldiers on Publick-houses, according to Law, to visit those Houses, inspect the Accommodations provided for the Men, see that they are good and sufficient, and oblige every publick House-keeper to receive and provide for the Officers and Soldiers that are or may be billeted on each House, in Proportion to the Number for which Quarters are required, either in the Publick-houses, or such others as the Keepers of them may procure; so that the Minds of the People may be quieted, and no just Cause of Complaint may arise, that Quarters, and the Necessaries in Quarters, are not duly provided, according to the Intention of the Legislature in passing that Act.

"The House have recommended it to the Provincial Commissioners to provide an Hospital for the Soldiers, which we make no Doubt will be done accordingly.* Signed, by Order of the House,

Isaac Norris, Speaker."

To this your Honour is pleased to answer as follows, viz.

"Gentlemen, December 18. 1756.

"The King's Troops must be quartered. With respect to the Insufficiency of the late Act, I refer you to my Message of the Eighth Instant, delivered immediately before the Passing of it;

*A Very convenient Guard-house was before provided at the Expence of the Province.[6]

---

that the whole Town would soon become a Hospital." The next day, Denny gave Bouquet a blank warrant to the sheriff to find private quarters for the sick if necessary. All three officials, however, seemed to consider the warrant principally as a threat to force the Assembly to provide additional quarters under law. *Pa. Col. Recs.*, VII, 358, 361–2.

6. The guard house had been under construction on July 14, 1756, when Benjamin Loxley received £12 12*s.* 2¼*d.* for boards for it, and apparently was completed by December 14 when Philip Syng was reimbursed £95 11*s.* 3*d.* "for sundry Accounts exhibited for making a Guard-house for the King's Troops." *Votes*, 1755–56, pp. 170–1.

and I see no Reason, from any Thing that has occurred since, to alter my Opinion. WILLIAM DENNY."[7]

On the whole we beg Leave to remark, That if any Thing more than the Act of Parliament requires be expected of us, we have never been explicitly informed what it is: That though your Honour is referred to by Lord Loudoun, as well acquainted with those Matters, you have never explained them to us: That when the Bill for extending the Act of Parliament hither was presented for your Concurrence, you made no Objection as to its Insufficiency, but that the Publick-houses could not accommodate the whole; which Objection we had afterwards Reason to think we had obviated to your Satisfaction. And lastly, That in your Message of Yesterday, you are not pleased to say that you will or will not favour us in our Request, that the Magistrates may be directed to see the Act duly executed, and good Quarters effectually provided; nor to point out any other or further Deficiency in the Act; but only tell us, as we think, somewhat abrubtly, *that the King's Troops must be quartered.*

May it please the Governor, we know that the King's Troops must be quartered, and are desirous they should have good Quarters. The Assemblies of this Province have in very late Instances shewn their Regard for the Soldiery, by voluntarily presenting Conveniencies and Refreshments to the Officers,[8] and furnishing Provisions and warm Cloathing for the Soldiers of the King's Forces, to the Amount of many Thousand Pounds.[9] We

7. This message reached the House on the same day it saw the odious quartering warrant: "Early the next day [December 18] the Sheriff waited on Col. Bouquet, and desired he might be trusted with the Writ for a short Time, in order to shew it to some of his Friends, who had great Influence on the Assembly, and might by their Petition prevent the Necessity of putting it into Execution, which wou'd have been very agreeable to all Parties. Instead of a Petition, the Writ itself was laid before the House in a clandestine manner, and very improperly by the Sheriff's Consent, which threw the House into a Ferment, and for the first Time since the Charter they sat all Saturday Afternoon and Sunday Morning." Denny to the Proprietors, April 9, 1757, 1 *Pa. Arch.*, III, 111. The sheriff, James Coultas, had been an officer under the Militia Act and otherwise seems to have been allied with BF politically, and thus would have tried to let the Assembly know of Denny's warrant before action was taken under it.

8. See above, VI, 208 n.

9. See above, VI, 391–2.

thought we had by the late Law provided well for their Quartering in this Province; especially as we had exactly followed the Act of Parliament made for the same Purpose. We cannot conceive it will, when well considered, be thought adviseable, to quarter the Soldiers by Force on private Houses rather than by Law on Publick-houses; and we apprehend, that if the bought Servants, which have been so lately taken from the King's good Subjects here, and no Satisfaction made their Owners, notwithstanding the Act of Parliament so expresly requires it,[1] are now to be thrust into their Houses, and made their Masters, some Commotions may arise, dangerous to the King's Peace. On these Considerations, and being desirous to preserve a good Understanding with your Honour, we beg you would be pleased to favour us with a Conference, that this Matter may, as soon as possible, be fully understood, and finally settled."[2]

To Peter Collinson

Duplicate:[3] Pierpont Morgan Library

Dear Friend Philada. Dec. 19. 1756

I have now the Pleasure of yours of the 7th and 10th. of September, and have received the old Book of Voyages, the Magazines for August, and Messrs. Hoadly and Wilson on Electricity.[4]

We have hitherto preserv'd a good Agreement with our new Governor; tho' it seems that some evil Counsellors about him would fain get him into a Quarrel with us; but I hope it will be prevented.[5]

1. See above, VI, 396–9.

2. December 19 being a Sunday, this message was delivered to Denny "when the Streets were full of People going to their respective Places of Worship." *Pa. Col. Recs.*, VII, 364. Though Denny found the message "a long Narrative filled with Abuses," he agreed to a conference with a committee of the Assembly the next morning. 1 *Pa. Arch.*, III, 112. See below, pp. 53–8, for the conference.

3. The original ALS not found; the duplicate is one of three prefacing BF's letter to Collinson of Jan. 31, 1757, received on March 15, 1757.

4. Collinson's letters have not been found, nor has the book on voyages been identified. See above, p. 25 n, for the book on electricity.

5. BF had reason to think there was "a good Agreement" with Denny; the governor had written Thomas Penn, Nov. 4, 1756, asking permission to ap-

Smith continues still in the Academy; but I imagine will not much longer, unless he mends his Manners greatly; for the Schools decline on his Account: The Number of Scholars at present, that pay, not exceeding 118, tho' they formerly were 200.[6]

The Air-Pump, &c. turn'd out agreable to Invoice, except, that the Stopcock Handle of one of the brass Hemispheres was wanting, and the 6 lb. of Quicksilver. These should be sent per the first Opportunity, together with Glasses instead of those which were broken, viz. The largest Receiver. The large Globe for weighing Air. The slender Barometer Tube; and the largest of the 3 Cylinders for holding Water in the Fountain Experiment. It would not be amiss to send 3 or 4 Barometer Tubes, such slender Things being very apt to break. And if the large Glass Vessels are not pack'd in separate Boxes, at least there should be Partitions in the Cases they are pack'd in. Since your Workmen are, by your Accounts, as dilatory as they are ingenious, I begin to be much concern'd for the great Trouble we have given you in these Affairs.[7]

I thank you for so readily paying my Drafts in favour of Mr. Strahan and the Society for Encouragement of Arts.[8] The Society sets out on noble Principles, and I hope they may be highly useful to the whole British Dominions and to Mankind.

---

prove a tax on lands, including those of the Proprietors', if the proprietary share of the tax was suspended for a year until the King's pleasure was known. Denny indicated very clearly that he thought such a tax just. Richard Peters, one of the "evil Counsellors," had a simple explanation of events: the Assembly and commissioners did with Denny "*what they please.*" To Penn, Dec. 11, 1756; both letters in Penn Papers, Hist. Soc. Pa. See the next document, however, for a quarrel between BF and Denny the day after this letter was written.

6. On Dec. 27, 1756, the Academy Trustees, including BF, "ordered that an exact Catalogue of the Youth at present in each of the Schools be prepared." According to the report, submitted March 5, 1757, 125 pupils were on the rolls. Montgomery, *Hist. Univ. Pa.*, pp. 227, 282. See above, p. 12 n, for BF's declining influence in Academy affairs.

7. BF had ordered £150 worth of scientific equipment for the Academy through Collinson on Aug. 27, 1755 (see above, VI, 171–2), and it had reached Philadelphia in early November 1756. The order lists and invoices have not been found.

8. See below, p. 69, for one of BF's frequent drafts on Collinson, and above, VI, 186–9, for the Society.

I am exceedingly obliged to Dr. Wright for the Regard he expresses for me in his Letter to you from Brussels, and for his ingenious little Piece on Thunder.[9] Pray return him my hearty Thanks.

Your honourable Friend's[1] Observation on what I wrote concerning our Militia Law, I don't well understand, perhaps because you have not sent the whole. If he doubted the Truth of what I said of the Numbers learning military Discipline under that Law, I send you enclos'd the printed Account or List of the Companies drawn from Secretary Peters's Account of Charge for issuing Commissions to the several Officers. The Companies consisted, one with another, of at least 100 Men each, and several Companies were added to the Militia after that List was printed.[2] If by "the ill Things he had lately heard from Pensilvania," he meant some Mischiefs done by the Indians, and therefore could not imagine we were in a better Posture of Defence, let me acquaint you, that if every Man in the Country was a Veteran Soldier, our sparse Manner of Settling on so extended a Frontier, would still subject us to Mischiefs from the Depredations of such an Enemy as the Indians are, who do every thing by Surprize, and lurk about for Opportunities of attacking single Houses, and small weak Neighbourhoods. But all that Pensilvania has suffer'd is charg'd to the Account of our not having a good Militia Law; tho' Virginia that has such a Law has suffer'd *more;* and New York, with such a Law and all the King's and New England Forces to assist her, has not been free from Scalping, besides losing Oswego. One might as justly charge to your Want of a good Militia Law in England, the Highway Robberies and Housebreakings which sometimes fill your Newspapers; and even blame your regular Forces for not prevent-

9. See above, p. 24 n.

1. This could have been any of Collinson's numerous friends in official circles; perhaps Board of Trade President Lord Halifax or Secretary of State Henry Fox. Norman G. Brett-James, *The Life of Peter Collinson, F.R.S., F.S.A.* (London, 1926), pp. 94–6.

2. BF probably sent the list of militia officers printed in *Pa. Gaz.*, March 25, 1756, showing 52 companies organized in the province. Another list compiled on Nov. 4, 1756, by Richard Peters, after the Militia Act had been disallowed, showed 31 associated companies, few of which contained a full complement of 100 men. 1 *Pa. Arch.*, III, 19–21. BF's letter to Collinson about the Militia Act has not been found.

ing them. We have now near 1500 Men on our Frontier, and yet People are sometimes scalp'd between Fort and Fort, and very near the Forts themselves. And if these Soldiers who have Arms continually in their Hands cannot always secure themselves, why should the Mischiefs done to the Farmers occasion a Doubt of the Truth of what I told you of our People's learning military Discipline under our Militia Law. For the Militia cannot be always under Arms, the Land must be till'd and Business follow'd; every House and Plantation cannot be guarded, and on the Frontier they are Miles distant, and so can afford little Aid to one another: Those Men, posted on the Frontier, are not the Militia, but what we call our *Provincial Troops,* being regularly inlisted to serve for a Term, and in the Pay of the Province; and do nothing but bear Arms like your Regulars. The *Militia* follow their respective Callings at home, muster only on certain Days to learn Discipline and are to be ready in Case of Invasion, &c. by any great Force; but are of little Use in hunting Indians; and therefore all the Colonies, in such Wars hire Men for the purpose who are fitter for it, and make it their Business. This Distinction between the *Provincial Troops* and the *Militia* of the Colonies, seems not to be understood in England; for even the Lords of Trade in their Report against our Militia Law, appear to have look'd upon them as the same, when they object, "that as our Militia was not oblig'd to march more than three Days out of the Province without their Consent, it might hazard the King's Troops that should be joined with them."[3] Whereas if any Expedition is undertaken in the Colonies in Conjunction with the King's Troops, it is not carried on by the Militia as such, but by listed Men hired expressly for the Service; these are called *Provincial Forces,* and under as absolute Command till that Service is ended, as the King's Troops; so that the Inconvenience objected to was not real. However, we are now to have a Militia Law like the other Colonies: The Bill is brought into the House, and I suppose will pass.[4] We shall, as we ought, do all that can reasonably

3. A paraphrase from the Board of Trade report, March 3, 1756, recommending disallowance of the Militia Act, read in Council in Philadelphia, Oct. 16, 1756. *Pa. Col. Recs.,* VII, 274.

4. BF was too optimistic; a new militia bill had been under consideration since October 1756 (see above, pp. 5–6), but though discussed repeatedly, it was not passed until March 30, 1757. Denny then proposed amendments giv-

be expected of us, to please as well as serve, our[5] Mother Country.

I am, with sincerest Respect and Affection, Dear Sir, Your most obedient humble Servant B FRANKLIN

Pennsylvania Assembly Committee: Report on a Conference about Quartering

Printed in *Votes and Proceedings of the House of Representatives*, 1756–1757 (Philadelphia, 1757), pp. 53–5.

Joseph Fox, John Hughes, Franklin, William Masters, and William Allen were appointed a committee to confer with Governor Denny on the quartering impasse. Before they were admitted to the chamber, Denny told the Council "he chose not to enter into any Altercation, nor to refute the many false Relations of Matters of Fact" in the Assembly message of December 19, but he would "insist that Quarters be instantly provided." He then showed the Council a message to the Assembly which charged it had been "indecent, frivolous, and evasive," and that beds were needed for 124 soldiers "who lie upon Straw," and quarters must be made ready for newly arriving recruits. After Denny called in the committee and showed it his message, "Mr. Franklin opened the Conference by making large Professions of the good Disposition of the House for the Army &ca." The report of the conference was entered in the Council minutes from the Assembly *Votes* with this comment: "N.B. The Committee's Report is not agreeable to Truth, and very artfully told, not mentioning several pertinent Matters said by the Governor and the Members of Council; and several offensive, indecent and rude Expressions, used by Mr. Franklin and others of the Committee, being entirely passed over. Upon the whole, there was abundance of Heat, Passion, and Rudeness, on the Part of the Committee."[6]

ing him the power to nominate officers and requiring conscientious objectors to declare their scruples in court, but the House rejected his proposals. *Votes*, 1756–57, pp. 105, 109. The amendments reveal what had become the real points of dispute: were the officers to be designated by the governor, and were those who refused to bear arms to be penalized or examined in some way?

5. BF here scratched out "Sovereign."

6. *Pa. Col. Recs.*, VII, 369–74. Denny later complained that the Assembly printed its report on the conference (in *Pa. Gaz.*, Dec. 23, 1756), "without my leave" and without comparing it with the minutes taken by the clerk of the Council (1 *Pa. Arch.*, III, 112), but since its minutes record the conference "as it stands in the Votes of the Assembly," (*Pa. Col. Recs.*, VII, 370), it would appear that no minutes were taken by the Council clerk.

[December 20, 1756]

That the Governor having been pleased to appoint this Day at Half after Twelve a Clock for the Conference, they had waited upon him accordingly, and found present Robert Strettell, Benjamin Shoemaker, Richard Peters, John Mifflin, and Benjamin Chew, Esquires, Members of the Governor's Council.

That the Committee had opened the Conference, by assuring the Governor of the good Dispositions of the House towards the Army, and their Intention that sufficient Quarters should be provided for them; but withal expressed the Concern it gave the House to hear, that his Honour had unnecessarily, as they apprehended, issued orders for Quartering them on private Houses by Force, and contrary to Law.[7]

To which the Governor was pleased to answer, that he was informed the Quarters in the Publick-houses were insufficient; that Beds were wanting for more than One Hundred Men.

The Committee then observed, That it was still the Opinion of the House, that the Publick House-keepers of this City generally were able to provide what was necessary for the Number billeted on them; and if they did not comply with the Law, the Magistrates should do their Duty, and fine them, as the Law directed. That if some of them were too poor, others were more able, and the Proportions should be regulated.

The Governor was pleased to say, it was not his Business to enquire where the Fault lay; it was plain the Soldiers were not well quartered; and they must not suffer.

The Committee then took the Freedom to remind the Governor, that the House could only prepare Laws; they had no Power to execute them. That they had provided a good Law for this Purpose, and the Governor had passed it. That the executive Powers of Government were vested in him. His Honour being pleased to say, It could not be expected of him, to go from House to House to see how the Law was executed; the Committee answered,

That the Complaint being laid before his Honour, Orders might properly issue from him to the Magistrates (who are under his Direction) to enquire into and redress it, by exacting a due Observance of the Law, and enforcing it by levying the Fines.

7. See the Assembly's message of December 19 (above, pp. 38–49) and its annotation for this and other matters mentioned during the conference.

The Committee then took Notice, that no Soldiers had yet been billeted on the Taverns in the Suburbs closely adjoining to the City, where there were many very capable of receiving them: That the neighbouring Towns could also accommodate a great Number.

The Governor replied, That the Quarters were demanded in the City, and it was his Duty to see the Orders executed; that if the Inhabitants thought it unequal, or a Hardship, they might apply to Lord Loudoun.

The Committee answered, That it were to be wished the Governor would consider himself somewhat more in his Civil Capacity as Governor of the Province. We expected of him, that he would be the immediate Father and Protector of the People, and if any Orders he received would in their Consequences be grievous to the People, he would represent the Matter properly in our Behalf: That if an Application to Lord Loudoun, to redress any Grievance, was necessary, we conceived it ought to be made not directly, but through the Governor, and that to do otherwise, would be inconsistent with the Respect due to the Governor. That we did request he would accordingly apply for Orders to quarter on the neighbouring Towns any farther Troops that might arrive here, more than our Publick-houses could well accommodate.

The Governor was pleased to say, he would do so when General Webb arrived,[8] for he thought it reasonable.

The Committee desired the Governor would be pleased to inform us, if any further or other Provision ought to be made for Soldiers Quartering, than what was mentioned in the Act of Parliament.

His Honour was pleased to say, that he knew of none; and that he had answered that Point in a Message he intended to send to the House this Day; which Message he held in his Hand.

8. Major General Daniel Webb (*c.* 1700–1773), successor to Thomas Dunbar as colonel of the 48th Regiment and third in command in North America under Lord Loudoun, had earned the colonists' scorn for his hasty retreat from the route to Fort Oswego after its capture by the French, and was to continue to be a vacillating, incompetent officer until his recall to England in December 1757. *DAB.* He had been assigned by Loudoun to enforce quartering in Philadelphia, but a palsy attack and the effect of Loudoun's written threats in gaining quarters, spared the city his presence. Pargellis, *Military Affairs*, 273, 292–3.

The Committee then asked, Whether any further Provision ought to be made for Quartering the Officers, than what the Act of Parliament required?

The Governor answered, None that he knew of. But afterwards mentioned something of Money given them in Flanders, by the Name of *Slope-Gelt;*[9] tho' he did not explain it, or seem to insist on it.

It was asked, What was to be understood by Quartering being extended farther in Time of War, than in Time of Peace.

The Governor answered, He knew not, unless it was Quartering on private Houses.

The Governor added, That before he left England, Complaint was made, that the Publick-houses at Canterbury were oppressed by too great a Number of Troops quartered on them, when the Invasion was apprehended, and it was proposed in Parliament to make them some Satisfaction by a Sum of Money, but he knew not whether it was done.[1]

The Committee replied, That in that Case the Parliament must have had the Grounds of Complaint laid before them, and been satisfied they were just. That no Complaint had ever been made to the House by our Tavern-keepers, though this same Law had been a Year in Use among us, before it was at this Time again re-enacted. That the House, on the Remonstrance of the Mayor and Aldermen, had required an Account of the Billeting, in order to satisfy themselves whether there was Cause of Complaint, but had not yet obtained it.

The Governor farther said, That in Time of War, and in Cases of Necessity, it was usual in England to quarter Soldiers on private Houses, and instanced Carlisle. That it was done in Scotland, in the Time of late Rebellion, notwithstanding the Law. That the Inhabitants of Westminster, and Newcastle, had at that Time voluntarily offered to quarter a great Number of Soldiers.[2]

9. Or "slap-gelt," a victualling and housing allowance sometimes permitted officers, but disapproved by Loudoun. Pargellis, *Lord Loudoun,* p. 145.

1. In this and other cases where exceptional burdens were placed on public-house keepers, Parliament passed relief measures for them. *Ibid.,* p. 188.

2. These instances occurred during the Scottish rebellion of 1745 where Denny had served with the English forces, and had, as Loudoun professed to believe, become "thoroughly acquainted with Quartering in England." *Pa. Col. Recs.,* VII, 340.

It was answered, That in Cases of Necessity, there was no Doubt but the Inhabitants of this Province would chearfully submit to it; but such Necessity did not appear to us; since there was Room enough in the Publick-houses of the Suburbs, and neighbouring Towns, and other Towns in the Province, for much greater Numbers than Quarters had yet been demanded for. That where it was voluntarily offered, Provision might be made to render it easy; but where Force was used, it was very different, as Families might be taken unprovided.

The Governor replied, That the General was the proper Judge of such Necessity; and the General thought it necessary to have the Soldiers quartered near together.

We replied, We were confident the General had no Inclination to oppress any of His Majesty's good Subjects; but if Necessity warranted Quartering on private Houses by Force, and contrary to Law; and Military Officers were the only Judges of that Necessity, they might say it was necessary to quarter the whole Army, not only in one City, but in one Square, or one Street; and thereby harrass the Inhabitants excessively. That the People of this Province were as good and as loyal Subjects as any in the King's Dominions, and as well affected to the Soldiery: That we had evinced this by doing more (as we conceived) at our own Expence, for the Army since they arrived in America, than any other Province whatever: That we hoped no Measures would be taken to create Differences between the Soldiery and the People, or to render the King's Service distasteful to those who had at present an hearty Affection to it: And further, that the Governor would listen to no Insinuations, nor be prevailed on to make any Representations of us to the contrary.

The Governor was pleased to say, He should represent nothing but Facts.[3]

A Report of the Surgeons of the Hospital, that the sick Soldiers in

3. The anger shown here may mark the occasion of the report by Richard Peters, who was present, that BF "behaved with great rudeness and Insolence . . . calling him [Denny] in express terms, a meer Bashaw or worse." But see above, VI, 489 n. Peters was the more disgusted because "an opulent City consisting of 2500 Houses" refused to shelter a few hundred of the King's troops sent for its protection. Peters to Thomas Penn, Dec. 26, 1756; Penn Papers, Hist. Soc. Pa.

the Taverns were badly accommodated, so that their Lives were in Danger, and the Health of the Inhabitants might be affected by the Spreading of their Distempers, being read by the Secretary;

The Committee mentioned, That an Hospital was ordered at the Province Expence for the Soldiers.

The Governor said, we had done it at last with an ill Grace.

His Honour was then reminded by one of the Committee, That when the Commissioners, on the first Application for an Hospital, had enquired of him what was the Custom in England, in that Particular; he was pleased to answer, It was the Custom for each Town or Corporation where Troops were quartered, to provide a Hospital at the Expence of the Town or City. That the Commissioners therefore, as the Province Money in their Hands began to run low, left that Matter to the Corporation of Philadelphia, who had Money in Bank, more than sufficient for that Purpose. But the Corporation declining it, the House recommended it to the Commissioners, who had ordered it.[4]

The Governor answered, It was the Custom in England, but the Corporations were not obliged to it. Though when they refused it, it was not well taken.

This the Committee report as the Substance of what passed at the Conference, to the best of their Remembrance.

4. After Denny found he "could neither get the new Hospital nor the old one, nor any House for an Hospital" for the soldiers, many of whom were ill, (*Pa. Col. Recs.*, VII, 359), the army doctors (surgeons) applied to the city authorities for aid, who in turn passed the problem on to the Assembly. On December 16 the Assembly asked the provincial commissioners to "make Provision for the Expence" of a hospital, along with "the necessary Utensils." *Votes*, 1756–57, p. 48. The Commissioners' accounts for 1757 show frequent payment for hospital expenses, and on Nov. 8, 1757, Joseph Fox was paid £350 "for Wood for the Barracks, and Rent of the King's Hospital." *Votes*, 1757–58, pp. 118–21. The patients at the Pa. Hospital had been moved from the "old" building, on Market Street, to the "new" building at Eighth and Pine Streets on December 17. This move, the smallpox menace, and the anti-proprietary bias of the Quaker-dominated Hospital Managers, probably all help explain the extreme difficulty experienced in securing hospital care for the sick soldiers. Above, IV, 108–11; Thomas G. Morton and Frank Woodbury, *The History of the Pennsylvania Hospital, 1751–1895* (Phila., 1895), pp. 13–15, 42.

Pennsylvania Assembly Committee: Report on the Governor's Message

Printed in *Votes and Proceedings of the House of Representatives,* 1756–1757 (Philadelphia, 1757), pp. 58–9.

When the Assembly met on December 21, the day after the acrimonious conference with Governor Denny, it considered the conference minutes and the written message Denny had presented at that time. After some debate, the Assembly expressed its displeasure with Denny's conduct in a message drafted on the floor of the House: its decent conduct had been slandered by Denny, who had only to enforce laws already passed to resolve the quartering problem, but if exact returns submitted to the House proved the need for more legislation, it would "take proper Measures to supply the Deficiency." In response Denny demanded such quarters as were furnished in Great Britain in time of war, the details of which were settled neither in law nor in precedent. Franklin and others were appointed on the 22d to consider this message, and two days later they brought in the report printed here.[5]

[December 24, 1756]

The Committee have considered the Governor's Message of the Twenty-first Instant, and are of Opinion, that in the first Paragraph, where it is said the Governor is glad to find the House have *at length* agreed to take proper Measures, &c. there is some Appearance of undue Reflection on the House, as if we had delayed or refused to take proper Measures to supply the Deficiency, in case the Publick-houses were not able to provide the Quarters; when the Truth is, That the House were always willing to do it, but were never, nor are yet satisfied that there could be such Deficiency, if the Law was properly executed.

The Committee farther observe, that the second Paragraph seems to insinuate, that notwithstanding *His Majesty requires, our Mother Country expects, and Lord Loudoun has demanded, in several Letters laid before us,* "that we do provide for all such Charges as arise from furnishing Quarters, and Necessaries allowed in Quarters, by Act of Parliament; in furnishing Carriages, Sloops, and all other necessary Means of Conveyance for His Majesty's Troops, whenever such Troops be stationed within, or shall be marching through,

5. *Votes,* 1756–57, pp. 55–9. If the Assembly message of the 21st was drafted by BF, as so many others were, neither the official minutes nor his Record of Assembly service indicate the fact.

this Province; and likewise Lodging, and such other Necessaries as are furnished in Quarters in Great-Britain in Time of War;" yet we had taken no Notice of such Expectations and Demands, nor made any Provision accordingly; whereas the Truth is, That both this and the last Assembly provided "for all such Charges as arise from furnishing Quarters, and the Necessaries allowed in Quarters in the Act of Parliament," by a Bill extending hither that very act, which received the Governor's Assent: That from the very first Demand the Assembly of this Province provided for furnishing Carriages, and other necessary Means of Conveyance for the King's Troops, by putting Money into the Hands of Committees, or into the Hands of the Governor and Commissioners for the King's Use, Part of which has been applied to those Purposes, whenever any Demand has been made for Carriages; and no Account of this Kind was ever refused Payment. A considerable Sum still remains in the Governor and Commissioners Hands, subject to such Demands; and the Supply Bill, now under the Consideration of the House, will make a further Provision:[6] To which we may add, that in the last Sixty Thousand Pound Bill the Sum of Ten Thousand Pounds was subjected to the Orders of Lord Loudoun, for any Part of the Service his Lordship should find necessary, but the House was obliged to strike it out by the Governor's refusing to pass the Bill for a larger Sum than Thirty Thousand Pounds.[7]

The Committee farther observe, That the Distinction between the Necessaries furnished in Quarters *in Time of Peace,* and those furnished *in Time of War,* is not yet understood by the House, nor have they been able to obtain from the Governor any Explanation of it, though they applied to his Honour for such Explanation both by a written Message, and by a Committee appointed expresly to confer with his Honour, "that this Matter might be fully understood." The House, by extending the Act of Parliament relating to Quarters, have provided for all that they understood to be necessary in that Respect, and for all that the Governor informed them was necessary. His Honour now is pleased to say, the Act of Parliament relates only *to a Time of Peace.* Whenever he shall be pleased to let us know what further Necessaries are required in Quarters

6. This bill passed the House, Jan. 22, 1757, but Denny rejected it. See below, p. 106.

7. See above, VI, 502–3.

in Time of War, the House will, no Doubt, consider that Matter, and do what shall appear reasonable.

As the Circumstances of the present Time call rather for Action than Altercation, the Committee are of Opinion, the House would do well to make no Answer to the Message in Question, but show their Disposition to Peace by their Silence, and apply themselves diligently to raising the necessary Supplies for His Majesty's Service, and to perfecting the Militia Bill now under their Consideration. This, their Opinion, however is humbly submitted to the House.[8]

Richard Peters to the Provincial Commissioners

Draft: Pennsylvania Historical and Museum Commission

Sunday Morn. 10 o Clock
26 Decr. 1756

Gentlemen

The Governor commands me to acquaint you that He has received a Letter by Express from Lord Loudun which obliges him to know if the Quarters and Necessaries in Quarters for the Officers and Men demanded by Colonel Bouquet on Friday last will be actually provided and the Hospital repaired and furnished on or before the first day of January.

His Honour desires a clear and precise Answer may be given as soon as you conveniently can before Night, the Express waiting

8. The Assembly promptly approved this report and resolved "That this House will, in order to prevent, as much as in them lies, any Disputes with the Governor at this critical Juncture, take no further Notice of his last Message relating to the Quartering of Soldiers or of his Honour's extraordinary Conduct in that Affair." The House then adjourned until Jan. 3, 1757, without the customary request for Denny's concurrence, a move Richard Peters considered a deliberate affront and neglect of duty, and which Denny later complained was done "notwithstanding the distressed condition and sickness of the soldiers who were raised and paid to defend them." This, Denny said, was "the highest Instance... of the Depravity of Human Nature" he had ever met with. *Votes,* 1756–57, p. 59; Richard Peters to Thomas Penn, Dec. 26, 1756, Penn Papers, Hist. Soc. Pa.; Denny to Penn, April 9, 1757, 1 *Pa. Arch.,* III, 112. In spite of the professions about "Peace" and "Silence" in the final paragraph of this report, the House ordered its long message of December 19 and the report of the next day's conference with Denny printed in *Pa. Gaz.,* Dec. 23, 1756.

to carry it to Lord Loudun.[9] I am Gentlemen Your most obedient humble Servant RICHARD PETERS

To Isaac Norris, John Mifflin, Lynford Lardner,
Benjn. Franklin, Joseph Fox, John Hughes,
William Masters Esquires

Lewis Ourry to ———[1]

ALS: American Philosophical Society

Sir Philadelphia Decr. 26th. 1756

By visiting the Quarters of the Men belonging to the first Battallion of the Royal American Regiment with the Mayor, Sheriff, and other Magistrates

I found that — — 94 Men laid on Straw
And that — — 73 had nothing to lay on

9. On December 24, the day of the Assembly's abrupt adjournment (see the previous document), a quartermaster's inspection showed that 36 of the soldiers quartered on public houses had no beds, and 47 had very bad ones. On the same day Col. Henry Bouquet, the commander of the first battalion of the Royal American Regiment, demanded of Denny that quarters be provided by January 1 for the additional men (approximately 500) who were to be recruited to bring the battalion to full strength. He insisted on the assignment of private houses in accordance with Denny's earlier warrant. 1 *Pa. Arch.*, III, 85–6; *Pa. Col. Recs.*, VII, 376. A copy of Bouquet's demand, attested by Peters, is among the Franklin Papers, APS. On Christmas night a letter from Loudoun ended the bickering: the soldiers *would* be quartered, by force if necessary, and "if the number of Troops now in Philadelphia are not sufficient, I will instantly march a number sufficient for that Purpose, and find Quarter to the whole." *Ibid.*, VII, 379. Loudoun had told the Duke of Cumberland that since the Pennsylvanians "have all along been so troublesome, and are now so obstinate," he intended to make an example of them and insist they furnish every last article of wartime quartering right down to firewood and beer. Pargellis, *Military Affairs*, 273–4. Thereupon, the Council advised that Denny should "immediately convene the Provincial Commissioners, and make of them a peremptory Demand for the Accommodation of the Soldiers." *Pa. Col. Recs.*, VII, 380. All except Isaac Norris appeared and heard Loudoun's threat, but, according to Peters, they were still in no mood to take action until "B.F.'s expressing his Sentiments in favour of a total Compliance, the rest immediately changed their Tone." Peters to Thomas Penn, Dec. 26, 1756, Penn Papers, Hist. Soc. Pa. See the next two documents for the Commissioners' agreement on quarters.

1. Lewis Ourry (1717–1779), of a refugee Huguenot family five of whose members served British arms, was commissioned lieutenant in 1747, came to America in 1756, and served under Col. Henry Bouquet in western Pennsyl-

and not Sufficient quantity of Covering, the Houses on which they are quarter'd not being capable of containing near the number billeted on them, nor conveniences for them.

The rest have good Beds, and Accomodations.

No Quarters fit for Officers.

Nor any provided for the Recruits daily coming in.

Ls. OURRY
Acting as Qr. Mast. to the first
Battallion of the R. A. Regt.

To Henry Bouquet[2] with Memoranda

Letter: Draft: Library of Congress. Memoranda: I and II: Library of Congress; III: American Philosophical Society[3]

After the commissioners agreed at Franklin's urging to meet all of Colonel Bouquet's and Lord Loudoun's demands for quarters, it remained

vania as a quartermaster and commissary officer until 1765. He was on friendly terms with BF's family in Philadelphia, and later with BF in London. Donald Cornu, "Captain Lewis Ourry, Royal American Regiment of Foot," *Pa. Hist.*, XIX (1952), 249–61; Ourry to Deborah Franklin, Sept. 26, 1765; Ann Ourry to BF, May 16, 1783, and Jan. 27, 1785. This letter, without addressee, seems to be a report to a superior officer, probably Governor Denny or Colonel Bouquet. Its presence among BF's papers suggests that it was passed along to him and the other commissioners to consider at their December 26 meeting.

2. Henry Bouquet (1719?–1765), Swiss-born French Protestant, served in Swiss regiments in Holland and Sardinia for twenty years before being commissioned lieutenant colonel in the Royal American Regiment in 1756. After a successful summer as a recruiter, he led the first battalion to its Philadelphia quarters in December where he not only pleased Richard Peters, but impressed BF as a man of "learning, ingenuity, and politeness." Following brief service in South Carolina, he returned in time to take part in the Forbes expedition and serve brilliantly in western Pennsylvania during the rest of the war and during Pontiac's Conspiracy, a contribution for which he was made a naturalized citizen of the grateful province. He was unexcelled in adapting European discipline and infantry tactics to the special conditions of the American wilderness. Shortly after the King thanked him publicly for his services and commissioned him brigadier in command of the southern district, he died of yellow fever in Pensacola. *DAB; PMHB*, LXII (1938), 41–51; Paul-Emile Schazman, "Henry Bouquet in Switzerland," *Pa. Hist.*, XIX (1952), 238, 244–8; Richard Peters to Thomas Penn, Dec. 26, 1756, Penn Papers, Hist. Soc. Pa.; BF to Alexander Garden, April 14, 1757, below, p. 183.

3. All these documents are in BF's hand except the last, which appears to be in that of Quartermaster Lewis Ourry.

only to decide the details: what quarters and "necessaries" would be provided, how soon, and for how many soldiers? Franklin and Bouquet drew up the points of agreement in accordance with the memoranda printed here, the commissioners acceded, and then Franklin sent Bouquet a note confirming the arrangements. Upon learning of the agreement, Denny wrote Loudoun, hoping it would be "entirely to your Lordship's Satisfaction," and Richard Peters was relieved that the "troublesome affair is brought at last to a right issue."[4]

Sir Sunday Evening [December 26, 1756]

I have the Pleasure to acquaint you, that every Thing will be provided agreable to the Memorandums made between us this Evening. I have the Honour to be with great Respect, Sir Your most obedient humble Servant

Col Bouquet

[MEMORANDA]

I

[December 26, 1756][5]

The Hospital is represented as not capable of holding 100 Sick; it is intended to inoculate those who have not had the small Pox, an additional Building is wanting as near as may be to the Hospital, for such as are Sick of that Distemper, which will be wanted no longer than till that is over.[6]

The Necessaries to be furnished in the Hospital, are mentioned in the List.[7]

The whole Men are to be quartered in Town, and tho' the Battalion is not full, it is expected to be so by Recruits continually coming in, and Quarters should be ready for them. If the whole Number of Beds cannot be provided by the first of January, at least One Hundred should be provided, filled with soft Hay or

4. *Pa. Col. Recs.*, VII, 380; Peters to Thomas Penn, Dec. 26, 1756. Fifteen days later Peters reported: "Col. Bouquet hinted that had he applied directly to B.F. and not to the Governor, matters would have been done at first to Lord Loudoun's Satisfaction, this is actually all he [BF] aims at." Peters to Penn, Jan. 10, 1757, Penn Papers, Hist. Soc. Pa.

5. The memoranda are undated, but clearly they were all drawn at the meetings on this date.

6. See above, p. 58 n. "The Hospital" referred to here is that provided by the commissioners for the troops, probably the old building on Market Street vacated by the Pa. Hospital on December 17.

7. See Memorandum III below.

Straw or Chaff, and covered with a Blanket, besides the Sheets and Blankets for Covering. The rest in three Weeks after.[8]

The Deficiencies in the present Quarters to be made good before the first of January.[9]

II

Col. Bouquet expects that an Allowance be made for Officers Lodgings, proportion'd to their Rank, as has been usual in Time of War.

Infantry per Month	Florins Pd.	For the Winter	
A Colonel	40.	Major Genl.	975
Lieut. Colonel	25	Aid de Camp	200
Major	25		
Captain	15		
Lieut.	6		
Adjutant	9		
Ensign	6		
Quarter Master	9		
Chaplain	7. 10		
Auditeur	6. 15		
Surgeon	6		
Provost.	5.		

The above is extracted from the Convention for the Winter Quarters of the British Troops in the Territories of the United Provinces.[1]

20 Stivers make a Florin

10 Florins and 15 Stivers make 20*s.* Sterling

8. The first battalion of the Royal American Regiment, fully recruited, would require quarters for 1100 men and 51 officers. 1 *Pa. Arch.*, III, 85–6. Since about 600 troops were already quartered, 500 additional beds would make "the whole Number." The commissioners' accounts for 1757 show frequent payments for bedding, rent, utensils, horse pasturage, beer, and sundries. *Votes*, 1757–58, pp. 118–19.

9. See the preceding document for Quartermaster Lewis Ourry's return of deficiencies.

1. Bouquet, who had been in the Dutch service, and British officers who had been among the troops often stationed in the United Provinces during the eighteenth century, were doubtless familiar with quartering conventions there; the particular one referred to here has not been identified. For the commissioners' proposals on allowances for officers' quarters, see below, p. 96.

Return of Necesaries wanted for the Hospital granted for the Sick of the 1st Battallion of the Royal American Regiment At Philadelphia[2]

III

		No. of Men
Beds and Bedding for two Men each	36	84
Ditto – – – –for Single Patients	12	
Pewter Bed Pans – – –	6	
Close Stools – – –	6	
Chamber Potts – – –	50	
Kitchen Utensils		
Copper Kettles for Cooking – –	6[3]	
Wooden Platters – – –	60	
Wooden Spoons – – –	60	
Pewter Porringers – – –	60	
Pewter Spoons – – –	60	
Tin Saucepans of different Sizes –	20	

With a Sufficient Quantity of Candles, Firing, and Utensils
Candlesticks
Knives and Forks.

William Denny to the Provincial Commissioners

Copy: Pennsylvania Historical and Museum Commission

Gentlemen, Philadelphia 29th: December 1756

Mr. Croghan, who has a Deputation from Sir William Johnson to manage Indian Affairs for this Part of the Northern District,[4]

2. This return is almost certainly the list referred to in Memorandum I above; it was probably submitted by Quartermaster Ourry for the guidance of the commissioners.

3. George Wescott received £5 12*s.* on May 10, 1757, for "six Copper Kettles" delivered to Commissioner Joseph Fox. *Votes*, 1757–58, p. 118.

4. Under Johnson's own exclusive commission to manage Indian affairs in the Northern Department, he had on Nov. 24, 1756, made George Croghan his deputy in Pennsylvania with instructions to secure Indian friendship, persuade braves to march with British armies in the spring campaigns, inquire into Delaware and Shawnee grievances, and find out the intentions of the Ohio Indians. When Denny read to the Council, December 14, a letter from Croghan announcing his authority and explaining his plans, that body "was not a little surprized at the Appointment" in view of Croghan's earlier difficulties in the province. *Pa. Col. Recs.*, VII, 354–6 (and see above, VI, 295 n.). He was

has proposed, for the immediate Service of this and the other Colonies, to send one or two Messengers to the Sasquehannah Indians at Otsaningo, and to Teedyuscung at Diahogo,[5] to come to meet him at Harris's Ferry, where he will endeavour to engage some of the most skilful and discreet of them to go to the several Shawonese and Delaware Tribes of the Ohio Indians, in order to sound their Inclinations with respect to this Province, and if they shall be found well disposed, then to invite them to a Conference in the Spring, at some Place to be left to their Choice. As Money will be wanted for this Service, I recommend it to you to allow a Part out of the Remainder of the Thirty Thousand Pounds to defray the Expences which will accrue by these Messages and the intended Necessaries at Harris's. This, which requires immediate Dispatch, is, I think, of so much Consequence as to merit a Preference to any other Matters. It is necessary that this Affair should be kept secret.[6] I am Gentlemen, Your very humble Servant, WILLIAM DENNY.

To the Provincial Commissioners.

---

asked to appear in Council on the 29th when "the State of Indian Affairs was fully considered." Since Denny had no funds at his disposal, the Council agreed to seek the commissioners' aid in executing Croghan's plans. *Pa. Col. Recs.*, VII, 382.

5. Indian towns on the upper east branch of the Susquehanna, near present-day Binghamton, N.Y., and Athens, Pa., respectively.

6. The commissioners received this letter on the 29th, and that evening two of them told Denny they could not grant the request since the £30,000 "were expended." *Ibid.*, VII, 383. On Jan. 4, 1757, the commissioners laid the letter before the House, where, after Denny had furnished copies of Croghan's instructions and plans, Speaker Isaac Norris was asked "to speak to George Croghan, concerning his Intentions of sending Messages to the Indians." Norris reported on the 6th that Croghan expected the government to defray the expense of sending "Messengers to Diahogo, to hasten the Meeting of the Indians intended to be held at Easton, in Pursuance of the late Conference with Teedyuscung." The Assembly promptly resolved to bear that expense (*Votes*, 1756–57, pp. 62–4), but perhaps pointedly said nothing about messengers to the Ohio Indians or a conference at Harris's Ferry. Two days later Croghan received £100 from Israel Pemberton and other members of the Friendly Association to pay for sending "Messengers to the Ohio Indians and obtaining a Conference with them." *Pa. Col. Recs.*, VII, 391. Thus, at least temporarily, Croghan secured the support of the usually discordant groups interested in Indian affairs: the governor and his Council, the Assembly, and the Friendly Association. Nicholas B. Wainwright, *George Croghan, Wilderness Diplomat* (Chapel Hill, 1959), pp. 118–21.

To Edward and Jane Mecom

ALS: American Philosophical Society

Philada. Dec. 30. 1756.

Dear Brother and Sister

You will receive this by the Hand of your Son Benjamin, on whose safe Return from the West Indies I sincerely congratulate you.[7] He has settled Accounts with me, and paid the Ballance honourably.[8] He has also clear'd the old Printing House to himself, and sent it to Boston, where he purposes to set up his Business together with Bookselling, which, considering his Industry and Frugality, I make no doubt will answer.[9] He has good Credit and some Money in England, and I have help'd him by lending him a little more;[1] so that he may expect a Cargo of Books and a Quantity of new Letter in the Spring; and I shall from time to time furnish him with Paper. We all join in Love to you and yours, I am Your Loving Brother

B Franklin

To William Strahan

ALS: Free Library of Philadelphia

Dear Sir

Philada. Dec. 31. 1756

This serves only to cover a Bill of Exchange drawn by B. Mecom on you, upon a Supposition that you have receiv'd Bills he sent you from Antigua for about £120 more than the Ballance of your Account.[2] If those Bills are not come to hand or not paid, you need not be at the Trouble of Protesting this Bill; but let it lie in your Hands till you hear farther from me. If those Bills are paid, then please to carry this £100 to my Account. B. Mecom has settled honourably with me, and bought my old Printing-House that he had at An-

7. On Benjamin Mecom's decision to give up his printing business in Antigua, see above, VI, 463–5.

8. Among the Franklin Papers in APS is Benjamin Mecom's bond to BF, Dec. 27, 1756, for the payment of £50 one year from date. In his will of April 28, 1757, made before sailing to England, BF bequeathed this bond with accrued interest to Benny, indicating thereby his intention to forgive the debt. The bond was never canceled as paid.

9. The Boston venture lasted until 1762 when he moved to New York.

1. See BF's letter to Strahan immediately below.

2. See above, VI, 467, 477.

tigua. He wants some new Letter which he now writes for. Lest his Bills abovementioned should fail, I have given him a Draft on my Friend Collinson for Fifty Pounds Sterling which he now sends to you. He purposes to set up in Boston.[3] My Respects affectionately to you and yours, particularly my Son Billy.[4] It gives me great Pleasure to learn by your last that he is become so capable of Business.[5] I am, Dear Sir, Your most obedient Servant

B FRANKLIN

Addressed: To / Mr Wm Strahan / Printer / London

From [Elizabeth Hubbart][6]

AL: American Philosophical Society

My Dear Papa [*c.* December 1756]

Now for the Story I promised in my last;[7] and I wish I had the nack of teling it in such a maner, as to afford you as many Hearty Laugh's, as I have had on the Occation. You must know then, that Littel mischievous Urching Cupid, has got a mighty odd whim in his Head, he has new strung his Bow, and let fly one of his Keenest Arrows directly ame'd; at the Heart of an Old Man (our Speaker Mr. Hubbards Father)[8] in his Eighty first Year, he Buryed his Wife about a Month ago, and has been for many years as Blind as a Beatel, yet nothing would do but he must have another Wife, well he imediately set about recolecting what Beauties he h[a]d formily

3. See immediately above.

4. A reference to the proposed marriage between William Strahan, Jr., and Sarah Franklin, which the two fathers often mentioned but which never took place.

5. Strahan's letter to BF not found; but on Sept. 11, 1756, Strahan had written to David Hall that by the departure of a senior employee he had lately had "a good Opportunity of bringing Billy forward in the Business, who now supplies his place extremely well, and vastly beyond my Expectation, or what could reasonably be hoped from one of his Years." APS.

6. Identified by the handwriting and by BF's reply, Jan. 13, 1757.

7. Not found.

8. Joseph Hubbard (1676–1761), blacksmith, brazier, landowner, deputy to the Mass. General Court, 1694–95, married in 1698 Thankful Brown, presumably the deceased wife of this story. Their son Thomas Hubbard (1702–1773), A. B., Harvard, 1721, became a wealthy Boston merchant; member of the General Court; speaker, 1750–59; councilor, 1759–72; treasurer of Harvard, 1752–73. *Sibley's Harvard Graduates*, VI, 490–5.

seen; and giving my Mama the preferance, the Parson[9] was set to woork to feel her Palts (no mischeif going forward but the Parson and the Deavel have a finger in the Pye you know) but they being very much Indisposed he was Obliged to think again, and after severiel Vain attempts, he at last thought of a Lady he had great hopes of! and as soon as Boux Phebus's Nap was out, he sent for his Granson, and told him to go to the Lady, and be sure to make a low Bow and say Madam, and give his Love to her; and tell her if She would favour him with a Visset, the Chorrote[1] should wate on her, but by no means to forget to make a low Bow, and say Madam, and I beleive he gave him a Copper to Quicken his Memory, for the arrent was so well done that the Lady wated on him in a few hours, when after a littel Conversation he was told she was going, he roas and by the help of a Servant, and his Hands Pawing about like a Cat a drowning he found the Lady Clasped her in his Arms; and they say almost stifeled her with Kisses, he beg'd She would retier with him to the Chamber, where we must leave them an hour or two—well the Lady is come down, and would you think it, they say her Capp, Hankercheif, and Apron, are very much Discompose'd. However the Preliminaries are all setteled, and they agreed to be Published the next day! the young Rogues say to prevent a greater discovery, but I beleive it was only to prevent his Hanging him self in his Garter, or some such Fattal accident, for he sent for his Son that Night, and desiered he might be put on the Clarks Book as early as possible the next Morning. His Son invain indeavoured to perswade him to defer it a littel, told him every Boy in the street was talking of it, and he thought in deacencey to his Mother's Memory he might Stay a littel longer, beg'd he would Consider on it if it was but for one Week. He indeed Acknowledged it was too soon, but then he desiered him to Consider (now you must imagine him ringing up his Face, like a Child that has lost its Sugar Teat) that he should lose a World of Happiness with the Lady in that Time, and a Week was an Age, with a good deal more such stuf, and that Tomorrow must, and should be the Day. And so it was, the Minit they ware out Pub-

9. Possibly Thomas Foxcroft (1697–1769) of the First Church, Boston, who performed the marriage described here.

1. Charrote: chariot, in the eighteenth century a light four-wheeled carriage with a coach box and rear seats only.

lished the Parson Joyn'd their Hands, the Coulars ware display'd, and the Gun's Fire'd, and after a Dance in the Evining, the Lambs were lade in Bed.[2] Now I think I have given you a very perticular Account of this Courtship, and Weding, but however light we pretend to make of this affair, it may have sad Consiqunces, and from this Success of Cupids he may intirely forget us, Unless you can think of Some Stratigem to prevent it.

Adiue And beleive me with the highest Esteem and affection Dear Sir [*Signature torn off*]

PS I had forgot to tell you he has an Estate of 10000 Pounds sterling, and besides the agrement he has promised to give the Lady a thousand Pounds O[ld] Tenor every ten Years he shall Live with her, and he is but Eighty one.

Queries on Frontier Settlement and Defense

MS not found; reprinted from William Duane, *Memoirs of Benjamin Franklin . . . with a Postliminious Preface* (Philadelphia, 1834), I, xvii.

Duane states that "we find the following notes made immediately upon his [Franklin's] appointment to the command" in Northampton County (Jan. 5, 1756), but the present editors know of no reason for assigning such a precise date. The calm tone of the queries suggests long-range planning rather than emergency; perhaps Franklin drew them up for one of the many meetings of the provincial commissioners in the sixteen months between Nov. 27, 1755, and his departure for England, April 4, 1757. During that time countless now forgotten plans for defense must have been proposed only to be discarded for equally numerous and also forgotten reasons. One such scheme, outlined in *Pa. Gaz.*, March 25, 1756, proposed a law banding farmers together in groups of "ten, twelve, or fourteen" in order that some men always be available for guard duty while others tilled the fields. Also recommended were communal arrangements modeled on Moravian practices, small fortifications, and arms supplied by the province. Whatever their specific relevance, the considerations here printed help to point up Franklin's concern and re-

2. The marriage intentions of Mr. Joseph Hubbard and Mrs. Elizabeth Adams were recorded Dec. 9, 1756, *Boston Marriages, 1752–1809*, Boston Record Commissioners' Report, XXX, 22. Foxcroft recorded the marriage (mentioning Hubbard's age as 81), Dec. 23, 1756, *New Eng. Hist. and Geneal. Reg.*, XLII (1888), 253. Harlan P. Hubbard, *One Thousand Years of Hubbard History* (N.Y., 1895), pp. 89–90, fails to mention this second marriage.

sponsibility for frontier settlement and defense during the Indian wars of 1755–57.[3]

[1756]

Considerations to be taken:

What number of men?

Should the post be fortified, and in what manner?

How long to be continued there?

Could they not be partly employed in raising their own provisions?

Could they have some lots of land assigned them for their encouragement?

What their pay? and from what funds?

How much the annual expense?

Is it certain that the late method of giving rewards for apprehending rioters will be effectual?

To whom does the land belong?

Anonymous: Musing near a Cool Spring

Transcript: Library Company of Philadelphia

Unsigned and undated, these verses have been copied into a Scrap Volume compiled by Pierre Eugène du Simitière. The latest event specifically mentioned is the building of Fort Allen in January 1756 (above, VI, 362–7), and the absence of any direct mention of Franklin's English mission implies a date earlier than the summer of 1757 and presumably even before the decision of the Assembly to send him to England (Feb. 3, 1757). Probably the verses were written during his period of great popularity in the spring and summer of 1756. Richard Peters admitted to Thomas Penn in April that "even two thirds of the church are gone off... in favor of him and his Politicks," and later described the escort

3. The editors have also considered the possibility that this paper relates to proposals made by the Proprietors in 1751 for establishing a settlement and blockhouse in the Allegheny country as a protection to Indian trade. Governor Hamilton had conferred with Speaker Norris "and some of the principal Members of the House" on the matter in February, and on August 21 the House had sent a message opposing the idea. But, since BF did not become a member of the Assembly until these discussions were nearly at an end, it seems unlikely that he would have prepared such a memorandum at that time. *Pa. Col. Recs.*, V, 514–15, 547.

given Franklin by the militia officers on his departure for Virginia (March 19) by saying that they had acted "as if he had been a member of the Royal Family or Majesty itself."[4] Franklin explained the situation to Collinson more simply. "The People happen to love me," he wrote. "Perhaps that's my Fault."[5] The unknown author of these verses was clearly one of those who loved him.[6]

[1756?]

Musing near a Cool Spring

"A wit's a feather and a cheif's a rod
An honest man's, the noblest work of God." Pope[7]

Dear patriot muse that honest man behold
Record his Acts in characters of gold.

Who plann'd the Scheme the Associates to unite?
Who wrote *plain truth* to bring that scheme to light?
Who bid Yon Academick structure rise?
"Behold the Man!" each lisping babe replies.
Who schemed Yon Hospital for the helpless poor?
And op'd to charitable use each folding door.
Our Countrys cause, what senator defends?
Void of all partial, or all private ends.
Who to his publick trust has firmly stood?
And built Fort Allen for his Countrys good.
Who form'd a Law our Forces to unite?
And diegn'd to execute that Law aright.
Who found out means our Treasury to supply?
Who would not suffer publick faith to die?

4. Peters to Penn, April 29, June 1, 1756, Penn Papers, Hist. Soc. Pa.

5. See above, p. 13.

6. Thomas P. Haviland (*PMHB*, LXXV (1951), 196–8) believes that the verses were composed in 1767 or 1768 and that the couplet beginning "Our Country's cause" refers to the English agency. The editors disagree; attention is focused too directly on BF's services in defense of Pennsylvania, 1755–56, and any similar poetical effusion composed as late as 1767 could hardly fail to make specific mention of his testimony before the House of Commons (February 1766) in favor of repealing the Stamp Act. The cited couplet seems to refer to his leadership in the Assembly on measures for defense.

7. *Essay on Man*, Epistle IV, 247–8; quoted in *Poor Richard Improved*, 1748, above, III, 262.

Who was the Man brave Braddock, did record?
"The only man that with him keep his word."[8]

'Twas He, whose name, the good and just will sound,
While patriot deeds on faithful records stand.

Great thy reward for all thy Labours done,
And at the great Tribunal will be known.
There will thy Genius other worlds survey,
And there adore the glorious God of day.
There Bacon Newton will our F——lin greet.
And place him in his Electrisic seat.
'Ore Uurope, Asia, Africk's, science'd Fame,
The Royal Medal will exalt thy name;
Transfer the Palm by thy great genius won
And proudly own America's great son.
If then thy sphere, to Electerise above,
Dart me one ray in pitty and in love
Oh! send thy influence, if permitted, send,
To guide my soul to my beloved Friend.

Poor Richard Improved, 1757

Poor Richard improved: Being an Almanack and Ephemeris . . . for the Year of our Lord 1757: . . . By Richard Saunders, Philom. Philadelphia: Printed and Sold by B. Franklin, and D. Hall. (Yale University Library)

Courteous Reader,

As no temporal Concern is of more Importance to us than *Health,* and that depends so much on the Air we every Moment breathe, the Choice of a good wholesome Situation to fix a Dwelling in, is a very serious Affair to every Countryman about to begin the World, and well worth his Consideration, especially as not only the *Comfort* of Living, but even the *Necessaries of Life,* depend in a great Measure upon it; since a Family frequently sick can rarely if ever thrive. The following Extracts therefore from a

8. General Braddock wrote Governor Morris, May 24, 1755, that "in every Instance, but in my Contract for the Pennsylvania Waggons I have been deceived and met with nothing but Lies and Villany." Morris laid this letter before his Council June 2, and its contents undoubtedly became generally known in Philadelphia soon after. *Pa. Col. Recs.,* VI, 400.

late Medical Writer, Dr. Pringle,[9] on that Subject, will, I hope, be acceptable and useful to some of my Readers.

I hear that some have already, to their great Advantage, put in Practice the Use of Oxen recommended in my last.[1] 'Tis a Pleasure to me to be any way serviceable in communicating useful Hints to the Publick; and I shall be obliged to others for affording me the Opportunity of enjoying that Pleasure more frequently, by sending me from time to time such of their own Observations, as may be advantageous if published in the Almanack. I am thy obliged Friend, RICHARD SAUNDERS

How to make a STRIKING SUNDIAL, by which not only a Man's own Family, but all his Neighbours for ten Miles round, may know what o'Clock it is, when the Sun shines, without seeing the Dial.[2]

Chuse an open Place in your Yard or Garden, on which the Sun may shine all Day without any Impediment from Trees or Buildings. On the Ground mark out your Hour Lines, as for a horizontal Dial, according to Art, taking Room enough for the Guns. On the Line for One o'Clock, place one Gun; on the Two o'Clock Line two Guns, and so of the rest. The Guns must all be charged with Powder, but Ball is unnecessary. Your Gnomon or Style must have twelve burning Glasses annex'd to it, and be so placed as that the Sun shining through the Glasses, one after the other, shall cause the Focus or burning Spot to fall on the Hour Line of One for Example, at one a Clock, and there kindle a Train of Gunpowder that shall fire one Gun. At Two a Clock, a Focus shall fall on the Hour Line of Two, and kindle another Train that shall discharge two Guns successively; and so of the rest.

Note, There must be 78 Guns in all. Thirty-two Pounders will be best for this Use; but 18 Pounders may do, and will cost less, as well as use less Powder, for nine Pounds of Powder will do for

9. On John Pringle see above, VI, 178 n. The extracts are not reprinted here.

1. See above, VI, 316–18.

2. This piece was reprinted in London the following year in the newly established *Grand Magazine of Universal Intelligence, and Monthly Chronicle of our Own Times*, I (Feb. 1758), 96, and evoked several humorous responses in later issues of the magazine.

one Charge of each eighteen Pounder, whereas the Thirty-two Pounders would require for each Gun 16 Pounds.

Note also, That the chief Expence will be the Powder, for the Cannon once bought, will, with Care, last 100 Years.

Note moreover, That there will be a great Saving of Powder in cloudy Days.

Kind Reader, Methinks I hear thee say, *That it is indeed a good Thing to know how the Time passes, but this Kind of Dial, notwithstanding the mentioned Savings, would be very expensive; and the Cost greater than the Advantage*. Thou art wise, my Friend, to be so considerate beforehand; some Fools would not have found out so much, till they had made the Dial and try'd it. Let all such learn that many a private and many a publick Project, are like this *Striking Dial*, great Cost for little Profit.

JANUARY. *I Month.*

CONVERSATION HINTS.[3]

Good Sense and Learning may Esteem obtain,
Humour and Wit a Laugh, if rightly ta'en;
Fair Virtue Admiration may impart;
But 'tis GOOD-NATURE only wins the Heart:
It molds the Body to an easy Grace,
And brightens every Feature of the Face;
It smooths th'unpolish'd Tongue with Eloquence,
And adds Persuasion to the finest Sense.

He that would rise at Court, must begin by Creeping.

Many a Man's own Tongue gives Evidence against his Understanding.

Nothing dries sooner than a Tear.

3. The "Conversation Hints" at the beginning of each month are taken, with omissions and changes, from Benjamin Stillingfleet, *An Essay on Conversation* (London, 1737), lines 219–465 *passim*, reprinted in Robert Dodsley, *A Collection of Poems* (London, 1748), I, 169–78 *passim*. The third couplet in the September extract does not appear in the original version or the Dodsley anthology.

When a Man looks back upon his Day, Week or Year spent, and finds his Business has been worthy the Dignity of human Nature, it exhilerates and revives him, enables him to pass his own Approbation on himself, and, as it were, to anticipate the *Euge,* the *Well done, good and faithful Servant,* he shall one Day receive from his great Master. But he that gives himself only the idle Divertisements of a Child, cannot reflect on Time past without Confusion; and is forced to take Sanctuary in a total Inconsideration, or run from one Amusement to another, to avoid Thinking, or answering to himself the Question, *What have I done?* Idleness, and its Amusements are in the End more tiresome than Labour itself.[4]

Uneasy both in Country and in Town,
They search a Place to lay their Burthen down:
One, restless in his Parlour, walks abroad,
And vainly thinks to leave behind his Load;
But strait returns; for he's as restless there,
And finds there's no Relief in open Air.
To's Country Seat another would retire,
And spurs as hard as if it were on Fire,
There soon begins to yawn, and stretch and snore,
And seeks the City which he left before.

FEBRUARY. *II Month.*

Would you both please, and be instructed too,
The Pride of shewing forth yourself subdue.
Hear ev'ry Man upon his fav'rite Theme,
And ever be more knowing than you seem.
The lowest Genius will afford some Light,
Or give a Hint that had escap'd your Sight.
Doubt, till he thinks you on Conviction yield,
And with fit Questions let each Pause be fill'd.

4. This paragraph is from Charles Palmer, *A Collection of Select Aphorisms and Maxims, with Historical Observations: Extracted from the Most Eminent Authors* (London, 1748), no. 587. BF has supplied the quotation from Matthew 25:21, following "Euge," and has modified and shortened the remainder of the passage. The verses which follow have not been identified.

And the most knowing will with Pleasure grant,
You're rather much reserv'd than ignorant.

'Tis easier to build two Chimneys, than maintain one in Fuel.

Anger warms the Invention, but overheats the Oven.

Is there any Duty in Religion more generally agreed on, or more justly required by God, than a perfect Submission to his Will in all Things? Can any Disposition of Mind, either please him more, or become us better, than that of being satisfied with all he gives, and content with all he takes away? None, certainly, can be of more Honour to God, nor of more Ease to ourselves; for if we consider him as our Maker, we dare not contend with him; if as our Father, we ought not to mistrust him; so that we may be confident whatever he does is for our Good, and whatever happens that we interpret otherwise, yet we can get nothing by Repining, nor save anything by Resisting.[5]

'Tis done, O Lord, the Idol I resign,
Unfit to share a Heart so justly thine;
Nor can the Heav'nly Call unwelcome be,
That still invites my Soul more near to thee:
Ye Shades, ye Phantoms, and ye Dreams adieu!
With Smiles I now your parting Glories view.
I see the Hand; I worship, I adore,
And justify the great disposing Power.

RULES of LAW fit to be observed in purchasing.
From an old Book.[6]

First, see the Land which thou intend'st to buy,
Within the Seller's Title clear doth lie.
And that no Woman to it doth lay Claim,
By Dowry, Jointure, or some other Name,
That it may cumber. Know if bound or free
The Tenure stand, and that from each Feoffee

5. Palmer, *Select Aphorisms*, no. 138, with variations. The verses which follow have not been identified.

6. Not found.

It be releas'd: That the Seller be so old
That he may lawful sell, thou lawful hold.
Have special Care that it not mortgag'd lie,
Nor be entailed on Posterity.
Then if it stand in Statute bound or no:
Be well advis'd what Quit Rent out must go;
What Custom, Service hath been done of old,
By those who formerly the same did hold.
And if a wedded Woman put to Sale,
Deal not with her, unless she bring her Male.
For she doth under Covert-Baron go,
Altho' sometimes some also traffick so.
Thy Bargain being made, and all this done,
Have special Care to make thy Charter run
To thee, thine Heirs, Executors, Assigns,
For that beyond thy Life securely binds.
These Things foreknown and done, you may prevent
Those Things rash Buyers many times repent.
And yet, when as you have done all you can,
If you'd be sure, deal with an honest Man.

Very good Rules, these, and sweetly sung. If they are learnt by heart, and repeated often to keep them in Memory, they may happen to save the Purchaser more Pence than the Price of my Almanack. In Imitation of this old Writer, I have Thoughts of turning Coke's *Institutes,* and all our Province Laws into Metre, hoping thereby to engage some of our young Lawyers and old Justices to *read a little.*

MARCH. *III Month.*

The Rays of Wit gild wheresoe'er they strike,
But are not therefore fit for all alike;
They charm the lively, but the Grave offend,
And raise a Foe as often as a Friend;
Like the resistless Beams of blazing Light,
That chear the strong, and pain the weakly Sight.
If a bright Fancy therefore be your Share,
Let Judgment watch it with a Guardian's Care.

It is Ill-Manners to silence a Fool, and Cruelty to let him go on.

Scarlet, Silk and Velvet, have put out the Kitchen Fire.

APRIL. *IV Month.*

'Tis like a Torrent, apt to overflow,
Unless by constant Government kept low;
And ne'er inefficacious passes by,
But overturns or gladdens all that's nigh.
Or else, like Trees, when suffer'd wild to shoot,
That put forth much, but all unripen'd Fruit;
It turns to Affectation and Grimace,
As like to Wit as Gravity to Grace.

He that would catch Fish, must venture his Bait.

Men take more pains to mask than mend.

One *To-day* is worth two *To-morrows*.

Since Man is but of a very limited Power in his own Person, and consequently can effect no great Matter merely by his own personal Strength, but as he acts in Society and Conjunction with others; and since no Man can engage the active Assistance of others, without first engaging their Trust; And moreover, since Men will trust no further than they judge one, for his *Sincerity*, fit to be trusted; it follows, that a discovered Dissembler can atchieve nothing great or considerable. For not being able to gain Mens Trust, he cannot gain their Concurrence; and so is left alone to act singly and upon his own Bottom; and while that is the Sphere of his Activity, all that he can do must needs be contemptible.[7]

Sincerity has such resistless Charms,
She oft the fiercest of our Foes disarms:
No Art she knows, in native Whiteness dress'd,
Her Thoughts all pure, and therefore all express'd:
She takes from Error its Deformity;
And without her all other Virtues die.

7. Not found. The verses which follow are from Stillingfleet, *Essay on Conversation,* lines 400–7, reprinted in Dodsley, *Collection of Poems,* I, 176.

Bright Source of Goodness! to my Aid descend,
Watch o'er my Heart, and all my Words attend.

MAY. *V Month.*

How hard soe'er it be to bridle *Wit,*
Yet *Mem'ry* oft no less requires the Bit:
How many, hurried by its Force away,
For ever in the Land of Gossips stray!
Usurp the Province of the Nurse, to lull,
Without her Privilege for being dull!
Tales upon Tales they raise, ten Stories high,
Without Regard to Use or Symmetry.

The way to be safe, is never to be secure.

Dally not with other Folks Women or Money.

Work as if you were to live 100 Years, Pray as if you were to die To-morrow.

It is generally agreed to be Folly, *to hazard the Loss of a Friend, rather than lose a Jest.* But few consider how easily a Friend may be thus lost. Depending on the known Regard their Friends have for them, Jesters take more Freedom with Friends than they would dare to do with others, little thinking how much deeper we are wounded by an Affront from one we love. But the strictest Intimacy can never warrant Freedoms of this Sort; and it is indeed preposterous to think they should; unless we can suppose Injuries are less Evils when they are done us by Friends, than when they come from other Hands.[8]

Excess of Wit may oftentimes beguile:
Jests are not always pardon'd—by a Smile.
Men may disguise their Malice at the Heart,
And seem at Ease—tho' pain'd with inward Smart.
Mistaken, we—think all such Wounds of course
Reflection cures;—alas! it makes them worse.
Like Scratches they with double Anguish seize,
Rankle in time, and fester by Degrees.

8. Neither this paragraph nor the verses which follow has been identified.

JUNE. *VI Month.*

A Story should, to please, at least seem true,
Be apropos, well told, concise, and new;
And whensoe'er it deviates from these Rules,
The Wise will sleep, and leave Applause to Fools.
But others, more intolerable yet,
The Waggeries that they've said, or heard, repeat;
Heavy by Mem'ry made, and what's the worst,
At second-hand as often as at first.

Pride breakfasted with *Plenty,* dined with *Poverty,* supped with *Infamy.*

Retirement does not always secure Virtue; Lot was upright in the City, wicked in the Mountain.

But sarcastical Jests on a Man's Person or his Manners, tho' hard to bear, are perhaps more easily borne than those that touch his Religion. Men are generally warm in what regards their religious Tenets, either from Tenderness of Conscience, or a high Sense of their own Judgments. People of plain Parts and honest Dispositions, look on Salvation as too serious a Thing to be jested with; and Men of speculative Religion, who profess from the Conviction rather of their Heads than Hearts, are not a bit less vehement than the real Devotees. He who says a slight or a severe Thing of their Faith, seems to them to have thereby undervalued their Understandings, and will consequently incur their Aversion, which no Man of common Sense would hazard for a lively Expression; much less a Person of good Breeding, who should make it his chief Aim to be well with all.[9]

Like some grave Matron of a noble Line,
With awful Beauty does Religion shine.
Just Sense should teach us to revere the Dame,
Nor, by imprudent Jests, to spot her Fame.
In common Life you'll own this Reas'ning right,
That none but Fools in gross Abuse delight:
Then use it here—nor think the Caution vain;
To be *polite,* Men need not be profane.

9. Neither this paragraph nor the verses which follow has been identified.

JULY. *VII Month.*

But above all Things, *Raillery* decline,
Nature but few does for that Task design;
'Tis in the ablest Hand a dangerous Tool,
But never fails to wound the meddling Fool:
For all must grant it needs no common Art
To keep Men patient while we make them smart.
Not *Wit* alone, nor *Humour's* self, will do,
Without *Good nature,* and *much Prudence* too.

Idleness is the Dead Sea, that swallows all Virtues: Be active in Business, that *Temptation* may miss her Aim: The Bird that sits, is easily shot.

Shame and the *Dry-belly-ach* were Diseases of the last Age; this seems to be cured of them.

In studying Law or Physick, or any other Art or Science, by which you propose to get your Livelihood, though you find it at first hard, difficult and unpleasing, use *Diligence, Patience* and *Perseverance;* the Irksomness of your Task will thus diminish daily, and your Labour shall finally be crowned with Success. You shall go beyond all your Competitors who are careless, idle or superficial in their Acquisitions, and be at the Head of your Profession. *Ability* will command *Business, Business Wealth;* and *Wealth* an easy and honourable *Retirement* when Age shall require it.[10]

Near to the wide extended Coasts of Spain,
Some Islands triumph o'er the raging Main;
Where dwelt of old, as tuneful Poets say,
Slingers, who bore from all the Prize away.[1]
While Infants yet, their feeble Nerves they try'd;
Nor needful Food, till won by Art, supply'd.
Fix'd was the Mark, the Youngster oft in vain,
Whirl'd the misguided Stone with fruitless Pain:

10. Neither this paragraph nor the verses which follow has been identified.
1. The Balearic slingers.

'Till, by long Practice, to Perfection brought,
With easy Sleight their former Task they wrought.
Swift from their Arm th'unerring Pebble flew,
And high in Air, the flutt'ring Victim slew.
So in each Art Men rise but by Degrees,
And Months of Labour lead to Years of Ease.

AUGUST. *VIII Month.*

Of all the Qualities that help to raise
In Men the universal Voice of Praise,
Whether in Pleasure or in Use they end,
There's none that can with MODESTY contend.
Yet 'tis but little that its *Form* be caught,
Unless its *Origin* be first in Thought;
Else rebel Nature will reveal the Cheat,
And the whole Work of Art at once defeat.

Tho' the Mastiff be gentle, yet bite him not by the Lip.

Great-Alms-giving, lessens no Man's Living.

The royal Crown cures not the Head-ach.

On the Freedom of the PRESS.[2]

While free from Force the Press remains,
Virtue and *Freedom* chear our Plains,
And *Learning* Largesses bestows,
And keeps unlicens'd open House.
We to the Nation's publick Mart
Our Works of Wit, and Schemes of Art,
And philosophic Goods, this Way,
Like Water carriage, cheap convey.
This *Tree* which *Knowledge* so affords,
Inquisitors with flaming Swords
From Lay-Approach with Zeal defend,
Lest their own Paradise should end.

2. Matthew Green, *The Spleen. An Epistle Inscribed to his particular Friend Mr. C.J.* [Cuthbert Jackson] (London, 1737), lines 396–421.

The *Press* from her fecundous Womb
Brought forth the Arts of Greece and Rome;
Her Offspring, skill'd in Logic War,
Truth's Banner wav'd in open Air;
The Monster *Superstition* fled,
And hid in Shades her Gorgon Head;
And *lawless Pow'r,* the long kept Field,
By *Reason* quell'd, was forc'd to yield.

This Nurse of Arts, and Freedom's Fence,
To chain, is Treason against Sense:
And *Liberty,* thy thousand Tongues
None silence who design no Wrongs;
For those that use the Gag's Restraint,
First rob, before they stop Complaint.

SEPTEMBER. *IX Month.*

Hold forth upon yourself on no Pretence,
Unless invited, or in Self-Defence;
The Praise you take, altho' it be your Due,
Will be suspected if it come from you.
If to seem modest, you some Faults confess,
The World suspect yet more, and never less:
For each Man, by Experience taught, can tell
How strong a Flatterer does within him dwell.

These Aspects[3] make it clear to me,
That rain and thunder there will be,
As sure as two and one make three.

Act uprightly, and despise Calumny; Dirt may stick to a Mud Wall, but not to polish'd Marble.

PARADOXES.

I. The Christians observe the *first* Day of the Week for their Sunday, the Jews the *Seventh* for their Sabbath, the Turks the

3. These lines follow a prophesy of cloudy and rainy weather.

sixth Day of the Week for the Time of their Worship; but there is a particular Place of the Globe, to which if a Christian, Jew, and Turk sail in one and the same Ship, they shall keep the Time for their Worship on different Days, as above, all the Time they are sailing to that particular Place; but when they arrive at that Place, and during the Time they remain at it, they shall all keep their Sabbath on one and the same Day; but when they depart from that Place, they shall all differ as before.

II. There is a certain Port, from which if three Ships depart at one and the same time, and sail on three particular different Courses, till they return to the Port they departed from; and if in one of these Ships be Christians, in the second Jews, and in the third Turks, when they return to the Port they departed from, they shall differ so with respect to real and apparent Time, that they all shall keep their Sabbath on one and the same Day of the Week, and yet each of them separately shall believe that he keeps his Sabbath on the Day of the Week his Religion requires.

OCTOBER. *X Month.*

No Part of Conduct asks for Skill more nice,
Tho' none more common, than to give *Advice:*
Misers themselves, in this will not be saving,
Unless their Knowledge makes it worth the having.
And where's the Wonder, when we will intrude,
An useless Gift, it meets Ingratitude?
Shun then, unask'd, this arduous Task to try;
But, if consulted, use *Sincerity.*

The *Borrower* is a Slave to the *Lender;* the *Security* to *both.*

Singularity in the right, hath ruined many: Happy those who are Convinced of the general Opinion.

Ambition to be greater and richer, merely that a Man may have it in his Power to do more Service to his Friends and the Publick, is of a quiet orderly Kind, pleased if it succeeds, resigned if it fails. But the *Ambition* that has *itself* only in View, is restless, turbulent, regardless of publick Peace, or general Interest, and the secret

Maker of most Mischiefs, between Nations, Parties, Friends and Neighbours.[4]

Let Satyr blast, with every Mark of Hate,
The vain Aspirer, or dishonest Great.
Whom Love of Wealth, or wild Ambition's Sway
Push forward, still regardless of the Way;
High and more high who aim with restless Pride
Where neither Reason nor fair Virtue guide;
And Him, the Wretch, who labours on with Pain
For the low Lucre of an useless Gain,
(Wise but to get, and active but to save)
May Scorn deserv'd still follow to the Grave.
But he who fond to raise a splendid Name,
On Life's ambitious Heights would fix his Fame,
In active Arts, or ventrous Arms would shine,
Yet shuns the Paths which Virtue bids decline;
Who dignifies his Wealth by gen'rous Use,
To raise th'Oppress'd, or Merit to produce,
Reason's impartial Voice shall ne'er condemn,
The glorious Purpose of so wise an Aim.

NOVEMBER. *XI Month.*

Be rarely warm in Censure or in Praise;
Few Men deserve our Passion either ways:
For half the World but floats 'twixt Good and Ill,
As Chance disposes Objects, these the Will;
'Tis but a see-saw Game, where Virtue now
Mounts above Vice, and then sinks down as low.
Besides, the Wise still hold it for a Rule,
To trust that Judgment most, that seems most cool.

Proportion your Charity to the Strength of your Estate, or God will proportion your Estate to the Weakness of your Charity.

4. Not found. The verses which follow are from William Melmoth, *Of Active and Retired Life* (London, 1735), pp. 4-5, but BF has here followed the version printed in Dodsley, *Collection of Poems,* I, 185-6, in which the last nine lines differ substantially from the first printing. BF probably took all the poetry by Stillingfleet, Green, and Melmoth in this almanac from Dodsley rather than from the originals.

The Tongue offends, and the Ears get the Cuffing.

Some antient Philosophers have said, that Happiness depends more on the inward Disposition of Mind than on outward Circumstances; and that he who cannot be happy in any State, can be so in no State. To be happy, they tell us we must be content. Right. But they do not teach how we may become content. Poor Richard shall give you a short good Rule for that. *To be content, look backward on those who possess less than yourself, not forward on those who possess more.* If this does not make you *content,* you don't deserve to be *happy.*[5]

CONTENTMENT! Parent of Delight,
So much a Stranger to our Sight,
Say, Goddess, in what happy Place
Mortals behold thy blooming Face;
Thy gracious Auspices impart,
And for thy Temple chuse my Heart.
They whom thou deignest to inspire,
Thy Science learn, *to bound Desire;*
By happy Alchymy of Mind
They turn to Pleasure all they find.
Unmov'd when the rude Tempest blows,
Without an Opiate they repose;
And, cover'd by your Shield, defy
The whizzing Shafts that round them fly;
Nor, meddling with the Gods Affairs,
Concern themselves with distant Cares;
But place their Bliss in mental Rest,
And feast upon the Good possest.

DECEMBER. *XII Month.*

Would you be well receiv'd where'er you go,
Remember each Man vanquish'd is a Foe:
Resist not therefore to your utmost Might,
But let the Weakest think he's sometimes right;

5. Not found. The verses which follow are from Matthew Green, *The Spleen,* lines 602–23.

He, for each Triumph you shall thus decline,
Shall give ten Opportunities to shine;
He sees, since once you own'd him to excel,
That 'tis his Interest you should reason well.

Sleep without Supping, and you'll rise without owing for it.

When other Sins grow old by Time,
Then Avarice is in its prime,
Yet feed the Poor at Christmas time.

Learning is a valuable Thing in the Affairs of this Life, but of infinitely more Importance is *Godliness,* as it tends not only to make us happy here but hereafter. At the Day of Judgment, we shall not be asked, what Proficiency we have made in Languages or Philosophy; but whether we have liv'd virtuously and piously as Men endued with Reason, guided by the Dictates of Religion. In that Hour it will more avail us, that we have thrown a Handful of Flour or Chaff in Charity to a Nest of contemptible Pismires, than that we could muster all the Hosts of Heaven, and call every Star by its proper Name. For then the Constellations themselves shall disappear, the Sun and Moon shall give no more Light, and all the Frame of Nature shall vanish. But our good or bad Works shall remain forever, recorded in the Archives of Eternity.[6]

Unmov'd alone the *Virtuous* now appear,
And in their Looks a calm Assurance wear.
From East, from West, from North and South they come,
To take from the most righteous Judge their Doom;
Who thus, to them, with a serene Regard;
(The Books of Life before him laid,
And all the secret Records wide display'd)
"According to your Works be your Reward:
Possess immortal Kingdoms as your Due,
Prepar'd from an eternal Date for you."

A Receipt for making Sweet Corn, and Suckahtash.

Take the Ears of Indian Corn when in the Milk, and boil them almost enough to eat, then shell it, and spread it on a Cloth very

6. Neither this paragraph nor the verses which follow has been identified.

thin, and dry it in the Sun till it shrinks to half its Bigness, and becomes very hard, then put it into any dry Cask, and it will keep the Year round. When you use it, you must put it into a Pot, and let it warm moderately over a Fire for three or four Hours, but which Means it swells considerably, then boil it till you find 'tis fit to eat. In order to make Suckahtash, 'tis only putting about a third Part of Beans with the Corn when you boil it.

Of the expected COMET.[7]

The great blazing-star or Comet, which appeared in 1531, 1607, and 1682, is expected by Astronomers to return and appear again in this Year, or the next, for its Periods are somewhat unequal, and so cannot be exactly ascertained like those of the Planets which are more regular and better known. According to its last Period, its next Perihelion should be in July 1757; but the Length of that before would make it October 25, 1758.

As these huge tremendous Bodies travel thro' our System, they seem fitted to produce great Changes in it. Mr. Whiston has gone a good Way towards proving that the Comet of 1668,[8] was, in one, of its Revolutions, the Cause of the Deluge, by coming so near this Earth as to raise a vast Tide in the Abyss, by which the Shell was broke, and the whole overflowed; the Comet too was then in its Approach towards the Sun, and he supposes its Atmosphere crouded with the watery Vapours it had gathered in those inconceivably cold Regions, into which it had fled off in its Aphelion, and so produced the mentioned Rains. The same Comet Sir Isaac Newton has calculated, when in its Perihelion December the 8th, was heated by its Nearness to the Sun to a Degree 2000 times more hot than red hot Iron, and would require 50,000 Years to cool again. This same Comet, Dr. Halley observed Nov. 11, was not above a Semidiameter of the Earth from the

7. Halley's Comet of 1682 was expected to return in 1757–58; it was actually sighted in 1758 but did not pass through its perihelion until March 1759. It is named for Edmond Halley (1656–1742), who calculated its orbit and predicted its eighteenth-century reappearance.

8. This should be 1680–81. In the 6th edition of his *New Theory of the Earth* (London, 1755), pp. 459–78, William Whiston (see above, III, 466 n) had explained the Flood by a near-collision between the earth and the comet.

Earth's Way;[9] so that had the Earth at that time been in that Part of its Orbit, something very extraordinary might have happened either by Water or Fire.

Should a Comet in its Course strike the Earth, it might instantly beat it to Pieces, or carry it off out of the Planetary System.[1] The great Conflagration may also, by Means of a Comet, be easily brought about; for as some of them are supposed to be much bigger than this Globe we live on, if one should meet with us in its Return from the Sun, all the Disputes between the Powers of Europe would be settled in a Moment; the World, to such a Fire, being no more than a Wasp's Nest thrown into an Oven.

But our Comfort is, the same great Power that made the Universe, governs it by his Providence. And such terrible Catastrophes will not happen till 'tis best they should. In the mean time, we must not presume too much on our own Importance. There are an infinite Number of Worlds under the divine Government, and if this was annihilated it would scarce be miss'd in the Universe.

GOD sees with equal Eye, as Lord of all,
A Hero perish, or a sparrow fall.
Atoms, or Systems, into Ruin hurl'd,
And now a Bubble burst,—and now a World![2]

How to preserve Meat in hot Weather, without Salt.

A Clean Cloth dipp'd in Vinegar, and wrapt close round a Joint of Meat, Dr. Boerhaave[3] says, will keep it good eight Days.

9. BF misquotes Halley, as quoted by Whiston and *Gent. Mag.*, XXVI (1756), 25; the comet, according to Halley, was "not above the semidiameter of the sun to the northward of the way of the earth"; that is 432,000 miles, not a mere 4000.

1. *In Serious Thoughts Occasioned by the Late Earthquake at Lisbon* (London, 1755), John Wesley had suggested that the wrath of God might be manifested by the expected comet's setting the earth on fire. He had, however, confused the comet of 1680–81, upon which Whiston had based his theory of the Deluge, with Halley's comet of 1682. Numerous writers in *Gent. Mag.* undertook to set the matter straight and avert unreasonable panic. See especially XXV (1755), 584; XXVI (1756), 24–7, 72, 413.

2. Alexander Pope, *Essay on Man*, I, 87–90, from which BF's reprinting varies slightly.

3. Hermann Boerhaave (1668–1738), professor of chemistry at Leyden.

How to stop Blood if a Man is wounded in the Woods.

Powder made of the rotten Heart of a Black Oak, apply'd, will do it immediately. Some Indians carry a little Bag of this Powder when they go to War.

There is also a Kind of Fungus, somewhat like a Horse's Foot, that grows on old Oaks which have been lopped; it should be gathered in August or September, and kept dry. The Way of preparing it, is, to take off with a Knife the white and hard Part, till you find a Substance so soft, as to yield under the Finger like shammy Leather. This is to be divided into Pieces of different Sizes and Thickness: Beat them with a Hammer, to give them a still greater Degree of Softness, so that they may be easily torn with the Finger.

If even a Limb be cut off, one of these Pieces will stanch the Blood, being only applied and pressed against the bleeding Arteries.

Some say, that this Fungus, or Agaric, as 'tis called, is best when it has a greyish Colour on the Outside; tho' the white is very good.

How to recover the Salt out of old Brine or Pickle, so as to be fit for Use again, and better than at first.

Fill an Iron Pot (the broader and shallower, the better) with your Brine or Pickle; mix a sufficient Quantity of Whites of Eggs with the Brine, to clarify it from its Impurities. Boil it at first gently, and when the Scum hath all arisen, take it off carefully. As soon as the Brine is skimmed, abate the Fire, and only retain a moderate Heat, sufficient to keep the Brine of a scalding Heat. When the Brine is fully depurated, add about a tenth Part of sour Whey, which will destroy the corrosive or Eating Quality of the Salt. Keep the Brine of a scalding Heat all the Time the Salt is graining or forming into Chrystals. When most of the Water is evaporated, and the Salt chiefly grained, take it from the Fire; and straining it with a Cloth from the remaining Water, you will have a clean and most excellent Salt for Use; which being fine, is fit for the Table; and will moreover preserve Meat good and sound, without corroding or consuming the Fat, as common Sea Salt is apt to do.

A General RULE to find the Contents of close Casks in Gallons, and Parts of a Gallon, Wine-Measure.

Take the Diagonal Line of the Inside of the Cask, from the Middle of the Bung, to the Bottom of the Head, by any straight Stick; which measure in Inches, and Parts of an Inch; cube that Number (that is, multiply it by itself, and multiply that Product by the same Number) then divide by 370, and the Quotient will be Gallons; and if there be any Remainder multiply it by 8, and continue the Division, and the second Quotient will be Pints.

Exam. I. Admit the Diagonal of a Cask be 21 Inches.

```
         21
         21
         --
         21
        42
        ---
        441
         21
        ---
        441
       882   Contents is
    370)9261(25 Gallons.
        740
        ----
        1861
        1850
        ----
          11
           8
        ----
          88 (0 Pints.
```

Exam. II. Suppose the Diagonal to be 31½ Inches.

```
  31.5          992.25
  31.5            31.5
  ------        --------
  1575          496125
  315           99225
  945          297675
  ------       ---------
  992.25       31255.875

    370)31255(84 Gal.
        2960
        ----
        1655
        1480
        -----
         175.8
             8
        ------
    370)1406.4(3 Pints.
        1110
        ----
         296
```

Answer, 84 G. $3\frac{296}{370}$ P.

i. e. 84½ Gallons fere.[4]

The above Rule is easy to the Memory, and will be found agreeable to most common Casks that are made here, or come from the West-Indies; so that any Person having a Rule divided into Inches, and Parts of an Inch, may by this become an expert Gauger.

4. Fere: approximately.

To Peter Collinson

Original ALS not found; duplicate: Pierpont Morgan Library

Dear Friend Philada. Jan. 1. 1757

I wrote you yesterday a Line or two[5] enclosing the second of a Set of Bills for £120 Sterling, drawn on Mr. William Anderson, Merchant, London, by Robert Lloyd, of Maryland.[6] I now send the first of the same Set. On the 27th past I drew on you for £50 Sterling in favour of Benjamin Mecom, which I doubt not will meet with due Honour.[7] I wish you and yours many happy New Years, being, Dear Friend Yours affectionately B F

To William Strahan

ALS: Rosenbach Foundation; duplicate: Huntington Library

Dear Sir Philada. Jany. 1. 1757

I wrote you a Line or two yesterday,[8] enclosing B. Mecom's 2d Bill for £100 Sterling drawn on you upon Presumption that you had received some Bills he had sent you, amounting to about £120 more than the Ballance of his Account. He has settled honourably with me, and bought the old Printing House he had at Antigua, which he has sent to Boston, where he purposes to set up his Business among his Friends and Relations; and has wrote to you to purchase him two new Founts, one of Long Primer and one of Pica, for which I have furnish'd him with a Bill on Mr. Collinson for £50 lest you should not have receiv'd his Money. I now send B. Mecom's third Bill. If you are not in Cash for him, you need not be at the Charge or Trouble of Protesting it, but only acquaint me. If you are, carry it to the Credit of my

5. Not found.

6. William Anderson, who dealt with many Maryland merchants, was married to Rebecca, sister of Maryland Receiver General Edward Lloyd. Her cousin Robert Lloyd (1712–1770) of Queen Anne Co. was a burgess and later speaker of the Maryland Assembly. *Md. Hist. Mag.*, VII (1912), 424–5, 427–8.

7. See above, p. 68, and the letter immediately below for BF's assistance to his nephew, Benjamin Mecom.

8. See above, pp. 68–9, and below, p. 216, for Benjamin Mecom's affairs.

Account. I wish you and yours many happy New Years, being, with great Esteem and Affection, Dear Sir, Your most obedient humble Servant B FRANKLIN

Mr. Strahan

Addressed: To / Mr. William Strahan / Printer / London

To Elizabeth Hubbart

ALS: American Philosophical Society

Dear Bess Philada. Jan. 13. 1757

Your Story is well told and entertaining.[9] Only let me admonish you of a small tho' common Fault of Story-tellers. You should not have introduc'd it by telling me *how comical* it was, especially a Post before you sent the Story it self: For when the Expectation is rais'd too high, 'tis a Disadvantage to the Thing expected.

But let us not be merely entertain'd by the Tale; let us draw a small Moral from it. Old Age, we see, is subject to Love and its Follies as well as Youth: All old People *have been* young; and when they were so, they laugh'd, as we do, at the Amours of Age. They imagin'd, 'tis like, that the Case would never be theirs. Let us spare 'em, then; lest the same Case should one day be ours. I see you begin to laugh already at my ranking myself among the Young! But you, my Girl, when you arrive at Fifty, will think no more of being old, than does Your affectionate Uncle

B FRANKLIN

My Love to your good Mama, and to Suky,[1] with my Thanks for her Care of you in your Illness. Tell her I now forgive her for selling her Good Luck.[2]

Miss Betsy Hubbard

9. See above, pp. 69–71.

1. "Mama" was Elizabeth, widow of BF's brother John, and "Suky" was her sister Susannah (b. 1726). Harlan P. Hubbard, *One Thousand Years of Hubbard History* (N.Y., 1895), p. 57.

2. Probably a lottery ticket.

Memorandum on Allowances for Officers' Quarters

Draft: Library of Congress

Jan. 20. 1757.

The Commissioners voted to allow the Officers of the King's Forces, instead of Quarters[3]

Quarters were demanded of the City of Philadelphia for a Number of Officers of the 1st Battalion of the Royal Americans and one Independent Company.

Billets were accordingly delivered out by the Mayor, on the Inns and other Publick Houses of the City, for the Number of Officers required.

The Officers express'd some Dissatisfaction with the Quarters assigned, as not being convenient or suitable to their respective Ranks. Private Gentlemen were dispos'd to take a Number of the Officers and accommodate them gratis in their own Houses; but the Officers to whom it was mention'd, declin'd accepting such Quarters as it would be laying themselves under an Obligation for a Matter to which they had an undoubted Right.

The Provincial Commissioners being inform'd of the Dissatisfaction of the Officers with their Quarters, and desirous that they should be agreably accommodated, propos'd to give Money in Lieu of Quarters, that every Officer might provide himself with such as he should approve of.

The Sums they propos'd to allow were	Per Week	
For a Colonel's Quarters	£1 0	0
For a Lieut. Colonel's Do.	19	0
For a Major's Do.	16	0
For a Captain's Do.	9	–
For a Lieut.'s or Ensign's Do.	6	–
For a Surgeon or Chaplain's Do.	6	–
For a Quarter-master or Adjutant's Do.	6	–

It was thought convenient Lodgings with Firing, and the other Necessaries in Quarters, (Provision only excepted) might easily

3. In this heading BF first wrote "for the Payment of" after "Forces," then struck out the words and substituted "instead of." For the dispute over quartering British troops in Philadelphia, see above, pp. 38–66.

be had in the City at these Rates. This Proposal was some Weeks since by the Commissioners laid before the Governor for his Approbation, and by him, communicated to the Officers. They have not yet express'd their Acceptance or Refusal of the Offer.[4]

B Franklin

Endorsed: Officers Quarters &c.

Timothy Horsfield[5] to the Provincial Commissioners

Draft (incomplete): American Philosophical Society

Bethlehem Jany. 21st. 1757.

Messrs. Franklin Fox Hughes &ca. &ca.
Gentlemen

The last week Jo Peeby and Lewis Montour Came here and produced His Honour the Governour's Pass to go to the Indian Countrey, requireing all Persons to Assist them with Such Necessary's they Stood in need of to prosecute their Journey.[6] In Obedience to His Honour I Accordingly help't them to Every thing they requird of Me, as per the Brethrens Account Mr. Edmonds will Lay before you.[7] Just, as they Sat out, Jo Peeby came to Me, with the Indian Man Nickodemas,[8] who lives over the Watter, and Said I have Bought a Hors of this Man for £6 and you must Send it to Philadelphia to the Gentlemen they will

4. The officers apparently accepted this proposal; on March 29 an order was signed to pay Lieut. Lewis Ourry £246 9*s.* for their allowances according to this scale. See below, p. 156.

5. See above, VI, 361 n.

6. Jo[seph] Peepy, a converted New Jersey Indian often employed as an interpreter, and Lewis Montour, brother of Andrew (above, V, 64 n), had been dispatched by George Croghan with messages for the Indians on the upper Susquehanna in early January; see above, pp. 66–7. Horsfield's account shows that he paid £1 2*s.* 5*d.* for some food, lodging, and sundries, and much wine furnished the Indians, Jan. 12–14, 1757. William C. Reichel, ed., *Memorials of the Moravian Church*, I (1870), 238, 281–3.

7. On William Edmonds, see above, VI, 362 n. The account he brought has not been found, but it probably duplicated that referred to in the note immediately above.

8. For Nicodemus, and for George Hayes, George Clouse, and John Smalling mentioned below, see above, pp. 31–2 n.

keep it for Me, and I Desire you will Write for the Money and pay it to Nickodemus. I thought it a Very Odd Affair, but did not think proper to find any fault with him, But Answerd him I will Write to the Gentlemen and when the Cash comes, I Shall pay him.[9] After About Two Months plague and trouble With the Savage Wretch G. Hays We are at Last (thank god) got rid of him, he went the Other day, as he tould me to Diaougo[1] to fetch is Wifes Children; I have sent you G. Clows's Account. But am Sorrey I had not time to get it put into English, Not knowing of Mr. Edmonds going but a Litle before he Sat out. The Poor Indian John Smalling Alias Lucas Deceasd last Week, he Was Very Penitent and as one of the Brethren that Visited him Informed me, he Departed with Much Assureance of his going to rest, his Wife, is amongst Our Indians In B[ethlehe]m.
[*The rest of the letter missing.*]

From John Waring[2]

ALS: American Philosophical Society

Sir Jan. 24. 1757.[3]

I trouble You with this [to inform you of?] the Death of a worthy Clergyman the [Reverend Henry?] Wheatley,[4] Lecturer

9. Horsfield charged 11*s.* 8*d.* for keeping Peepy's horse, January 13–28, and then 5*s.* more for sending it to Philadelphia; there is no record of payment for the horse. Reichel, *Memorials,* I, 290.

1. Tioga, now Athens, Pa.

2. John Waring (1716–1794), B.A., Cambridge, 1737; Anglican clergyman of London and long-time secretary of the Bray Associates. BF later knew him in England where they were fellow Associates both interested in Negro education. *Gent. Mag.,* LXIV (1794), 966, 1051; and references in later notes to this document. Waring wrote this letter in two installments; a section torn from the upper right hand corner of the first of two folio leaves has removed some words at the beginning of each part which have been supplied conjecturally by the editors. Four or five lines at the top of the second leaf have been torn off at the place indicated in the text.

3. This date is taken from the end of the second part of the letter; Waring may have intended it for both parts, or he may have had an earlier date on the section torn from the first part.

4. Henry Wheatley (d. 1756), B.A., Oxford, 1709, and vicar or lecturer at various churches in Middlesex and Bedfordshire. Joseph Foster, *Alumni Oxon. 1500–1714,* IV (London, 1892); *Gent. Mag.,* XXVI (1756), 262.

of St. Leonard Shoreditch, [who named?] me the Sole Executor of his last Will, by which [he leaves?] a Legacy to some of his Relations now (if alive) at Philadelphia in the following words: "I give and bequeath to Benjamin Franklin Esq. of Philadelphia in Pensilvania One hundred Pounds Sterling in Trust for John Cole Grandson of my late Brother John Wheatley of the same Place, and the elder Son of James Hunter which he has by the Mother of the said John Cole Daughter of my said Brother John Wheatley to be paid to them for their Use equally at the Discretion and Judgement of the said Mr. Franklin."[5]

Mr. Henry Wheatley died on the Sixth Day of Last may, of which I had sent You earlier Advice, but that being a Clergyman and consequently but little connected with mercantile Affairs, the last Ships saild before I was apprized of it, and I was the less sollicetous to write to You About this Legacy till I cou'd be pretty certain that I should be able to honour Your Draught. I am advised to desire the favour of You to send over a Letter of Attorney to Your Correspondent here to impower him to receive this Legacy and to give a proper Discharge for the same.[6] This I am told is the legal and consequently the most safe way, and, if You approve of it shou'd be glad it were observed. Shou'd the Legatee John Cole, or all James Hunters Sons by John Coles Mother, have been dead before Mr. Wheatley, in Such Case I presume that the Legacy lapses and reverts to the Residuary Legatee, whose Name

5. Later documents help to clarify this involved bequest. John Wheatley, brother of the decedent, had a daughter Mary who married, first, a man named Cole, by whom she had a son, John Cole, the first legatee. She married, second, James Hunter, by whom she had a son (name not indicated), the second legatee. BF reported to Waring, Feb. 17, 1758, that John Cole was now old enough to be bound as an apprentice and that he would arrange for this and for the Hunter boy's schooling until the latter too was ready for apprenticeship. Apparently this second legatee died at an early age without leaving full brothers, for on Feb. 10, 1773, BF wrote James Hunter (presumably the father) proposing to pay over £50 with fifteen years interest for the benefit of Hunter's daughter, who had "arrived at an Age when the Money may be of Use to her." Nothing more has been learned of this Philadelphia family. Another sheet among the Franklin Papers, APS, also contains this extract of Wheatley's will and a note that Waring was the executor.

6. Waring's letter reached Philadelphia after BF's departure for England, so, upon learning of it, he was able to receive the legacy through his London banker without employing an agent.

is John Rittermaster: I shall be glad of the favour of a Line from You on this Subject by the first Opportunity, and am Sir Your most humble Servant JN. WARING

[I know you are?] pleased with every Opportunity of doing [Good; for that?] Reason tis needless for me: Worthy Sir, to [relate to you?] what follows. I am a member of a Society [usually known?] by the Name of the Associates of the late [Dr. Bray, a?] Gentleman whose Memory ought to be dear [to all preser?]vers of piety in the Brittish Plantations [in America. The ob?]jects of our Attention as a Society are the [Instruct?]ion, and Conversion of the Negroes in the Plantations to Christianity and founding parochial Libraries for the Use of the Clergy in England and America:[7] We shall be much obliged to You if You will favour Us with Your Sentiments on the first Design, and let us know how and by what means those poor ignorant people may be most effectualy instructed whether the parochial Clergy *do* take any pains with them and what Helps and Assistances they may want to enable them to diffuse the knowledge of our Religion among them? As the Lately imported Negroes are Strangers to our Language, Little Good I fear can be done with them, but might Not the black Children born in the Province be taught to read and instructed in the Principles of Christian Morality, and if the planters woud permit them, pray What Sum Sterling, per Annum wou'd be a suitable Salary for a Sober honest Master?[8] Some few Years ago a pious Clergyman in Wales set on foot a Scheme of itinerant Schoolmasters; who after residing three Six or nine

7. "Dr. Bray's Associates for Founding Clerical Libraries and Supporting Negro Schools," an organization devised to carry on the various philanthropic and missionary enterprises of Dr. Thomas Bray (1656–1730) when he fell ill in 1723, was given legal authority to continue his work. For a short time at the end of the seventeenth century he had been commissary of the Bishop of London in Maryland. *DNB.*

8. The education and catechizing of free and slave Negro children had been sponsored by Anglicans in Philadelphia at least since 1749. Apparently through this inquiry of Waring's, BF began an active support of the work which lasted throughout his life. Edgar L. Pennington, "The Work of the Bray Associates in Pennsylvania," *PMHB*, LVIII (1934), 1–25, and Richard I. Shelling, "Benjamin Franklin and the Dr. Bray Associates," *PMHB*, LXIII (1939), 282–93. BF answered the questions posed by Waring a year later; see below, pp. 356, 377–8.

Months in one place, and teaching persons of all Ages to read, who came to them, removed to another, and did the Like there, by this means Six or Seven thousand persons (Young and old) for some Years past have been annualy taught to read and instructed in religious knowlege. Might not some Such Scheme be set on foot in Your province for the Service of the blacks? The Associates beg the favour of You to consult with the worthy Commissary[9] and some of the other Clergy in the Neighbourhood and favour Us with the Result of Your Deliberations. One word more Both Planters and Slaves, I am told have mistaken Notions concerning [*four or five lines missing*] might have a very good effect upon their [morals?] and make them more faithful and honest in their Masters Service, and Such of them only, from time to time, admitted to baptism as came recommended by their Masters for their good behaviour, or who shewed by the general tenour of their Conduct that they had right Notions of Religion. I fear I have tired Your patience, but when we converse at this Distance, it is necessary to say all that occurs upon the Subject, because there may Not be an Opportunity soon of sending a Supplement. Our fund at present is but Small, however I hope by the blessing of God we shall be able to furnish those worthy Clergymen who engage with zeal in this truly Christian Design with religious Books and tracts to enable them more effectualy to carry it on and perhaps also with some useful Books towards forming a parochial Library for the Use of themselves and Successors: We shall be very thankful to You or them for any Informations which may be of Service. Letters upon this Subject directed to mee in Wood Street Spitalfields London shall be duely laid before the Associates and punctualy answered. I am once More Sir Your most humble Servant JN. WARING

Addressed: To / Benjamin Franklin Esq, / at Philadelphia / in Pensilvania / America

9. Rev. Thomas Dawson, commissary of Virginia, president of the College of William and Mary; see above, VI, 431 n.

Provincial Commissioners to William Denny

MS not found; reprinted from 1 *Pennsylvania Archives*, III, 93–5.

Sir: Philada. Jany. 25th 1757.

The ammunition and other Things applied for by Captain Calender,[1] and allowed by the Commissioners, are sent up some time since, except three Drums which were not then to be had, but will be sent per the first Opportunity. With this your Honour will receive an Account of the quantity of Ammunition sent,[2] and thereby can judge whether more will be necessary, and how much, on Account of the Detachments sent to reinforce Colonel Armstrong.

On Perusal of the Return of the Persons appointed to inspect the Beef, we are of opinion that, if your Honour thinks fit, strict and positive Orders be sent to the Officers to keep the Men to the Provincial Allowance: at the same Time acquainting them, that if they allow more it shall be stopt out of the Officers Pay. It is very possible that the Beef may be not equal as they say to "some such" as Philadelphia Market affords; but of that prime Beef the Quantity in this Province is small, and too dear even for middling People to purchase, only the richer sort are able to buy it, and the whole Quantity of that Kind rais'd in the Province would in our

1. Robert Callender (d. 1776) of Carlisle, long associated with George Croghan in Indian trade and land speculation, had been commissioned captain in Col. John Armstrong's battalion of the Pennsylvania Regiment of provincial troops, Oct. 11, 1756. Above, V, 90, 105 n; Nicholas B. Wainwright, *George Croghan Wilderness Diplomat* (Chapel Hill, 1959), pp. 29–30, 51–5; *History of Cumberland and Adams Counties, Pa.* (Chicago, 1886), p. 306; 1 *Pa. Arch.*, III, 29, 89. Though his application and the various other requests and complaints from Armstrong's battalion mentioned below have not been found, in November 1756 some of its officers had made accusations against Adam Hoops and William Buchanan, commissary agents for the forces in Cumberland Co. Besides berating the quality of beef furnished the soldiers, Armstrong thought Hoops and Buchanan profiteered enormously from their contract: they furnished each man in the battalion four pounds of beef, three pounds of pork, 10½ pounds of flour, and ⅞ quart of hard liquor per week, a provision for which the commissioners paid them 5*s*. For 400 men for a year, this amounted to over £5000, but at prevailing prices quoted by Armstrong, the total cost to the contractors was less than £3000. *Ibid.*, III, 48–9, 54–6; *Votes*, 1757–58, p. 117.

2. Printed at the end of this letter.

opinion be insufficient to feed half Col. Armstrong's Battallion, and therefore we think they ought not to expect it. What is now prepared for them is equal to any they us'd to have, and they never before complain'd of the Quality of it.

As to the Drying of Beef and Pork, the Design must be to make the same Quantity of Nourishment lighter of Carriage for Marching or Ranging Parties. We therefore approve of it, and request your Honour would be pleased to give Directions to Col. Armstrong to cause a Quantity to be weigh'd out of the Casks, an Account taken of such Weight, the whole to be dry'd, and again weigh'd when thoroughly dry; and then distributed occassionally in Weights proportion'd to the Loss by Drying, for example, if one Fourth of the whole Weight be lost, then three Quarters of a Pound is to be given out instead of a Pound, and so in whatever other Proportion the Loss of Weight may be. For what is lost is only in the Watery part, the Nourishing Part all remaining after the Drying.

We send your Honour an Account of the Blankets that have been delivered to that Battalion,[3] by which it will appear they have been more than fully supplied. When they return'd from Kittanning, the Demand was for 300 supposed to be lost; they were immediately sent. Then 60 more were demanded, Those also were sent. Now 40 more are required, these are not sent. Because we find by our Accounts they cannot be wanted, unless the Men have been suffered to sell them: In which case we think the Officers should see them supplied at their or the men's Expence.

We are preparing an Account of the Provissions that Battalion has consumed, by which your Honour will perceive that we have some Reason to be disatisfied with the Conduct of the Officers in that Respect. We know not what Col. Armstrong means by the sundry Instances of our taking Umbrage at his Conduct, and shall enter into no Disputes with him, having on many Accounts a Respect for him and his Officers. But this we must remark, that for the Defence of their County all the Men, Arms and Ammunition have been allowed that they could desire; that the Officers were appointed as well as the Men taken into pay from among them-

3. Printed at the end of this letter.

selves; that the Contractors were reputable Inhabitants of their own County, with whom we had no connection; that we have no interest directly nor indirectly in the Contract; that the Provisions being bought in their County the Money of course center'd among them; that we have endeavoured on all occasions to have that Batalion well supplied in the same Manner, and on the same Terms with the other Troops of the Province; but so it happens that tho' we have given satisfaction every where else, we are perpetually teiz'd with Complaints from that Quarter, and from thence only.[4] No Officers of that Battalion that we know of are waiting in Town for the Settlement of their Accounts: The Accounts of the others we shall settle as fast as possible. We are, with the utmost Respect your Honours Most obedient Humble Servants

WM. MASTERS, JOHN MIFFLIN,
B. FRANKLIN, JOS. FOX,

To the Honourable Wm. Denny Esqr.

4. The military exploits and prestige of Col. John Armstrong (1717–1795) and his men seem to have become politically entangled: his partially successful attack on Kittanning, Sept. 7, 1756 (above, p. 4 n), had vindicated those who urged an aggressive, ruthless Indian policy, while his connection with the proprietary interest probably caused part of the commissioners' obvious irritation with him. On Oct. 15, 1756, the proprietary-dominated Philadelphia City Council had voted plate, medals, and a sum of money to Armstrong and his officers for their victory, and in January 1757, the Council transmitted the gifts, for which Armstrong offered public thanks, actions perhaps calculated to call attention to the commissioners' ingratitude toward military heroes. *Minutes of the Common Council of the City of Philadelphia, 1704 to 1776* (Phila., 1847), pp. 600, 604–5; *Pa. Gaz.*, Feb. 17, 1757. Armstrong spoke bluntly of his difficulties: "The Commissioners and we are at great odds. It seems to me as if the devil had gotten possession of Bennie Franklin" (to James Burd, Feb. 22, 1757). Later in the year, Capt. Thomas Lloyd of the Augusta Regiment also complained when the commissioners refused to send him more arms and blankets until he had accounted for those sent earlier: "They intended, I suppose, to pass an act that arms should never perish through time, age, and blankets never decay." [Thomas Balch], *Letters and Papers Relating Chiefly to the Provincial History of Pennsylvania* (Phila., 1855), pp. 68, 88. Armstrong later served prominently in the Forbes expedition to capture Fort Duquesne, and was judge of the Court of Common Pleas, brigadier general in the Revolution, and member of the Continental Congress. *DAB*.

An Account of Blankets sent to the W. Side of Sasqua. [Susquehanna] at diff[erent] times.

1755,

Dec. 23,

George Croghan had 16 Pieces which make 240 Blankets,[5]

1756,

June 24,			
Col. Armstrong	had 3 Pieces which make	45	"
July 10,			
Col. Armstrong	had 3 Pieces which make	45	"
Aug. 31,			
Col. Armstrong	had 3 Pieces which make	45	"
Sept. 28,			
Col. Armstrong	had 15 Pieces (20 in a P'e)	300	"
Decr. 8,			
Col. Armstrong	had 4 Pieces (15 in a P'e)	60	"
Besides which, George Stevenson charges for Steel,[6]		40	"
	Total,	775	

Dec. 16, Sent by Andrew Cox, one Box of Medicines, for the Use of Col. A's Battalion.[7]

Jan. 5, Sent by Robt Amos,[8] 850 Pounds of Lead, 400 Pounds Powder, 1000 Flints, 4 Water Engines, 17 Brass-kettles, 4 Hour Glasses, 6 Tin and 2 Horn Lanthorns, which were delivered to Col. Armstrong.

5. When he was sent to Cumberland Co. to build three stockades. See above, VI, 294–5.

6. George Stevenson (1718–1783), was a landowner and public official of York Co. In civilian life Capt. John Steel was Presbyterian minister at Carlisle; he served later as chaplain of the Augusta Regiment at Shamokin. George R. Prowell, *History of York County, Pa.* (Chicago, 1907), I, 496–7.

7. Though Cox has not been identified, he probably carried the "Medicines for Col. Armstrong's Battalion" for which Charles Osborne received £19 14*s*. 7½*d*. on Dec. 24, 1756. *Votes*, 1755–56, p. 172.

8. Not identified.

Pennsylvania Assembly: Remonstrance to William Denny

Printed in *Votes and Proceedings of the House of Representatives*, 1756–1757 (Philadelphia, 1757), pp. 73–4.

On Nov. 24, 1756, at the Assembly's request, Governor Denny had submitted an estimate of military expenses in the province for the coming year totaling over £127,000, and on December 15 the House resolved that £100,000 "be granted to His Majesty for the Service of the current Year." After several days' discussion, it was determined to tax "all Estates, real and personal," at rates which would raise the amount in one year "according to the Method and Way of raising County Rates and Levies." The concern for method of taxing reflected difficulties experienced under the £60,000 act of November 1755 in making fair and efficient property assessments and collections, a problem compounded if the Proprietors' estates were to be assessed and taxed under the new bill. On December 23, the Assembly rejected a proposal to let citizens submit lists of their taxable property, and resolved that one person be elected in each township to assist the constable in making returns of taxable property. The next day the House appointed Franklin and others to bring in an appropriate bill, and designated one member from each county except Northampton to provide tax lists of his constituents, paying particular attention to delinquencies. The Assembly then ajourned for the holidays.[9]

The committee presented the £100,000 supply bill, as the measure came to be called, on Jan. 5, 1757, and after discussion, amendment, and recommitment, submitted an altered bill on the 12th, but the Assembly rejected the "Mode of taxing" proposed. The next day, the House received a petition from Chester County which complained of the "unjust Returns commonly made" and urged that three freeholders be chosen in each township to make tax returns. A week earlier the Philadelphia County tax commissioners had complained of the time consumed in hearing appeals for tax abatements and the vexation of seizing the property of tax delinquents; under such circumstances these commissioners petitioned to be relieved of office if the Assembly passed a new and heavier tax to be assessed and collected in the same manner as that of November 1755. After five days' debate the House again rejected a motion to let taxpayers list their "several Particulars to be taxed," made two more alterations in the bill, and finally passed it on Jan. 22, 1757.[1]

9. *Votes*, 1756–57, pp. 31–2, 47, 57–9.
1. *Ibid.*, pp. 61, 67, 69–71.

Three days later, a committee of the Council designated to propose amendments consistent with the Proprietors' instructions reported that the bill was so "repugnant" that proper amendments would necessitate "almost a new Bill," and proposed instead that Denny return the bill noting its general departure from the instructions (previously laid before the House for its guidance) and urging passage of a bill the governor could sign.[2] Such a message was sent, and after a petty quarrel over its meaning and a review of earlier documents about the tax dispute, the Assembly adopted the Remonstrance printed below which its members, marching through the streets of Philadelphia ("to Alarm everybody with the Sight and Occasion"),[3] delivered *en masse* to Denny on January 28.[4]

May it please your HONOUR, [January 26, 1757]

The Representatives of the Freemen of Pennsylvania, in General Assembly met, do hereby humbly remonstrate to your Honour,

That the Proprietaries professed Willingness to be taxed, mentioned by your Honour in your Message of Tuesday last, can be intended only to amuse and deceive their Superiors; since they have in their Instructions excepted all their Quitrents, located unimproved Lands, Purchase Money at Interest, and in short so much of their vast Estate, as to reduce their Tax, as far as appears to us, below that of a common Farmer or Tradesman.[5]

2. *Pa. Col. Recs.*, VII, 395–7. The bill is printed in *The Statutes at Large of Pennsylvania* (Harrisburg, 1898), V, 597–607.

3. Richard Peters to Thomas Penn, Jan. 27, 1757; Penn Papers, Hist. Soc. Pa. Peters continued his reports of Denny's betrayal of the Proprietors' party in the letter; not only did Denny show signs of bending to the Assembly's will in order to receive his salary, but he had invited BF and the Norrises to his table "to introduce them to Colonel Stanwix, for whom he made an Entertainment for the purpose," while at the same time Denny "has taken no notice of my Brother not so much as given him one single Invitation." To Penn, Jan. 31, 1757, Peters Letterbook, Hist. Soc. Pa.

4. *Votes*, 1756–57, pp. 73–5. Though no committee was appointed to draw the Remonstrance, it is most unlikely that the Assembly would have departed from its usual practice of depending on BF's pen for a document as important as this.

5. Denny's message of January 25 had emphasized that the Proprietors were "willing their Estates should be taxed in the Manner that appears to them to be reasonable, and agreeable to the Land Tax Acts of Parliament in our Mother Country." See above, VI, 515–31, for an analysis of the Proprietors' tax instructions.

That though the Proprietaries Instructions are by no Means Laws in this Province, we have so far complied with them, as to confine the Sum given to be raised in one Year. And had we complied with them in the other Particulars, the Raising any Thing near the Sum required by the present Exigencies of the Province, would be absolutely impossible.

That the apparent Necessity of so large a Sum for His Majesty's Service, and the Defence of this His Province, founded upon the Governor's own Estimate, has obliged us to an Effort beyond our Strength, being assured that Hundreds of Families must be distressed to pay this Tax.

That we have, in the due Exercise of our just Rights by the Royal and Provincial Charters, and the Laws of this Province, and as an English Representative Body, framed this Bill, consistent with those Rights.

That the Bill is agreeable to Justice and Equity with regard to the Proprietaries, and is not repugnant to the Laws of our Mother Country, but as nearly agreeable thereto as our different Circumstances will permit, nor is it contrary to any Royal Instruction whatever.

That great as the Sum is, and hard for this People to pay, we freely offer it to our Gracious King for His Service, and the Defence of this His Colony from His Majesty's Enemies.

That the Proprietaries refusing to permit us to grant Money to the Crown, in this Time of War and imminent Danger to the Province, unless we will consent thus to exempt their Estates from the Tax, we conceive to be injurious to the Interests of the Crown, and tyrannical with Regard to the People.

That we do farther humbly conceive, neither the Proprietaries, nor any other Power on Earth, ought to interfere between us and our Sovereign, either to modify or refuse our Free Gifts and Grants for His Majesty's Service.

That though the Governor may be under Obligations to the Proprietaries, we conceive he is under greater to the Crown, and to the People he is appointed to govern; to promote the Service of the former, preserve the Rights of the latter, and protect them from their cruel Enemies.

We do therefore, in the Name of our most Gracious Sovereign, and in Behalf of the distressed People we represent, unanimously

DEMAND it of the Governor, as our Right, that he give his Assent to the Bill we now present him, for granting to His Majesty One Hundred Thousand Pounds for the Defence of this Province (and, as it is a Money Bill, without Alteration or Amendment, any Instructions whatsoever from the Proprietaries notwithstanding) as he will answer to the Crown for all the Consequences of his Refusal at his Peril.[6]

Pennsylvania Assembly: Appointment of Franklin as Agent to Go to England, and His Acceptance

Printed in *Votes and Proceedings of the House of Representatives*, 1756–1757 (Philadelphia, 1757), pp. 75, 76, 78.

The sequence of events resulting in the appointment of Franklin as agent to represent the Assembly in England in its disputes over the instruction on the taxation of proprietary estates and related grievances is indicated by the following extracts from the Assembly Journals. The Remonstrance of January 26 (see immediately above) was delivered to Governor Denny on the morning of the 28th; the House took his answer into consideration that afternoon and promptly adopted the resolution printed first below. The next morning it chose Speaker Norris and Franklin as its representatives. While they were considering the request, the Assembly, acting "by special Order," passed a new £100,000 supply bill, exempting proprietary estates from taxation, February 3,[7] and then called upon Norris and Franklin for their decisions. Then followed the actions which produced a momentous change in Franklin's career.

Resolved, N.C.D. [January 28, 1757]

That a Commissioner, or Commissioners, be appointed to go Home to England, in Behalf of the People of this Province, to solicit a Removal of the Grievances we labour under by Reason of Proprietary Instructions, &c.

6. Denny rejected the Remonstrance immediately and told the Assembly he would lay the supply bill before the King with his reasons for disapproving it. Thereupon the Assembly voted to send a commissioner or commissioners to England. *Votes*, 1756–57, p. 75; see the next document for BF's appointment and pp. 116, 152–3 n, for his account of the rejected measure and the eventual passage of a £100,000 Supply Act at Lord Loudoun's insistence.

7. See below, pp. 121, 152–3 n.

Resolved, N.C.D. [January 29, 1757]

That Mr. Speaker, and Mr. Franklin, be requested to go Home to England, as Commissioners, to solicit the Removal of our Grievances, occasioned by Proprietary Instructions, &c. And being accordingly requested thereto by the House, they desired some Time to consider thereof.

[February 3, 1757]

Mr. Speaker, and Mr. Franklin, being called upon by the House, to declare whether they would comply with the Request of the House in going Home to England, to solicit a Redress of our Grievances; . . .[8]

Mr. Franklin said, "That he esteemed the Nomination by the House to that Service as an high Honour, but that he thought, if the Speaker could be prevailed on to undertake it, his long Experience in our publick Affairs, and great Knowledge and Abilities, would render the Addition of another unnecessary: That he held himself however in the Disposition of the House, and was ready to go whenever they should think fit to require his Service."

Resolved,

That the unanimous Thanks of this House to Mr. Speaker, and Mr. Franklin, for their ready Compliance with the Request of the House, be entered on the Minutes.[9]

8. Norris pleaded ill health and his possible greater usefulness in Pennsylvania, but nevertheless put himself at the disposal of the House.

9. Dr. John Kearsley, Jr. (d. 1777), nephew of Dr. John Kearsley, above, v, 20 n, and later mobbed and imprisoned for his Tory views, did not share the Assembly's pleasure at BF's appointment: "They talk of Sending the Electrician home which is a new delay. He Jumps at going. I am told his office [of deputy postmaster general] shakes. However though he would not go but to Support this falling interest of his own, he is artfully Insinuating that he goes on his Countrys Service. Most Certain I am that he will go at his Countrys Expence for he is wicked enough to Blind the people." ALS to Robert Hunter Morris, Feb. 8, 1757, Yale Univ. Lib. Capt. Thomas Lloyd also sneered at the proposed mission of Norris and BF: "Two of the venerable sages of Pennsylvania are going home with their fingers in their eyes." [Thomas Balch], *Letters and Papers Relating Chiefly to the Provincial History of Pennsylvania* (Phila., 1855), p. 67.

An exchange between Richard Peters and Thomas Penn, however, affords the fullest view of BF's agency as seen by his opponents on both sides of the Atlantic before his departure. "Certain it is," wrote Peters, "that B.F.'s view is to effect a change of Government, and considering the popularity of

Resolved,

That this House will make Provision for defraying the Expence that may attend their Voyage, and the Solicitation of the Affairs of the Province in England; and that Mr. Franklin do first go over.

Resolved,

That Benjamin Franklin, Esq; be, and he is hereby appointed Agent of this Province, to solicit and transact the Affairs thereof in Great-Britain.

Pennsylvania Assembly Committee: Report on the Easton Conference

Printed in *Votes and Proceedings of the House of Representatives*, 1756–1757 (Philadelphia, 1757), pp. 75-6.

The serious charges of land fraud made at the Easton Indian Conference, November 1756,[1] made certain that its minutes would receive careful attention. The Assembly asked for a copy, Nov. 24, 1756, and Governor Denny transmitted it a week later. On December 14, he appointed a Council committee to investigate the charges, and on Jan. 25, 1757, surveyor Nicholas Scull (above, I, 177 n), who had been present at the Walking Purchase confirmation of 1737, stated before the Council that the walk was "fairly performed" and he knew of no charges of fraud made at that time. Perhaps to counteract this statement, the four commissioners who had been present at the Easton conference made

his character and the reputation gained by his Electrical Discoveries which will introduce him into all sorts of Company he may prove a Dangerous Enemy. Dr. Fothergill and Mr. Collinson can introduce him to the Men of most influence at Court and he may underhand give impressions to your prejudice. In short Heaven and Earth will be moved against the Proprietors." In reply, Penn was full of confidence: "I think I wrote you before that Mr. Franklin's popularity is nothing here, and that he will be looked very coldly upon by great People, there are very few of any consequence that have heard of his Electrical Experiments, those matters being attended to by a particular Sett of People, many of whom of the greatest consequence I know well, but it is quite another sort of People, who are to determine the Dispute between us." Peters to Penn, Jan. 31, 1757, Peters Letterbook; and Penn to Peters, May 14, 1757, Penn Papers, both Hist. Soc. Pa.

1. See above, pp. 12–23, on BF's attendance at the conference, and the matters discussed at it. See especially p. 19 n, for an explanation of the alleged fraud in the Walking Purchase.

the report printed below, which the Assembly ordered printed along with the minutes of the conference. They were for sale in Philadelphia by March 10, 1757.[2]

January 29, 1757

We the Committee appointed to attend the Governor at the Conferences with the Indians at Easton, in November last, have perused the Copy of those Conferences, drawn up and signed by the Secretary, and laid before the House;

And as we apprehend it of Importance to the Province, that the Complaints made by the Indians, whether justly founded or not, should be fully represented, and their Sense of them understood, we think it necessary to observe to the House, that we conceive the Warmth and Earnestness with which they insisted on the Wrongs that had been done them in the Purchases of Land, are much too faintly expressed in this Account of the Conference. That we were not present at the palliating Hearsay Accounts of the Walking Purchase, said to be given the Governor by Mr. Weiser, and Mr. Peters, on the Fourteenth of November; tho, by the concluding Paragraphs under that Date, it may seem as if we were:[3] But we well remember, that the Transaction of that Walk was at Easton universally given up as unfair, and not to be defended, even from the Accounts of some of our own People who were present at the Walking; even the Secretary, though he did say, that he *believed* Satisfaction was afterwards made the Indians, and that this was the only Instance in which any Foundation of Complaint had ever been given them, yet this he allowed was (in his own Words) *unworthy of any Government*.[4] We would farther observe, that when Teedyuscung claimed the Lands, even those

2. Above, p. 16 n; *Votes*, 1756–57, pp. 33, 35, 77; *Pa. Col. Recs.*, VII, 354, 399–400; *Pa. Gaz.*, March 10, 1757. On January 25 Denny refused a request from William Callender and Israel Pemberton, acting for the Friendly Association for Regaining and Preserving Peace with the Indians by Pacific Measures, that they be permitted to search the Council Minutes for information "of the true State of the Indian Claims." *Pa. Col. Recs.*, VII, 394–5, 397–8. A copy of Secretary Peters' letter, written at Denny's order, is among the Franklin Papers, APS.

3. See above, pp. 18–19.

4. Secretary Peters later explained that this remark was "Table Talk and Loose Hear-say." *Pa. Col. Recs.*, VIII, 251 n. BF called this defense a "Prevarication." "Separate Notes" to Isaac Norris, Sept. 16, 1758, Lib. Cong.

on which the Conferences were held, no Objection was made, that neither he, nor any with him, had any Right to them; nor did we ever understand his Reason for not accepting Satisfaction to be as represented in the second Paragraph under November 17, for that "*the People* to whom the Land belonged were absent;" but for that many of them were absent, and those who were absent had not impowered him to act for them in that Matter; but he would endeavour to bring them in the Spring.

The Offer of the Commissioners to furnish the Means of making the Indians immediate Satisfaction,[5] not being fully related, we think it necessary to add, that the Reasons we gave the Governor for that Offer, were, 1. The Absence and great Distance of the Proprietaries, who being the sole Purchasers of Land from the Indians in this Province, ought, if the Indians were injured in such Purchases, alone to make the Satisfaction; but their Agents here had not the necessary Powers. 2. For that Promises [such being proposed][6] of enquiring into Indian Complaints, and doing them Right hereafter, had been so often made in other Governments, and so little observed, we imagined they could be of no Weight, and would rather be looked upon as a Denial of Justice; and therefore, we thought it better, as their Demands are seldom very high, to make them immediate Reparation for the Injuries they supposed they had received, and we would furnish the Goods, and risk the Proprietaries repaying their Value to the Province. The Secretary then told us, that he thought our Proposal very considerate and well-judged; that he was sure the Proprietaries would think themselves obliged to us, and repay the Money with Thanks: The Offer was accordingly made, but not accepted for the Reasons abovementioned. We then waited upon the Governor in a Body, and acquainted his Honour, That as we had made the Offer in Behalf of the Province, not from an Opinion that the Province ought to be at such Expence, but from the apparent immediate Necessity of the Thing, and on Account of the Proprietaries Absence as aforesaid; so now, since the final Settlement of the Indians Claims was postponed to the Spring, and there would be sufficient Time to write to the Proprietaries, and obtain their Orders to their Agents for the Payment of such Sums as should be

5. See above, p. 22.
6. Brackets in the original.

found necessary, we looked on ourselves and the Province as totally disengaged from that Offer, and expected that the Proprietaries would be wrote to accordingly.[7]

BENJAMIN FRANKLIN, JOSEPH FOX,
WILLIAM MASTERS, JOHN HUGHES.

To Peter Collinson

ALS: Pierpont Morgan Library

Dear Sir Philada. Jan. 31. 1757

The preceding are Copies of my late Letters;[8] to which I have little to add, except to request you would send the Magazines mention'd in the enclos'd List,[9] which it seems are still wanting to compleat the Sets in the Library. It may be well enough to forbear sending the Universal Magazine for the future, it contains little of Value.[1] I inclose also an Almanack,[2] and some Sheets to compleat your Set of Votes for the last Year. The rest are in Mr. Bartram's Box.[3] Our Assembly have unanimously voted sending

7. In spite of the inaccuracies alleged in this report, the conference minutes seem to have been printed in the form set down by the official recorder, Secretary Peters, before Dec. 1, 1756. A fragmentary paper by Conrad Weiser suggests that he had a chance to correct them before they were put into final form by Peters. Among other things, Weiser seems to have caused some statements he probably thought the Quakers had put into a speech by Teedyuscung (above, p. 18 n) to be deleted, and he corrected some statements of his own about an Indian conference of 1743. 1 *Pa. Arch.*, III, 38–9.

8. Those of Nov. 22, Dec. 19, 1756, and Jan. 1, 1757; see above, pp. 23, 49, 94.

9. Not found, but see above, VI, 171, 456, for a previous order of magazines for the Library.

1. *The Universal Magazine of Knowledge and Pleasure* . . . published monthly by John Hinton . . . London.

2. *Poor Richard Improved* for 1757.

3. John Bartram had shipped Collinson 26 boxes, mostly filled with seeds, on the ship *Carolina*, Capt. Robert Duncan, which cleared Philadelphia for London before Feb. 3, 1757, perhaps also carrying BF's letters of January 31 to Collinson and William Strahan, and of February 1 to Robert Charles. Collinson reported receipt of the boxes, but not the letters, sent on the *Carolina* on March 18, 1757. Darlington, *Memorials*, pp. 211, 214. The *Votes* enclosed in the letter to Collinson were probably those for August–September 1756 during Denny's administration, advertised for sale in *Pa. Gaz.*, Feb. 10, 1757. A week before the *Gazette* had advertised the earlier *Votes* ("the rest") covering Robert Hunter Morris' administration.

me to England, to endeavour a Settlement of our Disputes; I have not determin'd yet to go, as they gave me some Days to consider of it.[4] It will be a good Work, whoever does it; for the Province at present is very unhappy. I am, Dear Friend, Your affectionate humble Servant B FRANKLIN

Addressed: To / Mr Peter Collinson / Gracechurch Street

To William Strahan

ALS: Huntington Library

Dear Sir, Jany. 31. 1757

The above is a Copy of my last.[5] I have now before me your Favour of Sept. 11.[6] I shall not fail on every Occasion to recommend you to my Friends on the Book Account.[7] I wish I could give you any Hopes of soon receiving your Debt of J. Read.[8] Mr. Hall, no doubt, writes you more fully concerning him. It gives me great Pleasure to hear so good an Account of our Son Billy.[9] In Return, let me tell you, that our Daughter Sally in indeed a very good Girl, affectionate, dutiful and industrious, has one of the best Hearts, and tho' not a Wit, is for one of her Years, by no means deficient in Understanding. She already takes off part of her Mother's Family Cares. This must give you and Mrs. Strahan Pleasure: So that Account is partly ballanced.

Our Assembly talk of sending me to England speedily.[1] Then

4. See above, pp. 109–11.

5. See above, pp. 94–5.

6. Not found, but Strahan's long letter to David Hall of the same date discusses some of the matters BF mentions here. APS.

7. Strahan had responded to Hall's complaint that books of little reputation did not sell in Philadelphia, and also reported he had recently lost the business of the Charles Town Library Society in South Carolina.

8. See above, III, 39 n, 316–17, for James Read's debt to Strahan. Strahan had told Hall "There is a great deal of Cant in his [Read's] Letters, which not being seconded by his Actions, is truly disgusting." He asked Hall to show BF a letter to Read he enclosed and, if both approved, to send it on.

9. Strahan told Hall his son William had entered his printing business and was doing "extremely well, and vastly beyond my Expectation, or what could reasonably be hoped from one of his Years." On BF and Strahan's plans for the marriage of Billy Strahan and Sally Franklin, see above, V, 439 n. Billy was now 17 and Sally 13.

1. See above, pp. 109–11.

look out sharp, and if a fat old Fellow should come to your Printing House and request a little Smouting,[2] depend upon it, 'tis Your affectionate Friend and humble Servant B FRANKLIN

PS I enclose B. Mecom's first Bill for £100 Sterling the 2d and 3d sent before.[3]

Mr. Strahan

To Robert Charles[4]

Draft: American Philosophical Society

Sir Feb. 1. 1757.

I receiv'd your several Favours of August 14. Sept. 18 Sept. 22. and Oct. 16.[5] By this Ship you will receive a Box containing sundry Copies of our last Years Votes,[6] to which are added as you advised, the Accounts of the Expenditure of the £55,000 and the subsequent £30000 also the Papers relating to the Employing foreign Officers.[7] There is also in the Box an authenticated Copy of our late Bill for granting £100,000 to the King's Use, and of the Vote appointing yourself and Mr. Patridge Agents, under the great Seal, with all the late Messages, &c.[8] You will see in the Votes a Copy of the Proprietary Instructions in which a Money Bill is made for us by the Proprietary, sitting in his Closet at 1000 Leagues Distance.[9] The Governor laid before us an Estimate of the neces-

2. Printer's slang for part-time or irregular work.

3. See above, p. 94.

4. On Robert Charles, Assembly agent in England, see above, VI, 230 n.

5. None found, but see above, VI, 481–3, for Charles's letter of Aug. 12, 1756, to the Assembly Committee of Correspondence, which mentions some of the matters to which BF responds here.

6. See above, p. 114 n.

7. Not identified, but see above, VI, 401–2, on the officers of the Royal American Regiment.

8. See above, pp. 106–7, for the passage of this bill and the Assembly's Remonstrance against Denny's refusal of it. At the Assembly's request, on January 28 Denny had ordered the great seal affixed to a copy of the rejected bill returned to the House. *Votes*, 1756–57, p. 75. The appointment of Charles and Partridge as agents "for the Year ensuing" was voted Oct. 18, 1756. *Ibid.*, p. 6. The "late Messages" were probably the long ones on quartering printed in *Pa. Gaz.*, Dec. 23, 1756 (see above, pp. 38–49), and perhaps MS copies of the Remonstrance and recent messages on the £100,000 supply bill.

9. See above, VI, 515–31.

sary Expence for defending this Province one Year, amounting to £125,000. We knew our Inability to bear the raising so great a Sum in so short a time; We deducted the least necessary Articles and reduc'd it to £100,000 which we granted, and sent up the Bill. Not that we thought this Province capable of Paying such a Tax yearly or anything like near it; but believing it necessary to exert ourselves at this Time in an extraordinary Manner to save the Country from total Ruin by the Enemy. The Governor, (to use his own polite Word) REJECTS[1] it. Your English Kings I think are complaisant enough in such Cases to say, *They will advise upon it.* We have no Remedy here, but must obey the Instruction, by which we are so confin'd as to the Time of Raising, the Property to be tax'd, the Valuation of that Property and the Sum per Pound to be Tax'd on the Valuation that tis demonstrably impossible by such a Law to raise one Quarter of the Money absolutely necessary to defend us. So ¾ths of our Troops must be disbanded and the Country exposed to the Mercy of our Enemies; rather than the least tittle of a Proprietary Instruction should be deviated from![2] I forbear to enlarge because the House have unanimously desired your Friend Mr. Norris and my self to go home immediately to assist their Agents in getting these Matters settled.[3] He has not yet determined, but if he goes, you will by him be fully informed of every thing, and my going will not in my Opinion be necessary: If he declines it, I may possibly soon have the

1. Denny had used this offensive word in his second return of the supply bill, after receiving the Remonstrance of January 26. *Votes*, 1756–57, p. 75.

2. The same day BF wrote this letter (probably later in the day), the Assembly resolved "That a new Bill be brought in for granting to His Majesty the Sum of One Hundred Thousand Pounds for the Defence of this Province and the Trade thereof, to be raised by a Tax on all Estates, real and personal, and Taxables, within this Province (the Estates of the Honourable the Proprietaries only excepted) in the Manner prescribed by the Act now in Force for granting Sixty Thousand Pounds to the King's Use"; thus conceding the major point of exempting the Proprietor's estates from taxation. *Votes*, 1756–57, p.77. Richard Peters took a jaundiced view of the concession, however: "The House is preparing a Bill on the Foot of your Instructions with a view to shew their Insufficiency and Mischevious Consequences." To Thomas Penn, Jan. 31, 1757; Peters Letterbook, Hist. Soc. Pa. See below, pp. 121–32, 145–52, for further arguments over the supply bill.

3. See above, pp. 109–11.

Pleasure of seeing you.[4] I am, with great Respect, Sir, Your most obedient humble Servant B FRANKLIN

Mr. Charles

To Richard Partridge[5]

Draft: American Philosophical Society

Sir [February 1, 1757][6]

It is long since I had any of your Favours. I should now have wrote you a long Letter, but that the House have desired the Speaker and myself to go immediately home in order to get our Differences with the Proprietaries Settled some way or other, and tis probable that one of us will soon have the Pleasure of seeing and conferring with you fully on all our Affairs. A Box goes in this Ship directed to Mr. Charles, in which are all our late Papers and your Appointment as Agent under the great Seal, &c. I am very respectfully, Sir, Your most humble Servant BF

Mr. Patridge

Pennsylvania Assembly: Reply to the Governor

Printed in *Votes and Proceedings of the House of Representatives,* 1756–1757 (Philadelphia, 1757), pp. 81–2.

Under the quartering act of Dec. 8, 1756, public-house keepers were required to accommodate soldiers billeted on them for 4*d. per diem,* a rate at which they lost money though they were subject to fines for refusing billets.[7] They petitioned the Assembly for relief on Jan. 3, 1757, and eight days later Franklin and others were appointed to bring in a bill to render "the Burden of quartering Soldiers more equal on the Publick Houses of this Province." Reported on January 18, amended three days later, and passed on the 24th, the bill provided for an additional payment of 4*d. per diem* to innkeepers for each soldier quar-

4. At this point in the draft BF first wrote and then struck out: "It is long since I have been favour'd with a Line from Mr. Partridge." See the document immediately following.

5. On Richard Partridge, co-agent with Robert Charles, see above, V, 11.

6. This draft is on the same page as the last part of BF's of this date to Robert Charles, which supplies the date and explains the matters mentioned in it.

7. See above, p. 46 n, for the innkeepers' predicament, and pp. 38–49, 53–66, for the quartering question generally.

tered on them, to be sunk by a further tax of *2d.* per gallon on all liquor sold at public houses in the province.[8] On February 3 Governor Denny proposed five amendments, four of which the Assembly promptly agreed to. They sent the bill back to him, but Denny responded on the 7th with a message insisting that the tax be extended to *all* liquor sold in the province; otherwise the innkeepers, far from being relieved, would be further distressed by the loss of business caused by the discriminatory tax against them. Franklin and John Hughes drafted the reply printed below which was reported on February 8 and sent to Denny the next day.[9]

May it please your HONOUR, [February 9, 1757]

By our late Law, extending several Sections of the Act of Parliament, intituled, "An Act for punishing Mutiny and Desertion, and for the better Payment of the Army and their Quarters," all the Publick-houses in this Province were subjected to the Billeting of Soldiers quartered within the same; and had the Circumstances of His Majesty's Service admitted of their being quartered equitably and proportionably on all those Houses, the Bill we presented to your Honour would not have appeared to us necessary. But since it has been thought fit, that the whole Number quartered in the Province, should be billeted in Philadelphia, and the Publick Housekeepers throughout the rest of the Province bear no Part of the Burden, this Bill was intended to render it more equal among them all; not to take it from them, and lay it upon the People, which would be the Case, should your Honour's proposed Amendment be acceded to; for if the Excise be made general, the Price must rise proportionally on the Commodity excised, and the Farmers and labouring People, who chiefly buy it of the Retailers, and consume it at their Harvests, and other Labour, must pay the Addition.

But the Publick-Housekeepers, who sell for the most Part by

8. *Votes*, 1756–57, pp. 62, 66, 69, 71–2; *The Statutes at Large of Pennsylvania* (Harrisburg, 1898), v, 288–90.

9. *Votes*, 1756–57, pp. 77, 79, 81–2; *Pa. Col. Recs.*, VII, 400, 406–8. Since the innkeepers paid a fee for licenses issued at the governor's pleasure, it is not surprising to find the Assembly inclined to keep the burden on a group thus allied with the proprietary interest. Richard Peters wrote Thomas Penn, Jan. 27, 1757, that the additional tax on public houses was designed to put some of them out of business and thus further reduce the fees paid to the governor. Penn Papers, Hist. Soc. Pa.

small Measure, and receive at the Rate of Ten Shillings per Gallon for Rum that perhaps costs them not more than Three Shillings, may, we think, afford to pay Two-pence a Gallon above the present general Excise of Four-pence, without any great Inconveniency; since the other Retailers, who are confined to sell by no less Measure than a Quart, cannot interfere with them in that most profitable Part of their Business.

We would beg Leave farther to observe, That at present the Soldiers billeted on the Publick-houses at Philadelphia, amount, on an Average, to about four for each House; and that the Expence of furnishing Quarters, and Necessaries in Quarters to each Man, at Four-pence *per Diem,* will in Three Months for four Men amount to Six Pounds; this the Publick-houses are at present supposed to be burdened with; but the Addition to their Excise, by the proposed Bill, would in few Instances exceed Thirty Shillings, and they would be repaid the Six Pounds. We conceive therefore, that the Payment of Thirty Shillings in a Year, could not occasion the Loss of a great Share of their Business, when the Payment or Expence of Six Pounds has no such Effect. And that dividing equally among the whole Number of Publick-houses, a Burden which at present lies wholly on a Part only, must, in the Nature of Things, make it lighter on that Part.

Whether the Fund proposed will be sufficient, we cannot say, as both its Produce, and the Continuance of the Soldiers here, are uncertain. If it should fall short, a future additional Provision may be made, when it shall be thought necessary. We therefore offer the Bill again to the Governor for his Assent: If he shall, upon Consideration of the Reasons above given, think fit to wave his Amendment, the Bill may afford those People some immediate Relief: If not, Affairs of greater Importance will not at present admit of our spending more Time about it.[1]

1. Upon delivery of this message, the Governor's Council unanimously declared its adherence to the amendment Denny had offered, but by March 5 opinion in the Council was divided. On the 14th, the day of Lord Loudoun's arrival in Philadelphia, Denny and the Council gave in, notice of approval was sent to the Assembly the next day, and the bill became law on March 17. *Pa. Col. Recs.,* VII, 416, 431, 436; *Votes,* 1756–57, pp. 100–1. Settlement of the innkeepers' claims was long delayed; on July 28, 1758, the provincial commissioners announced that, upon submission of proper accounts, they would make the payments provided for in this act. *Pa. Gaz.,* Aug. 10, 1758.

Pennsylvania Assembly Committee: Report on the Governor's Message

Printed in *Votes and Proceedings of the House of Representatives*, 1756–1757 (Philadelphia, 1757), pp. 86–90.

The supply bill passed by the Assembly and sent to Governor Denny on Feb. 3, 1757, differed in important respects from the rejected bill about which the House had remonstrated on January 26.[2] It was framed as a supplement to the £60,000 act of Nov. 27, 1755,[3] and thus did exempt the proprietary estates from taxation, but it retained the four-year period for sinking the bills of credit to be emitted and the provision for Assembly-appointed commissioners to control expenditures, conditions contrary to Denny's instructions from the Proprietors. The new bill also changed the nature of the tax drastically; instead of the 20 percent levy on polls, unimproved lands, and income from trade and services as well as on the income from estates real and personal which in the rejected bill had been calculated to yield £100,000 in one year, the new measure simply added a 5 percent yearly tax on the income from real and personal estates, to be in effect for four years, to the 2½ percent annual tax of the 1755 act.[4] To provide for immediate needs £45,000 in new bills of credit were to be struck at once; these were to be retired in annual installments during the next four years out of the proceeds of the tax. On February 8, Denny appointed James Hamilton, John Mifflin, and Benjamin Chew of the Council to draft objections to the new bill, which were agreed to on February 11, and delivered to the Assembly the next day.[5] Franklin and others were promptly appointed to draft a response, which they cast in the form of a report rather than a message to the governor. The Assembly made some unspecified changes and then approved it on the 17th as printed here.[6]

[February 17, 1757]

In Obedience to the Order of the House, we have considered his Honour's Message of Yesterday, refusing the Bill for granting

2. See above, pp. 106–9.

3. See above, VI, 257 n.

4. The rejected bill and the new act are in *The Statutes at Large of Pennsylvania* (Harrisburg, 1898), V, 597–607 and 294–302, respectively. The new measure also added another 10 shillings to the 10-shilling poll tax imposed by the act of 1755 upon all single freemen over the age of 21.

5. *Pa. Col. Recs.*, VII, 409, 413–16. The nature of these objections is indicated in the Assembly committee's report.

6. *Votes*, 1756–57, pp. 83–90.

One Hundred Thousand Pounds to His Majesty's Service; and as it appears to us, that Reasoning with the Governor can be of no possible Use, since though the House should convince his Judgment, they cannot change his Instructions, and by those he is determined invariably to adhere; we have chosen to throw our Remarks into the Form of a Report to the House, rather than that of a Message to his Honour. Not that we have any Thing to offer which the House is not already fully apprized of; but since the Message is probably intended to be read where the Motives on which the House have acted may not so well be known,[7] it seems convenient they should at least be found on our Minutes, that all may judge of them, who are any way concerned in the Consequences.

We would therefore observe in general, that the Governor having before refused two Bills, one for granting Sixty Thousand Pounds,[8] the other for granting One Hundred Thousand Pounds to the King's Use, for various Reasons unsatisfactory to the Assembly, the House, sincerely desirous to make an effectual Grant, chose to form the Bill in Question on the Plan of the Sixty Thousand Pound Act, passed by the late Governor, which, after a solemn Hearing before the Board of Trade in February last, had received the Royal Assent.[9] By this Means they hoped to avoid all Objections and Difficulties, especially as the Proprietaries were not by the Bill to be taxed. The Bill is a Supplement to the last mentioned Sixty Thousand Pound Act, and in raising and disposing of the Hundred Thousand Pounds granted, the same Modes are to be pursued as by that Act are directed. But unfortunately the Governor, we find, is dissatisfied with that Act also, and most of his Objections are levelled against it.

As to the Governor's first Reason, viz. The Danger of depreciating our Currency, if Forty-five Thousand Pounds should be struck in Addition to it, to be sunk in four Years, we may observe, that the Governor is allowed by the twelfth Article of his Instruc-

7. A reference to the review of the dispute expected to take place in England after BF's arrival there.

8. Passed by the Assembly, Sept. 8, 1756; see above, VI, 502–15.

9. The £60,000 act of 1755 was confirmed by the King in Council, July 7, 1756. *Acts of the Privy Council, Colonial Series,* IV, 336–7.

tions[1] to re-emit the Eighty Thousand Pounds, now current among us, with the Addition of Forty Thousand Pounds more, for sixteen Years, without any Provision against the Injuries the Estates of the Widows and Orphans might sustain thereby, or any great Solicitude for the Rise of Exchange upon Bills, provided the Proprietaries Quitrents are secured, by being made payable according to the Exchange between the Cities of Philadelphia and London, and that they have the Disposal of the Interest Money, as directed by this and the eleventh Instruction, which must be strictly complied with; on these Terms then, it seems, there is no Danger of depreciating the Money by an Addition of Forty Thousand Pounds, though no Part of that Sum, or the Eighty Thousand Pounds, were to be sunk in many Years to come. We would further observe, that in the Times mentioned by the Governor, when we had but Eighty Thousand Pounds current in Bills of Credit, there was current in the Province at least Four Hundred Thousand Pounds of Gold and Silver, most of which, with what has been yearly imported, is since drawn out of the Province for Payment of the Army at New-York and Halifax, and for Payment of our Debts to the Merchants in England; so that a Piece of Gold is now rarely received in Payment. In the mean time, the Produce of the Province, and its People, since that Eighty Thousand Pounds was first made current, are very greatly increased, and consequently the Demand for a Medium of Exchange encreased. The late Emissions have not in the least depreciated our Money, for Bills were sometimes higher when we had only Eighty Thousand Pounds current, than they have been at any Time since the new Emissions. And if those Emissions have, as the Governor supposes, prevented the Fall of Exchange, they have so far been of Advantage to his Majesty's Service, as the Government Bills have thereby fetched a better Price. In the last War we remember, the Crown lost vast Sums by the Fall of Exchange in America; occasioned by a Scarcity of Money, joined with a Plenty of Bills; and *some* who bought them up, when they had fallen from £165 to £125 Currency for One Hundred Pounds Sterling, may likewise *remember,* that they thereby made proportionable Profits.[2]

1. See above, VI, 515–31, for this and other proprietary instructions mentioned below.

2. I.e., the British service was penalized if, because of a tight local money

They may possibly desire now to have a like Opportunity. The Money pretended to be given to the Province, but unjustly withheld,[3] is perhaps designed, with the late collected Quitrents, to purchase Bills when they shall be sold at the expected low Rate a Scarcity of Money may reduce them to; but we think His Majesty's Service is to be preferred to the private Advantage of the Proprietary, and a few of his Friends that trade in Exchanges. The House, however, would as carefully as possible guard against any Depreciation of the Currency. They therefore proposed to strike only Forty-five Thousand Pounds of the Hundred Thousand Pounds granted, and that to be sunk in four Years, one Fourth Part in each Year. Nor would they have chosen to strike any Bills at all, if Taxes of any Kind could possibly produce Money soon enough to answer the present Emergencies of the Government. If a Depreciation should happen, they are sensible they must suffer with others, and some of them more than many others: But when they considered, that within the present Year the following Sums are to be sunk and destroyed, viz.

Of the £80,000 one sixth Part, or	£13,333	6	8
Of the £55,000 one fourth Part, or	13,750	0	0
Of the £30,000 one tenth Part, or	3000	0	0
And if this Bill for 45,000 had passed, one fourth Part of that likewise,	11,250	0	0
In all,	£41,333	6	8

they could not conceive there was the least Danger of a Depreciation, especially as more Soldiers were daily raising and arriving, and ten new Regiments are expected from England, which must necessarily occasion a still greater Plenty of Bills of Exchange, to be sold on Behalf of the Government. If the War should continue, they judged therefore that the Exchange could not rise;

supply, its sterling purchased but little Pa. currency, and speculators stood to make large profits if they could subsequently exchange the sterling bills for greater amounts of Pa. currency. The sharp appreciation in local currency had occurred in 1740–41 when supplies purchased for the British attack on Spanish possessions in the West Indies had brought large amounts of sterling to the province. Anne Bezanson, Robert D. Gray, and Miriam Hussey, *Prices in Colonial Pennsylvania* (Phila., 1935), pp. 323–5.

3. The £5000 gift of November 1755 was still only half paid more than a year later.

and though Peace should be suddenly restored, yet the necessary Sinking of all our Eighty Thousand Pounds Loan Money, all the Fifty-five Thousand Pounds, great Part of the Thirty Thousand Pounds, and all the proposed Forty-five Thousand Pounds, in the Terms of four, and at farthest six Years, would certainly prevent a Depreciation; therefore, in either Case, the Adding Forty-five Thousand Pounds only to our present Currency could not injure the Estates of Widows, Orphans, or any others.[4] We are indeed surprized to find it so much as suggested, that striking a Sum for the Defence of the Province, and His Majesty's Service, *to be sunk in four Years,* may subject us to the Displeasure of Parliament; when it is so well known, that the Act of Parliament, made expresly to restrain the four New-England Colonies, in the Affair of Paper-Money, allows even those Colonies to strike any Sum they may find necessary for that Purpose, if they provide Funds to sink it in *five* Years; and the Lords of Trade gave it as one Reason for allowing our late Act to strike Fifty-five Thousand Pounds, "that we had provided to sink it in *so short* a Term as *four* Years." This proposed stricter Restraint, in a Time of such imminent Danger, appears to us, therefore, not only to be unreasonable in itself, but to be founded on no Law, Opinion, or Instruction whatever from our Mother Country.

On the Governor's second Reason, *to wit,* The Uncertainty of the Act to which this Bill is a Supplement, in the Mode directed for laying the Tax, and its Defect, in not obliging People to give an Account of their Estates upon Oath, &c. we shall only remark, that the Mode directed by that Act, is the same that has ever been used in this Province, and is what the Commissioners and Assessors are accustomed to, and well understand. The Injustice sup-

4. Reporting to the Council on March 14, Benjamin Chew called this reasoning "most false, and calculated only to amuse the ignorant." Chew argued that since the Assembly would soon emit the other £55,000 to be spent under the £100,000 bill and that earlier emissions would be retired much more slowly than the Assembly assumed, there would in fact be a substantial increase in the amount of Pa. currency in circulation. *Pa. Col. Recs.,* VII, 438–9. He proved to be correct on this point, but the basic Assembly argument was sound; there was no inflation of Pa. currency at this time. In fact, it deflated gradually from the near "par" ratio of £170 to £100 sterling current in early 1757 to roughly £155 to £100 two years later. Bezanson, et al., *Prices in Col. Pa.,* pp. 329–31, 341.

posed, has not taken Place in the Execution of it; no one has complained of, or so much as apprehends such Injustice. The Assessors are upon Oath to tax all equally and justly; which they could not do, if they laid, as the Governor supposes they may, the Sixpence per Pound on the Capital Value of some Estates, and on the annual Income only of others.[5] Defects there may possibly be in this Bill, and even to us there appears a very considerable one, *to wit,* that the Proprietary Estate is not taxed; but this we cannot amend if we would; others, when found, a subsequent Act may remedy. A perfectly equal Tax never yet was, nor perhaps ever will be laid in any Country by any Law: But in no Country, that we know of, are People put to their Oaths to make them confess and declare the *full* and *true* Value of their Estates. It is inconsistent with the Laws of the English Constitution, might be ruinous to some who at present live in good Credit, impracticable to others who do not keep clear Accounts, and inconvenient to all. The Officers are therefore to make the best Returns that they can by Enquiry or otherwise obtain, and the Assessors the best Judgment they can on those Returns. By this Bill the People may *possibly* be taxed unequally, with regard to their Estates; but by the Excise Act they must *certainly* be so; yet to the Excise Act the Governor has given his Assent, without the least Objection on Account of such Inequality, and even recommends further Excises in the Message under Consideration.

The Governor's third Objection is, That a Tax for four Years on Lands or personal Estates, "is *contrary* to the Proprietary Instruc-

5. The act of November 1755 levied a tax of "six pence for every pound clear value" on real and personal estates, that is, a tax of 2½ percent on the income. Both the rejected £100,000 bill and the new one repeated the "clear value" phrase to make a distinction between it and the capital or total value of the estates, but there is no stipulation in any of the bills for determining what relation "clear value" should bear to capital value (*Stats. at Large of Pa.*, V, 202, 294, 598), and it is this omission which the Council protested as "indeterminate and uncertain." Apparently the calculation of "clear value" was made by the rates. Chew called the Assembly argument on this point "one of the first Instances in a civilised Government, where Use and Custom has been thought a sufficient Sanction to support and authorize Iniquity." *Pa. Col. Recs.*, VII, 414, 439. The Assembly erred in asserting there had been no complaints of inequity; see above, p. 106. *Pa. Col. Recs.*, VIII, 472–7, records a lengthy tax protest by proprietary agents in 1760 perhaps similar to complaints made by other taxpayers.

tions," which say, that he SHALL NOT give his Assent to any Act laying such a Tax for more than one Year. It is true the Instructions say that and more; they say the Governor SHALL NOT pass any Act to tax the Proprietary Quitrents, nor their located unimproved Lands, nor the Fines or Purchase Monies they have at Interest, which together make the Bulk of their Estate; nor shall he pass an Act to tax the located unimproved Lands of any other Person; nor to tax the *Value* of any other Estate, but the *Rent* or *Interest* of the Value only, and that at the low Rate of Three *per Centum per Annum;* nor on that Interest of Three *per Cent.* more than Four Shillings in the Pound. So that whatever the Necessities and Distress of the Province may be to raise Money for its Defence, his vast Estate in Quitrents, Money at Interest, and located unimproved Lands, are to be exempted, and shall not pay a Penny; and not only so, but the People themselves shall be hampered with new Restraints, and forbid to grant His Majesty what they find the present State of His Service, and the imminent Danger to the Colony, absolutely call for. If we may not lay a Tax for more than one Year, we can grant no more than one Year's Tax will produce. If this be indeed the Practice, Wisdom, and Policy of our Mother Country, whence arose its Debt of Eighty Millions? A Debt greater than all their Taxes can pay in many Years, tho', being rich, while we are poor, and just beginning to live, they have much more to tax than we have. Four Shillings in the Pound, on Three *per Cent.* will produce only the Hundred and Sixty-sixth Penny of the full Value of any Estate.[6] Suppose Four Shillings in the Pound on Five *per Cent.* which is the Hundredth Penny, should be found absolutely necessary to secure the Province from His Majesty's Enemies; or suppose even the Fiftieth Penny necessary; must the Country be destroyed, and the whole be lost, rather than these Instructions be departed from? So it seems. For "the Governor's Honour and Interest may suffer if he breaks them." Thus, by the Proprietaries shackling their

6. I.e., if the "clear value" or income of an estate (in many cases, the annual rent) is set at 3 percent of its total value, and if that income is then taxed at the rate of four shillings per pound (20 percent) the tax is but 3 percent of 20 percent, or 0.6 percent (1/166th part), of the total value. The tax in the rejected £100,000 bill had been 20 percent of the "clear value." *Stats. at Large of Pa.*, V, 598.

Governor with Instructions and penal Bonds, and not allowing him to use his own Judgment, or the Advice of his Assembly, on the most important Occasions, the People may be deprived of one of the most valuable Ends of Government, Protection, and the King's Province exposed to Destruction.

The Governor, by his Estimate laid before the House, required One Hundred and Twenty-seven Thousand Pounds, as necessary for the Service of the current Year. Let us endeavour to compute, by the best Lights we have, how much of this a Tax, laid conformable to the Proprietary Instructions, can possibly produce. All their Estate, except a Trifle, and all located unimproved Lands, to whomsoever belonging, are to be exempted. There remains then to be taxed, only the improved Lands, Houses, and personal Estates of the People. Now it is well known, from the Tax Books, that there are not in the Province more than 20,000 Houses, including those of the Towns, with those on Plantations. If these, with the *improved* Land annexed to them, and the personal Estate of those that inhabit them, are worth, one with another, Two Hundred and Fifty Pounds each, it may, we think, be reckoned their full Value; then multiply 20,000, the Number of Houses, by £250 the Value of each Estate, and the Produce is £5,000,000 for the full Value of all our Estates, real and personal, the unimproved Lands excepted. Now Three *per Cent.* on Five Millions, is but One Hundred and Fifty Thousand Pounds; and Four Shillings in the Pound on One Hundred and Fifty Thousand Pounds, being but a fifth Part, is no more than Thirty Thousand Pounds:[7] So that we ought to have near Seventeen Millions to produce, by such a Tax, One Hundred Thousand Pounds. If it be asked, how

7. Chew dismissed all this figuring as "founded on Conjecture only, and the supposed Value of Estates, it is not to be depended on." He then urged, as the Council had done before, that there be "proper Provision by a Law to enable the Officers to enquire into" the true value of estates, and thus "reduce the Thing to a Certainty." *Pa. Col. Recs.*, VII, 440. The Assembly estimates might be questioned on another ground: its November 1755 law levied but a 2½ percent yearly tax on income; using the £5,000,000 estimate of total valuation and 3 percent of that figure as "clear value," the tax would yield only £2250 per year and only £9000 for the full four years it was to be in effect. Though receipts from the "head tax" and the levy on some unimproved lands under the 1755 tax would have added to the receipts, it still seems likely that the £5,000,000 estimate was too low.

then we proposed to raise One Hundred Thousand Pounds in one Year by the Bill the Governor lately refused, it may be answered, That the Proprietary Estate was by that Bill to be taxed; and all located unimproved Lands were to be taxed; Polls were to be taxed; and the Produce of all Offices, Trades and Employments, were to be taxed, according to the usual Method of assessing them under the County Rate and Levy Act;[8] and yet, with all these Helps, we were sure the Country must have been greatly distressed by that Tax, and that it would hardly have been possible to raise it within the Year. How then shall we make up the Deficiency, when the Tax we are allowed to lay can produce no more than Thirty Thousand Pounds? The Governor is pleased to say, "by following the Example of our Neighbours in taxing Luxury, and laying Duties on such Things as may do the least Injury to Trade." Some of our Neighbours have indeed tried this Method; and what does it produce? The whole Produce of the Tax on the Luxuries of New-York, including the Duties on Wine, Rum, Brandy, and other distilled Liquors, Negroes, Cocoa and Dry Goods, from September 1, 1755, to September 1, 1756, amount to no more, as appears by their Votes now before us, than Three Thousand Two Hundred and Four Pounds, Nineteen Shillings and Two-pence; though that is an older Colony, and inhabited by People generally richer than ours, and almost all the Gold and Silver of the neighbouring Colonies has, within that Term, centered there, to support the Troops. Our chief Luxury, if it may be called a Luxury, is Rum, and that, with Wine, &c. is already taxed, and the Tax mortgaged for ten Years to come. This Colony is more remarkable for Industry and Frugality than for Luxury; and 'tis doubted whether, if all our Luxuries were abolished, and the full Price of them paid to the Treasury, it would produce any considerable Sum; much less must be produced by any Excise or Tax on them that they can bear. We may indeed create some new Offices and Officers, and embarrass Trade, or drive it from our Ports, but little Advantage can we expect to arise from such Taxes to the Publick.

On the Governor's fourth Reason, we shall only remark, that unimproved Lands near the Frontiers may indeed be diminished

8. Passed in 1725–26, and continued; *Stats. at Large of Pa.*, IV, 10–26.

in Value, yet those within the Settlements must rise as the Inhabitants retire inward from the Enemy. The high Price those Lands are, and have been, kept at, has forced out of our Country ten times more of our People than have been driven away by the Enemy, and thereby greatly weakened the Colony. The Monopolizing Lands, therefore, to lie uncultivated for a Market, is a publick Injury; and besides that such Lands can well afford it, they ought to be well taxed to oblige the Owners to sell out, for the Publick Utility. But the Tax laid on them by the Bill is vastly too low, the valuation being confined between Five and Fifteen Pounds per Hundred Acres, when some of those Lands, being the first and choicest Pickings of every Indian Purchase, will actually now sell for near Three Hundred Pounds per Hundred, the War notwithstanding. And though those near the Frontier may be diminished in Value, they are however still of considerable Value, and whatever that is, they should be taxed for it. The Assessors will duly consider such Diminution of Value wherever they find it, and all other Land of the same Kind that holds its Price, should certainly not be exempted for the diminished Value of a Part only. 'Tis kind, however, in the Proprietaries to favour their Wholesale Chapmen, and encourage the Trade, by endeavouring to screen, with their own, the Purchases of their Favourites.

The Governor's fifth Reason against passing the Bill is, that the Act, to which it is a Supplement, refers to the Act for raising County Rates and Levies, and he conceives it unparliamentary for one Act to refer to another; but all the necessary Powers and Duties should be contained in the Body of the Act, independent of any other. Were it unparliamentary, as the Governor says, yet the Act he objects to has received the Royal Approbation, and is executed without the Inconvenience supposed, having been long in Use, and well understood by the Officers. It is but a few Weeks since the Governor himself was pleased to pass an Act for extending hither great Part of an Act of Parliament, by referring to the Clauses only, without requiring them to be inserted in the Bill: And we conceive it far from being unparliamentary, as there are many Instances of one Act of Parliament referring to another. But there being no Instruction in that Case, the Governor had then no Occasion for the Use of this Objection.

On the sixth Reason we must observe, that to make it appear something stronger, it is said, the *whole* Sum of One Hundred Thousand Pounds is to be paid into the Hands of the Trustees; whereas the Bill directs only Forty-five Thousand Pounds of it to come into their Hands, and that either before it is properly Money, being but printed Paper, unsigned, or when it ceases to be Money, and is only to be burnt and destroyed. And as it would probably be drawn out of their Hands almost as fast as it could be signed, no farther Security than they are under for the Eighty Thousand Pounds, by the Eighty Thousand Pound Act, was thought necessary. Fifty-five Thousand Pounds of the One Hundred Thousand Pounds never goes into the Trustees Hands at all, but is to be paid to the Treasurer as it arises from the Taxes, and by him issued in Discharge of the Commissioners Orders for the King's Service: The Treasurer therefore is to give an additional Security by the Bill. When the Forty-five Thousand Pounds comes to be sunk, the Trustees can never have much of it in their Hands at a Time, as a fourth Part of it is to be yearly sunk and destroyed. And the Securities they are already under were deemed fully sufficient, especially as great Part of the Money now under their Direction will be sunk before that comes to their Hands.[9]

The Governor's seventh Objection is likewise against the Act that has been confirmed at Home;[1] we shall therefore only mention what we are informed was the Practice on that Act. The former Governor did at first counter-sign some Orders, but found the Practice too troublesome to be continued. The Mode has since been, for the Governor and Commissioners to agree on the Service for which Money is necessary; then the most considerable Contracts are laid before him for his Approbation, and those Agreements and Approbations are entered on the Minutes. The Commissioners afterwards only settle Accounts, which is troublesome enough, and give Orders for the Payment, in Pursuance of such previous Agreements and Contracts. They would be glad

9. Chew thought the fourth, fifth, and sixth responses by the Assembly "too trifling to require any Remarks upon them." *Pa. Col. Recs.*, VII, 440.

1. Denny had objected that, though the November 1755 act provided for the governor's approval of expenditures, it did not prescribe "any Means whereby it may appear that the Governor's Consent has been had and obtained." *Ibid.*, VII, 415.

if the Governor could be present at every Meeting of the Board, and assist in transacting the Business; but it would take up too much of his Time, and is therefore impracticable. And it would be useless to give him the Trouble of signing Orders, if he cannot spare Time to examine the Accounts on which the Orders are founded; especially as two of his Council have always been two of the Commissioners; and no Governor has complained that they have drawn Orders for improper Services.

What are the many other Parts of the Bill which are contrary to the Instructions, his Honour has not been pleased to specify, nor is it material, since if every one of those Instructions is not observed, the Bill cannot be passed. In fine, as this necessary Bill is exactly conformable to the Act so lately allowed by the Crown, and which is now in Practice, without the Inconveniencies objected; the Want of Compliance with those Proprietary Instructions appears to your Committee the true and sole Reason of its not passing. The other Reasons, as we conceive, are only introduced to save That the Shame of standing alone, and on Examination appear to be not so much *Reasons* as *Excuses*.[2] And we cannot but regret the Situation of a Governor who finds himself under the Necessity of making them, and pity the Counsellors who must approve of them. But much more are we the unhappy People of Pennsylvania to be pitied, who must perish by the Hand of the Enemy, or comply with Instructions, or rather Laws, made for us by ill-informed Proprietaries, at a Thousand Leagues Distance; Laws unsuitable to our Circumstances, impracticable in their Nature, or, if practicable, ineffectual.

Submitted by the Committee to the Correction of the House.[3]

2. Denny took umbrage at this distinction, noting its "Incivility" when it came to his attention. *Ibid.*, VII, 417.

3. The day after the House accepted this report, Daniel Roberdeau and Thomas Yorke were ordered to return the supply bill to Denny, summarize some of the principal conclusions of the report, and if he still refused his consent, the Assembly determined to "refer it to his Honour to pay the Forces by him raised, or to disband them, as he shall judge he can best answer for his Conduct to His Majesty, whose Colony we apprehend to be in imminent Danger, and for the Defence whereof we have in vain endeavoured to make the necessary Provision as far as lay in our Power." *Votes*, 1756–57, p. 92. Denny demanded a copy of the report, which, after some quibbling over a paper the governor had drawn earlier detailing his reasons for rejecting

From the Earl of Loudoun Copy: Huntington Library

Sir New York, February 20th, 1757.

As I have been informed by Mr. Colden,[4] that You have been enquiring when the packet for England was to sail, in Order to Your Taking Your Passage in her, I have taken this Opportunity to acquaint You, that there will be another packet to sail as soon as I return from Philadelphia, which I suppose will be about the 25th. of March. And as I have several very material Things to settle for the Security of Back Settlements of the Southern Provinces, I shou'd be extremely Glad if Your Affairs wou'd permit Your putting off Your Departure till the second packet sails, as I know Your Presence will be of great Use in forwarding whatever shall be found necessary to be done.[5]

I am, &ca.

Benjamin Franklin, Esqr. at Philadelphia.

---

the first £100,000 bill, was delivered to him on February 23. *Ibid.*, p. 97; *Pa. Col. Recs.*, VII, 417. This report and the messages preceding it were printed in *Pa. Gaz.*, Feb. 24, 1757. See below, pp. 152–3 n, for the eventual passage of the £100,000 supply bill.

Perhaps having advance knowledge of this report, Richard Peters gave vent to his feelings about Assembly messages: "all this Billingsgate Language which is used—all these Ebullitions of Passion, Malice and Wrath will do good I hope in the End ... I hear the Reports filled with such keen strokes against the Proprietaries are the performances of B.F. and were still more bitter before they underwent correction ... I am afraid that B.F. whose face at Times turns white as the driven Snow with the Extreams of Wrath may assert Facts not true. ... I have a very high Opinion of B.F.'s virtue and uncorrupted honesty but party Zeal throws down all the pales of Truth and Candour and lays all the Soul waste to Temptation without it knowing or suspecting it." To Thomas Penn, Feb. 14, 1757; Peters Letterbook, Hist. Soc. Pa.

4. Alexander Colden (above, VI, 359 n), postmaster at New York.

5. Loudoun had planned a council of war with the governors from Pennsylvania southward in Philadelphia on February 17, but subsequently postponed it to March 14. Pargellis, *Lord Loudoun*, p. 218. BF had already placed his sea stores on board the packet *Halifax*, Captain Morris, which left New York on March 15, but he agreed to stay in Philadelphia and meet Loudoun; see below, p. 143. The "second packet" with BF aboard did not sail until June 20, 1757.

To Jane Mecom

MS not found; reprinted from Jared Sparks, ed., *A Collection of the Familiar Letters and Miscellaneous Pieces of Benjamin Franklin* (Boston, 1833), p. 48.

Dear Sister, Philadelphia, 21 February, 1757.

I am glad to hear your son is got well home.[6] I like your conclusion not to take a house for him till summer, and if he stays till his new letters arrive, perhaps it would not be amiss; for a good deal depends on the first appearance a man makes. As he will keep a bookseller's shop, with his printing-house, I don't know but it might be worth his while to set up at Cambridge.

I enclose you some whisk seed; it is a kind of corn, good for creatures; it must be planted in hills, like Indian corn.[7] The tops make the best thatch in the world; and of the same are made the whisks you use for velvet. Pray try if it will grow with you. I brought it from Virginia. Give some to Mr. Cooper, some to Mr. Bowdoin.[8]

Love to cousin Sally, and her spouse.[9] I wish them and you much joy. Love to brother, &c. B. FRANKLIN.

To William Coleman[1]

Copy, MS minutes: Trustees of the University of Pennsylvania

Dear Friend Feb. 22d. 1757.

Recollecting Coll. Ludwell's Donation of £20 Sterling to the Academy,[2] I am desirous of settling it before I go (tho I have not

6. On Benjamin Mecom's plans to return to Boston and set up a printing office and bookshop there see above, p. 68. After some months of occasional work in the printing shop of Zachariah Fowle, Mecom operated a press of his own "opposite to the Old Brick Church" in Boston. His work was said to be "correct and good," though Isaiah Thomas thought him eccentric and somewhat dandified. Thomas, *Printing,* I, 143–4, 337–9, 349–52.

7. BF sent some of the same seed (*sorghum vulgare,* or broom corn) to Samuel Ward, Catharine Ray's brother-in-law, a month later. See below, p. 154.

8. Samuel Cooper and James Bowdoin. On both see above, IV, 69 n.

9. Jane Mecom's daughter Sarah (C. 17.5) had married William Flagg, March 18, 1756. Their first child, Jane (C.17.5.1) was born Jan. 25, 1757.

1. On William Coleman, BF's old friend and treasurer of the Academy, see above, II, 406 n.

2. For the gifts of Col. Philip Ludwell of £20 sterling to the Academy and

yet heard that his Bill, which I sent home, is accepted.) Therefore, and to save you the Trouble of paying that Interest Money to my Order, I inclose £1 11*s.* 3*d.*, which added to the Interest Money £32 18*s.* 9*d.* makes £34 10*s.* 0*d.* the Value of £20 Sterling at 72½ Advance per Cent. and so both these Matters are settled together, of which please to make a Memo. in your Book. I return your Receipt canceled. When the whole is come to your Hands, please to send the Coll. a Receipt, signed by you as Treasurer, under the Seal of the Academy, expressing, that it is for the generous Benefaction of the honourable Col. Ludwell of Virginia, to the Academy. Mrs. Franklin will forward it. As he was pleased to leave the particular Mode of applying it to me, I could wish it were put to Interest, and three Prizes purchas'd with the yearly Produce, to be distributed yearly for the three best Pieces of Writing (not exceeding 4 Lines each Piece) done by Boys under 14 Years of Age, who were taught at the Academy. One Prize of 18*s.* Value for the first. One Ditto of 13*s.* Value for the 2d. and one Ditto of 9*s.* Value for the 3d. Some useful Book neatly bound and gilt to be a Part of each Prize. But this I submit to the Trustees.[3] I am Yours affectionately B FRANKLIN

To William Coleman Esqr.

To William Parsons

ALS: American Philosophical Society

Dear Friend Philada. Feb. 22. 1757

I thank you for the Intelligence from Fort Allen, relating to the Indians.[4]

£10 to the Pa. Hospital, made through BF in September 1756, see above, VI, 532 n.

3. The Trustees' apparent failure to accept this advice may reflect BF's declining influence in Academy affairs. Reporting on the Trustees' meeting of Jan. 11, 1757, when the vacancy created by the death of Lloyd Zachary was filled, Board President Richard Peters told Thomas Penn that "in his room, to the mortification of Mr. Franklin, Mr. [Benjamin] Chew was elected.... BF blames the Trustees that they did not beforehand consult him on his Election, saying it was a piece of Justice due to him as he was the Father and principal support of the Academy, and this is true, but for all that it was not thought proper to gratify his Pride which now grows insufferable." Letter of Feb. 14, 1757, Peters Letterbook, Hist. Soc. Pa; Montgomery, *Hist. Univ. Pa.*, p. 316.

4. No such letter from Parsons to BF has been found, but on February 23

The Commissioners have not yet settled your Account, but I will press them to do it immediately.[5]

I have not yet heard from Mr. Stephenson but will write to him once more.[6]

And now, my dear old Friend, I am to take Leave of you, being order'd home to England by the Assembly, to obtain some final Settlement of the Points that have occasioned so many unhappy Disputes. I assure you I go with the sincerest Desire of procuring Peace, and therein I know I shall have your Prayers for my Success.[7] God bless you, and grant that at my Return I may find you well and happy.[8] I am, as ever, Dear Friend, Yours affectionately

B FRANKLIN

William Parsons Esqr

Endorsed: Feb: 1757 Mr. Franklin's Farewell Letter, mentioning his Acct. not being settled by the Comrs.

Pennsylvania Assembly Committee: Report on Grievances

Printed in *Votes and Proceedings of the House of Representatives*, 1756–1757 (Philadelphia, 1757), pp. 94–6.

On Feb. 17, 1758, fourteen days after Franklin's appointment as agent to England, the Assembly named a committee "to draw up the Heads of the several Grievances necessary to be represented Home to England for Redress."[9] Its report, submitted the 22d, was adopted and entered in the minutes the next day. Franklin was not a member of the committee since the report was in effect part of the instructions for his agency, but he carried a copy of it with him and later documents drawn in England show that it was often at his elbow.[1] It is printed here as a

one from Capt. Jacob Arndt (Orndt) commanding officer at Ft. Allen, to Parsons, Feb. 18, 1757, telling of Teedyuscung's proposal for another treaty at Easton, was read in Council. *Pa. Col. Recs.*, VII, 429.

5. No record of settlement appears in the commissioners' accounts.

6. See above, VI, 492–3, and below, p. 206, for BF's effort to help Parsons collect a debt through James Stevenson of Albany.

7. As Parsons was an adherent of the proprietary party, BF phrased this sentence in a way to be unobjectionable to his old friend.

8. Parsons died Dec. 17, 1757.

9. *Votes*, 1756–57, pp. 85, 94–6.

1. See below, pp. 171, 248–52.

summary of the disputes with the Proprietors in which Franklin as an assemblyman had taken a leading part, and as a foundation for his mission to England, especially pertinent because only a fragment of his formal instructions survives.[2]

Feb. 22. 1757.

In Obedience to the Order of the House, we have drawn up the Heads of the most important Aggrievances that occur to us, which the People of this Province with great Difficulty labour under; the many Infractions of the Constitution, in manifest Violation of the Royal Grant, the Proprietary Charters, the Laws of this Province, and of the Laws, Usages and Customs of our Mother Country, and other Matters, which we apprehend call aloud for Redress: They are as follow.

First. By the Royal Charter, which has ever been, ought to be, and truly is, the principal and invariable Fundamental of this Constitution, King CHARLES the Second did give and grant unto William Penn, his Heirs and Assigns, the Province of Pennsylvania; and also to him and his Heirs, and his or their Deputies or Lieutenants, free, full, and absolute Power, for the good and happy Government thereof, to make and enact any Laws, *according to their best Discretion, by and with the Advice, Assent, and Approbation of the Freemen of the said Country, or of their Delegates or Deputies,* for the Raising of Money, or any other End appertaining to the Publick State, Peace, or Safety of the said Country. By the Words of this Grant it is evident, that full Powers were granted to the Deputies and Lieutenants of William Penn, and his Heirs, to concur with the People in framing Laws for their Protection, and the Safety of the Province, according to their "best Discretion," independent of any Instructions or Directions they should receive from their Principals. And it is equally obvious to your Committee, that the People of this Province, and their Representatives, were interested in this Royal Grant, and, by Virtue thereof, have an original Right of Legislation inherent in them, which neither the Proprietaries, nor any other Person whatsoever, can divest them of, restrain or abridge, without manifestly violating and destroying the Letter, Spirit, and Design of this Grant.[3]

2. See below, p. 163, for this fragment.

3. The relevant extracts from the charters and laws referred to in this report will be printed in the next volume under date of April 24, 1758.

Nevertheless, we unfortunately find, that the Proprietaries of this Province, regardless of this sacred Fundamental of all our Rights and Liberties, have so abridged and restricted their late and present Governor's Discretion in Matters of Legislation, by their illegal, impracticable and unconstitutional Instructions and Prohibitions,[4] that no Bill, for granting Aids and Supplies to our most gracious Sovereign, be it ever so reasonable, expedient and necessary, for the Defence of this His Majesty's Colony, and Safety of His People, unless it be agreeable thereto, can meet with his Approbation; by Means whereof the many considerable Sums of Money which have been offered for those Purposes by the Assemblies of this Province, ever anxious to maintain his Honour and Rights, have been rejected, to the great Encouragement of His Majesty's Enemies, and the imminent Danger of the Loss of this His Colony.

Secondly. The Representatives of the People in General Assembly met, by Virtue of the said Royal Grant, and the Charter of Privileges, granted by the said William Penn, and a Law of this Province, have Right to, and ought to enjoy, all the Powers and Privileges of an Assembly, according to the Rights of the Freeborn Subjects of England, and as is usual in any of the Plantations in America; that it is an indubitable, and now an incontested Right of the Commons of England, to grant Aids and Supplies to His Majesty in any Manner they think most easy to themselves and the People; and that they are the sole Judges of the Measure, Manner, and Time of granting and raising the same.

Nevertheless, the Proprietaries of this Province, in Contempt of the said Royal Grant, Proprietary Charter, and Law of this Colony, designing to subvert the Fundamentals of this Constitution, to deprive the Assembly and People of their Rights and Privileges, and to assume an arbitrary and tyrannical Power over the Liberties and Properties of His Majesty's Liege Subjects, have so restrained their Governors by their despotic Instructions, which are not to be varied from, and are particularly directory in the framing and passing of Money Bills and Supplies to His Majesty, as to the Mode, Measure and Time, that it is impossible for the Assembly, should they lose all Sense of their most essential Rights, and comply with these Instructions, to grant sufficient

4. See above, VI, 515–31, for the Proprietors' instructions.

Aids for the Defence of this His Majesty's Province from the common Enemy.

Thirdly. In Pursuance of sundry Acts of General Assembly, approved of by the Crown, a natural Right, inherent in every Man, antecedent to all Laws, the Assemblies of this Province have had the Power of disposing of the publick Monies that have been raised for the Encouragement of Trade, and Support of Government, by the Interest Money arising by the Loan of the Bills of Credit, and the Excise. No Part of these Monies was ever paid by the Proprietaries, or ever raised on their Estates; and therefore, they can have no Pretence of Right to a Voice in the Disposition of them. They have ever been applied with prudent Frugality, for the Honour and Advantage of the Publick, and the King's immediate Service, to the general Approbation of the People. The Credit of the Government has been preserved, and the Debts of the Publick punctually discharged. In short, no Inconveniencies, but great, and many, Advantages have accrued from the Assembly's prudent Care and Management of these Funds.

Yet the Proprietaries, resolved to deprive the Assemblies of the Power and Means of supporting an Agent in England, and of prosecuting their Complaints, and remonstrancing their Aggrievances, when injured or oppressed, to His Majesty and His Parliaments, and to rob them of this natural Right, which has been so often approved of by their gracious Sovereign, have, by their said Instructions, prohibited their Governor from giving his Assent to any Laws for emitting or re-emitting any Paper Currency or Bills of Credit, or for raising Money by Excise, or any other Method, unless the Governor or Commander in Chief for the Time being, by Clauses to be inserted therein, have a Negative in the Disposition of the Monies arising thereby, let the languishing Circumstances of our Trade be ever so great, and a further or greater Medium become ever so necessary for its Support.

Fourthly. By the Laws and Statutes of England, the chief Rents, Honours and Castles of the Crown are taxed, and pay their Proportion to the Supplies that are granted to the King for the Defence of the Realm, and Support of Government. His Majesty, the Nobility of the Realm, and all His British Subjects, do now actually contribute their Proportion towards the Defence of America in general, and this Province in particular; and it is in a more especial Manner the Duty of the Proprietaries to pay their Proportion of a Tax for the immediate Preservation of their own Estates in this Province. To exempt, therefore, any Part of their Estates from their reasonable Part of this necessary Burthen, is as unjust as it is illegal, and as new as arbitrary.

Yet the Proprietaries, notwithstanding the general Danger to which the Nation and its Colonies are exposed, and great Distress of this Province in particular, by their said Instructions, have prohibited their Governors from passing Laws for the Raising of Supplies for its Defence, unless all their located, unimproved, and unoccupied Lands, Quitrents, Fines, and Purchase-Monies on Interest, the much greater Part of their enormous Estates in this Colony, are expresly exempted from paying any Part of the Tax.

Fifthly. By Virtue of the said Royal Charter, the Proprietaries are invested with a Power of "doing every Thing which unto a compleat Establishment of Justice, unto Courts and Tribunals, Forms of Judicature, and Manner of Proceedings do belong." It was certainly the Import and Design of this Grant, that the Courts of Judicature should be formed, and the Judges and Officers thereof hold their Commissions in a Manner not repugnant, but agreeable, to the Laws and Customs of England; that thereby they might remain free from the Influence of Persons in Power, the Rights of the People might be preserved, and their Properties effectually secured. That the Grantee William Penn, understanding the said Grant *in this Light,* did, by his original Frame of Government, convenant and grant with the People, That the Judges, and other Officers, should hold their Commissions during their good Behaviour, and no longer.

Notwithstanding which, the Governors of this Province have, for many Years past, granted all the Commissions to the Judges of the King's Bench, or Supreme Court of this Province, and to the Judges of the Court of Common-Pleas of the several Counties, to be held during their Will and Pleasure. By Means whereof, the said Judges being subject to the Influence and Directions of the Proprietaries and their Governors, their Favourites and Creatures, the Laws may not be duly administred or executed, but often wrested from their true Sense, to serve particular Purposes; the Foundation of Justice may be liable to be destroyed, and the Lives, Laws, Liberties, Privileges and Properties of the

People thereby rendered precarious, and altogether insecure, to the great Disgrace of our Laws, and the inconceivable Injury of His Majesty's Subjects.[5]

Your Committee further beg Leave to add, that besides these Aggrievances, there are other Hardships the People of this Province have experienced, that call for Redress. The Inlistment of Servants, without the least Satisfaction being made to the Masters, has not only prevented the Cultivation of our Lands, and diminished the Trade and Commerce of the Province, but is a Burthen extremely unequal and oppressive to Individuals; and should the Practice continue, the Consequence must prove very discouraging to the further Settlement of this Colony, and prejudicial to His Majesty's future Service. Justice therefore demands that Satisfaction should be made to the Masters of such inlisted Servants, and that the Right of Masters to their Servants be confirmed and settled. But as those Servants have been inlisted into His Majesty's Service for the general Defence of America, and not of this Province only, but all the Colonies, and the Nation in general have, and will receive, equal Benefit from their Service, this Satisfaction should be made at the Expence of the Nation, and not of this Province only.[6]

That the People now labour under a Burthen of Taxes, almost insupportable by so young a Colony, for the Defence of its long extended Frontier, of about Two Hundred Miles, from New-Jersey to Maryland, without either of those Colonies, or the Three Lower Counties, on Delaware, contributing their Proportion thereto, though their Frontiers are in a great Measure covered and protected by our Forts: And should the War continue, and with it this unequal Burthen, many of His Majesty's Subjects in this Province will be reduced to Want, and the Province, if not lost to the Enemy, involved in Debt, and sunk under its Load.

That notwithstanding this Weight of Taxes, the Assemblies of this Province have given to the general Service of the Nation

5. The Assembly probably had particular reference to Justice William Moore of Chester Co. The Assembly received eight petitions, January–March 1757, complaining of his conduct in office; referred to the Committee of Grievances, April 1, 1757. *Votes*, 1756–57, pp. 62, 86, 99, 106. See above, VI, 246–7, for his quarrel with the Assembly.

6. See below, pp. 224–8.

Five Thousand Pounds to purchase Provisions for the Troops under General Braddock; Two Thousand Nine Hundred Eighty-five Pounds, and Eleven-pence, for clearing a Road by his Orders; Ten Thousand Five Hundred and Fourteen Pounds, Ten Shillings, and One Penny, to General Shirley, for the purchasing Provisions for the New-England Forces; and expended the Sum of Two Thousand Three Hundred and Eighty-five Pounds, One Shilling, and Two-pence Halfpenny, in supporting the Inhabitants of Nova-Scotia, which likewise we conceive ought to be a national Expence.[7]

And that His Majesty's Subjects, the Merchants and Insurers in England, as well as the Merchants here, and elsewhere, did, during the last War, and will, during this present War, be greatly injured in their Property, Trade and Commerce, by the Enemy's Privateers on this Coast, and at our Capes, unless some Method be fallen on to prevent it.[8]

Wherefore your Committee are of Opinion, that the Commissioners intended to be sent to England to solicit a Removal and Redress of the many Infractions and Violations of the Constitution, should also have it in Charge, and be instructed to represent to our most gracious Sovereign, and his Parliaments, the several unequal Burthens and Hardships before mentioned, and endeavour to procure Satisfaction to the Masters of such Servants as have been enlisted, and the Right of Masters to their Servants established and confirmed, and obtain a Re-payment of the said several Sums of Money, some Assistance towards defending our extensive Frontier, and a Vessel of War to protect the Trade and Commerce of this Province.

Submitted to the Correction of the House, by

JOSEPH FOX, THOMAS LEECH, JOHN HUGHES, JOSEPH GALLOWAY, WILLIAM MASTERS, JOSEPH GIBBONS, THOMAS YORKE.[9]

7. See above, vols. V and VI, for these actions.

8. See below, p. 285.

9. These assemblymen, all BF's chief political allies, except Gibbons, are identified in vol. VI above, and this vol. p. 29 n, for Galloway. Gibbons, representative from Chester Co., 1748–62, was one of the Quakers who had voted in their support, 1755–56. *Votes*, 1755–56, pp. 54, 74.

To the Earl of Loudoun

ALS: Huntington Library

My Lord, Philada. March 3. 1757.

I thank your Lordship for the Information you have been pleas'd to favour me with, relating to the Sailing of the Pacquets.[1]

It was intended that I should take Passage in the first; But I shall now wait your Lordship's Arrival here, that if in any thing I can be of Service, I may be ready to obey your Lordship's Commands; being, with the sincerest Respect and Attachment, My Lord, Your Lordship's most obedient and most humble Servant

B FRANKLIN

Endorsed: Mr. Frankland Philadelphia March 3d 1757 Rec March 6t

To Catharine Ray

MS not found; reprinted from Jared Sparks, ed., *A Collection of the Familiar Letters and Miscellaneous Pieces of Benjamin Franklin* (Boston, 1833), p. 49.

Dear Katy, Philadelphia, 3 March, 1757.

Being about to leave America for some time, I could not go without taking leave of my dear friend.

I received your favor of the 8th of November,[2] and am ashamed, that I have suffered it to remain so long unanswered, especially as now, through shortness of time, I cannot chat with you in any manner agreeably.

I can only wish you well and happy, which I do most cordially. Present my best compliments to your good mamma, brother and sister Ward, and all your other sisters, the agreeable Misses Ward, Dr. Babcock and family, the charitable Misses Stanton, and, in short, to all that love me.[3] I should have said all that love you, but that would be giving you too much trouble.

1. See above, p. 133.

2. Not found.

3. The persons mentioned include Catharine's mother, Deborah Greene Ray; her brother-in-law and sister, Samuel and Anna Ward; her other sisters, Judith Ray Hubbart and Phoebe Ray Littlefield; Samuel Ward's three unmarried sisters, Hannah, Margaret, and Elizabeth; and Dr. Joshua Babcock of Westerley (see above, VI, 174 n). Among the various unmarried ladies in

Adieu, dear good girl, and believe me ever your affectionate friend, B. FRANKLIN.[4]

Authorization to William Frizzel to Carry Mail

ADS: Princeton University Library

General Post-Office, Philada. March 10. 1757.

I do hereby permit William Frizzel, to carry and deliver Letters between Philadelphia and Lancaster, and to receive the usual Postage for his own Use, till a regular Post shall be established for that Stage.[5] B FRANKLIN, Postmaster General

Endorsed: Benjn. Franklin's Comission to of [*sic*] Wm Frizzle to ride Post 1757

A Testimonial

Printed in *John Gordon's Mathematical Traverse Table, &c.* Printed in the Year 1758, and Sold by Mr. W. Dunlap, in Philadelphia, Mr. G. Noel, in New-York, Mr. B. Mecom, in Boston, and by the Author. (Yale University Library)[6]

John Gordon (1700–1778), a former Philadelphian now living near Princeton, N.J., managed to combine the trade of a bricklayer with the teaching of surveying and other mathematical arts.[7] In the spring of 1757 he announced his intention of publishing by subscription a set of tables to assist "Mariners, Merchants, and Surveyors" in their calcula-

---

the Stanton family of Newport it is uncertain which BF designated as "charitable."

4. This is the last known direct communication between BF and Catharine Ray until the autumn of 1762, although her correspondence with DF continued. She married William Greene, April 30, 1758. William G. Roelker, ed., *Benjamin Franklin and Catharine Ray Greene Their Correspondence 1755–1790* (Phila., 1949), pp. 29–30.

5. William Frizel (*sic*) announced in *Pa. Gaz.*, Aug. 24, 1758, that after riding stage to Lancaster "for upwards of two years," he was giving it up, and requested those who owed him for the carriage of newspapers, etc., to pay his successor, Ludwick Byerly.

6. Evans 8140.

7. Gordon gives a brief sketch of his career on the second page of the tables. An abstract of his will appears in 1 *N.J. Arch.*, XXXIV, 207.

tions. As a matter of timely importance he added that his work would also "be of great use to all Military Gentlemen in any Part of the World, in forming their Marches, or other important Schemes or Designs of an Army." To this announcement in the newspapers and to the prefatory statement in the book itself, when it appeared the next year, he appended a series of testimonials as to the utility of his tables.[8] The first three of these endorsements are printed here, comprising the comments of two New Jersey surveyors and of one from Pennsylvania, and, perhaps inevitably, one by Franklin. It will be noticed, however, that the last of these wisely offered no personal judgment on the value of Gordon's tables—a matter probably beyond Franklin's mathematical competence—but merely endorsed the endorser just before him.

New-Jersey, March 8th, 1757.

We are of Opinion that if the above Tables were printed and published, they would be of great Use to the Public, in Measuring of Land and other Branches of the Mathematicks.

JOHN LAWRENCE,
JONATHAN HAMPTON, } Surveyors.

I am of the above Opinion.

NICHOLAS SCULL, Surveyor Gen. of Pennsylvania.

Philadelphia, March 11, 1757.

The above written Mr. Scull is well known to be one of the best Judges of these Matters in this Province, and therefore any Opinion of mine, or Certificate, is unnecessary after his.

BENJAMIN FRANKLIN, Post Master General.

To the Earl of Loudoun: Answers to Criticisms of the Supply Bill

AD: Huntington Library

When news that Lord Loudoun intended to hold a council of war in Philadelphia reached there in mid-January 1757, it was apparent that

8. The advertisement first appeared in *Pa. Jour.*, April 14, 1757; it was reprinted in several succeeding issues and also appeared in *N.Y. Mercury* as late as May 20. The names and number of endorsers varied in the different advertisements; in the book itself there are nine testimonials, altogether bearing the names of fourteen individuals from Pennsylvania, New Jersey, and New York.

he and his plans would have a powerful effect on local affairs. It was reported, for example, that Governor Denny "proposes to lay Mr. F's Conduct before Lord Loudoun . . . [who] can and I hope will bring him to an Ecclaircissment on which it may be determined what further measures to take with him."[9] The postponement of the conference from February 17 to March 15 delayed decisions still further; the Council gave Denny their unanimous opinion, March 5, that the supply bill "should be detained till Lord Loudoun's arrival, as something might be expected to be said by him on the Subject which might extricate the Governor and Assembly out of the Difficulties attending the passing Such a Bill."[1] At the same time, Loudoun's request that the newly appointed Assembly agent not depart for England until after the general's visit to Philadelphia[2] foreshadowed the important role Franklin was to play in the conferences.

Word of the postponement did not reach the southern colonies in time to delay departures from them, so Governors Arthur Dobbs of North Carolina, Robert Dinwiddie of Virginia, and Horatio Sharpe of Maryland, and Col. George Washington, commander of the Virginia troops, waited in Philadelphia nearly a month for Loudoun's arrival.[3] Col. John Hunter, money agent; Christopher Kilby, contractor for supplies; Edmund Atkin, the Southern Indian agent; Col. John Stanwix; the colonels of the Pennsylvania battalions; George Croghan; and the Rev. Michael Schlatter were also among the dignitaries who gathered to consult with Loudoun. He also talked with Israel Pemberton and other prominent Philadelphians as well as with provincial officials.[4] The formal council of war with the four governors (including Denny) came to quick agreement on the support and disposition of military forces in the south for the 1757 campaign: Colonel Stanwix to command half a battalion of the Royal American Regiment and 1000 Pennsylvania provincials using Carlisle as his principal base; 1100 Virginia and Maryland troops to guard the frontier in those

9. Richard Peters to Thomas Penn, Jan. 10, 1757, Penn Papers, Hist. Soc. Pa. A month later, however, Peters wrote Penn that Denny had abandoned the plan.

1. *Pa. Col. Recs.*, VII 430–1.

2. See above, pp. 133, 143.

3. For these early arrivals, and their participation in the conferences, see R. A. Brock, ed., *The Official Records of Robert Dinwiddie* (Richmond, 1884), II, 587–606; William H. Browne, ed., *Correspondence of Governor Horatio Sharpe* (Baltimore, 1888), I, 518–37; and Douglas S. Freeman, *George Washington*, II (N.Y., 1948), 234–41.

4. Lord Loudoun's nearly illegible Notebooks, virtually a diary, record his conversations with these persons. Huntington Lib.

The Earl of Loudoun

provinces; and Lt. Col. Henry Bouquet to command half a battalion of Royal Americans and 1000 or more provincials in South Carolina to repel a rumored French attack there. Loudoun also dealt at length with such matters as officers' rank, supplies, and payment of troops.[5]

Though Franklin probably participated informally in this planning, Loudoun recorded conversations with him only about provincial affairs. On the first day he "Talked over the Situation of this Country [Pennsylvania] and the Deplorable State it appears to be in" with "Mr. Frankland," who "promises to do every thing in his Power."[6] The same day Loudoun sought the advice of Governors Dobbs, Dinwiddie, and Sharpe in "Setting Right the Affairs" of Pennsylvania, and asked Denny "to consider if any, or which of the Instructions [from the Proprietors on money bills] could be given up; and promised, on receiving the Governor's answer, he would ask the same of the Assembly, and endeavour to reconcile Matters, that there might be no longer Delay in raising the Sums necessary." After discussion in Council, Richard Peters and Benjamin Chew were appointed to "digest" the concessions agreed upon. The document they prepared, entitled "Propositions in Relation to the Money Bill now under the Consideration of the Governor of Pennsylvania," was submitted, amended, and approved on March 17. It dealt with eight objections to the bill, similar to, but not wholly identical with, the points raised in Denny's message of February 11 and rebutted by the Assembly committee's report of the 17th.[7] On three or possibly four of these he was now willing to yield if necessary, but on the others he offered no concessions.[8]

Meanwhile Franklin had been added hastily to the Assembly committee appointed to deliver a congratulatory address to Loudoun, done March 16, to which the general replied politely, but warned that unless "all Animosities and Differences should be laid aside . . . they must not blame him" for unwelcome consequences.[9] The same day Loudoun also warned that obstructionists "must Stand in a bad light at home," and on the 18th he told Israel Pemberton that Indian affairs had been taken out of the hands of the several provinces "and more so out of Private Societys,"[1] a pointed reference to the intrusion of the Quakers

5. Loudoun Notebooks; Sharpe to Lord Baltimore, March 23, 1757, *Correspondence of Gov. Sharpe*, I, 533; *Pa. Col. Recs.*, VII, 470–2.

6. Loudoun Notebooks. The earl's spelling of BF's name in the Notebooks and other papers is doubtful, but usually appears to be as it is rendered here.

7. See above, p. 121.

8. *Pa. Col. Recs.*, VII, 441–3.

9. *Votes*, 1756–57, pp. 100–1.

1. Loudoun Notebooks.

at recent Indian treaties. That evening, "Lord Loudoun, the Gentlemen Strangers in the Place, the Officers of the Royal Americans, and a Number of the principal Inhabitants of the Town, were genteelly entertained by the Corporation at the State-House."[2]

On March 19, Loudoun recorded that "whilst Mr. Frankland and I were talking over talking over [*sic*] the Affairs in Dispute between the Governor and the Assembly in order to trie to bring them to an agreement which the Governor had desierd I might trie with Mr. Frankland[,] when[?] Dinwiddie Called and afterwards Mr. Denny both which were called on at Mr. Frankland's Desier and we went throu the dispute over the Bill. Neither of them[?] agreed in the Facts which the other aledged but Mr. Frankland was much more acquainted[?] with the Affair than the Governor."[3] Probably at this time Loudoun showed to Franklin and Speaker Norris the Propositions approved by Denny and the Council on March 17 and a summary of the objections to the £100,000 supply bill and asked for a reply.[4] Their answer is printed here from the original in Franklin's hand among Lord Loudoun's papers.[5]

2. *Pa. Gaz.*, March 24, 1757.

3. Loudoun Notebooks. Perhaps to counter this good impression made by BF, Denny drew Loudoun's attention to Sir Charles Hardy's letter of Oct. 25, 1756, enjoining Morris and Denny to prevent publication of improper intelligence in the Philadelphia newspapers. Denny pointed out that this would be impracticable "unless your Lordship lays your Commands on the Postmaster, to be extremely cautious" and perhaps orders "that Articles of Intelligence should receive my [Denny's] Approbation, and not [be] published without Leave." *Pa. Col. Recs.*, VII, 447. This proposal for censorship is not mentioned in Loudoun's Notebooks nor was it carried into effect at this time. The attempt to control BF's conduct through threats to his office under the Crown continued in England, too. Thomas Penn wrote Richard Peters, April 9, 1757, that the Duke of Cumberland had "spoke to Sir Everard Falkner [Fawkener, BF's post office superior] by no means to support Franklin unless he acted another part." Penn Papers, Hist. Soc. Pa.

4. See above, pp. 106–9, 121–32, for earlier argument over the £100,000 supply bill, including references to two different sets of objections to it by Denny or members of his Council. Loudoun had requested, in addition to the list of concessions mentioned above, "all the Remarks, which in the opinion of the Council woud lye against the Bill, or the Assembly's long Defence of it." 1 *Pa. Arch.*, III, 118. These "Remarks," apparently under headings A–G, have not been found, but their substance is easily inferred from this reply to Loudoun and earlier recorded objections to the bill.

5. Appended to the text of the reply are extracts from various documents referred to in it. These extracts are not printed here but are explained in appropriate footnotes.

[March 21, 1757]

A. The Assessors are yearly chosen by the People, and if there is any Complaint of unequal Taxation, (which there always will be in every Country) it does not with us lie against the Assessors as unjust and partial, so much as against the Concealment of Estates, and the imperfect Manner of obtaining a Knowledge of them, which is intended soon to be remedied.[6] The Commissioners and Assessors who tax the People are oblig'd, by a Law pass'd in the 6th Year of the present Reign,[7] to lay their Assessments and Accounts before the Justices and Grand Juries of the County Courts, which has accordingly been done ever since that Law passed: Yet no Complaints have ever to this Day been made to the Assembly by any of the Courts, of any Injustice in the Assessors. And it seems extraordinary that this Matter should at this Time be press'd, by the Governor who is never tax'd, and by the Proprietors who exempt themselves from Taxes, while the People, who alone are affected by any Inequality, are as easy as they generally are in any Country. The Assembly, however, have already determin'd to prepare a particular Bill, to regulate the Assessing and Levying of Taxes[8]; but they chose to make Use of the old Method in the present proposed Tax, not because they fully approved of it, but because the King's Service required an immediate Supply, and the Changing of established Modes, in a Matter so interesting as that of Taxation, would, as they had found by Experience in the Attempt made this present Session, take up much Time, and might fail at last. The Mode directed in the £100,000 Bill now before the Governor, is the same that has been used in this Province from the Beginning, and the same that is

6. See above, p. 106, for the difficulty over evaluation of estates.

7. *The Statutes at Large of Pennsylvania*, IV (Harrisburg, 1897), 10–26. For Loudoun's information, BF copied and attached pertinent sections of this law.

8. A revised system of property valuation and assessment had been discussed fruitlessly in the Assembly since Dec. 15, 1756. Denny later reported that, as part of the agreement with Lord Loudoun which secured passage of the bill, "Mr. Franklin promised, . . . the loose Method of taxing, and the Number and Nomination of the Assessors, should be rectified in another future bill." To Thomas Penn, April 10, 1757; 1 *Pa. Arch.*, III, 118. On March 22, the Assembly appointed a committee "to bring in a Bill for obtaining a better Return of Property to render the Taxing of the Inhabitants of this Province more just and equal." *Votes*, 1756–57, p. 103. The issue was not settled during the continuation of proprietary government in Pennsylvania.

directed by the Act for granting £60,000 pass'd the last Year, is now practic'd in the Execution of that Act, and all the Officers concerned are well acquainted with it.[9] It seem'd therefore the Method most eligible on the present Emergency, which is become so pressing, that a Compliance with the Proposal in the first Clause, tho' it should on Consideration be found reasonable, is now impracticable. The Bill expressly mentions, that the Tax is to be on *all Estate both real and personal,* the Proprietary Estate only excepted.

B. The Committee for Disposing of the Money and Auditing the Accounts, *are* expresly named in the Bill, and two of them *are* of the Council.[1]

C. The Provincial Treasurer *is* required to give in a new Security by the present Bill; the Sum is also named in the Body of the Bill, to wit, £5000 and as the People must not only pay the Tax, but make good any Deficiency however arising, there is no doubt but Assemblies will always be ready to make such Provision as shall be found necessary to secure the Money in the Hands of their Treasurer, by a particular Bill for that purpose.[2]

D. As the present Money Bill is form'd, none of the Money can be issued without the Governor's Assent and Approbation, and it is in his Power at any time to regulate the Manner in which that Assent shall be signified.[3]

9. As evidence that the £60,000 act was acceptable in England, BF copied and attached extracts from the reports of the Board of Trade, March 3 and April 15, 1756, where it was at first objected to, but then approved.

1. The governor and his Council had complained frequently of the power granted the commissioners and their appointment by the Assembly, but as BF made clear in an extract from the proposed £100,000 bill attached for Loudoun's information, there was no uncertainty as to their identity. The Council propositions of March 17 insisted that all orders for payment be countersigned by the governor. *Pa. Col. Recs.*, VII, 442.

2. The governor in Council agreed to waive his objections on this point in the March 17 proposals. *Ibid.* BF copied and attached the provisions in the proposed bill relating to the treasurer's bond.

3. Denny had objected that though the supply bill had indeed required the governor's assent to expenditures, "yet the Commissioners alone have a power to draw Orders on the Trustees." *Ibid.*, VII, 415. See above, pp. 131–2, for the Assembly's response to this objection. BF copied and attached the relevant portion of the proposed bill, but this hardly met the Council's objections to the *procedures* developed under similar provisions of earlier supply acts.

E. The Governors of this Province have always had the Disposal of all Presents to Indians, and the Choice of all Commissioners appointed to make Treaties with them. The Assemblies never claim'd any Power of this kind. The Proprietaries are hereditary Governors of this Province; they have a noble Support in the Quit Rents; they ought therefore to govern the Province in person: But they live in England, make private Estate of the Quit Rents, and send Deputies to govern in their Stead. Their Deputies have also a Support, (which we have establish'd by Law) in the Money arising from Licences, &c. suppos'd to be near £1000 Sterling per Annum. Thus we actually pay *two* Supports, and yet have not the full Benefit of *one* Governor: For the Proprietors live at a great Distance, and cannot readily be apply'd to on any Emergency of Government, and their Deputy is so restrain'd, as that he cannot use his own Judgment. When our Lieut. Governors were at Liberty to act as Governors, and to pass such Laws as they found for the Benefit of the People, they have always received from the Assembly additional Yearly Marks of the People's Gratitude and Respect. Above £30,000 has been given by the Assemblies within these 30 Years, to Governors, out of the Funds which by Law the Assemblies had the sole Disposition of.[4]

F. The Assembly have great Respect for their present Governor, and if he would think fit himself to hear and answer their Complaints, it might probably be very agreable to the Assembly to have an Opportunity of laying them before him. But as there are some of his Council, who are suspected to be the Advisers of all the Measures, and even Procurers of the Instructions to be complain'd of as Grievances; Men who are look'd upon as Enemies to the House and to the People, attach'd to the Proprietors by profitable Offices held during Pleasure, it seems as if it could

4. In the propositions of March 17 Denny and the Council had complained that upon his arrival he had received from the Assembly an order on the provincial treasurer for £600, no part of which had yet been paid him. "As the Governor is constantly employed in the Business of the Government, to which he devotes his whole Time and Attention, he thinks it reasonable that some effectual Provision should be made for his Support in this Bill." *Pa. Col. Recs.*, VII, 442–3. Denny was apparently willing to leave the impression with Loudoun that this £600 was his only public source of income. He had not raised this point in his earlier exchanges with the Assembly itself about the £100,000 supply bill.

answer no good End, but rather tend to continue and increase Contention, if the Council are to consider those Complaints and advise the Answers.

G. The Naming of the Treasurer's Securities in the Body of the Bill, is unusual if not intirely new, and may be attended with Inconvenience:[5] For if the Securities, after consenting to be nam'd in the Bill, should change their Minds when the Law had pass'd, the Treasurer could not act without a new Law naming others; unless those named were compell'd under a Penalty to become Securities, which would seem extraordinary. If the Securities are such as the Governor has no Objection to on Account of Insufficiency it is all that appears to be necessary. And he is the sole Judge of their Sufficiency.[6]

Endorsed: Extracts and answers to Points Proposed to be amended in the Bill Receved from Mr Frankland at Philadelphia March 21t 1757 Rec. March 21t

5. See above, p. 131, for earlier argument over securities for officers handling public funds. The pending £100,000 supply bill contained the usual provisions for bonding the provincial treasurer; why the governor and his Council took this occasion to object to those provisions is unknown.

6. The tangled events of March 21 leading to the enactment of the supply bill have been the subject of inconsistent accounts by their participants. BF's recollection (Par. Text edit., pp. 392–4) that Loudoun asked him to persuade the Assembly to give in and that the bill was agreed upon because of his effective appeal to the House, is mistaken; the Assembly had already conceded on the taxation of proprietary estates, February 3, and the final and essential concessions were made by Denny, as Loudoun explained to William Pitt, April 25, 1757: "[The Pennsylvania] Assembly had proposed a Bill, the Governor thought he could not pass consistent with his Instructions from Mr. Pen; I took all possible pains with the leading Men of the Assembly, to accomodate this difference: The Council, that is Mr. Pen's Council of State (for they make no part of the Legislature) represented them very strong, the Members of the Assembly answered their Objections, on which I consulted with Lieutenant Governor Denwiddie, as a Man of great Experience in the Affairs of this Country, And as our Opinions agreed, that in the present situation of Affairs and the Consequences that must happen from no Money being granted, it was proper, the Governor should for this time, pass the Bill as it was presented by the Assembly; he did it on a Letter from me, containing my reasons for advising that Measure." Gertrude S. Kimball, ed., *Correspondence of William Pitt* (N.Y., 1906), I, 41. Denny's own report to Thomas Penn was substantially the same, but added that he passed the bill at Loudoun's insistence because BF had promised to secure amendments in

Provincial Commissioners: Order to Pay James Young[7]

DS: Yale University Library

Philada. March 23, 1757

To the Trustees of the General Loan-Office.

Gentlemen, No. 1.

Till the New Money to be struck by the One hundred Thousand Pound Act (this Day to be passed by the Governor and Assembly)[8]

---

the tax provisions of a future bill (note 8 above), and because news arrived from Ft. Augusta that 800 French and Indians were expected to attack that place. 1 *Pa. Arch.*, III, 118. According to the Council minutes, the express from Ft. Augusta arrived after noon on March 21, whereupon Denny consulted Loudoun, who urged him "not to make any further Opposition to the Supply Bill, but to pass it directly." Denny immediately informed the Assembly he would pass the bill, which became law on March 23. *Pa. Col. Recs.*, VII, 453; *Votes*, 1756–57, pp. 102–3. Whatever the exact sequence of events, Loudoun's official letter to Denny, written the afternoon of the 21st, indicates the pressures responsible for the passage: Loudoun found "the Publick Service in the Province entirely at a Stand" because of the dispute over the supply bill; that the consequently unpaid provincial troops were "in great danger of disbanding," a circumstance rendered more dangerous by the rumored attack; that it was "absolutely necessary" that Pennsylvania furnish its quota of forces to help defend the southern colonies; that he could not station any more of the King's troops in Pennsylvania; and thus, since there was not time "for new modelling another Bill," Denny was urged "to wave your Instructions for the present, and pass this Bill, that Money may be raised." *Pa. Col. Recs.*, VII, 453–4. That this chain of events represented a serious blow to the proprietary interest is clear from Penn's response to Peters' now missing letters describing them. At first Penn was defiant: "We shall not consent to be determined in any matter of consequence by his [Loudoun's] orders, they are to be given to the Army but not to us or his Majesty's Subjects in general" (May 14, 1757). Later Penn was surprised that Loudoun "should still have put so much confidence in Franklin" and have taken "Mr. Franklin's reflections on the Council for facts"; indeed, it was most remarkable, Penn wrote further, that "my Lord Loudoun would have treated you [Peters and the Council] in the manner he has done." July 9 and Aug. 13, 1757, Penn Papers, Hist. Soc. Pa.

7. See above, VI, 392–6, and this volume, pp. 3, 25, for orders for payment by the commissioners. Capt. James Young (1729–1779), Philadelphia official, commissary general and paymaster of Pa. Troops, 1756–65, and wagonmaster during the Revolution, married Mary Jane, daughter of Dr. Thomas Graeme. Charles P. Keith, *The Provincial Councillors of Pennsylvania* (Phila., 1883), p. 164.

8. See above, p. 152 n.

comes into your Hands, the Governor and Commissioners request you to advance Three or Four Thousand Pounds, to be replaced by the first of the new Money; as that Sum is immediately wanted for the Publick Service. What you shall so advance to be paid to James Young, Esqr. Paymaster of the Provincial Forces.[9]

William Denny[1]
John Mifflin B Franklin
Jon Hughes Jos Fox

£3.000. 0. 0 pd. See Js. Youngs Receipt on the Other Side.

Philada. March 24th 1757 Recd of Charles Norris one of the Trustees of the General Loan Office the Sum of Three thousand pounds on Account of the within Order. Jas. Young
£3000. 0. 0.

Endorsed: Govr. & Comrs Order, and James Youngs rect for £3.000. 0. 0 paid March. 23d. 1757

To Samuel Ward[2]

ALS: Nantucket Atheneum

Dear Sir Philada. March 24. 1757

I inclose you some of the Grain called Whisk Corn, or Broom Corn.[3] It must be planted in Hills like Indian Corn, 3 or 4 Grains in a Hill. It looks like Indian Corn when growing, till the Top comes out, of which they make the Whisk Brushes for Velvet, and excellent Brooms. The Grain is good for Bread, and for Fowls, Horses, &c. being a kind of Millet, and of great Increase. The Stalks &c. make excellent Thatch. It grows 10 foot high, and I believe must have a little more room than you commonly give

9. In response to the rumor of an attack on Ft. Augusta, Young was sent there to pay arrears due the troops. He arrived at the fort in early April and disbursed £2300, four months' pay for the men. The officers volunteered to forego their back pay for the time being so that the ranks could have what was available. *PMHB,* XXXVI (1912), 419.

1. Denny's signature on one of the commissioners' orders for money payments is unusual. It may signify an intention to assume a more active part in the disbursement of funds under the new act. On the previous practice, see above, p. 131–2.

2. On Samuel Ward, Catharine Ray's brother-in-law, see above, V, 504 n.

3. See above, p. 134, where BF told Jane Mecom that he had brought this seed from Virginia.

your Indian Corn; but plant it at the same time. When tis ripe, gather it; you may strip the Seed off by Hand, from the Whisk, or your Fowls will pick it off. Give my dear Friend Katy enough of the Tops to make a Whisk for her Mantelet; and with it, if you please, a Kiss from me, and my best Wishes. My respectful Compliments to Mrs. Ward and all Friends; I expect to sail next Week for England, where, if I can be of any Service to you, favour me with your Commands, directed to me at the Pensilvania Coffee House in Birchin Lane, London. I am, dear Sir, Your most obedient Servant B FRANKLIN

[*Instruction to post rider:*] Put this in the New London Bag

Addressed: To / Mr Ward / Mercht at / Westerly / Free / B FRANKLIN

From John Hughes[4] with Franklin's Receipt

I. MS not found; reprinted from *Pennsylvania History*, VI (1939), 15;[5]
II. ADS: Yale University Library

The minutes of the Society of Arts (see above, VI, 186-9 n) for the meeting of Sept. 7, 1757, note that Franklin attended and read the extract of a letter from John Hughes printed as No. I below; that Franklin paid in the donation; and that the Society voted their thanks to Hughes for his gift and to Franklin for his trouble. The date on Franklin's autograph receipt to Hughes, printed as No. II below, suggests the probable date of the original letter.

I

[March 24, 1757]

I herewith put into your Hands Thirty two Dollars which I desire you to present to the Society you mentioned to me some time ago, and be pleased to let them know I commit it to their Direction to be laid out either for the good of Great Britain or America as they think proper.

II

Receiv'd March 24. 1757 of Mr. John Hughes Thirty-two Dollars, being his Present to the Society for Promoting Arts and Manu-

4. See above, VI, 284–5 n.

5. In an article by Frank R. Lewis, "Benjamin Franklin and the Society of Arts."

factures; and Eight Dollars to be laid out in a Thermometer and Barometer, per me B FRANKLIN[6]

William Denny, Franklin, and the Provincial Commissioners: Order to Pay Lewis Ourry

ADS:[7] Historical Society of Pennsylvania

March 29. 1757

Pay to Lieut. Lewis Ourry, or Order, the Sum of Two Hundred and Forty-six Pounds Nine Shillings, being for the Discharge of the Quarters of 1 Col. 1 Lieut. Col. 1 Major, 7 Captains, 28 Subalterns, and 1 Surgeon, for 15 Weeks; 1 Capt. and 3 Lieuts. 17 Weeks; 2 Captains and 2 Lieuts. 3 Weeks, at the Rates in the Margin; it being according to Allowance made by the late Commissioners.[8]

	Per Week
Col.	20*s.*
Lieut. Col.	19*s.*
Major	16*s.*
Capts.	9*s.*
Subalterns	6*s.*
Surgeon	6*s.*

£246. 9*s.* 0*d.*

JOHN BAYNTON WILLIAM DENNY
JOHN MIFFLIN B FRANKLIN
JON HUGHES JOS: FOX
WM: MASTERS JOS. GALLOWAY

To The Trustees of the General Loan Office of the Province of Pennsylvania

6. An undated entry in BF's accounts shows that he paid £7 4*s.* to the "Society of Arts &c. on Account of Mr. Hughes, the Money he sent." Another group of entries, dated Oct. 14, 1757, record payment of "Nairn's bill for Barometer &c. £5 1*s.* 0*d.* of which the Barometer [cost] £1 16*s.* 0*d.* and one Thermometer £1 11*s.* 6*d.* Case and Porter 3*s.* [a total of] £3 10*s.* 6*d.* for J. Hughes." "Account of Expences" (below, p. 164), pp. 7, 5; *PMHB,* LV (1931), 105, 104. BF and Hughes were appointed to supervise premiums the Society offered to encourage silk culture in Pa., April 5, 1758. BF may have helped draft the statement about the premiums, printed in the *American Magazine* for July 1758. His interest in silk culture in Pa. continued throughout his life.

7. In BF's hand.

8. See above, p. 96, for the commissioners' proposal for allowances to the officers in lieu of quarters. Other than Governor Denny and BF, the signers

Bill to the Proprietors

ADS: Friends Library of the Society of Friends, London; also copy: Historical Society of Pennsylvania[9]

March 30, 1757

An example of the extent to which Franklin had conducted his printing, stationery, and bookselling business on credit is the bill he rendered to the Proprietors, March 30, 1757, before leaving for England. It includes 97 items running from 1734 to 1745; except for three undated items at the end, none of these charges had been paid when the bill was presented.[1] Twenty-eight of the entries were for advertisements in the *Gazette;* 26 were for printed forms of various sorts or for advertisements in quantities of several hundreds, apparently intended for distribution by hand;[2] 17 were for paper, blank books, and other stationery supplies; 14 for books and pamphlets; 5 for binding or gilding of books; the rest were miscellaneous. Franklin subtracted from the total charge the three undated items for which Richard Hockley, the Penns' receiver general, had paid, and indicated the amount due as £57 1*s.* 6*d.* He then wrote: "March 30, 1757. Errors excepted per B FRANKLIN."[3] Below this is Thomas Penn's direction: "I desire you will examine this account and if it does not appear by this Books that any of it has been paid that you will pay it as demanded and place to the account

---

of this order were the commissioners (together with Isaac Norris) named in the £100,000 Supply Act passed March 23. Since BF was not a commissioner under the new act, his signature probably indicates an endorsement to the new commissioners of the arrangements he had helped set up.

9. The copy, among the Penn Papers in Hist. Soc. Pa., carried none of the notations and endorsements mentioned in the headnote except BF's. It also indicates that the three undated items at the end were paid for by Lynford Lardner, not by Richard Hockley as in BF's original. It is endorsed: "Copy of B. Franklin's Bill £57:1:6."

1. All but nine of the items are recorded in Ledger A and B or in Ledger D. Most of the earlier entries also appear on the bill of 1734 printed in full above, I, 371.

2. Some of the advertisements in the *Gazette* or in handbill form, especially those relating to the payments of quitrents, were printed in both English and "Dutch" versions.

3. Hockley wrote to the Proprietors, June 25, 1757: "The day before Franklyn left this Town Mr. Peters sent for me and exhibited an account he had received from him against You amounting to £57 1*s.* 6*d.* commencing in the year 1734 and ending Feby. 1744/5 for sundries, stationery and printing which astonished me greatly." He proposed to withhold payment until he heard from Penn about the matter. Penn Papers, Hist. Soc. Pa.

of charge. London December 4. 1758. THO PENN To Richard Hockley and Edmd Physick[4] or to the Receiver General for the time being."[5] Hockley's "Examin'd R H" is opposite Franklin's total and Deborah Franklin's receipt is at the bottom of the page: "Receivd July 30th. 1759 Fifty seven Pounds one Shilling and Six Pence in full Ballance of the above Account £57 1. 6. D FRANKLIN." Thus two years and four months after Franklin submitted this bill and twenty-five years after the first charges were incurred, Thomas Penn's agent finally paid what was due.

Philadelphia Post Office Record Book, 1757-1764

MS record book: American Philosophical Society

[March 30, 1757]

When Franklin was preparing to leave for England his son William, who was going with him, resigned the Philadelphia postmastership, which he had held since June 1753 (see above, IV, 513). In his place Franklin appointed his wife's nephew-in-law William Dunlap (see above, V, 199 n, and below, p. 168), who had been a printer in Lancaster. Among the Franklin Papers is a paper-covered book of 174 pages (88 of them blank) which contains Dunlap's record of letters received in that Post Office from March 30, 1757, to Oct. 5, 1764. It is set up in the form prescribed for Book C in the instructions Franklin and Hunter prepared in 1753 for the local postmasters (see above, V, 172–4).

Dunlap fell far behind in settling his accounts and was removed from office in 1764, but, in spite of his financial unreliability, he kept this record of incoming mail faithfully and, it would seem, accurately. The detailed entries are not of sufficient general interest to justify printing the contents of the book in full, but an analysis of the records does provide a view of the postal system, with Philadelphia as a focal point, during these years after Franklin and Hunter had assumed the deputy postmaster generalship and had introduced reforms and improvements in the service.

4. Edmund Physick (1727–1804), agent of Thomas Penn in the colony and later surveyor general. *PMHB*, V (1881), 359–60.

5. Thomas Penn had written Hockley, Aug. 13, 1757: "As to Mr. Franklin's account, you must examine it if it has been paid, if not, and his Servants will attest it is due, it must be paid." On Feb. 10, 1758, he commented to Hockley: "Mr. Franklin has not said anything to me about his account, when he does I shall pay him if he desires it." Penn Papers, Hist. Soc. Pa.

Dunlap's records show that by 1757 a weekly post rider was setting out from Boston, usually on a Monday, carrying mail from that town and usually from others as far north as Portsmouth, N. H. Letters for Philadelphia normally arrived on a Wednesday, nine days after leaving Boston, together with other mail picked up at post offices in southern New England, New York, and New Jersey.[6] Beginning in June this service was expanded to twice a week through the season of good weather, though the nine days usually required for delivery from Boston remained the same.[7] On very rare occasions the trip took only eight days, but much more often, especially in the winter and early spring, it took as much as twelve to seventeen days. In such cases the schedule of later trips might be badly disrupted.[8]

Before the establishment of the second weekly trip from New England through to Philadelphia and thereafter during the winter months when it was not running, a separate weekly service normally left New York on Thursday and arrived in Philadelphia on the following Saturday. The trip rarely took more than two days. Thus correspondents in these two cities and in New Jersey towns along the route could count on semi-weekly service throughout the year.

By contrast the service from the south to Philadelphia was highly erratic. Theoretically, mail left Williamsburg every two weeks, except in winter, and took ten days to reach Philadelphia; this was cut to nine days by 1762. By the time the mail arrived it might also include letters from Fredericksburg, Dumfries, Alexandria, and Annapolis. In the winter the service operated only once a month at best and took much

6. An example of the schedule on this route is in a series of entries recorded in August 1761. Letters for Philadelphia were billed out by the postmasters of Portsmouth and Newbury on the 7th, Boston the 10th, Newport the 11th, New York the 17th, and Woodbridge and Elizabethtown the 18th, arriving in Philadelphia the 19th. On other trips the post rider might have nothing to deliver from one or another of these places but might bring letters from such offices as Salem, Marblehead, Providence, New London, New Haven, Newburgh (picked up at New York), Brunswick, Trenton, or Princeton.

7. The second weekly trip normally left Boston on Thursday and reached Philadelphia a week from the following Saturday.

8. This record book shows only incoming mail at Philadelphia; presumably schedules and length of time en route were similar for the outgoing mail. In estimating how long a person in Boston, for example, might expect to wait before receiving even an immediate reply to a letter he sent to Philadelphia, it should be remembered that outgoing mail might lie in the post office for several days before the post rider set out. Depending on the season of the year and the days of the week on which a letter and its reply were written, an exchange of communications between Boston and Philadelphia during these years probably took at least three weeks and doubtless often more.

longer, if indeed any mail came through from further south than Alexandria.[9]

Comparison of this volume with Franklin's record book of 1748–52, when he was postmaster of Philadelphia (see above, II, 182–3), shows little change in the southern mail service but a distinct improvement in that from the north. Before Franklin and Hunter took charge of the entire system the northern post was on a weekly schedule during the favorable season of the year and a biweekly schedule during the winter. Now mail came in regularly from New York twice a week and from New England once, throughout the year, and beginning in 1762 the New England service during the best months was put on the same much improved basis as that from New York. Except when weather conditions intervened (or possibly illness of a post rider), these schedules were maintained with substantial regularity. While the methods of recording the quantity of mail differed enough between the two periods to make exact comparison difficult if not impossible, it is also clear that the amount of mail coming to Philadelphia had considerably increased with the growth in population and the increased frequency of the service.

Philadelphia Post Office Accounts, 1757–1764

MS account papers: American Philosophical Society

In addition to the Philadelphia Post Office Record Book described immediately above, there survives among Franklin's papers a series of loose sheets, mostly but not all in his hand, relating to William Dunlap's financial accounts, March 30, 1757, to July 11, 1764, and the operations of the Philadelphia Post Office during his tenure. The most important document is a balance sheet Franklin prepared from these and other records. It is reprinted here in full since it shows the gross business of this office during approximately seven and a quarter years. The other records on these sheets are described in footnotes but various arithmetical calculations used in preparing the entries are not specifically noticed.

9. Something of a record may have been established by one parcel of letters billed at Williamsburg Nov. 30, 1761, which was joined either there or in transit by another packet billed from the same place on December 17; to this mail were added letters from Fredericksburg, Jan. 7, 1762, and from Annapolis, January 30, before the lot reached Philadelphia on February 3, nine weeks and two days after the first letters had been recorded at the Williamsburg office.

[March 30, 1757]

William Dunlap Postmaster of Philadelphia

Dr.

		£	s.	d.
No. 1	To the whole Amount of unpaid Letters received into his Office from March 30. 1757 to Oct. 29. 1763 viz. 368039 dwt: 16 gr. at 5*d.* Currency is[1]	£7667	9	11
	To undercharg'd Letters 78 dwt. is	1	12	4
No. 2	To the whole Amount of Paid Letters sent by him to other Offices 15568 dwt: 8 at Do.	324	6	5
	To the Postage of Way Letters receiv'd by him 1452 dwt. at Do.	30	5	0
No. 3	To Postage of paid Letters from Aug. 18. 1763 to Oct. 6. omitted above 228 dwt: at Do. is	4	15	0
		£8028	8	8

Cr.

	£	s.	d.
By the amount of Dead Letters return'd to the General Post Office 44201 Dwt. at 5*d.* is	920	17	1
By Letters overcharged 18780 Dwt. at 5*d.* is	391	5	0
By Letters forwarded 40273 Dwt. at 5*d.* is	839	0	5
By his Commissions at 10 per Cent on the net Proceeds £5877 6*s.* 2*d.* is	587	14	7
By Cash paid Riders to Michaelmas 1763	1297	10	0
	4036	7	1
Ballance	3992	1	7
	£8028	8	8

1. One set of figures also on these sheets shows, in pennyweight (dwt.) and grains and by quarterly report dates, the total quantity of unpaid letters received in the Philadelphia Post Office from June 25, 1757, through Oct. 1, 1763, the way letters (picked up by the rider along his route), the undercharged, overcharged, and forwarded letters, and the ship letters paid for, although the first and last of these categories are not entered for the whole period. The unpaid letters received—the most significant items in this set of figures—averaged 14,159 dwt. per quarter.

[Dr.]

To the above Ballance	3992	1	7
To Postage receiv'd of Mr. Plowman for Letters sent to Baltimore Office[2]	22	8	9
To Ballance of the 3 Quarters from Oct. 1763 to July 6. 1764	491	18	11½
	4406	9	3½[3]

[Cr]

By Cash paid Mrs. Franklin as per Account render'd to Mr. Hunter, from April 7. 1757. to May 17. 1761[4]	2051	15	7
By Do. paid ditto at sundry times to Feb. 26. 1763	810	16	0
By Do. paid Ditto at sundry Times to July 11. 1764	501	16	9
By his Account for Mails and Bills	48	6	0
and	1	10	0
By Cash paid Hift, and Woolen a Gratuity from Postmaster General[5]	50	0	0
	3364	4	4[6]
Ballance	1042	4	11½
	4406	9	3½[7]

2. Jonathan Plowman, a prominent merchant of Baltimore, was probably the local postmaster there at this time.

3. An error; the total should read £4506 9*s.* 3½*d.*

4. One sheet of these records, headed "Mr. Dunlap's Payments to Mrs. Franklin," lists, in columns, a series of 190 separate amounts. The only one dated is the last, marked May 17, 1761. Their final total, £2051 15*s.* 7*d.*, is noted: "Sum total paid by Dunlap to Mrs. Franklin." The payments ranged from a low of £4 to a high of £85; three-fourths were for £10 or less. For BF's orders to make weekly payments see below, p. 169.

5. The identity of the recipients and the occasion for the gratuity have not been discovered.

6. An error; the total should read: £3464 4*s.* 4*d.* The balance due in the line below should remain the same, however, because this error and that in the total of the debit entries cancel each other out.

7. The remaining sheet in this group, headed, in BF's hand, "W. Dunlap's Quarterly Accounts," contains a column of figures in pounds, shillings, and pence for each quarter from June 25, 1757, through April 1761, with a total of £2105 18*s.* 2*d.* None of the amounts matches any of the others in these records. There is a parallel column of numbers of undetermined purpose. At the bottom of this paper are some entries in two columns headed respectively

Pennsylvania Assembly: Instructions to Benjamin Franklin

MS (fragment): American Philosophical Society

On March 1, 1757, the Assembly named the same committee (plus William West) that had made the report on the Assembly grievances against the Proprietors[8] "to bring in a Draught of the Instructions of the House to Benjamin Franklin, Esq; one of the Commissioners now about to embark for England." Two days later they reported a draft and were ordered further "to collect all the Papers and Proofs necessary for the said Agent to take with him." On the 9th the instructions were read and discussed in detail, and on the 10th "The House having gone through with their Alterations and Amendments on the Instructions to Benjamin Franklin, Esq; Ordered, That the same be transcribed for a third Reading."[9] The instructions were not printed in *Votes* nor is there any record of further action on them by the Assembly. Diligent search has turned up nothing more than the one-page fragment printed here, which survives among those of Franklin's papers that his grandson Temple left with Dr. George Fox, of Champlost, near Philadelphia, when he went to England in 1791.[1] That the Assembly acted on the instructions and that they constituted an important foundation for Franklin's agency is evident from Isaac Norris' remark that he could add little upon Franklin's departure beyond the report and the instructions already received.[2]

[March 31, 1757]

INSTRUCTIONS TO BENJAMIN FRANKLIN Esqr. One of the Commissioners appointed by the Assembly of the Province of Pennsylvania to obtain Redress of those several Infractions of the Royal Grant and Proprietary Charter, and other Aggrievances, which the People of this Province very justly complain of.

In Assembly March 31st. 1757.

YOU are to proceed immediately to Great Britain in the first Packet Boat that sails from New York, or by the next convenient Opportunity after your Receipt of these Instructions.

If you shou'd be taken by the Enemy, you [are to] advise the House by the first opportunity with your [*remainder lost*].

"Recd by B.F." and "W H.," (William Hunter) which total £1822 1*s.* 10*d.* sterling and £2381 17*s.* 4*d.* sterling, which include references to James Parker, the Philadelphia office, and Alexander Colden. None of these entries is precisely duplicated in BF's "Account of Expences" (see below, p. 164).

8. See above, pp. 136–42.

9. *Votes*, 1756–57, pp. 97–9.

1. See above, I, xxi–xxii.

2. See below, p. 171.

Account of Expenses, 1757–1762

MS account book: American Philosophical Society

"Account of Expences of my Voyage to England Disbursements &c.1757"

[April 1, 1757]

At the beginning of December 1757 Franklin set down in an account book his expenditures between April 1 and the time he sailed from New York and all the expenses he could remember since reaching England. Against the latter he entered his cash in hand and what he had received from his London banker and other sources and found that he had spent in England about £34 for which he could not account. He continued to enter his expenses and again struck trial balances in the middle of December and January with somewhat better results. Thereafter he used this book to record sums paid out and other financial transactions without attempting to balance cash receipts with expenditures. The last dated entry is for Feb. 16, 1762, some six months before he sailed for home.

Franklin was far from uniformly systematic in making entries in this book, and there are many demonstrable omissions.[3] In May 1759 he examined a number of old "Accounts, Receipts, Letters, and other Memoranda of prior Dates, and which ought to have been entred before," and dutifully if belatedly recorded what he found. From time to time he also recorded a good many bills of exchange he received from America, noting sometimes that he had turned them over to his banker for collection. He also occasionally used this little volume as a receipt book, writing out a formal acknowledgment that he had paid a certain sum for an indicated account and then getting his landlady, Mrs. Margaret Stevenson, his coachman, T. Bowman, or some other payee to sign the statement. Again he sometimes entered a memorandum that he had received or paid out money for some other persons' account for a particular purpose and that he, Franklin, was either debtor or creditor for a specified amount.

For all its mixed character and its limitations as a record, this account book is most useful in showing Franklin's monetary transactions during the years of his first agency in England. It can be determined, for example, that ocean passage and sea stores for himself, his son, and two Negro servants cost fifty guineas sterling, that he paid twelve

3. For example, there are no entries of the expenses of his various journeys away from London during these years.

guineas a month to hire a coach in London, and that Mrs. Stevenson charged him £2 16*s.* a week for lodging and for the board of the two servants. His settlements with her indicate that she did a good deal of shopping for him, not only for household necessaries but also for goods to be sent back to Deborah and Sally or friends in America. It is not suprising to find that he bought a good many books and magazines, both for himself and for others, or that he ordered type and printer's supplies at various times for David Hall, James Parker, and Benjamin Mecom. His friend Isaac Norris sent him considerable sums of money to be invested in government stocks or annuities and he regularly credited the speaker with the interest as received. When in 1760 he received just under £30,000 from the Exchequer in payment of the parliamentary grant of 1758 for provincial troops in British service, he entered a series of memoranda showing what expenses he had incurred in the business, how much he had turned over to the agent for the Lower Counties on Delaware as their share, and how he had invested the balance belonging to Pennsylvania.

Many of the entries reflect transactions mentioned in his correspondence and they will be cited at appropriate points in this and later volumes. In 1931 George Simpson Eddy undertook to print the entire account book.[4] He made an affort to rearrange the entries that were out of their chronological order and in some cases condensed the wording to save space. A careful check with the manuscript shows, however, that the printed text omits a substantial number of entries and that in a few instances Eddy confused two which he seems to have thought were repetitions of the same transaction. Citation, therefore, will be to both the manuscript and the printed version, the former to be referred to as "Account of Expences," and the latter by citing the volume and page of the *Pennsylvania Magazine* on which the entry appears.

To Charles Norris

ALS: Historical Society of Pennsylvania

I.N.

Dear Sir Saturday Afternoon [April 2, 1757]

The enclos'd Account was settled by the late Commissioners, on which there is due to me £26 17*s.* 10*d.*[5] It will oblige me, if

4. "Account Book of Benjamin Franklin kept by him during his First Mission to England as Provincial Agent 1757–1762," *PMHB,* LV (1931), 97–133.

5. There is no order to BF for this amount in the records of either "the late Commissioners" or the new ones; it probably represents an unpaid bal-

without Inconvenience you can advance me the Money. The new Commissioners will at any time sign an Order for it; I am Yours affectionately B FRANKLIN

To Charles Norris Esqr.

[*In the margin:*]

26. 17. 10	B Franklin
90. 12. 0	Wm. Franklin.[6]
117. 9. 10	

Addressed: To / Chas Norris Esqr

Endorsed: B Franklins request to pay £27 17*s.* 10*d.*[7] Comrs Order for Guns furnishd the Province. &c. April. 2d. 1757

Per £1000 Entered

Receipt for Bills of Exchange

ADS: Historical Society of Pennsylvania

[April 3, 1757]

List of Bills of Exchange[8]

	Sterling
Scot & McMichael	£340. 0*s.* 0*d.*
Richard Wilson	310. 0*s.* 0*d.*
Alexr Lothian	100. 0*s.* 0*d.*
	£750. 0*s.* 0*d.*

ance of some larger order drawn under the £60,000 or £30,000 supply acts (see above, VI, 395–6, and this vol., pp. 3, 25), or Norris' notation "per £1000 Entered" may indicate a sum still due BF for money he had advanced while on the committee to spend £1000 for defense in the fall of 1755; see above, VI, 165, 170–1. The pencilled "I.N." at the top probably represents Speaker Isaac Norris' approval of the payment.

6. WF received £37 8*s.* 5*d.* from the Loan Office on April 2 for postage on public letters and £90 12*s.* 0*d.* the next day "for Writing done, and as Clerk to the Assembly." Norris Papers, Hist. Soc. Pa.

7. Obviously an error for £26 17*s.* 10*d.*

8. On the eve of his departure for New York and England, BF settled his

Receiv'd April 3. 1757 of the Trustees of the Loan Office, the above three Setts of Bills for Seven Hundred and fifty Pounds Sterling by Order of Assembly. B FRANKLIN

65 per Ct. Exchange

Endorsed: Benjamin Franklin his Rect for £750 in Sterlg Recd in Bills of Excha. at 65 per Ct. Exchange[9] £1237. 10*s.* 0*d.* paid April 14th 1757 Entered in Trustees accot. in the Votes 1757.

Memorandum Book, 1757–1776

MS account book: American Philosophical Society

[April 3, 1757]

Before leaving for England Franklin provided his wife with a long, narrow account book in which she was to record her expenditures during his absence. She made the first entry on April 3, even before he had gone. But later, like many wives—and husbands too—she was far from meticulous in recording everything she spent. There are comparatively few entries under specific dates; more often she would put down under one day, such as the first of the month, a whole series of payments which she had quite obviously made over a period of time. And she left empty pages, or parts of pages, on which she may have intended to record expenditures when she got around to it. On the very last page is a plaintive entry in her hand: "September the 1d took for famely expenses in Cash £6–0–0 as I am not abell to set down every penney. I think to doe this way."

Despite the incompleteness of this record, it does suggest some of Deborah's financial dealings during her husband's long absence. A few sample entries will illustrate the point:

———

public accounts and received an allowance "for transacting the publick Affairs of this Province in Great-Britain." He received the bills of exchange here listed as half payment of £1500 sterling voted by the Assembly for the expense of his mission on April 1, the other half to be remitted on his order. *Votes*, 1756–57, p. 107. On March 17 he had also received £201 4*s.* 3*d.* "for immediate Services" and £210 13*s.* 9*d.* "for establishing a Post to Winchester, &c." *Ibid.*, p. 166.

9. That is, the exchange rate was: £165 Pennsylvania currency equalled £100 sterling.

paid the womon that Irons for us	£ 1	—	—
paid the poor tax 15 and fier Componey 1–6	—	16	6
laid ought fullishley	—	10	—
and Generousley	—	10	—
paid for a pair of purpill shoes for Salley	—	7	6
a pound of anchovise	—	3	6
my Cash did not quite hold ought this month			
Salleys french master	—	10	—
a bras dogs and fier Shoefil fier and tong	7	15	—
for splittin sume large wood and Clering the Seller	—	9	—
a lim of veel	—	7	—
paid our tacks	8	8	—

At the top of the eleventh page is an entry in Franklin's hand: "Nov. 1. 1762. I arriv'd home from England. BF." He thereupon took over this book and all the later entries are his, not Deborah's. During the two years that he was at home he used it to record his major financial transactions and to set down memoranda about them. There are virtually no entries of what might be called petty cash disbursements. The last items in this series record that he left £100 with Deborah when he sailed again for England in November 1764 and £350 in cash and £200 in a bond with Samuel Rhoads, for which Rhoads signed a receipt indicating that these payments were "to be apply'd towards the Building of B. Franklin's House, if wanted."

The next entry reads: "1775 Left London March 20 to embark at Portsmouth for Philadelphia in the Pennsylvania Packet Capt. Osborne. Arriv'd at Philadelphia May 5." Franklin then began again to use this book in much the same way as he had done in 1762–64. The last dated entries are for Oct. 21, 1776, five days before he sailed for France on his diplomatic mission. He had already used a few blank pages at the very end of the book to set up debit and credit ledger entries with Mrs. Stevenson, his English landlady, and with the English banking firms with whom he maintained accounts during his periods in Philadelphia. A number of the entries he made in the main part of the book in 1775–76 shed considerable light on his personal affairs and on his public business during those years. They will be cited at appropriate points in later volumes of this edition.

To William Dunlap

ALS: American Philosophical Society

Mr. Dunlap Philada. April 4. 1757

I now appoint you Postmaster of Philadelphia, during our Absence, as it will be some present Employment for you till our

Return; when I hope to put you in a better Way, if I find you diligent, careful and faithful.[1]

I would not have the Office remov'd on any Account from my House during my Absence, without my Leave first obtained.[2]

And as Mrs. Franklin has had a great deal of Experience in the Management of the Post Office, I depend on your paying considerable Attention to her Advice in that Matter.

As I leave but little Money with Mrs. Franklin for the Support of the Family,[3] and have [*torn*] all [*torn*] of the Post Office for the [*torn*] Absence, I expect and [*torn*] account with her for, and pay her, every Monday Morning, the Postage of the preceding Week, taking her Receipt for the same, and retaining only your Commissions of Ten per Cent.[4] You should have a little Book for such Receipts.

Wishing you Health and Happiness I am, Your affectionate Uncle B FRANKLIN

Power of Attorney to Deborah Franklin

Printed form with MS insertions in blanks: American Philosophical Society

[April 4, 1757]

KNOW all Men by these Presents, That I *Benjamin Franklin of the City of Philadelphia Printer* Have constituted, made and appointed, and by these Presents do constitute, make and appoint, my trusty and loving Friend *and Wife Deborah Franklin,*

1. On the circumstances of this appointment and Dunlap's failure to live up to these expectations see above, p. 158.

2. *Pa. Gaz.*, March 31, 1757, announced that the post office was now removed to the house of the postmaster general in Market St. The issues of May 19 and later advertised books to be sold by William Dunlap at the post office. On June 10, 1758, BF wrote to Deborah: "The Post-Office, if 'tis agreable to you, may be removed to Mr. Dunlap's House, it being propos'd by our good Friend Mr. Hughes." Dunlap had acquired Chattin's printing house and began advertising his publications "at the Newest-Printing-Office." *Pa. Gaz.*, June 15, 1758. He announced in the issue of Dec. 21, 1758, that the post office was removed to his dwelling for the winter season.

3. The torn passage which follows may be conjecturally restored as: "and have left all the Receipts of the Post Office for the Payment of her Expenses during my Absence, I expect and require that you account with her, . . ."

4. For the record of these payments see note on "Mr. Dunlap's Payments to Mrs. Franklin," above, p. 162 n.

to be my true and lawful Attorney, for me, and in my Name and Stead, and to my Use, to ask, demand, sue for, levy, recover and receive, all such Sum and Sums of Money, Debts, Rents, Goods, Wares, Dues, Accounts, and other Demands whatsoever, which are or shall be due, owing, payable, and belonging to me, or detained from me any Manner of Ways or Means whatsoever by *any Person or Persons whatsoever or whomsoever* Giving and Granting unto my said Attorney, by these Presents, my full and whole Powers, Strength and Authority, in and about the Premises, to have, use and take, all lawful Ways and Means in my Name for the Recovery thereof, and upon the Receipt of any such Debts, Dues, or Sums of Money aforesaid, Acquittances or other sufficient Discharges, for me, and in my Name, to make, seal and deliver; and generally all and every other Act and Acts, Thing and Things, Device or Devices, in the Law whatsoever, needful and necessary to be done in and about the Premises, for me, and in my Name, to do, execute and perform, as fully, largely and amply, to all Intents and Purposes, as I myself might or could do, if I was personally present, or as if the Matter required more especial Authority than is herein given; and Attorneys one or more under *her* for the Purpose aforesaid, to make and constitute, and again at Pleasure to revoke; ratifying, allowing and holding, for firm and effectual, all and whatsoever my said Attorney shall lawfully do in and about the Premises, by Virtue hereof. IN WITNESS whereof, I have hereunto set my Hand and Seal, this *fourth* Day of *April* in the *twenty-ninth* Year of his Majesty's Reign, *Annoque Domini* One Thousand Seven Hundred and *Fifty-seven.*

Sealed and delivered in the Presence of us, B FRANKLIN
JACOB DUCHÉ[5]
JACOB DUCHÉ junr

Endorsed: Power of Attorney to D. Franklin

5. Jacob Duché (1708–1788), Philadelphia merchant, colonel of the Philadelphia County Regiment of militia, 1756, vestryman of Christ Church. His son Jacob Duché, Jr. (1738–1798), graduated in the first class of the College of Philadelphia, 1757, where he taught oratory after further study at Cambridge University and ordination as a deacon. The son entered the priesthood in 1762 and succeeded Richard Peters in 1775 as rector of the united parishes of Christ Church and St. Peter's. He was made chaplain of the Con-

From Isaac Norris

Letterbook copy: Historical Society of Pennsylvania

My Worthy Friend Benjamin Franklin, April 4th. 1757

The interfering in those Weighty matters you are charged with, either by an Attempt to explain what you are fully Master of or to add any thing of my own not already contained in the Report of the committee or the Instructions of the House to yourself,[6] would subject me justly to a censure I hope to avoid for if I had any thing material beyond those I would have offered it during the passage of the Instructions and whilst the Report of the committee was under the consideration of the Assembly, and yet I doubt not your prudence in the Application &c. we propose to make to the Proprieters if they can by any means be brought to understand their true Interests as it is and ought to be connected with the good of the People; I need not Inform you how often they have declared this Truth upon our Minutes nor how they explain away the Rights we claim under our Charters and tho' they do not say it themselves their Dependants[7] declare Openly enough those Charters confirm to the people such Rights as are indeed necessary for a new Settlement but ought to be abridged upon the first favourable Occaision that Offers tho' it is apparent those Gentlemen have this Disposition too deeply rooted I fear to be Intirely eradicated, yet I own it would give me great pleasure that you use all your abilities in this Case and by all the condescention consistent with your good Judgment which I am well assured will preserve you from being decieved with false appearances or evasive Temporary Expedients and it will be a prudent precaution to be well with our Agents[8] of which I make no doubt from the

---

tinental Congress but later changed his sentiments, urged the recall of the Declaration of Independence, and went to England in 1777. Most of his property was confiscated but he was finally allowed to return to Philadelphia in 1792. In his last years he was converted to Swedenborgianism. *DAB;* Edward D. Neill, "Rev. Jacob Duché, The First Chaplain of Congress," *PMHB,* II (1878), 58–73. On the changes in his attitude toward BF see below, p. 207 n.

6. See above, pp. 136–42, 163, for the Report and the Instructions.

7. That is, the Pa. officials and agents appointed by the Proprietors.

8. Robert Charles and Richard Partridge.

high Opinion of your knowledge and Experience in the publick Affairs of this Province. It will be a general advantage to America if any favourable Opportunity should present to obtain the Liberty of importing Iron to any Port of England, instead of confining it to the Port of London only.[9] And as this is a general American Concern the Agents of the other Colonies will undoubtedly join if there should be any Prospect of Success which might be pretty well guessed at upon an Application to some of the leading Members of the House of Commons before we engage in any considerable Expence upon it, for it may well be expected the City will oppose such a Bill whenever it shall make its Appearance in Parliament.

I have wrote on from the Inclination I have to take Leave and wish you a Prosperous Voyage rather than from any Apprehensions of the Necessity of giving either of us the Trouble of reading or writing a Long Letter upon a Subject you are so thoroughly apprized of. But if any Thing of importance should hereafter occur, you may expect to hear further from me as I Shall be pleased to have a Line or two whenever you have Leasure to communicate the Concerns of the Province, or your private Interests if I can be of any service to them; And in every Respect I sincerely wish you a successful Voyage. Your Assured Friend I N

I have given you the trouble of two Letters which you will be pleasd to excuse.

Gave to BF at Fairhill on his way to N York.[1]

See my Letter to BF April 7. 1757[2] Omitted here prius pag 69

9. The Iron Act of 1750, besides forbidding the erection of slitting or rolling mills, plating forges, or steel furnaces in the colonies, required all American pig or bar iron to enter at London and be stamped, etc., not more than ten miles from that place (23 George II, c. 29). Parliament lifted the import restriction to be effective June 24, 1757 (30 George II, c. 16); Arthur C. Bining, *British Regulation of the Colonial Iron Industry* (Phila., 1933), pp. 70–6, 83–4.

1. BF must have stopped at Fairhill, Norris' country home about four miles north of Philadelphia, on his way to Trenton, April 4, 1757; see chronology, p. 174.

2. Seen below, p. 175.

Israel Pemberton to John Fothergill[3]

Draft: Historical Society of Pennsylvania

Dear Friend [April 4, 1757]

As I am sensible thou art well acquainted with Benja. Franklin's Character a recommendation of him seems unnecessary, yet as I would not be deficient in respect to him and am Sincerely desirous he may succeed in the important Service he is engag'd in, I cannot but desire he may have some Share of thy Friendship and so far as his views and measures tend to the restoring peace and promoting the real Interest of Pensilvania I wish him all the assistance and hearty Concurrence thou and all my Friends can give him.[4] Our meeting for Sufferings writes to yours by this Packet and I think of saying something to thy dear Brother.[5] I am with true love and respect Thy real Friend

Endorsed: 4. 4mo. 1757 To Jno: Fothergill by B Franklin

To Deborah Franklin

ALS: American Philosophical Society

Franklin and his son left Philadelphia on Monday, April 4, but they did not reach New York until the morning of the 8th. Then began a long period of frustrating delay until the packet on which they sailed weighed anchor off Sandy Hook on June 20. The movements of mem-

3. See above, v, 424 n, for Pemberton, and iv, 126 n, for Fothergill.

4. Pemberton later explained the restrained tone of this letter; he wrote Fothergill that he hoped BF would "be capable of removing some difficulties you have been under on our Account, tho' I am sensible, as a religious Society we can expect little more from him than a more candid representation of our Conduct, in Public transactions than has been made by some others." Letter of July 1, 1757; Etting-Pemberton Papers, Hist. Soc. Pa. See below, p. 376 n, for the continuing coolness of leading Quakers toward BF's agency.

5. Samuel Fothergill (1715–1772), brother of Dr. John Fothergill, merchant, and itinerant Quaker preacher, had been in America on a religious mission, 1754–56, when he developed close ties with the Pembertons and other American Friends. The Philadelphia Meeting for Sufferings had been organized in 1756 on the model of one in London to give support to Friends who "suffered" for reasons of conscience. *DNB;* James Bowden, *The History of the Society of Friends in America* (London, 1854), ii, 277–8, 283–4; Sydney V. James, *A People among Peoples, Quaker Benevolence in Eighteenth-Century America* (Cambridge, Mass., 1963), pp. 141–215.

bers of the Franklin family during this interval appear so confusing that a chronology may be useful.[6]

April 4: Leave Philadelphia; arrive at Trenton "well before Night."

April 5: Leave Trenton; probably spend night at Brunswick; roads very bad.

April 6: Arrive at Woodbridge.

April 7: Arrive at Elizabeth Town; dine with Governor Belcher.

April 8: Arrive at New York in the morning.

April 8 to about May 7: Benjamin and William Franklin in New York. Deborah and Sally come to Woodbridge toward the end of this period. Loudoun records conversations with Franklin on April 9(?), 15, 25, 26, and 30.

About May 8 to 11: Entire family with New York friends on "a little excursion in the Jerseys," visiting Newark, Passaic Falls, and Colonel Schuyler's copper mines.

May 12 to about May 23: Benjamin and Deborah in Woodbridge; William and Sally in New York.

May 23 to June 4: Benjamin and William in New York. Sally returns to Woodbridge May 27, where she and Deborah apparently stay until about May 30 before returning to Philadelphia.

June 5 (Sunday morning): "At length we are going on board" the packet *General Wall*. Lord Loudoun is also on a sloop going to Sandy Hook to join Admiral Hardy on the *Sutherland*.

June 5 to June 20: The convoy, including the packets, anchored off Sandy Hook, uncertain about the location of the French fleet.

June 20: The convoy sails from Sandy Hook.

June 23: Loudoun writes to the Duke of Cumberland from "near the Nantucket Shoals," probably sending the letter by the *General Wall*, which is soon detached from the convoy to sail direct to England, while Loudoun with other ships proceeds to Halifax.

My dear Child, Trenton, April 5. 1757

We found the Roads much better than we expected, and got here well before Night. My kind Friend Mr. Griffitts's[7] Carriage

6. Sources for this chronology are letters by BF and his son printed below; others by William to Elizabeth Graeme mentioned in the headnote of the next document but one below, including those printed in *PMHB*, XXXV (1911), 417–18; XXXIX (1915), 261–3; Loudoun Notebooks (Huntington Lib.); and his letters and dispatches in Pargellis, *Military Affairs*, pp. 366–7, 370–9.

7. Probably William Griffitts (d. 1762), one of BF's associates in the affairs of the hospital. See above, V, 285 n, 315.

appearing too weak in the Wheels, I have accepted Mr. Martin's[8] obliging Offer, and take his Carriage forward from this Place, and he will return to Town in Mr. Griffitts's. About a Dozen of our Friends accompanied us quite hither, to see us out of the Province, and we spent a very agreable Evening together. I leave Home, and undertake this long Voyage more chearfully, as I can rely on your Prudence in the Management of my Affairs, and Education of my dear Child; and yet I cannot forbear once more recommending her to you with a Father's tenderest Concern. My Love to all. If the Roads do not prove worse, we may be at Woodbridge to night. I believe I did not see Mr. Dunlap when I came away, so as to take leave of him; my Love to him. Billy presents his Duty, and Love to all. I am, Your affectionate Husband B FRANKLIN

Give my hearty Thanks to Mr. Griffitts.

Addressed: To / Mrs Franklin / Philada.

From Isaac Norris

Letterbook copy: Historical Society of Pennsylvania

My Friend B Franklin April 7th. 1757

The Clerk calls upon me to sign the Indian Trade Bill now sent down by the Governor who adheres to his Amendments and as the House after agreeing to some of the Amendments now adhere to the Bill there is an End of that salutary provision to induce the Indians to come heartily into our Interest by making it their Own. We think it a Strange innovation that Committees of the Council should be brought into Laws, to settle Our Accounts and dispose of the public Mony but it is a Scheme those Gentlemen have been long aiming at, hitherto, without Effect.[9] I have

8. Not identified, but perhaps a son of David Martin of Trenton; see above, II, 407 n.

9. The Assembly had tried numerous times since November 1755 to secure the governor's approval of a bill to remedy abuses in the Indian trade; see above, VI, 253–5, 449–51. The declared objective, to regulate the trade in order to make friends rather than enemies of the Indians, was laudable enough, especially in wartime when Indian allies were of critical importance. The bills, however, all insinuated that traders operating under proprietary license had abused the Indians thus causing their hostility to the province, and all provided for such tight Assembly control of the trade that proprietary agents would be barred from it in the future. Furthermore, the governor

sent on the other Side a loose Schedule of My Account,[1] when I can get Home I will write more largely as Matters offer, And then I will close the Account of *Osborne's* Books[2] as it stands in my Books. I see Osborne is concernd in Two Books of practical Husbandry and of Practical Gardening be pleased to desire Osborne to send them to me (I mean if you think they are fit for my Library) and Robt. Charles will pay the cost on your shewing him this my Request for I have not wrote to him about it.[3]

My Brother spoke to you about the Book of Gardening under the Title of Eden &c. and I presume gave the whole long Title that he would have for his own Use. I would have both the Gardening and Agriculture being much inclined to amuse my Self among my

---

objected to the bills' "encroachment" on executive prerogatives. The Assembly sent a new bill to Governor Denny on March 12, which Lord Loudoun and Governor Dinwiddie of Virginia considered on the 21st, the same day that Denny in Council returned it to the Assembly with proposed amendments. The next day, after accepting only trifling changes, the Assembly sent the bill back, and on April 5 Denny again returned it, whereupon the Assembly dropped the matter after again declaring its unwillingness to give in. Among other things, the Assembly disapproved a proposal that a committee of the Council and one of the Assembly *together* audit the books of the Indian commissioners. *Votes,* 1756–57, pp. 100, 102–3, 107; *Pa. Col. Recs.,* VII, 444, 449–50, 455–9; 1 *Pa. Arch.,* III, 114–15, 119; Loudoun Notebooks, March 21, 1757 (Huntington Lib.). BF had been interested in regulating the Indian trade at least since 1753 (see above, V, 154), and the problem was to figure prominently in his English mission; see, for example, BF to Isaac Norris, June 9, 1759, on hearings before the Board of Trade, May 29, 1759, on the Pennsylvania Indian trade bill passed April 8, 1758.

1. Not copied into Norris' letterbook.

2. Thomas Osborne (d. 1767), foremost London bookseller of his day, but distrusted by both BF and Dr. Johnson for his exorbitant prices and sharp practices. Above, III, 318–19, 322; *DNB.*

3. In September 1758 BF bought from Osborne and sent to Charles and Isaac Norris copies of the following: *A Compleat Body of Husbandry containing the Soil . . . Natural and Artificial Manures, etc.* (London, 1756), and *Eden: or a Compleat Body of Gardening* (London, 1757), both works attributed alternatively to Thomas Hale and John Hill; and Edward Lisle, *Observations on Husbandry* (London, 1757). BF to Isaac Norris, Sept. 16, 1758 (Lib. Cong.); Osborne's bill to BF, receipted Sept. 27, 1758 (Hist. Soc. Pa.); Isaac Norris' accounts with Robert Charles and BF, under date of 1758 (Lib. Co. Phila.); "Account of Expences," p. 35; *PMHB,* LV (1931), 114. The uncertain authorship of the first two works listed is discussed in G.E. Fussel, *More Old English Farming Books . . . 1731 to 1793* (London, 1950), pp. 37–8.

Dirty Acres if I can contrive some way or other to stay a little more at Home. I am (after wishing you a good Voyage) Your Assured Friend I N

William Franklin to Elizabeth Graeme[4]

ALS: Morristown National Historical Park

At this time William Franklin appears to have been deeply in love with Elizabeth Graeme of Philadelphia. Seven of his letters written to her between his leaving Philadelphia with his father and their sailing from New York survive, and one written after they reached England. Those which give information about his father's movements and activities not found elsewhere will be printed in this edition.

My dearest Betsy Elizabeth Town, April 7, 1757

Our Horses are baiting, which gives me a few spare Moments. I seize them to let my Charmer know of my Welfare. We expected to have arriv'd at New York Yesterday, but the extreme Badness of the Roads prevented our getting farther than Woodbridge. Our Chaise Horses tir'd before we reached Brunswick, which oblig'd us to leave them and the Carriage behind, and to come forward on Horseback. We shall, however, God willing, this Day reach the Place of Embarkation. Every Morning since our Departure has had a lowering Aspect, but before Noon the Clouds have dispers'd, the Sun has shone, and the Remainder of the Day has prov'd most delightfully agreeable. The Morning of our Love, my dear Betsy, has likewise been and is still overcast, threat'ning a

4. Elizabeth Graeme (1739–1801) was the daughter of Dr. Thomas Graeme, Philadelphia physician and one of the provincial councilors, and his wife Ann Diggs, stepdaughter of the former governor Sir William Keith. The relationship between the young people was suddenly ended while William was in England, apparently through his initiative and to her distress. In 1772 she married a Scot, Henry Hugh Fergusson (or Ferguson), but separated from him during the Revolution when he became a Loyalist while she supported the American cause. *PMHB,* XXXV (1911), 415–17; XXXIX (1915), 257–60; LVI (1932), 1–2. Letters from BF, about which she wrote later, are now lost: "I have some of the kindest and fondest letters from Dr. Franklin wrote to me when he wished me to have been a member of his family, which had had [*sic*] vanity taken place, and I had had a mind to have shewn them, would have been circulated thro all the anecdote writers in Europe and America under the article traits of Dr. Franklin's Domestic Character." To Benjamin Rush, Dec. 23, 1797, Rush Papers, Lib. Co. Phila.

wrecking Storm; who knows but kind Heav'n may graciously permit a chearing Sun to scatter these Clouds of Difficulties which hang over us, and afford a Noon and Evening of Life calm and serene. I trust our Conduct will be such as to deserve this Mark of Divine Goodness; may we not then reasonably [hope for?] its Accomplishment. Drawing [*at least one line missing*].

I hope before I leave New York to hear of our dear Mamma's being in a fair Way of Recovery.[5] She has my most cordial Prayers; and believe me my dear Betsy, there is Nothing I more sincerely wish than the Prosperity of every Branch of your good Family. Pray let me be respectfully remembered to them.

An Invitation from Govr. Belcher to Dinner, cuts me shorter than I intended. That every Blessing may attend you is the ardent Prayer of, Dear Betsy, Your most affectionate WM. FRANKLIN

To Joseph Galloway

ALS: Yale University Library

Dear Sir, New York, April 11. 1757

I received the Exemplifications of the Royal Grant, Charter and Commissions at Bristol, and by the Post Copies of the two £100,000 Bills under Seal, and a Copy of the Indian Trade Bill, with Amendments, all in good Order.[6]

I am sorry the Indian Trade Bill is lost;[7] but it is some Advantage that the iniquitous Views of the Proprietor and his Creatures of the

5. Mrs. Graeme ("Mamma") had been ill for some time.

6. In Penn Official Correspondence, Hist. Soc. Pa., is a paper headed "Extract from Mr. Peters's Letter of 5. April 1757" and endorsed "An Account of what Papers B. Franklin brings over." Peters stated that, the day before he wrote, the Assembly obtained the governor's certificates to Recorder Charles Brockden's exemplifications of the following documents: the royal charter to William Penn; the Charter of Privileges of 1701; Governor Denny's commission and commission of property; a deed "Wm. Penn &c. to John Penn &c."; a quadripartite indenture of Sept. 23, 1731, between William Penn, Letitia Aubrey, John and Thomas Penn; and commissions to William Plumsted as register general, William Allen as chief justice, James Hamilton as prothonotary, Nicholas Scull as surveyor general, and Richard Hockley and Edmund Physick as receivers general. The governor's certificates were to the effect that faith and credit should be given to Brockden's exemplifications as recorder of deeds for the city and county of Philadelphia "in any Justice Court and thereout." On the Assembly's bills, see above, pp. 106, 121, 175.

7. See above, p. 175.

Council are so clearly discover'd by their Conduct on this Occasion. The Spirit that makes them so ardently aim at the Disposition of Money not their own, is the same with that which inclines lesser Knaves to rob and pick Pockets. They seem to have no Regard to the Publick Welfare, so the private Point maybe gained. 'Tis like Firing a House to have an Opportunity of Stealing a Trencher.

I wish Success to the Negociations with the Indians. Tis a good Sign that so many are come down.[8] The next Post will probably find us here; pray favour me with any farther Intelligence concerning them or our other Publick Affairs, that comes to your Knowledge.

I leave some Enemies in Pensilvania, who will take every Opportunity of injuring me in my Absence. However, as they are my Enemies, not on my own private Account but on that of the Publick, I seem to have some Right to ask the Care of my Friends, to watch 'em and guard my Reputation and Interest as much as may be from the Effects of their Malevolence.[9] I chearfully leave my dearest Concerns under that Care, having no Reason to doubt the Continuance of the Friendships I have so long experienc'd.

Your kind Wishes demand my sincerest Thanks. I suppose Billy writes.[1] I will not now take Leave of you, as I intend another Line or two per next Post. With great Esteem and Affection, I am, Dear Sir, Your most obedient and most humble Servant

B FRANKLIN

The List of Servants is not come.[2]

Mr. Galloway

Endorsed: Benja. Franklin's Letter April 11. 1747 [*sic*]. N York.

8. BF knew before he left Philadelphia that 150 or more Indians, mostly Iroquois, had come to Harris's Ferry for a treaty, and on April 3 William Parsons wrote Denny from Easton that 50 of Teedyuscung's followers were at Fort Allen. *Pa. Col. Recs.*, VII, 462; 1 *Pa. Arch.*, III, 104. In a letter to WF, June? 1757, APS, intended for BF's attention, Charles Thomson described the lengthy but inconclusive negotiations with the Indians at Lancaster in May; the minutes are in *Pa. Col. Recs.*, VII, 505–51.

9. Perhaps a hint that BF expected Galloway to write in his defense if necessary. Newspaper controversy, in which Galloway probably took part anonymously, resumed in the spring of 1758.

1. WF and Galloway were intimate friends and corresponded regularly while the Franklins were in England, but no letter of this date has been found.

2. See below, p. 227 n.

To Samuel Hazard[3]

Copy: American Philosophical Society

Sir Philada. April 11th. 1757[4]

Your Absence when the Business was to be done for Mr. Greeme, prevented your seeing Messrs. Stevenson's Letter at that Time, or the Account that was afterwards carried to your House by my Son.[5] I had however some Expectations that you would do what was desired of you by those Gentlemen, your Friends, and I readily did what seem'd immediately necessary to serve Mr. Greeme, on sight, of their Letters to you, tho' I had no Knowledge either of him or them; and never have wrote a Line to him on the Affair: But your Refusal of that as well as of Kneeland's Orders,[6] is sufficient, as you never assumed to be sure you are not oblig'd to pay.

The Case seems to be different with respect to the Prizes, which you now speak of as out of date: In July 1755, when you promised to account with me for them if I would furnish Mr. Hesselus[7] with Academy Tickets, they were as much out of Date as they are now: On that Promise, I immediately furnished those Tickets, and have ever since kept your Note and those Prizes together, to be ready for a Settlement, whenever you should call on me for

3. See above, VI, 87 n.

4. Obviously the copyist's error for either the place or the date; BF was in New York on April 11, 1757.

5. The business discussed in this letter is not clear and is not elucidated by any of BF's surviving correspondence. A John Greame, or Graeme, and Francis Harris of Halifax, Yorkshire, advertised woolen goods for sale through Francis Harris of Philadelphia, and a James Stevenson of Philadelphia also advertised cloths for sale in 1757, but these may not be the men referred to. *Pa. Gaz.*, July 21, Oct. 20 *et seq.* In 1753 Hazard advertised in *Pa. Gaz.* that he had tickets for sale for the lottery to build a steeple for the Second Presbyterian Church, Philadelphia, and in that year and the next he advertised tickets for the Connecticut Lottery to raise money for the College of New Jersey. The two Philadelphia Academy Lotteries, in which BF was concerned, were under way in 1754 and 1755 as well as others in the area, and it is probable that BF and Hazard were dealing in, or exchanging with each other, tickets to lotteries in which they were each interested.

6. Samuel Kneeland, Boston printer, had sold twenty lottery tickets to BF in 1755. Eddy, *Ledger "D,"* p. 78. Writing to his wife, May 27, 1757, BF sent on a letter from Kneeland ordering paper. See below, p. 218.

7. Probably John Hesselius (1728–1778), portrait painter, son of Gustavus Hesselius (d. May 25, 1755). See above, III, 299 n.

that Purpose: As to the Billet you mention to be "sent by me (after yours) signifying my Intentions to return the Tickets to Virginia, in consequence of which you settled with the Trustees of the College &c." I think it must be an absolute Mistake, and that I never sent you any such Billet: For why should I return the Tickets to Virginia, when they had (on your promise to allow the Prizes) been received by me as pay for the Academy Tickets I furnished to Mr. Hessilus; and therefore ought to be produced by me at our Settlement, in which you said you would account with me for them, i.e. in our Settlement for the Tickets I had of you: In short, I always expected that whatever Prizes were in the Tickets bought of you, would be allowed, when the Money for the Tickets was demanded; and it seems to me, that my delaying to make my Demand of the Prize Money till you should make your Demand of the Ticket Money ought not to deprive me of my Right, any more than your Delaying till this Time to make your Demand ought to deprive you of yours: And indeed, as the Prize Money did not amount to more than I owed for the Tickets, it did not seem necessary that I should demand Payment of my Prizes, they being already paid by Money in my Hands.

If I did not pay for the two Tickets you mention to have sold me besides the 6, they must now be paid for; I submit that to your Books.

I thank you for your good Wishes, and am glad to hear your Affairs are near being compleated, being Sir Your very humble Servant B FRANKLIN

To Mr. Saml. Hazard
Copy

To Henry Bouquet[8]

Draft: American Philosophical Society

Col. Bouquet
Dear Sir New York April 14. 1757

I thank you for the Letter you have favour'd me with to Pro-

8. On Col. Henry Bouquet, who had commanded the first battalion of the Royal American Regiment in Philadelphia the previous winter but was now ordered to South Carolina, see above, pp. 63 n, 147.

fessor Koenig.[9] I shall take care to deliver the other to Monsr. Guinand,[1] if I reach London.

I regret much, that thro' your Business and mine, I could enjoy so little of your Conversation at Philadelphia. How happy are the Folks in Heaven, who, 'tis said, have nothing to do, but to talk with one another, except now and then a little Singing—and Drinking of Aqua Vitae.

We are going different ways, and perhaps may never meet, till we meet there. I pity you for the hot Summer you must first undergo in Charlestown. I do all I can for your Relief, by recommending you to an ingenious Physician[2] of my Acquaintance, who knows the Rule of making cool, weak, refreshing Punch, not inferior to the Nectar of the Gods.

Just now I presume to make a Prayer to them, *That whatever I wish for my Friends, shall come to pass.* If this Prayer be granted, you may be sure of a pleasant Voyage, an agreable Campaign, Health, Honour and Happiness. But why should I think such Praying and Wishing necessary. The Gods will doubtless take Care of those they love. *A Dieux* then, Dear Sir, and believe me with Sincere Esteem, Respect and Affection, Your most obedient and most humble Servant B FRANKLIN

9. Probably Samuel Koenig (1712–1757), German-born professor of mathematics at The Hague and member of several learned societies on the Continent.

1. Possibly Henry Guinand, a London merchant, declared bankrupt in 1769; referred to in 1783 at the marriage of his daughter as "the late Hen. G. esq. of Calcutta." *Gent. Mag.*, XXXIX (1769), 511; LIII (1783), 715. The Swiss instrument maker and optician of this surname, whom Smyth (*Writings*, X, 555) seems to identify as the man referred to, was too young, having been born about 1745.

2. BF first wrote: "to two ingenious Physicians"; see the letters to Garden and Lining immediately below. The expert on concocting punch was probably Dr. Garden; BF and Dr. Lining are not known to have met personally at this time and testimonial on the punch seems too enthusiastic to have been based on mere hearsay.

To Alexander Garden[3] Draft: American Philosophical Society

Dr. Garden
Sir New York, April 14 1757

I am here waiting the Departure of the Pacquet in which I am about to embark for London, and by that means have Leisure to write a little to my Friends, which the distracted State of our Province, and the Hurry of Affairs I have been engag'd in, for some time prevented. I wish now that I had brought some of your ingenious Letters with me,[4] that I might have consider'd them fully: particularly what relates to the Element of Fire, and the Quantity receiv'd by the Earth from the Sun, &c. I have touch'd a little on this Subject of Fire, in mine of this Date to Dr. Lining, to which I beg Leave to refer you.[5] But Fire is full of Wonders, and as yet we know little of its Nature.

I forwarded your Pacquet and Letter to Mr. Clayton[6] as desired, and free of Charge to him. I purpose, God willing, to return from England by way of Carolina, when I promise myself the Pleasure of seeing and conversing with your Friends in Charlestown.

Col. Bouquet,[7] who does me the favour to deliver this to you, is a Gentleman whose Conversation you must be pleas'd with, and I am sure a Stranger, of Learning, Ingenuity and Politeness will not fail of your Civilities.[8] I therefore only take the Liberty of Introducing him to you, and leave the rest to your self.

I am, with great Esteem and Respect, Sir Your most obedient humble Servant B FRANKLIN

[*In margin in BF's hand*:] Dr. Lining and Garden Col. Bouquet.

3. On Dr. Alexander Garden of Charleston, S.C., see above, VI, 187 n. He and BF had become acquainted in 1754 in Philadelphia when he was visiting John Bartram.

4. None of Garden's letters to BF have been found.

5. See immediately below.

6. John Clayton (*c.* 1685–1773), an English-born botanist of Virginia. His work on the local plants became the basis for Gronovius' *Flora Virginica* (Leyden, 1739, 1743). On meeting him in Williamsburg in 1756 BF invited Clayton to send letters addressed to Bartram or Garden through his hands to save the postage. *DAB;* Darlington, *Memorials,* p. 409.

7. See immediately above.

8. Struck through in the draft: "and Friendship."

To John Lining[9]

Copy: Yale University Library; also draft (incomplete): American Philosophical Society[1]

Sir, New-York, April 14. 1757.

It is a long Time since I had the Pleasure of a Line from you. And indeed the Troubles of our Country, with the Hurry of Business, I have been engag'd in on that Account, have made me so bad a Correspondent, that I ought not to expect Punctuality in others.

But being just taking Passage for England, I could not leave the Continent,[2] without paying my Respects to you, and at the same Time taking Leave to introduce to your Acquaintance a Gentleman of Learning and Merit, Col. Henry Bouquet,[3] who does me the Favour to present you this Letter, and with whom I am sure you will be much pleased.

Mr. Professor Simpson of Glasgow, lately communicated to me some curious Experiments of a Physician of his Acquaintance, by which it appeared that an extraordinary Degree of Cold, even to Freezing, might be produced by Evaporation.[4] I have not had Leisure to repeat and examine more than the first and easiest of them, viz. Wet the Ball of a Thermometer by a Feather dipt in Spirit of Wine, which has been kept in the same Room, and has of

9. On Dr. John Lining of Charleston, S.C., see above, v, 521 n.

1. The copy, in BF's hand, is the one he sent to Ezra Stiles, June 2, 1757; see below, p. 233. Of the draft only the last leaf survives, containing less than a fifth of the text. The letter is printed as Letter XXVI in *Exper. and Obser.*, 1769 edit., pp. 341–9. Significant differences are noted.

2. *Exper. and Obser.* reads: "But being about to embark for England, I could not quit the Continent."

3. See the two letters immediately above.

4. Robert Simson (1687–1768), professor of mathematics at the University of Glasgow. His letter to BF has not been found, but the "curious Experiments" described were those of Dr. William Cullen (1710–1790), who became professor of medicine at Glasgow in 1751 and professor of chemistry at Edinburgh in 1755. His "Essay on the Cold Produced by Evaporating Fluids" was published in *Edinburgh Philosophical and Literary Essays*, II (1755), 145–75. Later Cullen became professor of physic at Edinburgh and was for years the mainstay of the Medical School there. BF met Cullen in Edinburgh in 1759. *DNB* under both Simson and Cullen; John Thomson, *An Account of the Life, Lectures, and Writings of William Cullen, M.D.* (Edinburgh and London, 1859), I, 53–7, 139–40.

Course the same Degree of Heat or Cold. The Mercury sinks presently 3 or 4 Degrees, and the quicker if during the Evaporation you blow on the Ball with Bellows; a second Wetting and Blowing when the Mercury is down, carries it yet lower. I think I did not get it lower than 5 or 6 Degrees from where it naturally stood, which was at that time 60. But it is said, that a Vessel of Water being plac'd in another somewhat larger containing Spirit, in such a Manner that the Vessel of Water is surrounded with the Spirit, and both plac'd under the Receiver of an Air-pump, on Exhausting the Air, the Spirit evaporating leaves such a Degree of Cold as to freeze the Water, tho' the Thermometer in the open Air stands many Degrees above the Freezing Point.

I know not how this Phenomenon is to be accounted for, but it gives me Occasion to mention some loose Notions relating to Heat and Cold, which I have for some Time entertain'd, but not yet reduc'd into any Form. Allowing common Fire as well as the Electrical, to be a Fluid, capable of permeating other Bodies, and seeking an Equilibrium, I imagine some Bodies are better fitted by Nature to be Conductors of that Fluid than others; and that generally those which are the best Conductors of the Electrical Fluid, are also the best Conductors of this; and e contra. Thus a Body which is a good Conductor of Fire readily receives it into its Substance, and conducts it thro' the Whole to all the Parts; as Metals and Water do; and if two Bodies, both good Conductors, one heated, the other in its common State, are brought into Contact with each other, the Body which has most Fire, readily communicates of it to that which had least; and that which had least readily receives it, till an Equilibrium is produced. Thus, if you take a Dollar between your Fingers with one Hand, and a Piece of Wood of the same Dimensions with the other, and bring both at the same Time to the Flame of a Candle, you will find yourself obliged to drop the Dollar before you drop the Wood, because it conducts the Heat of the Candle sooner to your Flesh. Thus, if a Silver Teapot had a Handle of the same Metal, it would conduct the Heat from the Water to the Hand, and become too hot to be used; we therefore give to a Metal Teapot a Handle of Wood, which is not so good a Conductor as Metal. But a China or Stone Teapot being in some Degree of the Nature of Glass, which is not a good Conductor of Heat, may have a Handle of the same

Stuff. Thus also a damp moist Air shall make a Man more sensible of Cold, or chill him more than a dry Air that is colder, because a moist Air is fitter to receive and conduct away the Heat of his Body. This Fluid entring Bodies in great Quantity, first expands them by separating their Parts a little, afterwards by farther separating their Parts, it renders solids fluid, and at length dissipates their Parts in Air. Take this Fluid from melted Lead, or from Water, the Parts cohere again, the first grows solid, the latter becomes Ice. And this is soonest done by the Means of good Conductors. Thus, if you take (as I have done) a square Bar of Lead, 4 Inches long, and 1 Inch thick, together with 3 Pieces of Wood planed to the same Dimensions, and lay them as in the Margin,

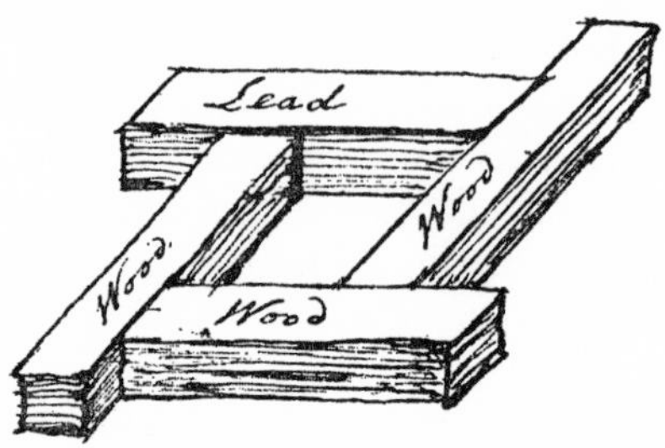

on a smooth Board, fix'd so as not to be easily separated or moved, and pour into the square[5] Cavity they form as much melted Lead as will fill it, you will see the melted Lead chill and become firm on the Side next the Leaden Bar, some Time before it chills on the other three Sides in Contact with the Wooden Bars; tho' before the Lead was poured in, they might all be supposed to have the same Degree of Heat or Coldness, as they had been exposed in the same Room to the same Air. You will likewise observe, that the leaden Bar, as it has cooled the melted Lead more than the wooden Bars have done, so it is itself more heated by the melted Lead. There is a certain Quantity of this Fluid, called Fire, in every living human Body, which Fluid, being in due Proportion, keeps the Parts of the Flesh and Blood at such a just Distance from each other, as that the Flesh and Nerves are suple, and the Blood fit for Circulation. If Part of this due Proportion of Fire be conducted away by Means of a Contact with other Bodies, as

5. *Exper. and Obser.* omits "square."

Air, Water, or Metals, the Parts of our Skin and Flesh that come into such Contact, first draw more near together than is agreeable, and give that Sensation which we call Cold, and if too much be conveyed away, the Body stiffens, the Blood ceases to flow, and Death ensues. On the other Hand, if too much of this Fluid be communicated to the Flesh, the Parts are separated too far, and Pain ensues as when they are separated by a Pin or Lancet. The Sensation that the Separation by Fire occasions, we call Heat, or Burning. My Desk, on which I now write, and the Lock of my Desk, are both expos'd to the same Temperature of the Air, and have therefore the same Degree of Heat and Cold; yet if I lay my Hand successively on the Wood and on the Metal, the latter feels much the Coldest; not that it is really so, but being a better Conductor, it more readily than the Wood takes away and draws into it self the Fire that was in my Skin. Accordingly, if I lay one Hand, Part on the Lock, and Part on the Wood, and after it has lain so some Time I feel both Parts with my other Hand, I find the Part that has been in Contact with the Lock, very sensibly colder to the Touch than the Part that lay on the Wood. How a living Animal obtains its Quantity of this Fluid called Fire, is a curious Question. I have shown that some Bodies (as Metals) have a Power of Attracting it stronger than others, and I have sometimes suspected that a living Body had some Power of Attracting out of the Air or other Bodies the Heat it wanted. Thus Metal hammer'd or repeatedly bent, grows hot in the bent or hammered Part. But when I consider'd that Air in contact with the Body cools it; that the surrounding Air is rather heated by its Contact with the Body; that every Breath of cooler Air drawn in, carries off Part of the Body's Heat when it passes out again: That therefore there must be in the Body a Fund for producing it, or otherwise the Animal would soon grow cold: I have been rather enclin'd to think that the Fluid, *Fire,* as well as the Fluid, *Air,* is attracted by Plants in their Growth, and becomes consolidated with the other Materials of which they are formed, and makes a great Part of their Substance. That when they come to be digested, and to suffer in the Vessels a Kind of Fermentation, Part of the Fire as well as Part of the Air, recovers its fluid Active State again, and diffuses itself in the Body digesting and separating it. That the Fire so reproduc'd by Digestion and Separation, continually leaving the Body, its

Place is supply'd by fresh Quantities arising from the continual Separation. That whatever quickens the Motion of the Fluids in an Animal, quickens the Separation, and reproduces more of the Fire, as Exercise. That all the Fire emitted by Wood and other Combustibles when burning, existed in them before in a solid State, being only discovered when separating. That some Fossils, as Sulphur, Seacoal, &c. contain a great deal of solid Fire; that Gunpowder is almost all solid Fire:[6] And that, in short, what escapes and is dissipated in the Burning of Bodies, besides Water and Earth, is generally the Air and Fire that before made Parts of the solid. Thus I imagin that Animal Heat arises by or from a Kind of Fermentation in the Juices of the Body, in the same Manner as Heat arises in the Liquors preparing for Distillation; wherein there is a Separation of the spirituous from the watry and earthy Parts. And it is remarkable, that the Liquor in a Distiller's Vat, when in its highest and best State of Fermentation, shows by the Thermometer,[7] as I have been informed, the same Degree of Heat with the human Body, that is about 94 or 96. Thus, as by a constant Supply of Fuel in a Chimney, you keep a warm Room, so by a constant Supply of Food in the Stomach, you keep a warm Body. Only where little Exercise is used, the Heat may possibly be conducted away too fast, in which Case such Materials are to be used for Cloathing and Bedding, against the Effect of an immediate Contact of the Air, as are in themselves bad Conductors of Heat, and consequently prevent its being communicated thro' their Substance to the Air. Hence what is called *Warmth* in Wool, and its Preference on that Account to Linen; Wool not being so good a Conductor. And hence all the natural Coverings of Animals to keep them warm, are such, as retain and confine the natural Heat in the Body, by being bad Conductors; such as Wool, Hair, Feathers, and the Silk by which the Silk-worm in its tender embrio State is first cloathed. Cloathing, thus considered, does not make a Man warm, by *giving* Warmth, but by preventing the too quick Dissipation of the Heat produc'd in his Body, and so occasioning an Accumulation.

There is another curious Question I will just venture to touch

6. For "that . . . Fire," *Exper. and Obser.* reads: "That some bodies are almost wholly solid fire."

7. For "shows by the Thermometer," *Exper. and Obser.* reads: "has."

upon, viz. Whence arises the sudden extraordinary Degree of Cold, perceptible on mixing some Chymical Liquors, and even on mixing Salt and Snow, where the Composition appears colder than the coldest of the Ingredients? I have never seen the chymical Mixtures made, but Salt and Snow I have often mixed myself, and am fully satisfied that the Composition feels much colder to the Touch, and lowers the Mercury in the Thermometer more than either Ingredient would do separately. I suppose with others, that Cold is nothing more than an Absence of Heat or Fire. Now if the Quantity of Fire before contain'd or diffus'd in the Snow and Salt, was expell'd in the Uniting of the two Matters, it must be driven away either thro' the Air or the Vessel containing them. If it is driven off thro' the Air, it must warm the Air, and a Thermometer held over the Mixture without touching it, would discover the Heat by the Rising of the Mercury, as it must and always does in warmer Air. This indeed I have not try'd; but I should guess it would rather be driven off thro' the Vessel, especially if the Vessel be Metal, as being a better Conductor than Air, and so one should find the Bason warmer after such Mixture. But on the contrary the Vessel grows cold, and even Water in which the Vessel is sometimes plac'd for the Experiment, freezes into hard Ice on the Bason. Now I know not how to account for this otherwise than by supposing, that the Composition is a better Conductor of Fire than the Ingredients separately, and like the Lock compar'd with the Wood, has a stronger Power of Attracting Fire, and does accordingly attract it suddenly from the Fingers or a Thermometer put into it, from the Bason that contains it, and from the Water in contact with the Outside of the Bason, so that the Fingers have the Sensation of extream Cold, by being depriv'd of much of their natural Fire; the Thermometer sinks, by having part of its Fire drawn out of the Mercury; the Bason grows colder to the Touch, as by having its Fire drawn into the Mixture, it is become more capable of drawing and receiving it from the Hand; and thro' the Bason the Water loses its Fire that kept it fluid, so it becomes Ice. One would expect, That from all this attracted Acquisition of Fire to the Composition, it should become warmer; and in fact, the Snow and Salt dissolves at the same Time into Water without freezing.[8]

8. *Exper. and Obser.* ends the letter here.

I doubt whether in all this I have talked intelligibly; and indeed how should a Man do so, that does not himself clearly understand the Thing he talks of. This I confess to be my present Case. I intended to amuse you, but I fear I have done more, and tired you. Be so good as to excuse it, and believe me, with sincere Esteem and Respect, Sir, Your most obedient humble Servant

B FRANKLIN

Endorsed in Stiles' hand: Copy Mr. Franklin's Letter to Dr. Lining. Apr. 14. 1757[9]

To Jane Mecom

ALS: American Philosophical Society

Dear Sister New York, April 19. 1757

I wrote a few Lines to you yesterday, but omitted to answer yours relating to Sister Douse:[1] As *having their own Way*, is one of the greatest Comforts of Life, to old People, I think their Friends should endeavour to accommodate them in that, as well as in any thing else. When they have long liv'd in a House, it becomes natural to them, they are almost as closely connected with it as the Tortoise with his Shell, they die if you tear them out of it. Old Folks and old Trees, if you remove them, tis ten to one that you kill them. So let our good old Sister be no more importun'd on that head. We are growing old fast ourselves, and shall expect the same kind of Indulgencies. If we give them, we shall have a Right to receive them in our Turn.

And as to her few fine Things, I think she is in the right not to sell them, and for the Reason she gives, that they will fetch but little. When that little is spent, they would be of no farther use to her; but perhaps the Expectation of Possessing them at her Death, may make that Person tender and careful of her, and helpful to her, to the amount of ten times their Value. If so, they are put to the best Use they possibly can be.

9. The draft is endorsed in BF's hand: "Letter to Dr. Lining on Fire &c."

1. Neither BF's letter of April 18 nor Jane Mecom's letter about their half-sister Elizabeth Douse (C.1) has been found. For the mortgage which BF held on Mrs. Douse's house and his disposition of it in his will of April 28, 1757, see above, V, 66–7, and below, p. 199.

I hope you visit Sister as often as your Affairs will permit, and afford her what Assistance and Comfort you can, in her present Situation. *Old Age, Infirmities,* and *Poverty,* join'd, are Afflictions enough; the *Neglect and Slight* of Friends and near Relations, should never be added. People in her Circumstances are apt to suspect this sometimes without Cause; *Appearances* should therefore be attended to, in our Conduct towards them, as well as *Realities.*

I write by this Post to Cousin Williams,[2] to continue his Care, which I doubt not he will do.

We expect to sail in about a Week, so that I can hardly hear from you again on this Side the Water. But let me have a Line from you now and then while I am in London. I expect to stay there at least a 12 month. Direct your Letters to be left for me at the Pensilvania Coffee House in Birchin Lane London.[3] My Love to all, from Dear Sister, Your affectionate Brother B FRANKLIN

PS. April 25. We are still here, and perhaps may be here a Week longer, Once more Adieu my dear Sister.

Addressed: To / Mrs Jane Mecom / at / Boston / Free / B FRANKLIN

Endorsed: Old Trees &c.

Commission to James Parker as Comptroller of the Post Office

Draft:[4] American Philosophical Society

Sometime after their appointment as joint deputy postmasters general in 1753 Franklin and Hunter had made William Franklin comptroller of the North American postal service, in addition to being postmaster of Philadelphia. The exact duties which they assigned to him in this position are not known since his commission and instructions have not

2. Jonathan Williams, who seems to have been relied on to look after several of his Franklin connections in the Boston area. See above, VI, 454. BF's letter to him "by this Post" has not been found.

3. Coffee houses bearing the names of various American colonies were favorite rendezvous and mailing addresses for residents of those colonies who visited London. Birchin Lane, running between Lombard St. and Cornhill, was in an area in which important Quaker activities were located.

4. In BF's hand.

been found. It is clear, however, that the comptroller was expected to assist the joint heads of the system in general oversight and probably had special responsibility for receiving and checking the reports and accounts of the local postmasters. With both Franklins about to leave America for England and with Hunter already there, it now became necessary to appoint someone to take direct charge of the service, and to give him substantial authority to act on behalf of the deputy postmasters general. For this responsible position Franklin chose his former employee and later partner James Parker, printer in New York and Woodbridge, N.J.,[5] and issued the commission and instructions printed here and in the next document. It was a happy choice; Parker was not only an able printer but, as events were to prove, an efficient administrator. The colonial postal system prospered under his control.

[April 22, 1757]

Benjamin Franklin and William Hunter Esquires,
His Majesty's Deputy Post-master General of all His Majesty's Dominions on the Continent of North America

To all to whom these Presents shall come, *Greeting. Know ye,* that we the said Benjamin Franklin and William Hunter, reposing special Trust and Confidence in James Parker, of Woodbridge in New Jersey, Gentleman, and having received good Testimony of his Fidelity and Loyalty to His Majesty, and of his Ability and Sufficiency to execute the Office and Duties required of a Comptroller of the General Post Office, manage and better regulate the Posts on the Continent in North America, his Inclination and Capacity to improve and advance his Majesty's Revenues therein [*crossed out:* and his Skill and Exactness in Accompts,] do by these Presents nominate and appoint him our Agent and Comptroller with full Power to transact, do and perform such Matters and Things for us and in our Name and Behalf, relating to the Management of the General Post Office on the Continent of North America, as we have given or shall give him in Charge, by our Instructions in Writing, and particularly to demand, receive, examine, correct, and allow, the Monthly Bills called Comptroller's Bills, and the Quarterly and General Accounts of the several Deputy Postmasters in every Province relating to the Postage of Letters; and to demand, recover, and receive, for us, the Ballances

5. On Parker see above, II, 341 n.

from such Accounts arising, and proper Discharges thereupon to give, and to do and perform every other Matter and Thing that to the Office and Duty of an Agent and Comptroller of the General Post Office doth or may appertain for and during such time as our present Comptroller William Franklin shall be absent from America, or until another shall be appointed by us to the same Office, Hereby strictly charging and requiring all Officers and others employed in and about the Posts already settled in any Part of his Majesty's said Provinces and Dominions in North America, or in Relation to the Revenue arising by the Post of Letters there, from time to time to give an Account of their Doings and Transactions therein to the said James Parker, and to observe and obey his Orders and Directions in Relation to their respective Offices, Trusts and Employments. *And* the better to enable the said James Parker to execute the Office and Trust reposed in him, we do hereby delegate unto him, in case of our Absence from the Continent of America, all our Power and Authority, to appoint Deputy Postmasters for the better managing and ordering the said Posts, in North America, and for collecting and improving the Revenue arising thereby, granting him full Power and Authority, so far as by Law we may, to suspend, remove or displace such Deputies and all and every other Person or Persons whatsoever, imployed or to be employed in the Management of the said Posts, or in the Collection of the said Revenue, who shall be guilty of any Neglect, Mismanagement, or Breach of Duty, in their Respective Offices or Employments, from the farther Execution of his or their Office or Offices.[6] And we do hereby Suspend the Commission of our present Comptroller and Agent William Franklin, now about to make a Voyage to England, until he shall return from thence, and resume the Execution thereof, when this present Commission is to cease, determine, and become void. In Witness whereof we the said Benjamin Franklin and William Hunter, have hereunto set our Firm[7] and caused the Seal of our Office to

6. At this point in the draft commission the following was first written and then struck out: "And we do hereby grant him the said James Parker, for his Care Pains and Trouble in the Performance and Execution of the Office and Trust hereby granted and committed unto him, the same Salary, Allowance, and Emoluments, as hath been heretofore allowed to, and enjoyed by our present Comptroller and Agent William Franklin, for the same Services."

7. Firm: signature, sign-manual. *OED*.

be affixed. Dated the 22d. Day of April 1757. In the thirtieth Year of his Majesty's Reign. FRANKLIN & HUNTER.

Endorsed: Copy of James Parker's Commission to appoint him Agent and Comptroller of the General Post-Office, dated April 22. 1757

Post Office Instructions to James Parker[8]

ADS: American Philosophical Society

Mr. James Parker [General Post O]ffice [in] North America April 22, 1757
Sir

As you have undertaken to execute the Office of Comptroller of the General Post Office during our Absence and that of the present Comptroller the following Instructions are necessary for your Observation viz.

[1.] [*Illegible*] Every Post Master on the Continent to send you a Comptroller's B[ill] containing an Account of the Letters paid and unpaid that he [has?] [*illegible*] sent to other Offices that so you may charge him or them with the same in your Books which you are to do on the Receipt of those Bills. If any Postmaster neglects to send his Comptroller's Bills you are to write to him and urge him to be punctual.

2. Every Post-Master ought to send you his Quarterly Account regularly, immediately after the Quarter Day; if any neglect this, you are likewise to write to them and urge them to Punctuality. When you receive those Accounts, you are to examine and compare them with your Comptroller's Book, and with the preceding Accounts received from the same Offices, correct the Mistakes and Errors, if any, and observe whether any new or uncustomary Charges are introduced.

3. As there is an Inconvenience in the Accounts kept, when different Quarter Days are observed by different Offices, you are to endeavour to bring them all to the Observation of the same Quarter Days, viz, Lady Day, or March 25. Midsummer at June 24. Michaelmas or Sept. 29. and Christmas or Dec. 25. the same

8. These instructions must have been drawn up by BF alone, since Hunter was in England at this time. Tears and discolorations make some lines in the MS virtually illegible.

being the Quarter Days used in the General Post Office in Great Britain.

4. After the Quarterly Accounts are corrected and rectified, you are to carry the Ballances due from the several Postmasters to the Debit of their respective Accounts in your Comptroller's Book; and endeavour to collect and receive all such Ballances from time to time as they arise, directing them to be remitted to you in such Specie and Manner as to you shall seem most advantageous to the Office; giving Credit to the several Postmasters in your Books likewise for the Ballances or other Sums you from time to time receive.

5. The Money receiv'd from the several Offices, after deducting a Commission of 7½ per Cent which is allow'd you for your Care and Trouble in the Premises, you are to remit to us or either of us while we remain in England, in good Bills of Exchange, till you shall have farther or other Orders.

6. If any Postmaster should in our Absence die, or resign his Office, misbehave therein, or neglect the Duties there[of] or remove out of the Town or Country where his Office was usually kept, you are to appoint another to execute the same pro tempore till you receive farther Direction from us in that Matter; taking Care that such Deputy by you appointed do not act but under the usual and legal Securities and Qualifications.

7. You are to communicate a Copy of our additional Instruction relating to the Carriage of Newspapers per Post to the several Post Offices and their respective Riders and endeavour by all prudential Methods in your Power that the same be observed and executed.[9]

8. We have Reason to believe that the Office is injur'd greatly by the present Rider between Philadelphia and Frederickburgh in Virginia.[1] And, if, after the Allowances that will now be made him and the Advantages he will receive by Carrying Newspapers, he refuses to give the Security and take the Qualification required

9. The additional instruction on the carriage of newspapers in force on this date has not been found, but see below, p. 390, for an instruction on the same subject, and probably to the same effect, dated March 10, 1758.

1. This may have been Thomas Franklin (no relation), of whom David Hall complained to BF, July 4, 1757 (see below, p. 238). Parker was apparently unable to effect any substantial improvement in the southern service during his tenure as comptroller.

of other Riders, you are hereby directed to remove him and appoint another; and if he should after such removal presume to ride and carry Letters contrary to the Act of Parliament, you are to cause him to be prosecuted, at our Expence.

9. If you find it necessary to take any Journeys for the better executing your Office of Comptroller, and in Compliance with these Instructions, you are to keep an Account of your Expences in such Journeys, which Accounts being reasonable, shall be allow'd you, together with a suitable Consideration for your Time and extraordinary Trouble.

10. There is a Post Office in Nova Scotia, under our Direction, but the Officer has never sent us any Account.[2] You are to write to him, and acquaint him, that no Account from his Office has ever come to our Hands since he received his Commission, which was about the Beginning of 1754, and desire he would forward to you an Account of his Office from that time to the End of the last Quarter, with all Expedition. Many Letters from different Parts of the Continent are sent to Boston Office for Nova Scotia, and forwarded thither by Sea, no Person appearing in Boston to pay the Postage; so that a good deal of Money, it is thought, arises at present in that Office, while the Army is canton'd in so many different Parts of America. Mr. Hubbard's's[3] Accounts will show how much of what has been charg'd to his Office is forwarded to Nova Scotia, and Mr. Colden's[4] will show whether any have been forwarded thither by Sea from New York.

11. You will inquire into the State of the Post Office at Burlington and endeavour to put it on such a Footing as may render it useful to the Inhabitants, and beneficial to the General Post Office.[5]

12. While we stay in England you are to write to us per every

2. A post office was established at Halifax in the spring of 1755. Its service from and to the rest of the continent and England was by ship via Boston or New York and continued for many years to be irregular and unreliable. William Smith, *The History of the Post Office in British North America 1639–1870* (Cambridge, Eng., 1920), pp. 33, 176; Thomas H. Raddall, *Halifax Warden of the North* (Toronto, 1948), pp. 61–2.

3. Tuthill Hubbart, postmaster at Boston in succession to his stepfather, BF's brother John, in 1756.

4. Alexander Colden, postmaster in New York.

5. Jonathan Thomas had been postmaster at Burlington earlier (see above, V, 422–3), but whether he still was in 1757 is uncertain.

Pacquet or other convenient Opportunity, acquainting us with your Proceedings in the Premises, and informing us of every Thing that may require our farther or more particular Direction.[6]

13. In general, you are to inform yourself from time to time whether the Posts continue to keep their Stages regularly, and whether the respective Postmasters give such due Attendance at their Offices as is satisfactory to the Publick; and to endeavour the Rectification of every thing that you find amiss, so that Correspondence may not be impeded or interrupted by any Neglect or Mismanagement in the Post Offices, or Misconduct of the Riders, nor any just Cause of Complaint be given to the Merchants or others who correspond per Post.

So wishing you Health and Success we remain, Your assured Friends FRANKLIN & HUNTER

Memorandums for Mr. Parker.

To enquire of Mr. Tuthill Hubbard, what is done in the Recovery of Mr. Huske's Bond;[7] and if recover'd to desire Mr. Hubbard to remit us the Money.

To enquire of Ditto what Sums he has receiv'd from the Eastern Offices, that Credit may be given them, and Mr. Hubbard charg'd with the same.

To enquire of Messrs. Peat & Hurd[8] whether they have paid

6. Virtually all the communications between Parker and BF during the latter's first mission to England have disappeared. From BF's next departure in 1764 until Parker's death in 1770, however, the comptroller's surviving letters to his superior, many dealing with postoffice business, are numerous, often very long, and, in Smyth's words, "a constant wail of distress."

7. On Ellis Huske, postmaster at Boston before John Franklin, see above, IV, 318 n.

8. Thomas Peat (or Peet) (1698–1760) and Ebenezer Hurd (1703–1788), both of Stratford, Conn., were for many years the post riders on the New York to Saybrook section of the New England route. Hurd carried the mail for 48 years. After Peat's death one of his sons apparently took over, for in 1773 Hugh Finlay, on a postal inspection trip, complained bitterly that Peat and Hurd constantly carried "way letters" and executed other private commissions for inhabitants along their route for their personal profit, thereby greatly delaying the mail service and depriving it of proper income. Samuel Orcutt, *A History of the Old Town of Stratford and the City of Bridgeport, Conn.* (Fairfield Co. Hist. Soc., 1886), II, 1223, 1263; Dena D. Hurd, *A History and Genealogy of the Family of Hurd in America* (N.Y., 1910), pp. 39–41; *Journal kept by Hugh Finlay . . .* [1773–1774] (Brooklyn, 1867), pp. 37–9, 41–3.

any Money on our Account to Mr. Holt,[9] and how much, that Mr. Holt may be charg'd with it.

To get the Quarterly Account from Trenton Office,[1] that ended Sept. 29. 1756, that the State of it may be entred in your Books, the said Account being lost or mislaid.

To enquire of Hartford Postmaster for Account between Nov. 1755 and April 12. 1756, the same not being to be found at present among the Office Papers.

To receive of Mr. James Thompson, late Postmaster of New Brunswick,[2] the remainder of his Note, now left with you.

Endorsed: [*Words cut off*] Comptroller 1757

To Joseph Galloway

ALS: Yale University Library

Dear Sir, N York, April 25. 1757

The List of Servants is come to hand.[3] I suppose 'tis as compleat as it could at present be made, but it has many Blanks in it. I purpose to talk with my Lord upon it to day, as well as upon the Affair of the Indian Trade Bill, which I have always had much at heart; and shall let you know the Result.[4]

We are still waiting for my Lord's Dispatches, and still uncertain when we shall have them. 'Tis an uneasy Situation; but we must have Patience.

A Fleet of Transports is forming here for the Expedition,[5] and the Embargo continues. No fresh News from England; except that by a Vessel into New-England, which brings Papers to the

9. On John Holt, postmaster of New Haven, see above, v, 441 n.

1. The names of the postmasters at Trenton and Hartford (immediately below) at this time have not been found.

2. Probably the man of that name who by June 1756 was living in New Brunswick and in 1761 advertised his inn and tavern there. 1 *N.J. Arch.*, XX, 38, 601, 602, 648.

3. The list is among Lord Loudoun's papers; see below, p. 224-8, for it and BF's conferences with Loudoun on compensations for indentured servants enlisted in the army.

4. See above, p. 175. Though BF conferred with the general on the 25th, Loudoun did not record any conversation about the trade bill.

5. By the end of April Loudoun had gathered 30 transports to carry his troops to Halifax where he intended to join Admiral Francis Holburne for an attack on Louisbourg. Pargellis, *Lord Loudoun*, pp. 236–7.

28th of February, it is said there is an Account that the Admirals were on board, but the Fleet not sail'd.[6]

With great Respect and Esteem I am, Dear Sir, Your affectionate humble Servant B FRANKLIN

Mr. Galloway

Endorsed: April 25. 1757 B. Franklin's Letter

Last Will and Testament ADS: The Franklin Institute, Philadelphia

[April 28, 1757]

I Benjamin Franklin of the City of Philadelphia, Printer, being in my usual Health of Body and Mind (blessed be God) do this twenty-eighth Day of April, in the Year 1757, make, publish, sign and seal, this my last Will and Testament, viz.[7]

I will that all my just Debts, if any there are at the Time of my Decease, be paid as soon as may be after that shall happen.

I give to my Nephew James Franklin, Son of my Brother James Franklin, two small Tenements which I have in Germantown, near Boston, and One Hundred Dollars in Money; the Tenements to him and his Heirs and Assigns for ever.[8]

I give to my dear Sister Jane Mecom, the Mortgage I have on my Sister Douse's House and Lot in Boston, with said Douse's Bond, and every Demand I have against my said Sister Douse's, Estate.[9] Only I will that my said Sister Douse be never disturbed in the Possession of the said House and Lot during her Life, tho' she should not be able to discharge the said Mortgage or pay the Interest arising on the same.[1]

6. Holburne's fleet sailed from Spithead on February 17, left Ireland May 8, and arrived in Halifax July 9. *Ibid.* Garbled news of the first of these events had reached Cape Ann, was relayed to Boston, and appeared in the *N.-Y. Mercury,* May 2, 1757.

7. For BF's (mutilated) will of June 22, 1750, see above, III, 480–2.

8. James Franklin (C.11.4), son of BF's brother James, to whom be had been apprenticed as a boy, had in turn been educated by and apprenticed to BF. See above, II, 261–3. On BF's lots and tenements in Germantown, at Braintree, Mass., see above, V, 119 n.

9. On the mortgage and bond BF's eldest half-sister Elizabeth Douse (C.1) had given him Sept. 27, 1753, see above, V, 66–7.

1. See BF's comments on this matter to Jane Mecom, above p. 190.

Also I give to my Sister Jane Mecom the Share of my Father's Estate, and the particular Legacy which he left me by his Will, and also the Debt due to me from that Estate.[2]

Also I give to my Sister Jane Mecom, my least Silver Tankard.

I give to my Nephew Benjamin Mecom, Son to my Sister Jane Mecom, a Bond I have of his for Fifty Pounds Sterling, with the Interest that may be due thereon at the Time of my Decease.[3]

I give to my Son William Franklin, a Lot of Ground which I have in Arch Street, and my Pasture Ground in the Northern Liberties, with the Improvements that are or may be thereon at the Time of my Decease, to him and his Heirs and Assigns forever.[4]

Also I give to my said Son William Franklin, all my Library, Books, Pamphlets, Letters and Manuscripts whatsoever; except such as relate to my Accounts, or Bonds, Notes and other Securities of my Estate.

Also I give to my said Son William Franklin, my Air Pump with its Apparatus, and all my Natural Curiosities.

Also I give to my Son William Franklin One Thousand Pounds in Money, to be paid him by my Executors within One Year after my Decease; deducting only such Sum or Sums as may by any Means become due to me from my said Son after the Date of this Will.

I give to my Daughter Sarah Franklin One Thousand Pounds in Money; to be put out to Interest for her till she shall arrive at the Age of Twenty-one Years, and then to be paid to her with the Interest.[5]

Also I give to my said Daughter Sarah Franklin, my Share in the Library of the Library Company of Philadelphia.[6]

And I give to my loving Wife Deborah Franklin, One Thousand

2. Josiah Franklin died Jan. 16, 1745. In his will, dated Oct. 20, 1744, and probated Aug. 7, 1750, he bequeathed to BF a sum in New Tenor Massachusetts currency to the value of £30 Old Tenor and one ninth of the residue of his estate, which was to be distributed following his wife's death. Suffolk Co. Registry of Probate, Boston, vol. 44, pp. 222–3.

3. For Benjamin Mecom's bond, dated Dec. 27, 1756, see above, p. 68 n.

4. For BF's acquisition of these properties in 1741, see above, II, 310–11.

5. Sarah Franklin was now in her fourteenth year.

6. On the founding of the Library Company in 1731 and its incorporation in 1742, see above, I, 208–10, and II, 345–7.

Pounds in Money, to be paid within One Year after my Decease. And I also give to my said Wife during her natural Life, my Right to two Houses and Lots in Market Street, now in Possession of her Mother Sarah Read, to possess and enjoy the same after her said Mother's Decease; and after my Wife's Decease, I give the same Houses and Lots to my Daughter Sarah Franklin, her Heirs and Assigns forever.[7]

And I give the adjoining Lot, which I took on perpetual Ground Rent of Samuel Preston Moore, to my said Daughter Sarah, her Heirs and Assigns for ever.[8]

But if my said Daughter Sarah should die before she comes of Age, and without lawful Issue, in such Case I will that the Eastermost House and Lot, One Half of which was given me by my Wife's Mother Sarah Read, and the other Half I purchased of John Croker, be sold, and the Money divided equally among the Children and Grand Children of Frances Croker, the deceased Sister of my Wife; and that the Westermost House and Lot which I purchased of my Brother-in law John Read, together with the Lot I took from Samuel Preston Moore, do go to my Son William Franklin, his Heirs and Assigns for ever.

My Electrical Apparatus I give to Yale College at New-haven in Connecticut.[9]

And all my Household Goods and Furniture of what kind so ever, Plate excepted, I give to my Wife, to be used and disposed of as she may think proper. And I will that she have the Use of all my Plate during her Life, and that at her Decease the same be equally divided between my Son and Daughter before-named, or

7. These were the two half-lots with their buildings, originally owned by DF's father, John Read, which Sarah Read had transferred to her son John and her daughters DF and Frances Croker and their husbands in April 1734. They had immediately given her back life-time leases to the properties. BF had bought the Croker interest Oct. 12, 1745, and John Read's house and lot, Nov. 15, 1751. See above, I, 362–70; III, 44–5; IV, 208–9.

8. BF had acquired this property, adjoining that he had recently bought from John Read, on March 25, 1752. See above, IV, 295–6.

9. In 1751 BF had urged President Clap to procure a subscription for "a compleat Apparatus for Natural Philosophy" and offered to contribute "the Electrical Part" himself. Although little seems to have come of this proposal, BF did give the college one piece of electrical apparatus at some time before February 1755. See above, IV, 213; V, 499–500.

in case of the Death of either of them, the Survivor to have the whole.

And the Income arising out of my Printing House, according to the Terms of the Agreement between my Partner David Hall and me, during the Continuance of the Partnership,[1] I will have divided and paid in three equal Parts, one Part to my Wife, one Part to my Son William, and one Part to my Daughter Sarah; but so, as that in case either of my said Children die without Offspring before the Expiration of the said Partnership, then the Part of the Income accruing to such Child is to go to the Survivor. And if my Wife die before the Expiration of the said Partnership, then the Share of the Income thereof hereby allotted to her, is to go to my said Children, or to the Survivor of them, or to the Issue of such Survivor. And in case of the Death of my Wife, and of both my Children without Issue, then I give the said Income to the Children and Grandchildren of my Brother James Franklin, deceased, the Children and Grand Children of my Sisters Mary Homes and Sarah Davenport, deceased; the Children and Grandchildren of my Sisters [*in margin:* Mary Homes] Lydia Scot and Jane Mecom, to be equally divided among them all.[2] And after the Expiration of the Partnership, I will that the said Printing House, Types and Materials thereto belonging, be sold, and the Money arising by such Sale divided in the same Manner as the Income thereof is herein directed to be divided. But the Part of the Income arising to my said Daughter Sarah, before and until she comes of Age, I would have put out to Interest by my Executors, and the Interest apply'd to her Education.

And whereas my Nephew Josiah Davenport did some time since convey to me the Rent of an House and Lot in Third Street, to secure to me the Repayment of a Sum of Money I had paid for

1. The articles of agreement with David Hall, dated Jan. 1, 1747–8, provided that the partnership was to continue until Jan. 21, 1766. See above, III, 263–7.

2. James Franklin (C.11) had died in 1735, leaving five children who attained adulthood. Mary Franklin (C.10), wife of Robert Homes (or Holmes), had died in 1731, leaving only one son still living in 1757; her other children had died without issue. Sarah Franklin (C.12), wife of James Davenport, had died in 1731; all her five children had issue. Lydia Franklin (C.16) had married Robert Scott in 1731 and had one daughter. Jane Franklin (C.17) had married Edward Mecom in 1727 and had twelve children of whom nine were still living in 1757. See Genealogy, above, I, lix–lxii.

him, with Interest; I will that the said Interest be paid or allowed by my Executors towards the Support and Education of my said Nephew's Child which lately had the Misfortune of losing its Sight by the Small Pox.[3]

And I give to my Sister Lydia Scot, Twenty Pounds.

And I give to my Brother-in-law John Read's Son John Five Pounds, and to his Son Franklin Read Ten Pounds.[4]

And I give to Francis, Son of William and Deborah Dunlap, Ten Pounds,[5] And to each Child of Josiah Davenport, Ten Pounds.

And I give to William and Deborah Hall, Children of my good Friend and Partner David Hall, each Ten Pounds.[6]

And I give to Samuel and Jane Parker, Children of my good Friend James Parker, each Ten Pounds.[7]

And I give to the eldest Son of my Kinsman Jonathan Williams Ten Pounds.[8]

And I will that my Negro Man Peter,[9] and his Wife Jemima, be free after my Decease.

3. Josiah Davenport (C.12.4), who had settled in Philadelphia as a baker in 1750 (see above, III, 388, 475), wrote DF, March 22, 1759 (APS), that he had turned over the lease to BF and two bonds of £100 each as security; he was about to sell the house to his tenant and wished to discharge the unpaid balance of his debt before executing the deed. His unfortunate child was probably one of his daughters, Sarah or Deborah, by his second wife, the former Ann Annis. There was a smallpox epidemic in Philadelphia in the spring of 1757. *Pa. Gaz.*, April 7, 1757.

4. DF's brother John's sons, John K. and Franklin, were entered in the Philadelphia Academy in 1756 and 1762, respectively. Montgomery, *Hist. Univ. Pa.*, p. 548.

5. Francis Dunlap, first child of William and Deborah Dunlap (DF's niece), was born Feb. 8, 1755, and baptized in Christ Church, Philadelphia, Feb. 26, 1756. *PMHB*, XV (1891), 488.

6. William and Deborah Hall were born Jan. 20, 1752, and Oct. 20, 1754, respectively. *Ibid.*, XVI (1892), 364.

7. Samuel Franklin Parker (*c.* 1746–1799), often mentioned in his father's later correspondence with BF; and Jane Ballareau Parker (d. 1831), who married Gunning Bedford, Jr., before 1773.

8. Josiah Williams (C.5.3.1) (1747–1772) was the eldest child of Jonathan Williams and Grace Harris (C.5.3), daughter of BF's half-sister Ann. Their two other sons, Jonathan, Jr. and John are not mentioned here, but Jonathan, Jr. was later intimately associated with BF in France.

9. Peter had gone to Virginia with BF in 1756. See above, VI, 425 n. Either he (or possibly a son of the same name) accompanied him to England and gave him general satisfaction there.

And the Residue of my Estate, Goods and Chattels, and Money that may be remaining in the Hands of my Executors, or received by them from Debts outstanding at my Decease, after Payment of my Debts, Legacies and Funeral Expences, I would have divided, paid and ordered in every respect in the same Manner as is herein directed concerning the Income and Produce of my Printing House.

And if by any unforeseen Change in my Circumstances, my Estate should appear to my Executors to be incapable of paying the abovementioned several Legacies in Money to my Wife and Children, either in the Quantity or Time prescribed, I will that no Preference shall be given, but a proportional Abatement or Payment made of each.

And I appoint my trusty, loving and faithful Friends David Hall and James Parker, to be Executors of this my last Will and Testament. And I desire my good Friends William Coleman, Hugh Roberts, and Philip Syng,[1] to assist them with their Advice from time to time where it may [be] needful in the Settlement of any of my Affairs. And I earnestly recommend to my little Family, the Continuance of Peace, Love, and affectionate Performance of mutual Duties to their Lives End. But if any Dispute should arise among them, or between them or any of them and my Executors, relating to my Estate or any Part thereof, or to the Intention of this my Will in any [res]pect, I would have the same submitted to the Determination of my said three Friends, and that their Determination be final.

And now humbly returning sincere Thanks to God,[2] for producing me into Being, and conducting me hitherto thro' Life so happily, so free from Sickness, Pain and Trouble, and with such a Competency of this World's Goods as might make a reasonable Mind easy; that he was pleased to give me such a Mind, with moderate Passions, or so much of his gracious Assistance in Governing them; and to free it early from Ambition, Avarice and Superstition, common Causes of much Uneasiness to Men: That he gave me to live so long in a Land of Liberty, with a People that I love; and rais'd me, tho' a Stranger, so many Friends among

1. Among BF's earliest friends in Philadelphia; Coleman and Syng had witnessed his will of 1750.

2. This eloquent final paragraph is repeated verbatim from the will of 1750.

them; bestowing on me, moreover, a loving and prudent Wife and dutiful Children: For these, and all his other innumerable Mercies and Favours, I bless that BEING of BEINGS who does not disdain to care for the meanest of his Creatures. And I reflect on those Benefits received, with the greater Satisfaction, as they give me such a Confidence in his Goodness, as will, I hope, enable me always in all Things to submit freely to his Will, and to resign my Spirit chearfully into his Hands, whenever he shall please to call for it; reposing my self securely in the Lap of God and Nature, as a Child in the Arms of an affectionate Parent.

B FRANKLIN [*seal*]

Signed, sealed published and declared by the said Benjamin Franklin, as and for his last Will and Testament, in the Presence of us.[3]
JAMES CHILD
JON HUGHES
JNO SIBBALD

Memorandum. The above Will is all written by my own Hand, at New York, while waiting for a Passage to England. When I cancelled my former Will.

B FRANKLIN

To Deborah Franklin

ALS: American Philosophical Society

My dear Child New York, April 29. 1757

I wrote to you yesterday per Post.[4] This is only to acquaint you, that I am determined against going in the first Pacquet.[5]

3. Of these witnesses James Child and John Sibbald advertised themselves in *Pa. Gaz.* as ship captains and merchants. In August Sibbald announced that he was outfitting "the Ship Pennsylvania's Frigate," which sailed, apparently on a privateering voyage, on August 17. *Pa. Gaz.*, Aug. 4, 18, 1757. Probably Child was in New York in connection with the furnishing of transports and supplies for Loudoun's expedition and Sibbald on the equipment of his new ship. On John Hughes see above, VI, 284 n.

4. Not found.

5. As events proved, this decision made no difference in the date of BF's sailing, because Loudoun held all three packets that arrived from England until he himself sailed on his abortive expedition against Louisbourg in June. The general had begun a long letter to the Duke of Cumberland four days before BF wrote this, but did not conclude it until June 3, two days before both he and BF embarked. Pargellis, *Military Affairs*, pp. 343–61.

Send me the Indian Sealskin Hussiff,[6] with all the Things that were in it. It will be an acceptable Present to a Gimcrack great Man in London, that is my Friend. In the right hand little Drawer under my Desk, is some of the Indian Lady's Gut Cambrick; roll it up as you would a Ribband; wrap it in Paper, and put it into the Housiff with the other Things.

Among my Books on the Shelves, there are two or three little Pieces on the Game of Chess; One in French bound in Leather, 8vo. One in a blue Paper Cover, English;[7] two others in Manuscript; one of them thin in brown Paper Cover, the other in loose Leaves not bound. If you can find them yourself, send them: But do not set anybody else to look for them. You may know the French one, by the Word ECHECS in the Titlepage.

I wrote you fully about the Accounts Books; so add only my Love to all Friends, from Your affectionate Husband

B FRANKLIN

Addressed: To / Mrs Franklin / Philada. / per favour of / Mr McMichael[8]

To William Parsons

ALS: American Philosophical Society

Dear Friend, New York, May 3. 1757

I have just time to bid you Farewell; and to acquaint you, that Mr. Nugent[9] is at present in the Service in Ireland, but 'tis thought the Regiment he belongs to, will be one of those ordered to America with the expected Fleet. He is a Relation of Col. Bradstreet's;[1] who is daily expected here, and tis said can give me the best Account of Nugent. If I learn any thing farther before

6. Hussif or hussive (housewife): a pocket-case for needles, pins, thread, scissors, etc. *OED*. The intended recipient has not been identified.

7. This may have been Philip Stamma's pamphlet *The Noble Game of Chess; or a new and easy method to play well in a short time* (London, 1745), which BF ordered from Strahan, Sept. 22, 1751, but later said he did not need because David Martin, his principal antagonist at chess, had died. See above, IV, 196, 323. The other works on the game have not been identified.

8. Probably a member of the Philadelphia mercantile house of Scott & McMichael.

9. On Richard Nugent, lieutenant in the 15th (Amherst's) Regiment of Foot, ordered to America in December 1757, see above, VI, 492 n.

1. On Col. John Bradstreet, see above, VI, 473–4 n.

I sail, I will acquaint you with it. I am, Dear Friend, Yours affectionately B FRANKLIN

Wm Parsons Esqr

Addressed (mostly cut off): Free B F[RANKLIN]

Endorsed: May 3d 1757 B. Franklin Richard Nugent
Mr. Franklin's Letter concerning Richd. Nugent[2]

From Jacob Duché, Junior[3] ALS: American Philosophical Society

Sir Philada. May 6. 1757

As you kindly offered me your best Services before you left Philadelphia, which, as I had then no Commands to trouble you with; I declined the Honor of accepting, I now beg Leave to make Use of the Liberty you permitted me, to request you to take Charge of the inclosed Letters. I believe you are personally acquainted with the Gentlemen to whom they are directed, and may perhaps have an Opportunity of seeing them yourself. I wish you the highest Success in your laudable Undertakings, as I am well convinced that all your Actions hitherto have been immediately for the Public Good, and trust that in your future Conduct, you will still have that noblest of Ends in View.[4]

I am, Sir, Your assured Friend and very humble Servant

JACOB DUCHÉ JUNR.

P.S. My Father sends his Compliments and best Wishes to you.

Addressed: To / Benjamin Franklin Esqr.

Endorsed: Jac. Duché junr May 6. 57

2. In a letter to Timothy Horsfield, June 13, 1757 (APS), Parsons mentions receiving this letter.

3. See above, p. 170 n.

4. Duché was nineteen years old at the time of writing this commendation. Eleven days later he graduated in the first class of the College of Philadelphia. At the time of the newspaper controversies a year earlier he had been one of four students who had presented to the College Trustees a paper in support of Provost Smith, although his father was one of those Anglicans whom Peters had called "mere Franklinists." See above, VI, 456–7 n; Montgomery, *Hist. Univ. Pa.*, pp. 272–3. The present letter suggests that young Duché might by now have become a "Franklinist" himself, but less than a year later he was again supporting Smith.

From ———[5] AL (incomplete): American Philosophical Society

The accurate determination of longitude by a ship at sea long remained an unsolved problem.[6] Several theoretically possible methods were advanced during the two centuries and a half after Columbus, but when put to actual test none proved both practicable and sufficiently reliable to serve the needs of mariners, especially of those embarked on long east-west voyages, such as the crossing of the ocean. So urgent did the matter become that several large prizes were offered for the discovery of an accurate and usable method. Among these the British Parliament offered in 1714 a prize of £20,000 for any method capable of determining a ship's longitude within half a degree, with proportionately smaller prizes for methods of lesser exactitude; grants were also provided to assist promising experiments. The act placed the administration of the scheme in the hands of commissioners commonly called the Board of Longitude.[7]

The most promising method—and the one which ultimately won the prize—was by the construction of a timekeeper more reliable than any previously built, which, once set to accord with the local time at some point of known longitude, such as the Royal Observatory at Greenwich, England, could be carried on shipboard and compared with the local time at sea as found by celestial observation. The time when the sun or moon, for example, will be at a certain position in the sky at Greenwich on a given date can be predicted and set down in a table prepared in advance, and, since the earth revolves through one degree every four minutes, it becomes a simple calculation to convert the difference between Greenwich and local ship's time into degrees, minutes, and seconds of longitude east or west of Greenwich.[8]

5. The author of this letter has not been identified. He was obviously a Philadelphia clock- and watchmaker who was not personally acquainted with BF. The wording of his letter suggests that he was a man of limited education, or, at least, that a writer's pen was not one of the tools he could use most successfully. In the list of clockmakers of Philadelphia given in George H. Eckhardt, *Pennsylvania Clocks and Clockmakers* (N.Y., 1955), pp. 168–99, the following appear to be possibilities: Johann Ent, Augustine Neisser, Thomas Stretch, and Christopher Witt.

6. Much of this headnote is based upon Rupert T. Gould, *The Marine Chronometer Its History and Development* (London, 1923), esp. pp. 1–70.

7. An Act for providing a Publick Reward for such Person or Persons as shall discover the Longitude at Sea, 12 Anne c. 15.

8. For example, if the timekeeper shows Greenwich time to be 1:00 P.M. at the moment when observation from the ship shows local time to be exactly noon, the ship is precisely fifteen degrees west longitude from Greenwich.

That is, it is a simple matter if the timekeeper is unaffected by the ship's motion, even in a heavy storm, or by changes in temperature, humidity, gravity (at different points on the earth's surface), or other external conditions. It may gain or lose somewhat if that gain or loss is constant and has been ascertained in advance, but it must not fluctuate erratically. To determine the longitude of a ship within half a degree, after six weeks at sea, the timekeeper must be accurate to approximately three seconds a day throughout the voyage. And an error of considerably less than half a degree in determining a ship's position in unpropitious weather has often spelled disaster.[9] At the time of the Act of 1714 no timekeeper made could come close to meeting these conditions when taken to sea.

Inevitably the huge rewards offered by Parliament attracted the attention not only of mathematicians and ingenious mechanics, as they were intended to do, but also of cranks and visionaries, some of whom were as sure that they had solved this problem as they were that they could square the circle or create perpetual motion. The unknown writer of this letter to Franklin may indeed have been something of an ingenious mechanic, as he clearly esteemed himself to be, but even if one discounts heavily his inability to express himself with entire clarity, it seems necessary to class him with the many enthusiasts who bombarded the Board of Longitude with unworkable schemes for solving not only the problem officially before it but others quite outside its province.

It is an interesting coincidence, however, that the man who ultimately did win the parliamentary £20,000 for his chronometer, John Harrison (1693–1776), was at this very time completing one of his preliminary models in England and planning the device, finished in 1759, which won him the first half of the grand prize.[1] And there is

9. Relationship between degrees of longitude and nautical miles varies with the latitude. A nautical mile (1.1516 statute miles) equals one degree of longitude at the equator. Half a degree at the 40th parallel, the latitude of Philadelphia, is roughly 23 nautical miles.

1. Harrison's earlier timekeepers won him the Copley Medal of the Royal Society in 1749. His timekeeper No. 3 was finished in 1757 and he began at once to construct No. 4, which Gould calls "the most famous chronometer that ever has been or ever will be made" (*Marine Chronometer*, p. 49). It was placed on a naval vessel in 1761, carried on a voyage to Jamaica, tested there, returned to England on another ship, and proved to have a total unpredicted error during five months and two ocean crossings of only 1 minute, 53½ seconds of time or 28½ minutes of longitude. A second trial in 1764 showed even less error and the Board of Longitude reluctantly (because its members suspected a fluke) agreed to award Harrison £10,000. A protracted dispute

perhaps a touch of irony in the fact that Harrison, the son of a Yorkshire carpenter with virtually no formal education, could not put his ideas on paper any more effectively than could Franklin's Philadelphia correspondent. There is no evidence that Franklin ever brought this letter to the attention of the Board of Longitude after he reached England. He did, however, pay Harrison 10*s*. 6*d*. on Dec. 1, 1757, "to see his Longitude Clock."[2]

Worthey Sir Philada. May 10th. 1757

Not Haveing the Happiness of your Acquaintance I have at the instigation of Some of My Freinds and your Acquaintance Made bold to beg one Favour of you that is when in England to Lay this Letter before the Royal Society[3] which is to give them to under Stand that I have invented and try'd a Clock and have made a watch up of the Same Motion as the Clock which I Give this Name too for a Sort of a Description of its moving Power; its a Geometrical Celendrical Concave Triangle Horizontial Watch or Clock. I have taken the Clock Slung or Suspended it by a String and twist or work it how you will it goes as unaltriable as a fix'd Clock. The Way I first Discoverd it was indeavouring to Correct the Disadvantages of Common and Horizontial Watchess which are Great. Not only this I have Discovird but Have found a Principal or Cause in Nature to make a machine that will Go of its owne Cause for Stop your the wheel take your finger away it goes but When I add more wheels so as to make minutes Hours and Seconds it Stops but am in hopes by the Blessing of Almighty God—to bring it in a Short time to Perfection So as to Move on the Same Cause of the Watch and Clock for I Can Make the Watch as Well as the Clock Strike true Seconds. I have further invented a Watch or improved one So as to make it wind it Self up as it Goes. This I found out When apprentice as Well as a Collet for turning Watch or Clock Wheels Which were I in England as the work Men was to See it their is None of them

followed but finally, through the intervention of King George III, a special act of Parliament appropriated to him the second half of the grand prize in 1772. Including grants to assist his experiments, Harrison received a total of £22,550 from the Government for his work. *Ibid.*, pp. 40–70.

2. "Account of Expences," p. 8; *PMHB*, LV (1931), 106.

3. It would appear from this and later passages that the writer thought it was the Royal Society, rather than the Board of Longitude, which was to make awards for discovering a method of determining longitude.

but would Give a Guinea a Peice for it Saves a man half his Time in makeing a Clock or Watch for it fits Different Size arbours and Never Casts them. What has made me So Shy of Not Communicating it before was this my Good Friend Ls Es[4] I Shewe'd it to being a Curious man he Directley Privateley went to work and Sett others and Came to me for a Second Sight but Luckeley I Gest what he was after and was Confirm'd for then he Said he would Get a Patent for it but Wee Should Go halves in the Profit but their is No trusting Such men When one Detected in so base an Action. I have made a Great Number of Machines of one kind or other for the Despatch of Work that Would be too tedious to Mention time being Short. The afforesaid Ls Es thought to Amuse me out of Gilding and Polishing Which I have Brought to a Great Perfection and Said it was for a freind of his in Carolina but I repaid him in his owne Kind and Gave him the Receip he Gave me and Says he I told you I knew how to Do it as Well as you and So thought to Gett Some of my Practical Remarks but Was Mistaken for I had Receive'd an affront from a bigots of ED[5] of my owne Profesion about the trifeling Dial. I Must Acknowledge he is a better Nitting Nedle Case Maker than a Clock Watch or mathematical instrument Maker Witness Govenor Tinker[6] Reflecting telescope Which I made a New Mirror and alterd the focus of the Glassess he Spoild. Excuse me for this affront has Cause me to Ask the fa[vour] of the Gentlemen of the Society. NB Ls Es intended the Gilding &c for E, d. What is ment by the Perpetuial Motion and Londitude and what Reward[7] for I am Determind Never to Stir on uncertanties being in a Good Trade at Present but will Lett them Die With me if they

4. Possibly Lewis Evans is intended here, though the editors have found no evidence to show that he was the sort of man who would be guilty of the duplicity here charged.

5. Probably Edward Duffield (1720–1801) clock- and watchmaker of Philadelphia, 1741–47, and later of Lower Dublin, Philadelphia Co. He made at least one clock for BF, was elected to the APS, and was one of the executors of BF's last will.

6. John Tinker (d. 1758), governor of the Bahamas from 1740 to his death, visited Philadelphia in the fall of 1754 and attended the Academy exercises on November 12. *Pa. Gaz.*, Nov. 14, 1754.

7. Evidently the writer, like numerous others, believed erroneously that the Act of 1714 provided rewards for discovering perpetual motion as well as a method of determining longitude.

Cannot make it Worth my Wile to emprove to their Desir'd Satisfaction Which if I am Incouragd I am in No Doubt but by the Blessing of Almighty God I Shall in Due time do for I Can Say I Never Craved a favoir of the almighty God of Wisdom but in Due time I had my Desired end answer'd. Now Gentlemen Ile Give you as Plaine a Description of my Clock and Watch as I Dare Venture at Present.

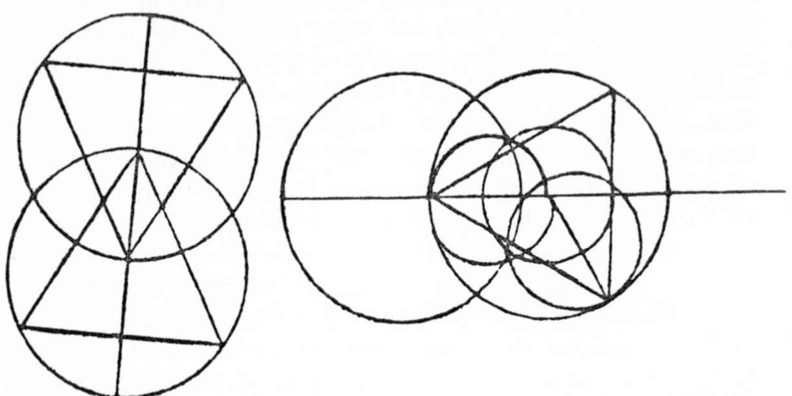

This I first made goe with two Globs and two Triangles but Now Goes With a Single of Each for the more Convenencey of Putting it into Watch Work.

Now Gentlemen I have Given you a Draught of it Exacttley How I Draw it on Steel and Brass and file and turn it Putt it to Geather and it shall ware time out of mind for Letts Reason a Common Watch has two Braking Pins Which Causess it to Hurrey and Go So much faster at Some times and So Slow at others. The Horizontial ones has remedyd this Misfortune but has one as Great that is if they are un[*illegible*] in Winding She Will Stop a Little[8] [Dirtey?] is the Same and the Worst Take of[f] the Regulating Spring or you Cannot move the Celinder. If you

8. While the writer's exact meaning cannot be determined, this is clearly a reference to a common failing of early clocks and watches, which stopped when the motive power (whether a spring or a weight) was being rewound. The difficulty had been overcome by Jeremy Thacker in 1714 and again independently by John Harrison in 1735 by the addition of an auxiliary spring called the "maintaining power." Gould, *Marine Chronometer*, pp. 34, 44.

Press the Wheel so as to Break it and the Nex thing It is not till further [*sic*] for I shall Describe my owne but this I can assure you this of mine is Such that it moves So Light that your 1 or 2 Pinion Shall be wore out Sooner than the Regulating Cause that is the Triangles and Globes besides the force Given is Such that Without the Regulating Spring you Cannot Stop them. No Longer than you hold your finger or Point against the Moveing Cause though I make it Go true time without a regulating Spring I mus Needs Say that if you Saw one you would Say as Samuel Kirk said the most ignorant man in the World Would be Convins'd its So Demonstriable to Sight that I Cannot Describe it With my Pen. You Can No more Err in Makin the Size of Each triangle and Globe than in Makeing a Pinion of 6 to a Wheel of 48 for to Make it Ware well it must be the Height of [*illegible*] and an [?] but How to Regulate this. [*Remainder missing*].

William Franklin to Elizabeth Graeme

ALS: American Philosophical Society

My dearest Betsy, New-York, May 12, 1757

I am this Moment return'd from an Excursion of four or five Days in the Jerseys.[9] The Mail is made up and the Post just upon his Departure. I detain him just to acknowledge the Receipt of two Letters from you, which I have not Time to read thro'.

This is all that I can possibly say at present; your Regard imagine the rest, for Your truely affectionate FRANKLIN

9. In a letter dated May 16, William describes this excursion more fully: "Our Stay here was so tedious that my Father determined upon a little Excursion in the Jerseys. Our Party consisted of some Gentlemen and Ladies of this Place, and my Mother and Sister, who had come to Woodbridge in Expectation of spending a few Days with my Father before his Departure. Our Ride was to Newark, Passayak Falls, and to Col. Schuyler's Copper Mines. The face of the Country, its many Improvements, the Variety of romantic Prospects which almost everywhere abound afforded me far greater Pleasure than any Thing I had ever seen before. Indeed I had not the least Idea that Views so agreeably enchanting were to be met with in America." The letter goes on at length to explain how busy he has been and how much he regrets her not having taken an opportunity that arose to come to New York. *PMHB*, XXXIX (1915), 262–3. On the Passaic Falls and Colonel Schuyler's estate, see above, III, 465–6.

To [Peter Franklin][1] ALS: American Philosophical Society

Dear Brother, Woodbridge, N Jersey May 21. 1757

I have been now near 6 Weeks waiting for the Sailing of the Pacquet, and know not yet when she is like to sail.

I received yours of the 7th Inst.[2] with the Invoice and Memorandum, which I shall endeavour to comply with. As to the Pay, I expect not to meddle with your Paper Currency; for I always lose by it.[3] With the Goods I shall send Directions about the Time and Manner of Payment.

My Love to dear Sister[4] and Thanks for your and her kind Wishes and Prayers, is all at present from Your affectionate Brother B FRANKLIN

My Wife is here, but Billy and Sally are at New York. If they were present they would join with her in Love to you, Duty, &c.

Endorsed: Brother & Sisters Letters & my Coppies

The Price Currant [Janury?] you of the Last Payment.[5]

To the Earl of Loudoun ALS: Huntington Library

My Lord, Woodbridge, N. Jersey.[6] May 21. 1757

Having determined not to go in the first Pacquet, I retired hither about two Weeks ago, to have Leisure for Settling some private Affairs before the Sailing of the second; which is the Reason I have not for some time been to pay my Respects to your Lordship.

In your present Multiplicity of important Business, I would not be too importunate. But if your Lordship should think it fit, and can spare a few Minutes to appoint some Persons of Credit in

1. This letter is almost certainly to Peter Franklin (C.9), merchant and shipmaster of Newport, BF's only surviving brother. None of his living brothers-in-law, James Davenport, Edward Mecom, and John Read, followed an occupation which suggests his asking BF to send goods from England.

2. Not found.

3. Rhode Island currency was notoriously inflationary and unstable, although the parliamentary act of 1751 had halted some of the earlier excesses.

4. Peter Franklin's wife was the former Mary Harmon.

5. This endorsement, written very lightly, is virtually undecipherable.

6. See above, p. 174, for BF's visit to Woodbridge and other activities while awaiting passage to England.

Pensilvania, or direct Governor Denny to nominate them, to enquire into the Claims of the Masters whose Servants have been taken into the Service from that Province, and report thereon to your Lordship when the Campain shall be over, it would in the meantime quiet the Minds of the Sufferers, as well as show your Lordship's Regard for Justice.[7]

I hear it is reported, that the second Pacquet is to accompany the Fleet, and that the third may probably be sooner in England. If this is so, a Hint of it from your Secretary would be esteem'd a great Favour,[8] by him who has the Honour to be, with the sincerest Respect and Attachment, My Lord, Your Lordship's most obedient and most humble Servant B FRANKLIN

Rt. Honble. Earl of Loudoun

To Jane Mecom

MS not found; reprinted from Jared Sparks, ed., *A Collection of Familiar Letters and Miscellaneous Pieces of Benjamin Franklin* (Boston, 1833), pp. 52–3.[9]

Dear Sister, Woodbridge, New Jersey, 21 May, 1757.

I received your kind letter of the 9th instant,[1] in which you acquainted me with some of your late troubles. These are troublesome times to us all; but perhaps you have had more than you should. I am glad to hear that Peter is at a place where he has full employ.[2] A trade is a valuable thing; but, unless a habit of industry be acquired with it, it turns out of little use; if he gets *that* in his new place, it will be a happy exchange, and the occasion not an unfortunate one.

It is very agreeable to me to hear so good an account of your

7. See below, pp. 224–8, for the negotiations over indentured servants.

8. BF commented at length in the autobiography about Loudoun's long delay in dispatching the packets; Par. Text edit., pp. 394–404.

9. While Duane (*Works*, VI, 16–17) printed this letter several years before Sparks did, his version contains apparent misreadings and omits the postscript entirely; hence the Sparks text is reprinted here.

1. Not found.

2. Peter Franklin Mecom (C.17.6), now eighteen, had been apprenticed to his uncle John Franklin as soapmaker and tallow chandler. His present "place" is not known, except that he was concerned with the making of soap. See below, p. 221.

other children; in such a number to have no bad ones is a great happiness.[3]

The horse sold very low indeed. If I wanted one to-morrow, knowing his goodness, old as he is, I should freely give more than twice the money for him; but you did the best you could, and I will take of Benny no more than he produced.[4]

I don't doubt but Benny will do very well when he gets to work; but I fear his things from England may be so long a coming, as to occasion the loss of the rent.[5] Would it not be better for you to move into the house? Perhaps not, if he is near being married.[6] I know nothing of that affair, but what you write me, except that I think Miss Betsey a very agreeable, sweet-tempered, good girl, who has had a housewifely education, and will make, to a good husband, a very good wife. Your sister and I have a great esteem for her, and if she will be kind enough to accept of our nephew, we think it will be his own fault, if he is not as happy as the married state can make him. The family is a respectable one, but whether there be any fortune I know not; and as you do not inquire about this particular, I suppose you think with me, that where every thing else desirable is to be met with, that is not very material. If she does not *bring* a fortune she will help to *make* one. Industry, frugality, and prudent economy in a wife, are to a tradesman, in their effects, a fortune; and a fortune sufficient for Benjamin, if his expectations are reasonable. We can only add, that, if the young lady and her friends are willing, we give our consent heartily, and our blessing. My love to brother and the children. Your affectionate brother, B. FRANKLIN.

P.S. If Benny will promise to be one of the tenderest husbands in the world, I give my consent. He knows already what I think of Miss Betsey. I am his loving aunt, DEBORAH FRANKLIN.

3. Jane Mecom had given birth to twelve children, of whom nine were still living.

4. Van Doren (*Franklin-Mecom,* p. 58) explains that BF had furnished Benny Mecom with a horse, presumably for the trip from Philadelphia to Boston the previous winter, to be sold after reaching home.

5. On Benjamin Mecom's plans to set up a printing office and bookshop in Boston, see above, p. 68.

6. Benjamin Mecom married (exact date unknown) Elizabeth Ross, almost certainly the daughter of John Ross (d. 1754), former mayor of Elizabeth Town, N.J. Van Doren, *Franklin-Mecom,* pp. 58–9.

To Ezra Stiles

ALS: Horace Howard Furness Memorial Library, University of Pennsylvania

Dear Sir, New York, May 23. 1757

I have been waiting here near Six Weeks for the sailing of the Pacquet, and know not yet when that will be.[7] From London I will send you the Account you desire of the Verification of the Meridian of France;[8] and one of the best Thermometers I can procure. If in any thing else I can do you pleasure, signify it by a Line directed to me at the Pensilvania Coffee House in Birchin Lane. I shall always be glad to hear of your Welfare, being, with sincere Esteem and Regard, Dear Sir, Affectionately yours

B FRANKLIN

Addressed: To / The Revd Mr Ezra Stiles / at Newport / Rhode-Island / Free / B FRANKLIN

Endorsed: Benja Franklin Esqr. May 23. 1757. Recd. 28 May 1757. Wrote to Mr. Franklin in London Mar. 30. 1758—by Capt. Gallatly.

To Deborah Franklin

ALS: American Philosophical Society

New York, Friday, May 27. 57

My dear Debby Afternoon

Mr. Parker being doubtful this Morning, whether the Rain would permit his setting out to day, I had prepared no Letter to send per Sally when he took a sudden Resolution to go. Mr.

7. WF wrote to Elizabeth Graeme on this same day: "I am just now informed, that we are likely to embark to morrow or next Day at farthest. This occasions me a great Deal of Hurry as I did not expect that the Fleet could possibly be ready till the next Week. But such Dispatch has been made by my Lord and Sir Charles that all the Forces are on Board the Transports, and most of them fell down to the Hook." But he added a postscript: "Perhaps another Post may reach me. If it should not my Letters will be forwarded by the first Pacquet." Darlington Memorial Library, Univ. of Pittsburgh.

8. César François Cassini de Thury, *La Méridienne de l'Observatoire royale de Paris, verifiée* (Paris, 1744; Suite des Mémoires de l'Académie royale des Sciences, année MDCCXL).

Colden[9] could not spare his Daughter, as she helps him in the Post Office, he having no Clerk.

I inclose only the 4th. Bills, which you are to put up safe with my Writings; the first Set I take with me, the second goes in Radford, and I now send the third by Bonnel.[1]

All the Pacquets are to sail together with the Fleet, but when that will be is yet uncertain. For yesterday came in three Privateers with several Prizes,[2] and by them there is Advice, that the French Fleet which was in the West Indies, is gone to the Northward, and now 'tis question'd whether it will be thought prudent for these Transports to sail, till there is certain Advice that the Grand Fleet is arrived from England. This, however, is only Town Talk.

I send Mr. Kneeland's[3] Letter. Pray forward the Paper he writes for per first Opportunity.

I send a Memorandum receiv'd from Joseph Crocker,[4] with a Note on the Back of it.

I leave it to yourself, whether to go home directly or stay a little longer. If I find we are not like to sail for some time I shall perhaps step down again to Woodbridge and try to finish my Work. But it may be that your longer Absence from home will be attended with some Inconvenience.

I am making up a Bundle of Papers to send you. Put them into my Room.

I can hear nothing yet of the Cloaths.

9. Alexander Colden, postmaster of New York, at whose house Sally Franklin had been visiting.

1. Radford (or Ratford) was captain of the *Earl of Leicester*, Bonnell of the *Harriott*, both packet boats. As noted in the postscript of this letter, Radford died a few days later.

2. The privateers *Johnson*, *Hawke*, and *Charming Sally* brought into New York as prizes, May 26, three ships, a brig, and a snow, with "very valuable" cargoes of sugar, cotton, indigo, and coffee, which were promptly offered for sale in the city. *N.-Y. Mercury*, May 30, 1757.

3. See above, p. 180.

4. Joseph Croker (or Crocker) was a connection of DF through her sister Frances, wife of John Croker. A mason and stonecutter, he executed the lettering on the stone BF erected in Boston for his parents' graves. See below, p. 229. One of a party of workmen sent to build a house for Teedyuscung, he was killed and scalped by Indians precisely one year after BF wrote this letter. *Pa. Col. Recs.*, VII, 134–5.

I have been very low-spirited all Day; this tedious State of Uncertainty and long Waiting, has almost worn out my Patience. Except the two or three Weeks at Woodbridge, I know [not when] I have spent Time so uselessly as since I left [Philadelphia].

I left my best Spectacles on the Table. Please to send them to me.

Saturday Morning

Jemmy[5] got here early and tells me Mr. Parker and the Children got well down.

In my Room, on the Folio Shelf, between the Clock and our Bed Chamber, and not far from the Clock, stands a Folio call'd the Gardener's Dictionary, by P. Miller.[6]

And on the same Side of the Room on the lowest Shelf, or lowest but one, near the Middle, and by the Side of a little Partition, you will find standing or rather lying on its fore Edge, a Quarto Pamphlet, cover'd with blue Paper call'd a Treatise of Cyder-making.[7]

Deliver those two Books to Mr. Parker.

Sunday Afternoon

Yesterday while I was at my Lord's, with whom I had the Honour to dine, Word was brought in, that 5 Sail of French Men of War were seen off Egg Harbour[8] the Day before, and as some of the French Prisoners lately brought in in the Prizes reported that such a Number of Men of War sailed with them from the West Indies to go to the Northward, it might be suppos'd to be them if the Account from Egg Harbour was true. If on Examination it should be found true, and the French take it in their Heads to cruize off this Port with such a Force, we shall then be shut up here for some time, for our Fleet here is not of Force sufficient to venture out. If this story be not true, yet 'tis thought by some we shall hardly sail till there is certain Advice of the English Fleet's being arriv'd at Halifax, and perhaps not till a Convoy comes from thence hither to guard us.[9] So I am

5. Not identified; possibly a servant of James Parker.

6. Philip Miller, *The Gardener's Dictionary*, 6th edit., in one vol. (London, 1752).

7. Sir Hugh Stafford, *A Treatise on Cyder-Making* (London, 1753). See above, V, 268 n.

8. Probably Great Egg Harbor, at the present Ocean City, N.J.

9. BF puts the general quandary properly, but on the 28th, the day he dined

wavering whether I had not best go down again to Woodbridge, and finish my Books.

I spent the Evening last Night with Mr. Nichols's Family,[1] who all desired their Compliments to you and Sally.

I send one of the French Books translated.[2]

Monday Morning. Our going is yet uncertain. I believe I shall put every thing on board to morrow, and either go down again [to Wood]bridge, or send for the Trunk of Books hither, to employ myself till we have [Word to board?].

I have wrote to Sister Jenny, and [hope] to quiet [*torn*] them. Family Quarrels are the [*torn*] most indiscreet [and sca]ndalous of [Quarrels. So?] let me beg of you my dear [Wife not] to have any [Part in] this. Write [*torn*] about in in my Absence.[3] [Your] loving [Husband] B FRANKLIN

---

with Loudoun, the decision had been made to sail for Halifax in spite of the risk, and on the 29th Loudoun learned that the French fleet probably was bound directly for Louisbourg, perhaps the source of BF's comment in the postscript of this letter. Loudoun Notebooks (Huntington Lib.); Gertrude S. Kimball, ed., *Correspondence of William Pitt* (N.Y., 1906), I, 70–2.

1. Richard Nicholls, former postmaster of New York. See above, II, 407 n.

2. This is probably *Mémoire contenant le précis des faits, avec leur pieces justificatives . . .* (Paris, 1756), containing documents on Anglo-French affairs, 1749–56, including some captured from Washington and Braddock, notably Washington's "journal" taken at Fort Necessity in 1754. Copies of the French work were found on prizes at sea and brought into Philadelphia and New York. James Chattin advertised in *Pa. Gaz.*, Feb. 17, 1757, the forthcoming publication by subscription of a translation, and he announced its readiness May 26, under the title *A Memorial containing a summary Account of Facts, with the Authorities, in Answer to the Observations sent by the English Ministry to the Courts of Europe* (Evans 7897). In the *N.-Y. Mercury*, June 6, 1757, Hugh Gaine announced an independent edition then in press, which would be sold cheaper than the Philadelphia version (Evans 7896). There is also a New York edition in the same year bearing the imprint of J. Parker and W. Weyman (Evans 7895). Washington, in Philadelphia at the time of Chattin's first announcement, investigated and declared that the French text of his "journal" was a distorted version of his notes, March 31 to June 27, 1754, with omissions and unjustified elaborations. He prepared a hasty correction which Chattin offered his subscribers as an appendix to his edition. *Pa. Gaz.*, May 26, 1757; Douglas S. Freeman, *George Washington,* II (N.Y., 1948), 236–7.

3. For what can be deduced concerning this family quarrel see the next document.

Postscript. I wish you would, per next Post, write a Letter to Sister Jenny, and recommend a Reconciliation. Capt. Radford is at length dead.

The Report of French Men of War off the Coast is vanished.

Addressed: To / Mrs Franklin / at / Woodbridge

To Jane Mecom

MS not found; reprinted from Duane, *Works*, VI, 18–20.

Dear Sister, New York, May 30, 1757.

I have before me yours of the 9th and 16th instant;[4] I am glad you have resolved to visit sister Dowse oftener; it will be a great comfort to her, to find she is not neglected by you, and your example may, perhaps, be followed by some other of her relations.[5]

As Neddy is yet a young man, I hope he may get over the disorder he complains of, and in time wear it out.[6] My love to him and his wife and the rest of your children. It gives me pleasure to hear that Eben is likely to get into business at his trade.[7] If he will be industrious and frugal, 'tis ten to one but he gets rich, for he seems to have spirit and activity.

I am glad that Peter is acquainted with the crown soap business, so as to make what is good of the kind.[8] I hope he will always take care to make it faithfully, never slight manufacture, or attempt to deceive by appearances. Then he may boldly put his name and mark, and in a little time it will acquire as good a character as that made by his late uncle, or any other person whatever. I believe his aunt at Philadelphia, can help him to sell a good deal of it; and I doubt not of her doing every thing in her power to promote his interest in that way. Let a box be sent to her (but not unless it be right good) and she will immediately

4. Neither letter found.

5. See above, p. 190.

6. Edward Mecom, Jr. (C. 17.2), Jane's eldest living son, aged 26, a saddler, suffered from tuberculosis; he died Dec. 7, 1758.

7. Ebenezer Mecom (C. 17.4), Jane's third eldest living son, aged 22, a baker.

8. On Peter Franklin Mecom (C. 17.6), see above, p. 215 n. For the Franklin family's manufacture of green soap, stamped with a crown as a sign of quality, see above, I, 348 n.

return the ready money for it. It was beginning once to be in vogue in Philadelphia, but brother John sent me one box, an ordinary sort, which checked its progress. I would not have him put the Franklin arms on it;[9] but the soapboilers arms he has a right to use, if he thinks fit. The other would look too much like an attempt to counterfeit. In his advertisements, he may value himself on serving his time with the original maker, but put his own mark or device on the papers, or any thing he may be advised to as proper; only on the soap, as it is called by the name of crown soap, it seems necessary to use a stamp of that sort, and perhaps no soapboiler in the king's dominions has a better right to the crown than himself.

Nobody has wrote a syllable to me concerning his making use of the hammer, or made the least complaint of him or you.[1] I am sorry however that he took it without leave. It was irregular, and if you had not approved of his doing it, I should have thought it indiscreet. *Leave* they say is *light,* and it seems to me a piece of respect that was due to his aunt to ask it, and I can scarce think she would have refused him the favour.

I am glad to hear Jamey[2] is so good and diligent a workman; if he ever sets up at the goldsmith's business, he must remember that there is one accomplishment without which he cannot possibly thrive in that trade, (i.e. *to be perfectly honest*). It is a business that though ever so uprightly managed, is always liable to suspicion; and if a man is once detected in the smallest fraud it soon becomes public, and every one is put upon their guard against him; no one will venture to try his hands, or trust him to make up their plate; so at once he is ruined. I hope my nephew will therefore establish a character as an *honest* and faithful, as well as *skilful* workman, and then he need not fear employment.

And now as to what you propose for Benny I believe he may be, as you say, well enough qualified for it, and when he appears

9. On the Franklin arms, see above, II, 229–30 n.

1. The editors are as much in the dark as was BF concerning this family argument. It may be related in some way to the quarrel mentioned in the final paragraph of this letter.

2. Clearly an error in transcription by Duane for "Johnny." Jane's son John Mecom (C. 17.7), aged 16, was apprenticed to his cousin William Homes (C. 10.1), a Boston goldsmith, and later followed that trade. Her son James (C. 17.10) was born in 1746 and died at the age of four months.

to be settled, if a vacancy should happen, it is very probable he may be thought of to supply it;[3] but it is a rule with me, not to remove any officer that behaves well, keeps regular accounts, and pays duly; and I think the rule is founded on reason and justice. I have not shown any backwardness to assist Benny, where it could be done without injuring another. But if my friends require of me to gratify not only their inclinations, but their resentments, they expect too much of me. Above all things I dislike family quarrels, and when they happen among my relations, nothing gives me more pain. If I were to set myself up as a judge of those subsisting between you and brother's widow and children, how unqualified must I be, at this distance, to determine rightly, especially having heard but one side. They always treated me with friendly and affectionate regard, you have done the same. What can I say between you, but that I wish you were reconciled, and that I will love that side best that is most ready to forgive and oblige the other. You will be angry with me here, for putting you and them too much upon a footing, but I shall nevertheless be, Dear sister, your truly Affectionate brother,

B. FRANKLIN.

To Isaac Norris

Draft: American Philosophical Society

Sir, New York, May 30. 1757.

After waiting here above Seven Weeks for the Sailing of the Pacquet, the Time of her Departure is no more ascertain'd now than it was the Day of our Arrival.

The Pacquets it is now said are all three to sail with the Fleet; the two first to be dismiss'd soon after the Fleet is at Sea; the third to go with the Fleet to the Place of Rendezvous, and not to be discharg'd till the Arrival and Junction of the Fleet from England.

3. Apparently Jane and other members of her family wanted BF to appoint Benjamin Mecom (C. 17.3) postmaster of Boston in place of Tuthill Hubbart, whom BF and Hunter had named to the position following the death of his stepfather, BF's brother John. See above, VI, 422. From what follows in this paragraph and from BF's letter to DF, May 27 (printed immediately above) it appears that there was a good deal of bad feeling between the Mecoms on the one hand and John Franklin's widow and stepchildren on the other. Doubtless the fact that the postmastership had gone to a stepnephew rather than to one of BF's blood relatives enhanced the ill will.

But this is not certain: Resolutions change as Advices are receiv'd or Occurrences arise.[4] And it is doubted whether the Fleet will sail from hence till there is certain News of the Arrival of that from [Englan]d. Since there is Intelligence that Beaufremont's Squadron is gone from the W. Indies to the Northward.[5]

I have had the Honour of several Conferences with my Lord on the Subject of the Servants.[6] His Lordship objects first that it

4. BF first included here in the draft, and then struck out, two uncompleted passages which together indicated that, when he "went from hence to Woodbridge, where I retir'd for about three Weeks, the better to settle some more of my own Affairs," he asked Loudoun to send him a "timely Hint" as to when the packet was to sail. Later he had received word that it was to depart on May 23; "But she is still here." See the postscript below.

5. The three packets, the *General Wall* (on which BF sailed), the *Earl of Leicester*, and the *Harriott*, did proceed according to BF's report. Rumors that Vice Admiral Chevalier de Bauffremont's fleet lay off New York persisted, but in fact it had arrived off Cape Breton Island on May 28, and three days later was anchored in Louisbourg harbor. When Loudoun finally sailed, June 20, he still did not know exactly where either the French or English fleet was. Pargellis, *Lord Loudoun*, pp. 237–8; Gipson, *British Empire*, VII, 101–4; Loudoun Notebooks, Huntington Lib.

6. See above, VI, 396–400, 474–5, for earlier difficulties over enlistment of indentured servants. At his last meeting with BF in Philadelphia, March 26, Loudoun had recorded that "Having been assured by Lt. Col. Bouquet that the Assembly were to pay all the Indentured Servants listed in the Province of Pennsylvania[,] as he had been [often informed?] by the Principal Men of Philadelphia [*illegible*] I asked Mr. Frankland about it.

"Mr. Frankland says he knows of no Intention they have of paying any thing for Indented servants[.]

"I asked what was the Meaning of the £10,000 he wrote to Mr. Pownal the Assembly had Raised for the King's Use [see above, VI, 503].

"He sade the Governor would not pas that Bill but [he was at the?] time [being] in Conjunction with the other Provinces but as none of the others came into that publick fund, they had no thoughts of it.

"That the [Reason for desiering?] a Receipt from the Officer that Enlisted an Indented Servant was that the Committee of [Grievances?] might be able to make a list of them that they might applie Home for Redress.

"I sade in [if?] that affair of Recruiting was immediately under me in the first Instance I thought it extraordinary they should applie home before they First tried whether I would settel it with them and desiered to See the List they had made up.

"He told me it was not finished but I should have a Coppy as soon as it was made out." Loudoun Notebooks.

On March 28, the Assembly ordered that a list of sums due masters for enlisted servants be prepared "with all convenient Dispatch." *Votes*, 1756–

appears by the List, which I laid before him that many of the Servants were inlisted in General Braddock and Gen. Shirley's time; with those he has nothing to do. 2dly. That many were inlisted before the Act of Parliament appointed Satisfaction to be made to the Masters; and as all the Lawyers agree, that the Right to take them without Pay was clearly in the King before the Act, no Satisfaction should be made or expected for those. 3d. That the particular Proofs of the Loss of each Servant, and of his being inlisted in the K's Service do not appear. 4th. That the Affair is now so intricate and perplex'd, that it would take more time to examine and settle it than he can possibly spare. 5th. That if his Officers had done wrong in not paying for the Servants as they took them, the Fault was our own; it was owing to some principal People among our selves, whom he could name, who had always assur'd the Officers the Assembly intended to pay for the Servants; and by that Means led them into the Error. His Lordship made several other Observations and Objections, all which I answered and endeavoured to remove as well as I could;[7]

57, p. 105. BF received the list in New York by April 25, and that day conferred with Loudoun about it, (see above, p. 198, and see note 7 below for an explanation of the list). Places where the account of the conversations in Loudoun's Notebook adds to BF's summary are noted below. Though Loudoun recorded meetings with BF on April 9, 15, 25, 26, and 30, he set down remarks about indentured servants only on the 25th, at a conference also attended by Maj. Gen. James Abercromby.

7. Loudoun seems to have been firmly convinced that Pennsylvania had at one time agreed to reimburse masters, since he again asked about the £10,000 granted him in the rejected £60,000 bill of September 1756, and said that recruiting officers did not give certificates to masters since they were not asked for in view of the general assumption that the province would take care of any just claims. An advertisement in *Pa. Gaz.*, Nov. 18, 1756, may have encouraged this assumption; it asked masters "who have in any manner suffered by the late Enlisting of Servants and Apprentices" to report particulars to local assemblymen or the Committee of Grievances for the "Consideration" of the Assembly. Loudoun also objected again to the application for redress in England without first making a proper complaint to him, and he upbraided BF for the failure of Pennsylvania to carry out the terms of the new act of Parliament regulating recruitment (see above, VI, 400 n). Loudoun further pointed out that he had asked for the list of claimants in Philadelphia, and now, a month later, he was given an improper and incomplete list. To BF's suggestion that Denny appoint persons to investigate claims, Loudoun replied that the recruiting officers would have to be heard as well as the claimants, and since

but there is, I believe, one at Bottom, which it is not in my Power to remove, and that is the Want of Money. The Expences of an American War necessarily run very high;[8] and are complain'd of by some in England; and his [Lordship is un]willing to discourage the Ministry at home by large [demands?]. He will therefore mix none of those of his Predecessors with his own, makes the most frugal Agreements, and avoids all Payments that he can avoid with Honour. For Instance, there is a Ballance not very large, due to me on my Account of Waggons and Forage Supply'd to General Braddock. I presented the Account to his Lordship, who had it examin'd and compar'd with the Vouchers, and on Report made to him that it was right, order'd a Warrant to be drawn for the Payment. But before he sign'd it, he sent for me, told me that as the Money became due before his time he had rather not mix it in his Accounts; it would be the same thing to me to receive it in England; he believ'd it a fair and just Account and as such would represent it home, so that I should meet with no Difficulty in getting it paid there. I agreed to his Lordship's Proposal, and the Warrant was laid aside.[9]

---

the officers were off on summer campaigns, nothing could be done at present. Loudoun Notebooks. If Loudoun conveyed the same impressions to BF that he recorded in his diary, the latter could scarcely have avoided the conclusion that Loudoun thought Pennsylvania had defaulted on a promise to pay the injured masters and had deceitfully thrown together a hasty list of claims it hoped to impose upon the King's commander. Loudoun may very well have implied that BF acted a bad part in presenting such fraudulent claims. If so, this might explain why BF spoke so contemptuously of Loudoun in the autobiography (Par. Text edit., pp. 400–2), after having been much in his confidence and spoken so well of him during their months of association in New York and Philadelphia.

8. At this point BF first wrote and then crossed out "and the expected Cash is not yet arrived, and the long Embargo has slacken'd the Sale of Bills."

9. Loudoun recorded in his notebook, April 26, that BF's unsettled account of £17 12*s.* 6*d.* should have been presented to Commissary General Robert Leake along with the other wagon charges. Four days later Loudoun said he "again" told "Mr. Frankline" he would not settle the wagon accounts, not only because he insisted on separating his affairs from those of Braddock and Shirley, but also because the charge was excessive for the service performed. This conversation is probably the source of BF's later comment that Loudoun had accused him of having profiteered in the wagon affair (Par. Text edit., pp. 402–4), though it is surprising that BF should here report to Norris that the account had been approved.

I once propos'd to his Lordship that if he would appoint[1] or desire Gov. Denny to appoint some Persons of Credit in Pensilvania to examine the Claims of the Masters, and report to his Lordship at the End of the Campaign, it might for the present make the Minds of the Sufferers more easy, and he could then order Payment for such Part as he should find right for him to pay, and we might endeavour to procure Satisfaction elsewhere for the rest. His Lordship declin'd this, saying that he knew not who to appoint, being unacquainted with the People; that he did not care to trouble Govr. Denny with it; of whom he must ask it as a Favour; and besides, Auditors in the Plantations, of Accounts against the Crown, had in many Instances been so shamefully partial and corrupt, that they had lost all Credit. If he appointed Auditors, they must be some of the Officers [of] the Army, who were acquainted and understood the Affair, and at present they were engag'd in other Duty.

I will not trouble you with a Detail of all I said to his Lordship on this Affair tho' I omitted nothing material that occurr'd to me. But I find he is for keeping the Matter in Suspense, without either promising Payment or refusing to pay; perhaps till he receives Direction about it from home. He does not seem to like however that I should make any Application there relating to it; and chuses to keep the List in his Hands, till his Return from the Campaign.

The List is indeed so very imperfect, that I could not promise my self much from laying it before him. Of many Servants it is not noted by what Officers, or in what Company or even in what Regiment they were inlisted; of others the Time they were bound for, or had served, or had still to serve, is omitted: Of others, no Notice is taken of the Price they cost. Nor is there any Distinction of Apprentices. Tho' perhaps the Account is the best that could be obtained the Time and other Circumstances considered.[2] Upon

1. BF wrote the first part of this sentence "I intimated to his Lordship that if he would appoint Parsons as," but then changed it to the form here printed. Apparently BF did suggest his old friend William Parsons as a fit person to review the claims, but then decided not to tell Norris about it.

2. The list sent to BF and put into Loudoun's hands survives among the general's papers at the Huntington Lib. Entitled "List of Servants, Belonging to the Inhabitants of Pensilvania, and taken into His Majesty's Service, For whom Satisfaction has not been made by the officers according to Act of Par-

the whole, as the Enquiry, if it is ever made by my Lord's Order, will be by Officers of the Army, they being in his Lordship's Opinion the fittest Persons and most impartial; as all Inlistments before the Commencement of his Command, will be rejected, and also all before the Act of Parliament; As very clear Proofs of every Circumstance, when the Servant was inlisted, by what Officer, of what Regiment, &c. &c. will be insisted on, and the Recruit[ing] Officers at the Time took such effectual Care to prevent in many Instances, the Masters knowing any thing of those Circumstances;[3] I am enclin'd to think very little Benefit will be produc'd by such Enquiry; and that our Application home for some Allowance on that Account will be better founded on what the Assembly after their own Enquiry have thought themselves oblig'd to pay, than on such an imperfect List as has been sent me. This however I submit. And if it should be still thought proper to apply in England on the Footing of that List another Copy must be sent by some future Opportunity.

His Lordship has on all Occasions treated me with the greatest Goodness,[4] but I find frequently that strong Prejudices are infus'd into his Mind against our Province. We have too many Enemies among our selves; I hope in time Things will wear a better Face.

Please to present my humble Respects to the House, and believe me, with great Esteem, Sir &c.

---

liament," and endorsed "Philada April 21st 1757 This List is not yet compleat, the Claims continuing to come in daily," the list records claims for 612 servants amounting to £3652 0*s.* ½*d.* Pennsylvania currency, or £2272 7*s.* 1*d.* sterling. For complete entries, the list records the name of the master and the servant for whom a claim is entered, the total time of the servant's indenture, the time served, the time of service due, the total amount paid for the servant, and, calculated from these figures, the amount due the masters for service lost. The list also records the regiment or company in which the servant enlisted, though in over 200 of the 612 entries that information is missing, and some of the entries are incomplete in other particulars. In no case is the date or place of enlistment or the name of the recruiting officer noted.

3. BF here wrote and then crossed out "for fear of Arrest."

4. BF here wrote and then crossed out "and given me frequent [opportunity?] of justifying our Pro[ceedings?]." In addition to the conferences with BF, mentioned above, Loudoun recorded conversations with him on April 15 and 30 about postal service to Albany. Loudoun Notebooks.

P.S.[5] Sunday morning June 5. At length we are going on board: All the Pacquets as I wrote above fall down together; and tis said the Fleet will certainly sail to morrow—But how little those Notices are to be depended you will see by the enclos'd wrote and sent to me at Woodbridge two Weeks ago by Capt. Conyngham, one of my Lord's Aid de Camps[6] by my Lord's Order.

Epitaph of Josiah and Abiah Franklin

Printed in *The New-England Magazine of Knowledge and Pleasure*, I (1758), 58.

Franklin composed an epitaph for the stone which he erected on the brick monument over his parents' grave in the Granary Burying Ground in Boston.[7] Though the exact dates of composition and placement of the stone are unknown, it is probable that he attended to the matter shortly before his departure for England, since his nephew Benjamin Mecom printed the inscription in August 1758 with this explanation: "The following EPITAPH was taken from a Tomb-Stone of Pennsylvania Marble, lately erected in the Burial-Place opposite to the Manufactury-House, in Boston. The *Letters* are very well formed: For this Specimen of superior Ability in his Business the *young* Artist deserves Commendation; though he that cut the Stone, is now in the *same State* with those whom it is intended to commemorate: He was lately shot dead by some lurking Indians on the Frontiers of Pennsylvania."[8]

By 1826 the inscription on the stone had been largely effaced and the monument was "in a state of dilapidation." A group of Boston citizens, led by Dr. John C. Warren, subscribed $940 and, with the permission of the Boston City Council and Franklin's heirs in Philadelphia, erected a new granite monument in the form of a twenty-foot pyramid.[9] The name FRANKLIN is carved on one side and below it

5. On a separate sheet. Though not certainly a postscript to this letter to Norris, it is included here since its second sentence repeats information BF had written and then crossed out on the first sheet of this letter.

6. Capt. James Cunningham of the 45th Regiment. Pargellis, *Lord Loudoun*, p. 167.

7. Par. Text edit., pp. 26–7.

8. *New-Eng. Mag.*, I, 57. The unfortunate young artist was Joseph Croker; see above, p. 218 n.

9. The documents relating to this action are in Mass. Hist. Soc. *Proc.*, XLV (1912), 484–93. John Collins Warren (1778–1856) was the eldest son of John Warren (1753–1815), Boston patriot and surgeon, and nephew of Joseph Warren (1741–1775), killed at the Battle of Bunker Hill. The new monument

a bronze tablet repeats, with slight modifications, the words of the epitaph. A further inscription explains that "The original inscription having been nearly obliterated / A number of citizens / Erected this monument, as a mark of respect / for this / illustrious author, / MDCCCXXVII." The text given below is as Mecom printed it. Variations in the autobiography and in the 1827 tablet are indicated in footnotes.

JOSIAH FRANKLIN,
And
ABIAH, his Wife,
Lie here interred.
They lived lovingly together in Wedlock
Fifty-five Years;
And without an Estate or any gainful
Employment,
By *constant Labour,* and *honest*[1] *Industry,*
(With GOD's Blessing)[2]
Maintained a large Family
Comfortably,[3]
And brought up thirteen Children and
Seven Grand-children
Reputably.[4]
From this Instance, Reader,
Be encouraged to Diligence in thy Calling,
And distrust not PROVIDENCE.

He was a pious and a prudent Man,
She a discreet and virtuous Woman.

Their youngest Son,
In filial Regard to their Memory,
Places this Stone.

J. F. born 1655, died 1744.
A. F. born 1667, died 1752.[5]

---

was designed by Solomon Willard (1783–1861), architect of the Bunker Hill Monument, and was made of the same Quincy granite.

1. The autobiography omits "*honest.*"
2. The 1827 inscription omits "(With GOD's Blessing)."
3. The 1827 inscription reads "comfortable."
4. The 1827 inscription reads "respectably."

To Deborah Franklin

ALS: American Philosophical Society

[My dear Child][6] New York, June 2. 1757

I have just received yours of the 29th [past. I have made] fresh Enquiry about the Clothes and [Sugar but have yet to] hear a Syllable of them. The brass [Engine at length] came by itself, and was deliver'd to the [?] House, with the three small Parts belonging [to it] by a tall Man whom she does not know; but no Clothes, Sugar, or anything else. There was no Direction upon the Engine,[7] and I wonder how it found its Way. Perhaps there was none on the other things, so that the Person who has them in Custody knows not where to deliver them. I wish I had them, but am not now like to get them while I stay; so do you enquire for them.

You do not tell me whether you take the Trunk of Books with you; but I suppose you do.[8]

It is now said, we are all to go on board tomorrow and fall down to the Hook. I hope it will be so, for having now nothing to do, my Stay here is extremely tedious.

---

5. The autobiography and the 1827 inscription both add their ages. In the same cemetery plot are buried Josiah Franklin's first wife Ann (d. 1689); their two infants both named Joseph (C.6, d. 1688; and C.7, d. 1689); Josiah and Abiah's child Ebenezer (C.13, d. 1703); Josiah's brother Benjamin (A.5.2.7, d. 1727; see above, I, 3–4); and Hannah Franklin (d. 1748), wife of BF's first cousin Samuel (A.5.2.7.1).

6. A large piece is torn out of the inner top corner of the folded sheet on which this letter is written. Missing words have been supplied conjecturally within brackets wherever this seemed possible. Sparks (*Works*, VII, 145) omitted, without indication, all of the first paragraph after "29th" in the first line and all of the paragraph beginning "[There is nothing]," and combined into his first paragraph the four intervening short ones and that concerning "Mr. Normandy" which follows his second omission. He also omitted the postscripts and made minor emendations in the remaining text. Bigelow (*Works*, III, 194) copied from Sparks. Smyth (*Writings*, III, 405) in general followed Sparks but indicated the first two major omissions by the use of suspension points, cited his source as the MS in APS, and followed it more literally in other details.

7. Not identified.

8. See above, p. 220.

Please to give my Respects to Mrs. Moore,[9] and assure her that I will take care of her Letters.

You will find sundry Parcels that came from London, some directed for the Library Company, some for Mr. Bartram. Deliver them if not deliver'd.

[There is nothing] extraordinary in my Letters from London. Only [Mr. Collinson] writes me, that sundry Instruments for the Academy [to the Amount of £ ?] 15*s.* 6*d.* were taken in Riddel, that he had £40 insur'd [on them in Lond]on to receive:[1] He had wrote me a long Letter by [?] forwarded me one from Pere Beccaria of Turin;[2] [but these were] lost.

[Desire] Mr. Normandy[3] to send after me, a fresh Memorandum [of what] he wanted, Mr. Collinson having lost the former.

[I] hope my dear Sally will behave in every thing to your Satis[faction] and mind her Learning and Improvement. As my Absence [will] make your House quieter and lessen your Business you will have the more Leisure to instruct her, and form her.

I pray God to bless you both, and that we may once more have a happy Meeting. God preserve, guard and guide you.

It is a doubt whether your next Letters will reach us here. Billy joins with me in Love to all Friends, presents his Duty to you and Love to his Sister. My Duty to Mother and Love to all the Family. I shall endeavour to write to you once more, before we sail, being as ever, my dear Child Your truly affectionate Husband

B FRANKLIN

9. Hannah Hill Moore, wife of Samuel Preston Moore (see above, IV, 295 n), physician and provincial treasurer of Pa.

1. Probably part of the instruments the Academy Trustees had voted to buy in July 1755, some of which had arrived in November 1756. See above, VI, 172 n, and this volume, pp. 23, 50. The *Lydia,* Captain Riddel, was reported as being in the Downs, bound for Philadelphia, Oct. 16, 1756. Captain Falconer arrived in the *St. George,* Jan. 31, 1757, and reported that the *Lydia* had been captured by a French privateer during her passage and carried into Morlaix with a valuable cargo. *Pa. Gaz.,* Jan. 6, Feb. 3, 10, 1757.

2. Giambatista Beccaria, the Italian physicist. See above, V, 359 n.

3. Possibly John Abraham Denormandie (see above, p. 37 n) or his son of the same name.

Sally should write to Mrs. Colden. Mrs. Nichols presents her Compliments, and says Sally will make a fine Woman.[4]

[*In the margin:*] [The Parcels a]re directed to the Library Company under [?] send it to Mr. Coleman's.[5]

[?] only stoop'd so much I was sorry to [see it. I hope she] will break herself of it.

To Ezra Stiles

ALS: Yale University Library

Dear Sir, New York, June 2. 1757

Having waited here near Eight Weeks for a Passage to England, we are at length told we shall certainly sail tomorrow.

For your Amusement I enclose you a Copy of a Letter I lately sent to a philosophical Friend in Carolina.[6] I shall not forget your Thermometer,[7] and shall be glad to hear from you when in England. I am, Dear Sir, with great Esteem, Your most obedient Servant B FRANKLIN

Addressed: For / The Revd. Mr Ezra Stiles / at / Newport / Per Mr James / Franklin.

Endorsed: Recd. 9th. June 1757. Ansd. a second Time Mar. 30. 1758[8]

4. Mrs. Alexander Colden, wife of the New York postmaster, and her mother, Mrs. Richard Nicholls. Sally had stayed with the Coldens during her New York visit.

5. William Coleman. See above, II, 406 n.

6. To Dr. John Lining; see above, pp. 184–90.

7. When BF returned to Philadelphia in 1762 he brought a thermometer which he then sent to Stiles. BF to Stiles, Dec. 19, 1762, Yale Univ. Lib. Stiles's careful thermometric observations, 1763–95, were probably made on this instrument. Edmund S. Morgan, *The Gentle Puritan: A Life of Ezra Stiles, 1727–1795* (New Haven, 1962), pp. 134–6.

8. Stiles replied to BF, July 12, 1757, discussing the letter to Lining, but the ship on which he sent his long communication was captured. He wrote again March 30, 1758, and that letter, too, was lost through enemy action, but partial drafts of both letters survive in the Stiles Papers. See below, pp. 239–43, 393–7.

William Franklin to Elizabeth Graeme

ALS: New York Public Library

My dearest Betsy New York, June 2, 1757

By one Accident or other we are still in N. York. But I know not how to complain of my Detention; for has it not afforded me the Pleasure of another Letter from my Betsy. A Letter for which I cannot be enough thankful. I must answer it in short; the Time of our Departure being now positively fix'd to this Afternoon.[9] The Name of our Pacquet is, *The General Wall,* Capt. Lutwych, Commander.[1] My Lord says she shall not be taken to Halifax, but accompany the Fleet for 3 or 4 Days only, in order to take on board Duplicates of his Dispatches sent by *the Earl of Leicester,* which is to sail directly for England. Capt. Bonnel, in the *Harriot* Pacquet is to go with the Fleet to Halifax, there to wait till they proceed upon the Expedition. I believe but few, if any, Letters sent by the Pacquet are opened. If you direct for me to the Care of Peter Colinson, Esqr. F.R.S. in London, I make no Doubt of your Letters coming safe.

My Lord, and Sir Charles, go in a 50 Gun Ship to Halifax;[2] and Genl. Abercrombie[3] in the Nightingale a 20 Gun Ship, Capt. Campbell, Commander. The whole of this Grand Armament seems at length destined for Louisbourg only!

Once more adieu. Adieu, my dearest Betsy. I need not repeat (for you must know) how much I am Your most affectionate

W. Franklin

9. Actually the two Franklins did not embark until the 5th.

1. In his "Account of Expences," BF records having paid "Capt. Lutwydge, Passage Money including Sea Stores &c. £55" sterling. Later in this account book is the following signed receipt: "Recd. May 5. 1758 of Benjamin Franklin Four Pounds Sixteen Shillings and Six pence, which with Cash and Stores recd. before, make Fifty Guineas, being in full for his and Son's Passage with their Servants, per me W. Lutwidge." "Account of Expences," pp. 2, 16; *PMHB*, LV (1931), 102, 110. Lutwidge died in action against the French, 1761. *Pa. Gaz.*, May 21, 1761.

2. The Earl of Loudoun and Rear Admiral Sir Charles Hardy sailed on the *Sutherland.*

3. Maj. Gen. James Abercromby (1706–1781), second in command under Loudoun; see above, VI, 459 n.

P.S. I have not seen Mrs. Abercrombie[4] for this Week past; she having gone down to the Hook with her Husband, and intends to remain on board with him till the Sailing of the Fleet.

To Miss Graeme

Addressed: To / Miss Eliza Graeme / In / Philadelphia

David Hall's Remittances to England, 1757–1765

MS account book: American Philosophical Society

[June 2, 1757]

The partnership agreement with David Hall, Jan. 1, 1748, provided that Hall was to pay one half the net income of the printing office to Franklin at every monthly clearing of accounts.[5] Apparently such strict regularity did not prove feasible and Franklin did not insist upon it. During his prolonged trip to England, however, he did expect Hall to send him bills of exchange at reasonable intervals covering, in round figures, the amounts due. In the record book labeled "Accounts Current Book David Hall Commencing Anno 1748," Hall devoted folios 19, 24, and 29 to a listing of the bills of exchange he sent to his senior partner in England. In each instance he noted the drawer of the bill he had bought, the English firm or public office on which it was drawn, the amount in pounds sterling, and the ships (usually with the captains' names) by which he had sent the original bill and other copies. The dates run from June 2, 1757, to April 12, 1762, with one single entry of Feb. 25, 1765, soon after Franklin had gone back on his second mission as agent for the Pennsylvania Assembly. With the exception of this final item all the bills of exchange are mentioned in the surviving correspondence between the partners during Franklin's absence.[6] While the particulars of the individual bills hardly need to be printed here, a summary of Hall's remittances may be useful in connection

4. Margaret, wife of Capt. James Abercromby (or Abercrombie) of Philadelphia, commander of the ship *Peggy*, which probably was in Loudoun's convoy about to sail for Halifax and Louisbourg. They were friends of the Graeme and Stedman families of Philadelphia, and after the captain was lost at sea in 1760, Mrs. Abercromby married Charles Stedman, whose first wife had been a sister of Elizabeth Graeme. *Pa. Gaz.*, Sept. 22, Oct. 13, 1757; *PMHB*, XXXIX (1915), 267 n. The mariner is not to be confused with Maj. Gen. James Abercromby or either of two other officers of that name then in New York, or with James Abercromby, colonial agent of Virginia in London.

5. See above, III, 265.

6. A few of these bills are also recorded in BF's "Account of Expences."

with that correspondence, which will appear at appropriate dates in this and later volumes:

Date	Sterling			Date	Sterling		
1757, June 2	£100	0s.	0d.	1759, Feb. 28	£100	0s.	0d.
July 4	100	0	0	March 24	100	0	0
Sept. 4	100	0	0	June 18	200	0	0
Oct. 18	100	0	0	Dec. 15	200	0	0
(Nov. 12	100	0	0)[7]	1760, March 5	200	0	0
1758, Jan. 6	100	0	0	April 18	100	0	0
Feb. 4	100	0	0	1761, Feb. 9	200	0	0
April 24	100	0	0[8]	June 1	100	0	0
April 24	149	12	5	1762, April 12	300	0	0
July 22	100	0	0	1765, Feb. 25	150	0	0
Nov. 13	100	0	0	Total	£2799	12s.	0d.[9]
1759, Jan. 18	100	0	0				

To [Peter and Mary Franklin][1]

MS not found; extracts reprinted from Parke-Bernet Galleries Catalogue, Sale No. 134 (Oct. 25–6, 1939), p. 26, no. 133; and Charles D. F. Burns Catalogue, No. B937/1, p. 22, no. 672.[2]

[New York, Saturday, June 4, 1757]

I enclose you an Order of Cousin James's on Mr. Collins for 35 Dollars.[3] Please to receive them, and send them per first safe hand

7. This bill, drawn by William Cooper of Boston on Messrs. Yeldin, White & Smith, merchants and ironmongers of London, was protested. BF returned it, June 10, 1758, and Hall credited his account accordingly. It is therefore not included in the total of the remittances shown in this listing.

8. This was included in a bill for £325 which Hall sent to William Strahan with instructions to pay £100 of the proceeds to BF.

9. In James Parker's report on the state of the account between BF and Hall, June 14, 1765, he credited Hall with "Account of Money paid by D. Hall for Bills of Exchange sent to England to B.F. from June 1757. to Feb. 1765. as per D. Hall's Accounts examined per JP £4776 19*s.* 6*d.*" Parker's figures represented Pa. currency, not sterling.

1. The compiler of the Parke-Bernet catalogue believed that this letter "to his brother and sister" was probably addressed to Edward and Jane Mecom. The contents, fragmentary though they are, persuade the editors that the addressees were almost certainly Peter Franklin (C.9), merchant and ship-master of Newport, and his wife Mary.

2. All but the final sentence is from the Parke-Bernet catalogue.

to my Wife. If you can get it in Gold, it may be enclosed in a little Packet and sent per Post . . . Billy presents his Duty. . . . I pray God to preserve you both.

From David Hall Letterbook copy: American Philosophical Society

Dear Sir. Philadelphia July 4th. 1757

My last to you was by the Rebecca, Captain Arthur (via Liverpool) covering the second Copy of the £100. Bill.[4] Inclosed you have now the third Copy of the same Bills, in Case of Miscarriages; and you have likewise inclosed the first Copy of another Bill for the same Value, on the same Gentlemen,[5] which I hope will come safe to Hand. The Exchange of this last the same as the first 67½.

In my letter per Arthur, I promised to send you the Copy of a Letter, I lately received from Mr. James Hunter of Fredericksburgh,[6] relating to our Virginia Customers which is as follows.

Gentlemen. Fredericksburgh 26th May 1757.

Whenever you are pleased to send me a list of the Ballances due on your Gazettes, I will collect the Same for you and Mr. Franklin without any Gratuity. I would recommend to you in future to discontinue the Gazettes to those who do not pay for the whole

3. James Franklin (C.11.4), Newport printer, nephew of Peter and BF. In BF's accounts is a credit entry to James for this order, converted into currency at £13 2*s.* 6*d.* Eddy, *Ledger "D,"* p. 57. Henry Collins (1699–1765), was an eminent Newport merchant, patron of the artists Smibert and Feke and civic leader. Henry W. Foote, *John Smibert Painter* (Cambridge, Mass., 1950) p. 145; Carl Bridenbaugh, *Cities in the Wilderness* (N.Y., 1938), frontispiece and pp. 459–60.

4. The *Rebecca,* Capt. Joseph Arthur, Sr., cleared Philadelphia at the expiration of the embargo, June 27, and arrived in Liverpool before August 11. *Pa. Gaz.,* June 30, 1757; *London Chron.,* Aug. 9–11, 1757. See facing page for Hall's payments to BF in England.

5. Messrs. Thomlinson, Hanbury, Colebrooke, & Nesbitt, merchants in London. Record of Hall's Remittances, APS.

6. Probably James Hunter (d. 1785), Scots merchant, later an iron founder and wealthy slaveholder, not to be confused with numerous other Hunters, mostly also named James, or William, of Fredericksburg. R. Walter Coakley, "The Two James Hunters of Fredericksburg," *Va. Mag. Hist. and Biog.,* LVI (1948), 3–21.

Year at Entrance, and I am of Opinion you will find no considerable decline in your Customers thereby. I am sure the Subscribers on my list would readily agree.

Thomas Franklin[7] is the Rider between Williamsburgh and this place, and he hath not shown me the Names of his Subscribers, if they be good, it may not be so convenient for him to finger the Entrances If you be inclineable to serve them. You may load a Waggon with Papers for Virginia if the Pay is not demanded till the Year's End.

From what you see this Gentleman writes, I believe it will be best to follow his Advice, and take none but those who pay as he directs.

By the last Post I receiv'd a letter from Mr. Christopher Chamney[8] in Virginia wherein he tells me he has lately paid, Eight Pounds Sixteen Shillings that Currency to Mr. John Stretch, Money received by him from different People on Account of our Gazette. I answered him that we were much obliged to him for the Trouble he had taken about our Affairs; but, as I had heard, from several Gentlemen, that that Person had refused to take Money for us, or to be concern'd at all with our Papers, should take it kind if, for the future, he would send any Thing he might receive for us by Letter, or order his Correspondent here (if he had any in this Place) to pay us. This I thought proper to do, as I heard you say you did not like Mr. Stretch's receiving for us. I am, Yours,

DH.

To Benjamin Franklin Esqr London

Copia

Via NY per Halifax Packet Boat[9]

Original per the Pennsylvania Cap Lyon[1]

7. Not identified; certainly not a relative of BF.

8. Neither Chamney(?) nor Stretch has been identified. See below, p. 390, for instructions to postmasters about delivery of and payment for newspapers.

9. The packet *Halifax* was scheduled to leave N.Y. for Falmouth Aug. 4, 1757, but did not sail until the 27th. *Pa. Gaz.*, July 28, 1757; *Colden Paps.*, v, 180.

1. The *Pennsylvania*, Capt. Charles Lyon, left Philadelphia before July 7, was taken by a French privateer and then recaptured by an English one, but finally late in August was again taken by the French and carried into St. Malo. *Pa. Gaz.*, July 7, Oct. 20, and Nov. 24, 1757; *London Chron.*, Aug. 30–

From Ezra Stiles

AL (incomplete): Yale University Library

Dear Sir Newport July 12th. 1757.

Just before you sail'd from New York, you was so good as to inclose to me a Copy of your philosophic Letter to a Friend in Carolina,[2] for which please accept my Thanks. The Philosophy of *Light* and *Fire, Heat* and *Cold* has hitherto been a Mystery to me. Even the luminous Emanations of a burning Candle I never could solve in my own Mind. I am half persuaded that *Light* is an Element different from *Fire;* which last is an Element which always produces Heat; as does somtimes, tho' not always the former; unless perhaps there may be such a Connexion between their Operations, that the one excites the other, when perhaps the sole Operation of the Fluid Light would not produce the Sensation of Heat in us. The Glow Worm, Rotten Wood, tainted Flesh, and the Head of a Fish, are all *luminous,* but not *hot:* The Flame of a Candle is however *luminous* and *hot.* The Fluids of *Fire* and *Light* if at rest are imperceptible—their Motions are accompanied with Sensations in us. The Fluid of Heat (to speak improperly) or rather, Fire, could its Motion be excited alone, and by itself only, perhaps might remain invisible: but if such be the Connexions of Nature, that Motion of *Fire* excites or is generally accompanied with a Motion of the Fluid *Light,* which is ambient in the same Space, it produces, as we say, *Light.* But if any Body, metallic or other, cut off the Connexion of mutual Action between the two Elements upon one another, the Motion of one only is excited, the other remains at rest. Iron admits a great degree of Heat before it becomes Luminous. Indeed I have tho't whether all Motion of the fiery Fluid does not excite a Motion of the luminous one: but that the Surfaces of the Bodies containing Fire already excited or put in Motion in them, that these Surfaces are differently suited to emit and reflect the differently colored Light (the Rays being originally and in themselves differently colored) some Surfaces suited to

---

Sept. 1, 1757. This capture resulted in the loss of one letter from DF to her husband (see below, p. 274), as well as a packet of valuable papers Richard Peters sent Thomas Penn including records of Lord Loudoun's meetings in Philadelphia, March 15–27, 1757; see above, pp. 145–53. Penn to Peters, Sept. 5, 1757, Penn Papers, Hist. Soc. Pa.

2. To Dr. John Lining; see above, pp. 184–90.

emit or reflect Rays of one Kind, some of another, some none at all, as the sooted Surfaces of Iron Potts, Kettles &c.—and whether the Action of excited Fire, distending the superficial Pores of Bodies, do not produce all the different Kind of thin Plates, necessary to exhibit the various colored Light—not unlike what is effected in the different Distention of Globules or Bubbles of Water, blown up by a Pipe, or in the variously tinged Clouds in general, or those in particular in which is exhibited the Rainbow.

The Surface of an unpolished Bar of Iron is not suited to reflect Light, I mean copiously, 'till violent Motion of Fire included in it originally (as all Bodies may be possessed of a mean Quantity) or added injected [*sic*] into it by the Action of the external motioned Element of Fire—till this violent Motion, by a stated Law, shall have, not only excited the included Light (of which it also possesses a mean Quantity), but distended the superficial Pores, so as to render the Plates which constitute the Surface so thin as readily to emit the excited internal Light already prepared to be transmitted; or reflect the excited external surrounding Light in like manner prepared for Reflection; or lastly, Rays of different orders alternately to reflect and transmit, as in Clouds and particularly the Rainbow. In a burning Coal, or glowing Iron, and glowing melted Metals, the Surfaces are so changed as to reflect copiously, almost all the Light, whence they in this State appear White, or a luminous Glow: This is when there is the greatest Degree of Heat, and consequently when the Pores are most distended, and when the plates are thinnest. When the action of the Fire is less vehement, the Bodies exhibit other Colors—generally *Red,* or such a Mixture of Rays as make a luminous *Whitness:* (I mean by *Luminous,* to distinguish it from the Whitness of Wall, Paper &c.). If I mistake not, the Red Rays refract and reflect the easiest—this may help us to infer the Degree of Distention, or Thinness of Plates. A pretty violent Fermentation of the Fluid Fire (exciting also Light) produced *Red;* a Ferm[ent]ation still more violent produces a Glowing white. In the last Case Rays of all Kinds are copiously emitted, in the former those of the *red* only. The glowing White is reflected or emitted from the thinnest Plates.

The sooty Surfaces of Pots and Kettles cant be made to reflect, till the Action of Heat be so Violent, the Heat so intense, as to seperate and throw off the Soot, and perhaps by melting the Iron or Brass cause it [to] be luminous in the Manner above described.

Tho the Action of Fire may produce Motion in Light and render it visible; yet the Action of Light does not always excite Motion in the Fluid Light. As in the Glow Worm &c. The Light in such Bodies is not attended with Heat, is cold. The Rays of the Sun however, when collected by a convex Lens, excite Motion in the Fluid of Fire and renders it perceptible. But the general Law of these mutual Operations we are ignorant of.

Oleaginous Substances, beyond all others, feed and propagate Fire already excited. The violent Collision of dry Sticks of Wood excite it, and indeed feed it; but it soon separates and dissipates the Parts, permitting all their little Moisture to escape and fly off, Leaving only the dry Ashes impregnated with a few Salts too heavy for Evaporation by Adhesion to the rarified ascending air. Oyls feed the Fire much longer. Fire excited, if it has Nothing to operate upon, soon runs into Equilibrium with the common Fluid, and, as we say, dies: but if supplied with dissipable Matter, it acquires greater Force by Action; and being thus furnished with Business for Action, it perseveres 'till it has accomplished all.

Fire exited set to a Lamp of Oyl, or to a Candle, never leaves it till by its Action it has dissipated the whole. The Motion of Fire communicating or exciting Motion in the surrounding Element of Light, the Light becomes visible in the Flame of the Lamp and Candle. And the Motion of Fire continued by being fed with Oyl or Tallow supplied thro' the Wick, the Motion of Light in the surrounding Flame or its Accumulation is continued. I should be glad of a more satisfactory Solution.

The undulatory Vibrations of the luminous Fluid, thro' Action of the Sun in the Center, may produce Light in any part of the System, where are Corpuscles or solid Bodies with Surfaces suited to reflect these Vibrations. As these Vibrations, tho never so contrary and across in their Directions, produce no Confusion: so neither those between the 2 Elements *Light* and *Fire*. Newton was of opinion that the Comets, when in the hither Parts of their Trajectories, dispensed beneficent Influences to the System. Perhaps when having passed their Perihelions and ascending charged with great Quantity of solar borrowed Heat and parts of their Bodies in more violent Motion, may communicate an extensive Agitation, on each side the Tract thro' which they run off, which may serve as necessary Purposes among the Elementary Fluids in the System, as the Tides in the Ocean.

Perhaps there are many Elements, or Kinds of Fluids, in our System, besides Water, Fire, Air, Light—Perhaps Cold may not be the Absence or Cessation of Motion only in Water, Air, Fire &c.; Is it impossible that it should itself be another Element or free passing permeating Fluid? which itself produces the Sensation of Cold in us? and which, in more than a mean Quantity insinuating itself among the other Elements, obstructs their Motion, congeals them? May not *volatile Salts,* Sulphur and the several Sorts of *Aromatics* which flow or float freely thro' Atmospherial Space at least, be so many different Elements? Salt is diffused thro' the Ocean. They may be confined; Portions may be detatched from the common pervading Mass; Communication may be cutt off: the same may be said of Water, Fire, Air, &c. Ocean Water is as full of Salt as of Light, Air &c. *Water* and *Air* obstruct one another: so *Air* and *Salts*. If *Salts* must be supposed sharp pointed; mayn't *Fire* with the same propriety? If *Salts* attract one another, tend to a coalescence; dont a Drop of Water attract Water? If *Water* floats in Air, dont *Nitre*? But then you'll say, dont Birds, Insects, and infinite Animalcula float there too? and are they so many Elements?

There are Elements common to the System, as Light, Heat, Aether: There are Elements peculiar to each planetary Globe, as Water, at least, perhaps the electrical Fluid, and perhaps some animal Fluid which may be the universal Principle of animal Life, the magnetic Effluvia, and aromatic Effluvia which circulate from Vegitables into the ambient Air and again reimbibed by Animals, and Vegitables. And in general all the other different Species of subtle inanimate Matter, so fine as to pass the minute Porosity of Bodies, in perpetual Circulations under the Appointment of general Laws, whether their Particles be globular or angular.

But it matters not as to the Term *Element;* the Question is, whether there ben't a Species of fine Subtle Matter that freely permeates Bodies, Fluids &c., which yet of itself when detatchd from any or all other Matter, Applied to our Bodies produce the Sensation of COLD? and whether a certain Mixture of this Matter with Water &c. produces Ice, Snow, and all the Phoenomena of COLD? As salts dissolve cogulated Blood; or rather as Runnet reduces

Milk to a Coagulum, so this Element, when in more than mean Quantity, produces Ice &c.[3]

N.B. This is about half of a Letter which I sent to B. Franklin Esqr. in London, by the Brig. Prince of Orange Edward Jackson Captain, who sail'd from this Port for London July. 14. 1757. and was taken and carried into Bayonne.[4]

To Deborah Franklin

MS not found; extract reprinted from WTF, *Memoirs*, I, 133 n.[5]

[Falmouth, July 17, 1757]

The bell ringing for church, we went thither immediately, and with hearts full of gratitude, returned sincere thanks to God for the mercies we had received: were I a Roman Catholic, perhaps I should on this occasion vow to build a chapel to some saint; but as I am not, if I were to vow at all, it should be to build a *light-house.*

William Franklin to Elizabeth Graeme

ALS: New York Public Library

Falmouth July 17, 1757

I have now the Pleasure to inform my dearest Betsy that her Franklin is safely arriv'd in England about two Hours ago, after a Passage of 27 Days. I am so much hurried in getting our Things

3. Though some of Stiles's theorizing in this letter shows keen insight, the conclusion of his recent biographer seems on the whole judicious: "Stiles was exploring one of the blind alleys of science." Edmund S. Morgan, *The Gentle Puritan: A Life of Ezra Stiles, 1727–1795* (New Haven, 1962), p. 135.

4. See below, p. 397, for another letter of Stiles's also captured by the French.

5. Attached as a footnote to BF's account of his voyage to England in William Temple Franklin's edition of the autobiography, and prefaced: "In a letter from Dr. Franklin to his wife, dated at Falmouth, the 17th July, 1757, after giving a similar account of his voyage, escape, and landing; he adds . . ." See Par. Text edit., pp. 404–10, for BF's story of the voyage, referred to by Temple Franklin, and the following document for WF's description of their narrow escape.

ashore, and enquiring for Horses and Carriages for transporting us up to London, that I have not Leisure to give you any of the Particulars of our Voyage. I design to do it however by the very first Opportunity. In general, we were highly favour'd with Winds, were several Times chac'd, and met with no Accident, except the Night before our Arrival, when we narrowly escap'd running ashore on the Rocks of Scilly, owing to our not having discover'd the Light ashore till it was almost too late to avoid them.[6] Altho' our Passage cannot, when compar'd to most others, be deem'd a very disagreeable one, yet I cannot but be [of] Opinion that let the Pleasures of this Country be ever so great, they are dearly earn'd by a Voyage across the Atlantick. Few are the Inducements that will tempt me to pass the Ocean again, if ever I am so happy as to return to my native Country.

I question if I shall have it in my Power to write again by this Pacquet, as 'tis said she will sail sometime this Week;[7] so that no Post after our Arrival in London can possibly reach her.

I must beg you to say for me to your good Family, and let my great Hurry plead in Excuse for your seeing so soon the Name of your affectionate WM: FRANKLIN

For Miss Graeme.

Addressed: To / Miss Elizth. Graeme / In / Philadelphia

6. See the preceding document. The Scilly Islands and adjacent rocks, 25 miles west of Land's End, were the scene of many accidents. A variable northwesterly current (now called Rennell's Current) across the mouth of the English Channel, caused by strong west winds in the Bay of Biscay and imperfectly understood in 1757, sometimes set ships headed into the channel as much as fifty miles off their dead-reckoning course. Furthermore, the lighthouse on one of the larger islands "never appeared clear and bright" to at least one experienced mariner, and was too far from the rocks most likely to endanger eastbound ships. "Observations on a Current that often prevails to the Westward of Scilly; endangering the Safety of Ships that approach the British Channel. By James Rennell, Esq. F.R.S.," *Phil. Trans.*, LXXXIII (1793), Part II, 182–200; and "Some farther observations . . ." *Ibid.*, CV (1815), 182–202. Bishop Light was erected in 1858 to remedy these defects.

7. The packet *Earl of Leicester* sailed from Falmouth August 8 and reached New York on September 10. She probably carried this letter and the one from BF to DF immediately above and also BF's extended preface for the 1758 *Poor Richard* almanac (see below, p. 328). The packet *General Wall* did not leave Falmouth until September 2 and reached New York October 15. *London Chron.*, Aug. 9, 1757; *N.-Y. Mercury*, Sept. 12 and Oct. 17, 1757.

To Deborah Franklin ALS: American Philosophical Society

My dear Child London, July 27. 1757

We arrived here well last Night, only a little fatigued with the last Day's Journey, being 70 Miles.[8] I write only this Line, not knowing of any Opportunity to send it; but Mr. Collinson will enquire for one, as he is going out.[9] If he finds one, I shall write more largely. I have just seen Mr. Strahan, who is well with his Family. Billy is with me here at Mr. Collinson's, and presents his Duty to you, and Love to his Sister. My Love to all. I am, my dear Child, Your loving Husband B FRANKLIN

Mr. Collinson says there was a Vessel going to New York, if not gone this Line will go by her.[1]

Addressed: To / Mrs Franklin / in / Philadelphia

8. BF remembered in the autobiography that on their 300-mile trip from Falmouth he and WF "only stopt a little by the Way to view Stonehenge on Salisbury Plain, and Lord Pembroke's House and Gardens, with his very curious Antiquities at Wilton." He added that they "arriv'd in London the 27th of July 1757," but this letter makes clear that they actually reached the city on the evening of the 26th. Par. Text edit., p. 410. He spent £32 13*s.* on the journey and for "some expences" in London. "Account of Expences," p. 2; *PMHB,* LV (1931), 102.

9. As early as June 5, 1757, BF had been "dayly" expected by Collinson, either at his place of business "in Grace Church Street at the Red Lyon" (near London Bridge), or at Ridgeway House at Mill Hill near Hendon, eight miles northwest of London, where Collinson lived and maintained his superb garden of botanical curiosities. This letter suggests that BF and WF were Collinson's guests their first night in London or that they called upon him the morning after arrival. There is an entry, July 27, in his account book of £22 13*s.* 6*d.* "for expences at the Bear Inn till provided with lodgings." This was a famous tavern at the Southwark end of old London Bridge (torn down in 1761). The lodgings, arranged for by the Pennsylvania agent Robert Charles, were at the home of Mrs. Margaret Stevenson, No. 7 Craven Street, where BF paid 11*s.* 5*d.* for dinner on July 30, when presumably he moved in. Mrs. Stevenson's house was on the right side of Craven Street as one walked from the Strand towards the Thames; it was near Charing Cross, the government buildings in Whitehall, and the Houses of Parliament. "Account of Expences," p. 3; *PMHB,* LV (1931), 102; *Colden Paps.,* V, 150, 154; Henry B. Wheatley, *London Past and Present* (London, 1891), I, 135–6, 472–3.

1. The ship was probably the *St. George,* Capt. James Johnston, which had arrived at Deal by August 1, sailed under convoy to Portsmouth on the 7th, and waited there another month for a westbound convoy. She arrived in New

From John Bartram

Letterbook copy: Historical Society of Pennsylvania

Dear Benjamin July the 29th. 1757

I now take the Freedom of thy usual Benevolence and favour of thy wife to inclose this letter in hers[2] hopeing this way we may keep the chain of friendship bright while thee art diverting thy self with the generous conversation of our worthy friends in Europe and adding dayly new acquisitions to thy former extensive stock of knoledge by thair free comunication of thair experimental improvements while thy poor yet honest friend Bartram is daly in mourning for the Calamities of our provinces. Vast sums spent and nothing done to the advantage of the king or countrey. How should I leap for Joy to see or hear that the British Oficers would prove by thair actions the zeal and duty to thair Prince and nation thay so much pretend in words.[3] I am not unsensible of the burden thee art charged with and perhaps thee may meet with some that is not so sincear as our dear Peter whome Captain Lyon tould me in A gratefull zeal was he believed one of the best men in London.[4]

Pray my dear friend bestow A few lines upon thy ould friend such like as those sent from Woodbridge.[5] They have A Magical power of dispeling malancholy fumes and chearing up my spirits, they are so like thy facetious discource in thy southern chamber when we used to be together. We have had this summer Abundance of thunder which hath done much damage. Several houses hath

York on December 4, also carrying a letter from Collinson to Cadwallader Colden asking him to inform DF of BF's safe arrival. *London Chron.*, Aug. 2 and 9, and Sept. 8, 1757; *Pa. Gaz.*, Nov. 24 and Dec. 8, 1757; *Colden Paps.*, V, 211–12.

2. Probably DF's letter of July 31, not found, but which BF acknowledged on November 22; see below, p. 274.

3. Philadelphia newspaper accounts of Indian attacks all along the Pennsylvania frontier sometimes mentioned their occurrence almost within sight of forts and parties of soldiers. Nor had the British regulars stationed at Carlisle under Col. John Stanwix prevented attacks in the immediate vicinity of that town. *Pa. Gaz.*, July-August 1757.

4. See above, p. 238 n, for the capture of the ship *Pennsylvania* and its captain, Charles Lyon, who frequently carried letters to and from Peter Collinson.

5. No letters to Bartram written during BF's visit at Woodbridge, N.J., May 12–23, 1757, have been found.

been much shattered. In one house 2 young women was killed one of which had a child in her lap two weeks ould which was found on the floor and stil liveth. All in the room was so stupefied that thay [can't] give any account how thay was hurt. One saith he saw A ball of fire break [into the room, and] spread about. Several was singed as with fire.

From Ferdinand John Paris[6]

Copy: Historical Society of Pennsylvania

Hampstead[7] Friday Afternoon past 4.
Sir, 12. Augst. 1757.

In Consequence of my Letter to You, of the 10th. Instant,[8] I am now to acquaint You, that it's believed the Youngest of the Pro-

6. Ferdinand John Paris (d. 1759), admitted to the Inner Temple, 1715, for nearly forty years specialized in representing colonial affairs before the Board of Trade. He acted as legal advisor to the Penn family as early as 1720. In 1731 he was appointed London agent for the Pa. Assembly, but in 1740 his close connection with the Proprietors led to his discharge. Shrewd, energetic, haughty, skilled in the procedures acceptable to the various ministries, and in the use of every technicality, he was a formidable opponent, and, as the Penns' spokesman and penman, the man with whom BF as Assembly agent had to contend. BF found him "A proud angry Man [who] . . . had conceiv'd a mortal Enmity to me." Thomas Hutchinson called him "one of the first rate" solicitors, but "one who had a peculiar talent at slurring the characters of his antagonists. Many of his briefs which I have seen abound in this way." Mabel P. Wolff, *The Colonial Agency of Pennsylvania 1712–1757* (Phila., 1933), pp. 39–41, 78, 88–9; *London Mag.*, XXVIII (1759), 684; Par. Text edit., p. 414; Thomas Hutchinson, *The History of the Colony and Province of Massachusetts-Bay*, Lawrence Shaw Mayo, ed. (Cambridge, Mass., 1936), II, 292. At about the time he wrote this letter Paris received a report which doubtless contributed to his "enmity" to BF: "Mr. Franklin will be in England [soon], Exhibiting his complaints against the Proprietors, as is thought and expected by many that sent him; but I imagine his own schemes are very different from those of his Employers. He is a sensible Artfull man, very knowing in American affairs, and was his heart as sound as his head, few men would be fitter for Publick trust; But that is far from being the Case, He has nothing in view but to serve himself, and however he may give another turn to what he says and does; Yet you may be assured that is at the bottom, and in the End will shew itself. One motive among others, that Possibly induced him to chuse this Embassy, might be his apprehensions of danger from the back inhabitants, who in case of any remarkable blow from the french and

Continuation of this note and notes 7 and 8 are on next page.

prietarys[9] is some where from Home, and has not received, at least he has not answered, his Brother's Letter, touching the Appointment for to Morrow; Which, therefore, must go off; And they will take the first Opportunity to fix some other Time, Of which, You shall have due Notice, from, Sir, Your most humble Servant F: J: P:

Benjamin Franklin Esqr.
12. August 1757
Copp Mr. Paris's Second Letter to Mr. Franklin.

To the Proprietors: Heads of Complaint

Two copies: Historical Society of Pennsylvania[1]

"I believe I shall be able to deal very well with Mr. Franklin," wrote Thomas Penn when first informed of the Assembly's plan to send him as agent to England. To undercut his mission, Penn sought assurance from the Duke of Cumberland that Postmaster General Sir Everard Fawkener would "by no means support Franklin" in opposing the Proprietors, and he sowed seeds of jealousy, so he thought, between the new emissary and long-time agent Richard Partridge; Penn told Partridge he "did not desire to have any conversation with him [Franklin]—This did not displease him [Partridge] and we parted mighty good Friends." In a final move to thwart Franklin's agency, Penn

Indians, would in my opinion have sacrafised him and his associates." Robert Hunter Morris to Paris, July 4, 1757; Yale Univ. Lib.

7. At this time a country village northwest of London.

8. Not found; see the next document for BF's first meetings with the Proprietors.

9. Richard Penn, younger brother of Thomas. Although the brothers were legally joint Proprietors, for over ten years Richard had left the management of affairs almost entirely in his brother's hands.

1. The first copy (printed here), including the signature, is in WF's hand; only the date (placed originally at the bottom) is in different writing, probably that of the clerk who copied Paris' letter to BF immediately above. This might be the copy Thomas Penn sent Richard Peters on Sept. 5, 1757, but more likely BF had it made for his own purposes. The second copy, unsigned and in the hand of Thomas Penn's clerk, was sent to Peters on Nov. 14, 1757, and is docketed by Peters "received 28th March 1758." The original paper given to the Proprietors on Aug. 20, 1757, and later signed by BF, has not been found.

urged James Hamilton to come to England to help refute Assembly arguments.[2]

Meanwhile, Franklin busily prepared his own case: "I went to visit Dr. Fothergill, to whom I was strongly recommended, and whose Counsel respecting my Proceedings I was advis'd to obtain. He was against an immediate Complaint to Government, and thought the Proprietaries should first be personally apply'd to, who might possibly be induc'd by the Interposition and Persuasion of some private Friends to accomodate Matters amicably.[3] I then waited on my old Friend and Correspondent Mr. Peter Collinson, who told me that John Hanbury,[4] the great Virginia Merchant, had requested to be informed when I should arrive, that he might carry me to Lord Granville's,[5] who was then President of the Council, and wish'd to see me as soon as possible. I agreed to go with him the next Morning. Accordingly Mr. Hanbury called for me and took me in his Carriage to that Nobleman's,

2. Penn to Richard Peters, March 15, April 9, and May 4, 1757; and to James Hamilton, July 7, 1757; Penn Papers, Hist. Soc. Pa. See above, pp. 110–11 n, for other comments on BF's mission to England.

3. London Friends seem to have hoped strongly for such an accommodation: Thomas Crosby wrote James Pemberton, Oct. 18, 1757, that "I have not seen Benjamin Franklin, but hear that he hath had several Meetings with Thomas Penn, who 'tis said, discovers a Disposition to Hearken to Reason." Pemberton Papers, Hist. Soc. Pa.

4. John Hanbury (1700–1758), of a large merchant and manufacturing family, frequently involved in Quaker politics, and at this time, in partnership with John Thomlinson, money contractor for British armies in North America. Hanbury was described as "the greatest tobacco merchant of his day, perhaps in the world. This gentleman, though one of the people called Quakers, was no less remarkable for his connection and intimacy with the first nobility of the kingdom, particularly with the old Duke of Newcastle, the very learned Lord Grenville [*sic*], Gregory Sharpe, Sherlock Bishop of London, Hoadley Bishop of Winchester, Sir Charles Hanbury Williams, his relation, and most of the Lords spiritual and temporal of the Newcastle and Pelham administration." Newspaper of 1789, quoted in H. F. Barclay and Alice W. Fox, *History of the Barclay Family* (London, 1934), III, 251. See also B. Burke, *The Landed Gentry of Great Britain,* 16th ed.; *The Official Records of Robert Dinwiddie* (Richmond, 1883), I, 101–2.

5. John Carteret, first Earl Granville (1690–1763), at this time president of the Privy Council. *DNB.* His second marriage, 1744, was to Lady Sophia Fermor, sister of Lady Juliana, wife of Thomas Penn. This relationship gave him a connection not only with the Penns but with English Quakers which he seems to have retained even after the disputes between the leaders in the Pa. Assembly and the Proprietors reached fever pitch during BF's agency. See below, p. 376 n.

who receiv'd me with great Civility; and after some Questions respecting the present State of Affairs in America, and Discourse thereupon, he said to me, 'You Americans have wrong Ideas of the Nature of your Constitution; you contend that the King's Instructions to his Governors are not Laws, and think yourselves at Liberty to disregard them at your own Discretion. But those Instructions are not like the Pocket Instructions given to a Minister going abroad, for regulating his Conduct in some trifling Point of Ceremony. They are first drawn up by Judges learned in the Laws; they are then considered, debated and perhaps amended in Council, after which they are signed by the King. They are then so far as relates to you, the *Law of the Land;* for THE KING IS THE LEGISLATOR OF THE COLONIES.' I told his Lordship this was new Doctrine to me. I had always understood from our Charters, that our Laws were to be made by our Assemblies, to be presented indeed to the King for his Royal Assent, but that being once given the King could not repeal or alter them. And as the Assemblies could not make permanent Laws without his Assent, so neither could he make a Law for them without theirs. He assur'd me I was totally mistaken. I did not think so however. And his Lordship's Conversation having a little alarm'd me as to what might be the Sentiments of the Court concerning us, I wrote it down as soon as I return'd to my Lodgings."[6]

Sometime between August 13 and 16,[7] reported Thomas Penn, "Mr. Franklin came according to his appointment to pay me a visit previous to his entering upon Business. He professed his desire to do every thing in his Power to settle the differences that subsisted between us and the Assembly. We spoke of things generally, my Brother being in the Country on a Tour, I did not think it proper to do otherwise. The next day he came to Town, and we sent for Mr. Franklin, and appointed the 20th. of last Month to receive what he had to offer, which he proposed to do in the way of conversation, but as we had told him, it was absolutely necessary to have what he demanded in writing, he

6. Par. Text edit., pp. 410–12. BF's notes have not been found, but he gave a similar summary of Granville's remarks and his own reaction to them to James Bowdoin, Jan. 13, 1772. A longer account of Granville's comments went to Isaac Norris, March 19, 1759, but BF said nothing about his reply in that letter.

7. Though F. J. Paris wrote BF canceling the meeting with Penn on the 13th (see immediately above), and Penn himself wrote that day that he had not yet seen BF, they nevertheless might have met later on the 13th; if not, the meeting took place on one of the next three days since Penn wrote on the 17th that he had seen BF. Penn to Peters, Aug. 13 and 17, 1757, Penn Papers, Hist. Soc. Pa.

delivered a loose Paper not address'd to any body called heads of Complaint, a Copy of which I send you but I think it shou'd not be made publick."[8]

London Augst. 20, 1757.

HEADS OF COMPLAINT

1. That the reasonable and necessary Power given to Deputy Governors of Pennsylvania by the Royal Charter, Section 4th. and 5th. of making Laws with the Advice and Consent of the Assembly, for Raising Money for the Safety of the Country and other Publick Uses, "according to their best Discretion," is taken away by Proprietary Instructions enforced by penal Bonds, and restraining the Deputy from the Use of his best Discretion; tho' being on the Spot, he can better judge of the Emergency State and Necessity of Affairs, than Proprietaries residing at a great Distance; by Means of which Restraints sundry Sums of Money granted by the Assembly for the Defence of the Province, have been rejected by the Deputy, to the great Injury of His Majesty's Service in Time of War, and Danger of the Loss of the Colony.

2. That the indubitable Right of the Assembly, to judge of the Mode, Measure and Time of Granting Supplies, is infringed by Instructions that injoin the Deputy to refuse his Assent to any Bill for Raising Money, unless certain Modes, Measures, and Times in such Instructions directed, make a Part of the Bill; whereby the Assembly, in Time of War, are reduced to the Necessity of either losing the Country to the Enemy, or giving up the Liberties of the People, and receiving Law from the Proprietary; and if they should do the latter in the present Case, it will not prevent the former; the restricting Instructions being such, as that, if comply'd with, it is impossible to raise a Sum sufficient to defend the Country.[9]

3. That the Proprietaries have injoined their Deputy, by such Instructions, to refuse his Assent to any Law for raising Money by a Tax, tho' ever so necessary for the Defence of the Country, unless the greatest Part of their Estate is exempted from such Tax. This, to the Assembly and People of Pennsylvania, appears both unjust and cruel.

8. Penn to Peters, Sept. 5, 1757; Penn Papers, Hist. Soc. Pa.

9. See above, pp. 126–9, for an explanation of this point.

The Proprietaries are now requested seriously to consider these Complaints, and redress the Aggrievances complain'd of, in the most speedy and effectual Manner; that Harmony may be restored between the several Branches of the Legislature, and the Publick Service be hereafter readily and fully provided for.[1]

B FRANKLIN,
Agent for the Province
of Pensilva.

From William Sturgeon[2] Extract:[3] American Philosophical Society

[Philadelphia, Aug. 22, 1757]

Mrs. Franklin favoured me with the Sight of a Letter wrote to you by one Mr. Waring,[4] in which your Thoughts are desired on the important Subject of instructing the Negroes in the Principles of Christianity. As I have the Honour of being employ'd by the Society, a[s] Catechist to the Negroes in this City I take the Freedom to make mention of the Affair to you. When I first arrived here, few or none of the Colour were Christians; but by the Blessing of God, several of them, after proper Instruction, have

1. In November, on the advice of Paris, the Proprietors "put the Paper into the Hands of the Attorney and Solicitor General for their Opinion and Counsel upon it, where it lay unanswered a Year wanting eight Days." Par. Text edit., p. 414. But see below, p. 366 n, for the earlier reply from the solicitor general. On Nov. 27–28, 1758, the Proprietors and Paris addressed a reply on the Heads of Complaint to the Assembly. BF summarized the intervening negotiations in a letter to Isaac Norris, Jan. 19, 1759. The points in dispute, of course, had been covered repeatedly in the Assembly messages of 1755–57.

2. William Sturgeon (*c.* 1722–1770), B.A., Yale, 1745, ordained as an Anglican clergyman, 1747, went to Philadelphia as assistant minister of Christ Church and teacher of Negroes, partly supported by the Society for the Propagation of the Gospel and the Bray Associates. BF and others commended his work, but William Smith violently accused him of political partisanship, and in 1766 he resigned his Christ Church pastorate. Dexter, *Biog. Sketches*, II, 61–3.

3. In BF's hand, enclosed with his letter to John Waring, Jan. 3, 1758; see below, p. 356.

4. See above, p. 98, for this letter which reached Philadelphia after BF had left for England. DF evidently opened it and showed it to Sturgeon as the man best able to answer the questions in it.

been baptised, and are regular Communicants of our Church; and others who do not communicate, behave orderly, and attend the Service of the Church.

I am forced chiefly to instruct them by the Ear; but if a School could be opened for their Use under the Care and Inspection of the Minister, or some other prudent Person or Persons, the Work would in time become easy, and much Good might be done to them, and several of the lower Rank of White People.

Post Office Account with William Hunter

MS memorandum: American Philosophical Society

Pasted on page 26 of Franklin's Ledger, 1764–1775, is a small slip of paper on which he wrote a memorandum which appears to have nothing to do with the accounts to which it has been attached. Although the memorandum as a whole is dated 1772, it is printed here at the date of the earliest item on it.

London, May 5, 1772

Hunter

1757	Aug 29.	31.	10.	0
	Do	42.		
	Oct. 27	20.	0.	0
		400.	0.	0[5]
1758	May 3	35.	0.	0
	Aug. 26	40.	0.	0
	Nov. 21	100.	0.	0
1759	Mar. 1	191.	5.	0[6]

5. In BF's "Account of Expences," p. 7; *PMHB*, LV (1931), 105, are the following entries (in tabular form) under date of Dec. 1, 1757: "Paid Mr. Hunter sundry Sums, viz 30 Guineas 40 Do. in two Drafts on Banker £73. 10*s*. Note, these, with what he had before makes 100 Guineas. Another Draft for £400 Another Do for £20."

6. The two items of May 3 and August 26 are not found in BF's "Account of Expences," but on p. 37 (also in *PMHB*, LV, 116) occurs the following (also in tabular form): "Mar. 1. [1759] Paid Mr. Hunter £191 5*s*. 0*d*. which with £100 paid in Nov. last makes £291 5*s*. 0*d*. being his Proportion of Post Office Money receiv'd by me since Aug. 10. 1757. the Post Office Account being previously settled to that time."

The above Sums taken from Banker's Book (Brown & Sons) all above the Line are settled in the Post Office Account between W. Hunter and me. Query, How were the subsequent Sums settled.

From David Hall   Letterbook copy: American Philosophical Society

Dear Sir   Philadelphia, 14th Septemr 1757

I make no Doubt but long before this comes to hand, you have received the first and Second Copies of the second Hundred Pound. I sent you one by Capt. Arthur, Via Liverpool, the other by Capt. Lyon.[7]

Inclosed I have now sent you the first Copy of another Bill, for One hundred Pounds, the Exchange the same as the others, Sixty Seven and a half, which you will please to own the Receipt of, as soon as it reaches you, and likewise of what has been sent before. As there are only three setts of Hunter's Bills[8] shall send but two of them, till I hear of one at any Time being intercepted.

We shall begin in a Week or two more from this Date, to expect to hear from you in Case you have had the Good Luck to escape the Monsieurs, which by what we have heard lately, seems to be a pretty difficult Matter to do, as they cover the seas in a Manner with their Privateers &c. Yours &c.   D H

To Benjamin Franklin Esqr. via Liverpool per Industry Cap. Nuttle
Copy Via Liverpool per the Philadelphia Capt. Ferguson Jr
[?]   per the Carolina Cap. Duncan

Wrote at the same time under Cover to his Father to Mr. William Franklin.[9]

7. See above, p. 237, for these payments, and p. 236, for a summary of Hall's remittances to BF in England.

8. According to the summary of Hall's remittances, this bill was "drawn by Mr. John Hunter of New York on Messrs. Thomlinson, Hanbury, Colebrooke & Nesbitt. Merchants In London endorsed by Mr. John Nelson." See above, VI, 223 n, for Hunter and Nelson, both of whom were associated with the London merchants mentioned here.

9. Not found.

William Franklin to the Printer of The Citizen

I. Printed in *The Gentleman's Magazine*, XXVII (September 1757), 417–18.
II. Printed in *The London Chronicle: or, Universal Evening Post*, No. 113, Sept. 17–20, 1757, pp. 275–6.

Soon after beginning his negotiations with the Proprietors, Franklin became convinced that they "were repeatedly publishing scandalous and malicious Falshoods against the Assembly and People of Pennsylvania" in the English press. A letter in *The Citizen, or General Advertiser*, Sept. 9, 1757, aspersing the Assembly and the Quakers, provided the immediate occasion for a reply, but, because it might appear improper for the Assembly's chief negotiator with the Penns to engage in such a newspaper controversy, the response appeared over the signature of William Franklin.[1] It was published in *The Citizen*, September 16, reprinted in *The London Chronicle*, September 17–20 (Number II below), and repeated in *The Citizen* on the 23d.[2] *Gentleman's Magazine* printed it in the September issue (distributed in October) with an extended introduction prepared by the Franklins (Number I below). On Dec. 8, 1757, *The Pennsylvania Gazette* reprinted the letter as it had appeared in the September 23 *Citizen*,[3] and in a further demonstration of Franklin's assiduous propagandizing, it was inserted as an appendix in Richard Jackson's *An Historical Review of the Constitution and Government of Pennsylvania*, which appeared in London in June 1759 under Franklin's guidance and sponsorship. An introduction in this work praised the letter's good effect: "since that Time [September 1757] no one has ever offer'd to publish the least Thing in Contradiction; altho' before, scarce a Week elaps'd without the

1. See below, pp. 290–1, for WF's explanation of the circumstances of this publication.

2. This short-lived London newspaper appeared as *The Citizen, or Morning Post* from Sept. 16, 1756, to Aug. 30, 1757, and as *The Citizen, or General Advertiser* from then until its demise, Dec. 31, 1757. BF paid one guinea to have the letter printed. "Account of Expences," p. 5; *PMHB*, LV (1931), 104. Only incomplete files of *The Citizen* survive and the editors have been unable to locate in England or the United States copies of any of the three pertinent issues in September 1757. The text of WF's letter (Number II below) is therefore taken from *London Chron.*

3. *The Citizen* provided a new introduction for this September 23 reprint, which *Pa. Gaz.* repeated: "The great Demand for the following Letter, occasions our reprinting it, for the Satisfaction of the Public; and to shew how ready we are in communicating to our Readers any Thing worthy their Attention; by exposing the Artifices of those who would, in a remote Land, overthrow the native Rights and Liberties of Englishmen."

News-Papers furnishing us with some anonymous Abuse of that Colony."[4]

I

In our Magazine, Vol. xxv. p. 87 [487]. Vol. xxvi. p. 28. we have given a very particular account of the disputes between the assembly of Pennsylvania and the late Governor Morris,[5] which had exactly the same cause, and produced exactly the same effects, as the late dispute between this Assembly and Mr. Denny.

The acting governor, who is only lieutenant governor, besides the royal instructions, receives instructions from the proprietaries. By these proprietary instructions the governor is required not to pass any bill for taxing their quit rents, their located unimproved lands, and their purchase money at interest, but the assembly have ever been determined to frame no money bill, in which these quit rents, lands, and money shall be exempted, for the following reasons.

1st, Because they conceive that neither the proprietaries nor any other power on earth, ought to interfere between them and their sovereign, either to modify or refuse their free gifts, and grants for his majesty's service.[6]

2d, Because though the governor may be under obligation to the proprietaries, yet he is under greater to the crown, and to the people he is appointed to govern, to promote the service of his majesty, and preserve the rights of his subjects, and protect them from their cruel enemies.[7]

3d. Because a tax laid comformable to the proprietary instructions, could not possibly produce the necessary supply. By these

4. *Historical Review*, pp. 438–40. Dr. John Fothergill praised the letter's style and its good effect in silencing opponents of the Assembly, but suggested a reservation: "I know not whether it did not serve to render the Proprietors more inflexible." To Israel Pemberton, June 12, 1758, Pemberton Papers, Hist. Soc. Pa.

5. See above, VI, 278 n, for mention of earlier *Gent. Mag.* accounts of events in Pennsylvania.

6. This paragraph (from the Assembly's Remonstrance of Jan. 26, 1757; see above, p. 108) and most of the others in this introduction are almost verbatim extracts from Assembly documents (drafted by BF) attacking the Proprietors.

7. Also from the Remonstrance of Jan. 26, 1757.

instructions all the proprietors estate, except a trifle, and all located unimproved lands, to whomsoever belonging, are to be exempted. There remains then to be taxed, only the improved lands, houses, and personal estates of the people. Now it is well known, from the tax books, that there are not in the province more than 20,000 houses, including those of the towns with those on plantations. If these, with the improved lands annexed to them, and the personal estate of those that inhabit them, are worth, one with another, £250 each, it may, we think, be reckoned their full value; then multiply 20,000 the number of houses, by £250 the value of each estate, and the produce is £5,000,000 for the full value of all our estates, real and personal, the unimproved lands excepted. Now three per cent. on five millions is but one hundred and fifty thousand pounds; and four shillings in the pound on one hundred and fifty thousand pounds, being but a fifth part, is no more than thirty thousand pounds; so that we ought to have near seventeen millions to produce, by such a tax, one hundred thousand pounds.[8]

4th. Because the bill* which they have prepared, without the exceptions required in the proprietaries instructions, is exactly conformable to an act lately passed by a former governor, and allowed by the crown.[1]

It is indeed matter of equal astonishment and concern, that in this time of danger and distress, when the utmost unanimity and dispatch is necessary to the preservation of life, liberty, and estate, a governor should be sent to our colonies with such instructions as must inevitably produce endless dispute and delay, and prevent the assembly from effectually opposing the French upon any other condition, than the giving up their rights as Englishmen.

The assembly, indeed, have been stigmatized as obstinate, fanatical, and disaffected; and reproached as the authors of every calamity under which they suffer. A paragraph in one of the

*In the bill which passed in March last,[9] the proprietary estate was not taxed, that matter being intended to be referred to the determination of superior authority in England.

8. From an Assembly committee report of Feb. 17, 1757; see above, p. 128.

9. See above, pp. 152–3 n.

1. This point is made, though in different words, in the committee report of Feb. 17, 1757.

public papers, which lately echoed the charge that has been long urged against them, has been answered by Mr. William Franklin of Philadelphia, who is now in England. We shall insert the paragraph and reply at large, as we cannot exhibit any other representation with equal authority.[2]

II

Pennsylvania Coffee-house
London, Sept. 16, 1757.

To the Printer of the Citizen.

Sir,

In your Paper of the 9th Instant, I observe the following Paragraph, Viz. "The last Letters from Philadelphia bring Accounts of the Scalping the Inhabitants of the Back Provinces by the Indians: At the same Time the Disputes between the Governor and the Assembly are carried to as great a Height as ever, and the Messages sent from the Assembly to the Governor, and from the Governor to the Assembly, are expressed in Terms which give very little Hopes of a reconciliation. The Bill to raise Money is clogged, so as to prevent the Governor from giving his Consent to it; and the Obstinacy of the Quakers in the Assembly is such, that they will in no Shape alter it: So that, while the Enemy is in the Heart of the Country, Cavils prevent any Thing being done for its Relief. Mr. Denny is the third Governor with whom the Assembly has had these Disputes within a few Years."[3]

As this Paragraph, like many others heretofore published in the Papers, is not founded on Truth, but calculated to prejudice the Public against the Quakers and People of Pennsylvania, you are

2. Following this paragraph *Gent. Mag.* goes directly into the quotation of the paragraph from *The Citizen* of September 9, without reproducing the opening words and phrases of the original and reprints the rest of WF's letter in its entirety. In all the surviving printings the date lines appear at the end with WF's signature, instead of at the beginning as here.

3. The full text of the piece to which WF replied has not been located in any printed or MS source, nor has its author been identified. News of frontier warfare and messages between the governor and the Assembly appeared frequently in London newspapers; e.g., *London Chron.* had printed the long messages of January–February 1757 on Aug. 3 and 15, 1757, and a shorter exchange of June 25 on September 3. See above, p. 246, for Indian attacks in Pennsylvania during July 1757.

desired to do that injured Province some Justice, in publishing the following Remarks;[4] which would have been sent you sooner, had the Paper come sooner to my Hands.

1. That the Scalping of the Frontier Inhabitants by the Indians is not peculiar to Pennsylvania, but common to all the Colonies, in Proportion as their Frontiers are more or less extended and exposed to the Enemy. That the Colony of Virginia, in which there are very few, if any Quakers, and none in the Assembly, has lost more Inhabitants and Territory by the War than Pennsylvania. That even the Colony of New York, with all its own Forces, a great Body of New-England Troops encamp'd on its Frontier, and the regular Army under Lord Loudoun, posted in different Places, has not been able to secure its Inhabitants from Scalping by the Indians; who coming secretly in very small Parties skulking in the Woods, must sometimes have it in their Power to surprize and destroy Travellers, or single Families settled in scattered Plantations, notwithstanding all the Care that can possibly be taken by any Government for their Protection. Centinels posted round an Army, while standing on their Guard, with Arms in their Hands, are often kill'd and scalp'd by Indians. How much easier must it be for such an Enemy to destroy a Ploughman at Work in his Field?

2. That the Inhabitants of the Frontiers of Pennsylvania are not Quakers, were in the Beginning of the War supplied with Arms and Ammunition by the Assembly, and have frequently defended themselves, and repelled the Enemy, being withheld by no Principle from Fighting; and the Losses they have suffer'd were owing entirely to their Situation, and the loose scattered Manner in which they had settled their Plantations and Families in the Woods, remote from each other, in Confidence of lasting Peace.

3. That the Disputes between the late and present Governors, and the Assembly of Pennsylvania, were occasioned, and are continued, chiefly by *new* Instructions from the Proprietors to those Governors, forbidding them to pass any Laws to raise Money for the Defence of the Country, unless the proprietary Estate, or much the greatest Part of it, was exempted from the Tax to be

4. The political disputes, defense measures, and other matters mentioned below are dealt with fully elsewhere in this and the preceding volume of this edition.

raised by Virtue of such Laws, and other Clauses inserted in them, by which the Privileges long enjoyed by the People, and which they think they have a Right to, not only as Pennsylvanians, but as Englishmen, were to be extorted from them, under their present Distresses. The Quakers, who, tho' the first Settlers, are now but a small Part of the People of Pennsylvania, were concerned in those Disputes only as Inhabitants of the Province, and not as Quakers; and all the other Inhabitants join in opposing those Instructions, and contending for their Rights, the Proprietary Officers and Dependants only excepted, with a few of such as they can influence.

4. That though some Quakers have Scruples against bearing Arms, they have when most numerous in the Assembly, granted large Sums for the King's Use (as they expressed it) which have been applied to the Defence of the Province; for Instance, in 1755, and 1756, they granted the Sum of £55,000 to be raised by a Tax on Estates real and personal, and £30,000 to be raised by Excise on Spirituous Liquors; besides near £10,000 in Flour, &c. to General Braddock and for cutting his Roads, and £10,000 to General Shirley in Provisions for the New England and New-York Forces, then on the Frontiers of New-York; at the same Time that the Contingent Expenses of Government to be otherwise provided for, were greatly and necessarily enhanced. That however, to remove all Pretence for Reflection on their Sect, as obstructing military Measures in Time of War, a Number of them voluntarily quitted their Seats in Assembly, in 1756; others requested their Friends not to chuse them in the ensuing Election, nor did any of that Profession stand as Candidates, or request a Vote for themselves at that Election, many Quakers refusing even to vote at all, and others voting for such Men as would, and did, make a considerable Majority in the House, who were not Quakers; and yet four of the Quakers, who were nevertheless chosen, refused to serve, and Writs were issued for new Elections, when four others, not Quakers, were chosen in their Places; that of 36 Members, the Number of which the House consists, there are not at the most above 12 of that Denomination, and those such as are well known to be for supporting the Government in Defence of the Country, but are too few, if they were against such a Measure, to prevent it.

5. That the Bill to raise Money said in the above Article of News, to be so clogged as to prevent the Governor from giving his Assent, was drawn in the same Form, and with the same Freedom from all Clogs, as that for granting £60,000 which had been passed by the Governor in 1755, and received the Royal Approbation; that the real Clogs or Obstructions to its passing were not in the Bill, but in the above-mentioned proprietary Instructions; that the Governor having long refused his Assent to the Bill, did in Excuse of his Conduct, on Lord Loudoun's Arrival at Philadelphia, in March last, lay his Reasons before his Lordship, who was pleased to communicate them to one of the Members of the House,[5] and patiently to hear what that Member had to say in Answer, the Governor himself being present; and that his Lordship did finally declare himself fully satisfied with the Answers made to those Reasons, and to give it as his Opinion to the Governor, that he ought immediately to pass the Bill, any Instructions he might have to the contrary from the Proprietors notwithstanding, which the Governor accordingly complied with, passed the Bill on the 22d of March, and the Money, being £100,000 for the Service of the current Year, has been ever since actually expending in the Defence of the Province; so that the whole Story of the Bill's not passing, the clogging of the Bill by the Assembly, and the Obstinacy of the Quakers preventing its Passage, is absolutely a malicious and notorious Falshood.

6. The Assertion of the News-Writers, "That while the Enemy is in the Heart of the Country, Cavils prevent any Thing being done for its Relief," is so far from being true: That First, the Enemy is not, nor ever was, in the Heart of the Country, having only molested the Frontier Settlements by their Parties. Secondly, More is done for the Relief and Defence of the Country, without any Assistance from the Crown, than is done perhaps by any other Colony in America; there having been, soon after the War broke out, the following Forts erected at the Province Expence, in a Line to cover the Frontier, viz. Henshaw's Fort on Delaware, Fort Hamilton, Fort Norris, Fort Allen, Fort Franklin, Fort Lebanon, Fort William Henry, Fort Augustus, Fort Halifax, Fort Granville, Fort Shirley, Fort Littleton, and Shippensburg Fort,

5. BF; see above, p. 148.

besides several smaller Stockades and Places of Defence, garrisoned by Troops in the Pay of the Province, under whose Protection the Inhabitants, who at first abandoned their Frontier Settlements, returned generally to their Habitations, and many yet continue, though not without some Danger, to cultivate their Lands: By these Pennsylvanian Troops, under Col. Armstrong, the greatest Blow was given to the Enemy last Year on the Ohio that they have received during the War: in burning and destroying the Indian Town of Kittanning, and killing their great Captain Jacobs, with many other Indians, and recovering a Number of Captives of their own and the neighbouring Provinces:[6] Besides the Garrisons, in the Forts, 1100 Soldiers are maintained on the Frontiers in Pay, being armed and accoutred by the Province, as ranging Companies.

And at Philadelphia, 15 Iron Cannon, 18 Pounders, were last Year purchased in England, and added to the 50 they had before, either mounted on their Batteries, or ready to be mounted, besides a Train of Artillery, being new Brass Field Pieces, 12 and 6 Pounders, with all their Appurtenances in extreme good Order, and a Magazine stored with Ammunition, a Quantity of large Bombshells, and above 2000 new Small Arms lately procured, exclusive of those in the Hands of the People. They have likewise this Summer fitted out a 20 Gun Province Ship of War, to scour the Coast of Privateers, and protect the Trade of that and the neighbouring Provinces,[7] which is more than any other Colony to the Southward of New England has done. Pennsylvania also, by its Situation, covers the greatest Part of New Jersey, all the Government

6. In *An Historical Review,* a note appended to the reprint of this letter asserted that the Kittanning expedition had been carried out over the objections of the governor, and that its success was a vindication of the provincial commissioners' plan to use ranging companies rather than garrisoned forts to defend the frontier. The governor's alleged devotion to garrisons and militia forces was cited as proof that what he *really* sought was the *power* which would go with large bodies of men under his command; his disdain of the Kittanning expedition, on the other hand, proved his neglect of measures truly calculated to defend the province. Pp 440–1. But see above, pp. 102–3, for Col. John Armstrong's quarrel with the commissioners.

7. The *Pennsylvania,* a frigate, Capt. John Sibbald, was purchased and outfitted by the provincial commissioners in the summer of 1757, and sailed on August 24 to protect the shipping lanes in and around Delaware Bay. *Pa. Gaz.,* Aug. 18 and 25, 1757.

of the Delaware Countries, and great Part of Maryland, from the Invasions of the Indians, without receiving any Contribution from those Colonies, or the Mother-Country, towards the Expence.

The above are Facts, consistent with the Knowledge of the Subscriber, who but lately left Philadelphia, is now in London, is not, nor ever was, a Quaker, nor writes this at the Request of any Quaker, but purely to do Justice to a Province and People, of late frequently abused in nameless Papers and Pamphlets published in England. And he hereby calls upon the Writer of that Article of News to produce the letters out of which, he says, he has drawn those Calumnies and Falshoods, or to take the Shame to himself. WILLIAM FRANKLIN.

From David Colden[8]

Draft: New-York Historical Society

Sir Septr. 18th. 1757

About the time you left America I was employed in endeavouring with my Fathers assistance to form an Explication of the Phenomena of Electricity, on his Principles of Action in Matter; some conceptions had occurred to me in pursuing the Experiments made by you and Mr. Canton[9] which gave me reason to hope it might be effected, on very simple principles. If you were at this time with us, I make no doubt what I have wrote on that subject, and which I now take the liberty to send you, would be much more correct. However I am so unwilling to have it appear in publick, before you have had an oppertunity of judging it, that I have desired my Cousin Alexander Colden[1] to leave it with you some time for your consideration: the favour which I have formerly had of corresponding with you on this subject gives me assurance that you will take the trouble of considering it and of letting me know your sentiments of it. I shall esteem it a great feavour Sir

8. Son of Cadwallader Colden and the author of a defense of BF's theories of electricity against the criticisms of the Abbé Nollet; see above, V, 135–44.

9. See above, V, 149–54, 516–19; also VI, 483, where the younger Colden mentions receiving a copy of BF's experiments made in pursuance of Canton's.

1. The son of Cadwallader Colden's brother James; he was a merchant in London, interested in science, and something of a protégé of Peter Collinson. David's letter to his cousin, Sept. 23, 1757, is in *Colden Paps.*, V, 185–7.

that you make corrections in any part that may appear to want it. I had much rather not have it published, than that it should afterwards appear unworthy the notice of the Judicious; but if it meets with your approbation I shall reckon myself very safe in the publication. I must beg you to let my Cousin see what you write me on this occasion, that he may know how to order the Printing, for I shall desire him to delay it, in case you make any material objections, till I have an oppertunity of obviating them, or recalling my error. Your advice to my Cousin in any thing concerning this Peice shall be most gratefully acknowledged by Sir Yrs.[2]

To Benjn Franklin Esqr.

From Isaac Norris

ALS: American Philosophical Society; also letterbook copy: Historical Society of Pennsylvania

Philada. October 17th. 1757

Respected Friend Benjn. Franklin

I was pleased to hear of your safe arrival by a short agreeable Letter from Exeter, which I had the pleasure of receiving about a Month ago.[3] The small but violent Party continues the same political Systems here expecting, I suppose, to be supported by Power and Influence at Home, where you will have the trouble to watch and disconcert their Misrepresentations.

As the Proprietary Purchases were to be explained at the last Treaty at Easton[4] they were under a Necessity of exerting their

2. This letter, captured by the French, never reached BF. Colden wrote him again on this matter, Oct. 26, 1758. No copy of the "Explication" has been found.

3. Not found, but presumably written about July 20 during BF's journey from Falmouth to London.

4. From July 25 to August 7, 1757, about 300 Indians, led by Teedyuscung, met at Easton with George Croghan, Governor Denny, six members of his Council, numerous assemblymen, interpreters, and perhaps 100 Quakers headed by Israel Pemberton. Though the treaty was officially conducted by Croghan as Sir William Johnson's deputy, the negotiations followed much the same pattern as those of the previous fall (see above, pp. 15–23); Teedyuscung, under the influence of Pemberton and his colleagues, continued to blame the Indian troubles on proprietary land frauds, while Richard Peters

Utmost Efforts to put forward the best Appearances, and did indeed venture further than I could have believed, If I had not been an Eye and Ear Witness of the Conduct of some of the Gentlemen, who were, on good Grounds, supposed to have the principal management of the Conferences there. Circumstances, which could not be made a Part of the Minutes, were carried on without the necessary Disguise in which Geo. Croghan condescended to become a Necessary Tool. The Law of this Province not yet confirmed in England,[5] the meanness of his former Course of Life and his present involved Situation, all probably, contributed to induce him to conduct himself as he did on this Occasion in Opposition to his former repeated Promises to me before it came to a Trial.[6] The Treaty laid before the House is in the Name of Geo. Croghan who is there supposed to be making his Report to Sir Wm. Johnson but what share he had in those Minutes, besides what they were compelled to make and collate at the publick Conferences, you who are acquainted with our Indian Minute Makers, need not be informed.[7] The Committee by Order of the

and Conrad Weiser steadfastly defended the earlier agreements. The integrity of the official recorders was impugned by a demand that Teedyuscung be permitted to have his own "secretary" and by an insistence that all deeds conveying Indian lands to the Proprietors be made public. Teedyuscung and his followers served Quaker ends for several days, becoming so imbued with self-righteousness as to threaten to massacre the proprietary officials. The Quakers quickly calmed them down, and when other Indian chiefs showed impatience with Teedyuscung's quarreling over ancient land sales, he suddenly gave up the disputes and proclaimed peace, thus undercutting the Quaker charges and allowing friendly relations to be formally re-established. The treaty is printed in Carl Van Doren and Julian P. Boyd, eds., *Indian Treaties Printed by Benjamin Franklin, 1736–1762* (Phila., 1938), pp. 189–212, 307, and there are full accounts of it in the biographies of Croghan, Weiser, Teedyuscung, and Pemberton cited elsewhere in these volumes.

5. The law of Dec. 1, 1755, protecting Croghan from his creditors; see above, VI, 295 n.

6. Among the Franklin papers at APS is a copy of a long memorandum drawn up by Norris at Croghan's request, July 25, 1757, and explaining what Norris alleged were injustices in proprietary purchases of Indian land, 1686–1742—quite possibly a response to Croghan's promise to seek full discussion of land grievances at the conference. Norris may have sent this copy to BF for use in pressing the Indian claims in England.

7. Croghan had sided with proprietary officials in some but not all of the disputes at the Easton treaty. Norris' feeling that Croghan had betrayed him

last Assembly will by this Conveyance transmit the Indian Minutes and Deeds as laid before the House by Charles Thompson[8] their Secretary, allowed and admitted by the Governor and George Croghan, with his Notes thereon.[9] But as the Governor has never offered him the Deed of 1718[1] I have ordered our Clerk to procure a certified Copy from the Office to be annexed to the Treaty. The printed Treaty of 1728 is not to be procured here tho it is probable R. Charles has it among his Papers;[2] I have two bound up with other Treaties, one of which I leave with my Brother in town and there is another belonging to the Assembly as we find upon search among the publick Papers but we have not been able to procure another. These Treaties being so scarce and not generally recollected by the People who whilst the Indians continued quiet, gave too light Attention to the Indian Purchases as

---

probably came from Croghan's increasing conviction that Assembly and Quaker interference had encouraged Delaware resistance to the Iroquois dominance upon which Johnson rested his Indian diplomacy. Nicholas B. Wainwright, *George Croghan Wilderness Diplomat* (Chapel Hill, 1959), pp. 127–34.

8. Charles Thomson (1729–1824), born in Ireland and landed an orphan in Pennsylvania in 1739; taught school in Philadelphia, 1750–60, and acted as agent, penman, and advisor for the Indian-Quaker group which opposed proprietary dealings with the Indians. BF arranged for the publication of his *An Enquiry into the Causes of the Alienation of the Delaware and Shawanese Indians,* in London in 1759. In 1760 Thomson forsook teaching for trade and politics, and he was in the forefront of every Pennsylvania protest against British rule from the Stamp Act to the Declaration of Independence. In 1774 be began fifteen years' uninterrupted service as secretary of the Continental Congress, a post at which he made a signal contribution to American independence, earning the gratitude and affection of Washington and John Adams among others. He failed to receive an office under the new Constitution, and retired to his home near Philadelphia where he spent his remaining years in scriptural studies which reflected his life-long devotion to the Presbyterian Church and resulted in highly regarded publications. *DAB;* Lewis R. Harley, *The Life of Charles Thomson* (Phila., 1900).

9. On Sept. 29, 1757, the Assembly had ordered these documents sent to its agents in order that "a true Representation of the Complaints of the . . . Indians against the Province . . . may be laid before his Majesty for his Royal Determination." *Votes,* 1756–57, p. 161.

1. Secretary Richard Peters had resisted making any of the deeds public, and managed to prevent divulgence of this one. Council meeting of Aug. 1, 1757; *Pa. Col. Recs.,* VII, 687–9.

2. BF's fellow agent, Robert Charles, long a close friend of Norris', had been receiving official Pennsylvania papers for years.

a Matter belonging to the Proprietarys only, might give Occasion to the witholding the Deed of 1718 and it was not known that it was recorded till after the Treaty at Easton. If what Isr[ae]l Pemberton told me is true, that Deed was actually produced to the Council during the Conferences and by them resolved not to be given with the other Deeds; (as you will find it was not) upon which One of the Counsellors entered his Dissent, but this to yourself only as I do not know what Use Is. Pemberton intends to make of this Anecdote, or upon what Terms he had it from his Kinsman the Counsellor.[3]

I shall herewith send the Copy of James Logans Letter to Thomas Watson dated the 20th of November 1727[4] by which it will appear that he (who best knew the Indian Purchases) owns the Lands about 3 or 4 Miles above Durham were not then purchased of the Indians. To this I shall add another Letter from J. Logan to my Father concerning the Manner heretofore used by some of our Land jobbers before they were purchased of the Indians. This conduct by long perseverance at length so exasperated the Indians that Governor Thomas in his Message to the Assembly on the 24th Augt. 1742 [Votes Vol 3 pagg. 481 seq][5] acknowledges they had wrote threatning Letters to the Proprietarys and the Magistrates that they would maintain the possession of their Lands by Force tho' by what has since happened it appears they were then Overawed by the Mohawks 'till the Unfortunate conduct of the British Arms in America has since given the Delawares an Opportunity of acting openly both against the Mohawks and those they apprehended their Oppressors within this Province. As the Proprietary Purchases are now found to concern every Freeholder who enjoys his Lands under them the Last Assembly appointed a Com[mitt]ee to make search for them thro' the Council

3. Though the 1718 deed is not mentioned in the minutes of the August 1 meeting, Councilor William Logan, Israel Pemberton's cousin, had urged that *all* deeds for Indian lands be made public. *Ibid.*, p. 688. At Thomson's request, a copy of the deed was provided on Aug. 30, 1757. 1 *Pa. Arch.*, III, 256, 262.

4. Printed on p. 23 of Thomson's *Enquiry*. The book is a full but partisan account of the land fraud charges made in this paragraph. The letter from James Logan to Isaac Norris, Sr., mentioned in the next sentence has not been found or further identified.

5. Brackets in the original.

Minutes, but were refused[6] as the Com[mitt]ee of Friends had been before so that we have hitherto only picked up such as had been recorded whilst it was yet improbable that the Indian clamours would ever reach the Royal Ear. John Penn soon after his Arrival here in the Year 1734[7] made large Sales of Land to Geo. McCall[8] and others, and Among the Rest made sale of One Hund[red] Thousand Acres of Land which was mostly located in the Forks of Delaware. A considerable time before the Day and halfs Walks by which the Proprietarys lay Claim to those Lands in Virtue of a Deed (as tis called) dated the 28th 6 mo 1686 and which seems to be ramm'd down the throats of the Delawares by the Treaty held by Governor Thomas in June and July 1742.[9] When these Lands were sold and located it became necessary to make Titles, and whether those Titles are good or not with Respect to the Indians is now the Dispute for which they have, unhappily for the purchasers, brought an Indian Ejectment. I have One of these Lottery Schemes[1] (very scarce) and I believe my Friend R. Charles must have one to which I refer your Curiosity.

I need not say any thing of our late Elections. The House have only met and chosen a few of their old Officers.[2] But as New scenes open upon us almost every Day I should be pleased to hear the Sentiments of proper Judges upon our (Carlisle or) Cumberland Election which for any thing I recollect at present is Variety in America.[3] Did not our most Fundamental Law oppose it in point

6. On July 12–13, 1757; *Votes*, 1756–57, pp. 160–1.

7. See above, I, 381, for the arrival of John Penn, then the senior Proprietor, in Philadelphia.

8. George McCall (*c.* 1695–1740), wealthy merchant and landowner, had purchased 14,000 acres of land from John Penn on June 20, 1735, in what is now Montgomery Co. *PMHB*, III (1879), 452–4.

9. See above, p. 19 n, for the so-called Walking Purchase.

1. A lottery for 100,000 acres of land advertised by the Proprietors in 1735, but never drawn because it did not fill. Those who had purchased tickets were given lands in the Delaware and Lehigh valleys. Thomson, *Enquiry*, pp. 31–2; Norris memorandum, July 25, 1757, APS.

2. Of the 36 members of the old Assembly, 31 (including BF) had been reelected on Oct. 1, 1757, and on the 14th and 15th the old officers were reelected, including Norris unanimously chosen as speaker. *Votes*, 1757–58, 3–4.

3. Col. John Stanwix, commanding officer of the British regulars stationed at Carlisle, had been elected, with the support of the proprietary interest, to the Assembly from Cumberland Co. 1 *Pa. Arch.*, III, 288.

of Residence it would be paying the highest Compliment to an Assembly of Pensylvania that the true Guardians of English Liberty should Concern themselves in our Affairs and kindly condescend to partake with us the Care of protecting the just Rights of this injured oppressed Colony. The N. Castle Convention tis said is likely to meet this Year; what they will do, or what may be expected from them, except the renewal of their Militia Law, I know not; but as that Assembly could not find time to meet all last Year, perhaps it may be thought Reasonable they should now lay some sort of a Tax upon themselves towards their own Defence but as every Thing that may be reasonably expected is not therefore performed I cannot in prudence further depend upon it[4] than upon the Free Gift which still lyes in the Condition you left it with a Ballance of Two thousand Pounds to be paid whenever it can be got.[5] I am Your Affectionate Friend ISAAC NORRIS

I am shorter upon Indian Affairs than I should otherwise think necessary as C. Thompson informs me he has wrote on that Subject fully to Wm. Franklin[6] to whom pray make my best Respects and Complements acceptable. IN

October 18th. We have gone thro' the Choice of our Agents, as last Year. I propose to write both to RC and RP.[7]

19th

By the Post of this Day I received a Letter of an Old Date from R. Partridge and soon after Is[rae]l Pemberton brought Partridges Letter to him of the 24th of Augt by the Packet, our House is dissatisfied that the Account of our Publick Affairs should be at the pleasure of private Intelligence and shewd some Resentment upon it among the Members but we have thot fit to continue him in the Agency as I have already wrote. Colo. Stanwix [is] not yet come [here?] nor do we know any thing from him since his Elec-

4. See below, p. 282 n, for the Delaware Assembly.

5. See above, VI, 480 n, for the incomplete payment of the Proprietor's gift. The letterbook copy ends here.

6. Charles Thomson wrote at length, mostly about the Lancaster Conference of May 12–20, 1757, to WF in a letter probably dated in June(?) 1757, and he also wrote about the Easton treaty in a letter not found but mentioned in one of Jan. 2, 1758; APS.

7. The Assembly re-appointed BF agent, and Robert Charles and Richard Partridge his assistants, on October 18. *Votes*, 1757–58, p. 6.

tion. We have Just now again sent up the Indian trade Bill and may possibly hear the Fate of it before this Vessel goes, but I do not chuse to delay the closing this Letter lest I should miss this Conveyance.[8] The Com[mitt]ee of Correspondence propose to send the Vote of Assembly last Year under the Great Seal and with it the Treaty as laid before the House by Charles Thompson with his Notes thereon.[9]

From David Hall Letterbook copy: American Philosophical Society

Dear Sir Philadelphia, 19th October 1757

My last to you by the Carolina Captain Duncan,[1] contained the second Copy of a Bill of Exchange for £100. which I hope is come safe to hand.

You have now inclosed the first Copy of one other Bill for £100. (which will make the fourth Hundred remitted you since you left Philadelphia)[2] the Receipt of which you will please to own by the first Vessel after it comes to hand, and likewise for that before sent. This last I had for Sixty-five, the others I think I acquainted you Cost Sixty Seven and a Half. &c.[3] D H

Inclosed is a Copy of the first letter of Advice relating to the above Bill of Exchange.

To Benjamin Franklin Esqr. per the Myrtilla Capt Budden Copy per Philadelphia Capt Stewart Via Liverpool

8. The Indian trade bill passed the House on the 19th, but Denny returned it the next day with amendments which the Assembly refused to accept. It was pending when the House adjourned, despite Denny's objection, on October 21. *Ibid.*, pp. 6–8; *Pa. Col. Recs.*, VII, 759–62, 768. See the next document for the probable conveyance of this letter by Capt. Richard Budden.

9. In view of "some material Omissions in, and considerable Differences between" the official minutes of the recent Easton treaty and those taken by Thomson, the House ordered that Thomson's minutes be printed along with a report by the Assembly delegates to the treaty. *Votes*, 1757–58, p. 8. Van Doren and Boyd, *Indian Treaties*, p. 307, explains the various versions of this treaty.

1. See above, p. 254.

2. For the record of Hall's payments to BF in England, see above, p. 236.

3. That is, the cost of sterling exchange had dropped. While Hall had bought the earlier bills at a cost of 67½ (£167 10*s*. Pa. currency for a £100 sterling bill), this one now cost only 65 (£165 Pa. currency for the £100 sterling bill).

To John Fothergill[4]

Draft: American Philosophical Society

Dear Doctor Tuesday morning, [October, 1757?][5]

I took the 30 grs. of Comp[oun]d Powder of Contrayerva[6] you prescribed, and had a good Night.

I had no Headach in the Morning, as when I took the Hartshorn Drops;[7] and therefore did not cup.[8]

But I have had all Day yesterday, a Giddiness and Swimming in my Head, which, every time I rise up, or turn suddenly, makes me stagger a little.

I hear a humming Noise in my head, and seem now and then to see little faint twinkling Lights. And my Head feels tender.

Will Abstinence be sufficient to remove this Disorder: or do you still advise Cupping, and any thing farther, for Your affectionate Friend[9]

Dr Fothergill

From John Bartram

Extract:[1] The Royal Society

[Philadelphia, November 12, 1757]

Here is a visible Aurora Borealis; at 7 a Clock it was about two hours high, to the northward pretty bright. Soon after Day light

4. Dr. Fothergill was BF's physician in the protracted illness here described.

5. As BF told DF November 22 (see below p. 272), his illness continued for about eight weeks. While this draft is not fully dated, the similarity of the symptoms to those he described to his wife suggest that it was written during this time, perhaps in October 1757.

6. Counter herb; antidote to poison; specifically, a tropical American aromatic root used as a stimulant or tonic.

7. Ammonia water made from shavings of the horn of a hart (deer).

8. To cup: to bleed for therapeutic purposes. BF later reported to DF that he had been cupped on the back of the head during this illness.

9. What may be parts of the initials "BF" are faintly discernable in a torn corner of the MS.

1. In BF's hand; he apparently made this extract to read before the Royal Society, Feb. 25, 1762; it was printed in *Phil. Trans.*, LII (1762), 474. BF had entitled the paper "Extract of a letter from Mr. John Bartram of Philadelphia to Mr. Franklin in London dated Nov. 12. 1757," but when published the final words were revised to read ". . . to Benjamin Franklin LL.D. F.R.S. relating to a remarkable Aurora Borealis."

disappeared it was much more East, where it was redder with some faint streamers, whose Points reached near 45 Degrees Elevation, which soon disappeared, and the Light descended by Degrees under the Pole, and by 10 a Clock was near extinct. I should be very glad to know whether (and how) it appeared this Night with you, which may assist in some Philosophical Enquiries. I have not observed any this Fall before. Yesterday the Weather was cool and clear, and the Wind pretty strong at North; and I believe this the coldest Evening we have had this Fall, tho' this Week we had Ice as thick as a Dollar.[2]

From David Hall Letterbook copy: American Philosophical Society

Sir Philadelphia 20th Novemr 1757

My two last to you by Capt. Budden to London, and Capt. Stewart to Liverpoole,[3] contained the first and second Copies of a Bill of Exchange for £100. Sterling, which I hope are come to hand and paid.

Inclosed you have now the first Copy of another Bill of Exchange for One Hundred Pounds more,[4] of which with the others before sent, please to advise me, when you have got the Money. I am &c. D H

To Benjamin Franklin Esqr.

To Deborah Franklin

ALS (mutilated): American Philosophical Society; parts reprinted from Duane, *Works,* VI, 20–4.[5]

My dear Child, London, Nov. 22. 1757

During my Illness which continued near Eight Weeks, I wrote you several little Letters,[6] as I was able; the last was by the

2. See below, p. 358, for BF's reply. No other reports of this aurora have been found.

3. See above, p. 270.

4. According to Hall's accounts of payments to BF in England (above, p. 236), this bill, later protested, was drawn by William Cooper of Boston and sent by the ship *Betty-Sally,* Capt. Edward Snead, which *Pa. Gaz.,* Nov. 17,

Pacquet which sailed from Falmouth [above a week since: in that I informed you that my intermitting fever which had continued to harrass me, by frequent relapses, was gone off, and I have ever since been gathering strength and flesh. My doctor, Fothergill, who had forbid me the use of pen and ink, now permits me to write as much as I can without over fatiguing myself, and therefore I sit down to write more fully than I have hitherto been able to do.

The 2d of September I wrote to you that I had had a violent cold and something of a fever, but that it was almost gone. However, it was not long before I had another severe cold, which continued longer than the first, attended by great pain in my head, the top of which was very hot, and when the pain went off, very sore and tender. These fits of pain continued sometimes longer than at others; seldom less than 12 hours, and once 36 hours. I was now and then a little delirious: they cupped me on the back of the head which seemed to ease me for the present; I took a great deal of bark, both in substance and infusion, and too soon thinking myself well, I ventured out twice, to do a little business and forward the service I am engaged in, and both times got fresh cold and fell down again; my good] Doctor grew very angry with me, for acting so contrary to his Cautions and Directions, and oblig'd me to promise more Observance for the future.[7] He attended me very carefully and affectionately; and the good Lady of the House[8]

1757, reported as cleared for London, but apparently her departure from the Delaware River was delayed long enough to receive this letter.

5. Large sections are now missing from the MS, but have been supplied, enclosed in brackets, from Duane's printed version.

6. Not found.

7. Apparently one of BF's indiscretions during this period was to sit to C. Dixon for his portrait miniature. See frontispiece.

8. Margaret (Mrs. Addinell) Stevenson (*c.* 1706–1783), a widow residing at No. 7 Craven St., Strand, took BF, WF, and their two Negro servants, Peter and King, as lodgers immediately upon their arrival in London (see above, p. 245 n), a congenial arrangement BF maintained throughout his years in England. Nothing is known of her husband or of her life before the summer of 1757; after that time, however, she and her daughter Mary (Polly), furnished BF with a good-natured, generous, lively home, and became intimate with the Franklins on both sides of the Atlantic. Whitfield J. Bell, Jr., "'All Clear Sunshine': New Letters of Franklin and Mary Stevenson Hewson," APS *Proc.*, C (1956), 521–36. Among many other payments to Mrs. Stevenson in

nursed me kindly; Billy was also of great Service to [me, in going from place to place, where I could not go myself, and Peter was very diligent and attentive. I took so much bark in various ways that I began to abhor it; I durst not take a vomit, for fear of my head; but at last I was seized one morning with a vomiting and purging, the latter of which continued the greater part of the day, and I believe was a kind of crisis to the distemper, carrying it clear off; for ever since I feel quite lightsome, and am every day gathering strength; so I hope my seasoning is over, and that I shall enjoy better health during the rest of my stay in England.

I have now before me, your letters of July 17, July 31, August 11, August 21, September 4, September 19, October 1, and October 9.[9] I thank you for writing to me so frequently and fully; I believe I have missed none of your letters yet, but those by Lyon, who was taken.[1]

You mention Mr. Scott's[2] being robbed, but do not say to what value; was it considerable? I have seen Mr. Ralph, and delivered him Mrs. Garrigues's letter.[3] He is removed from Turnham Green; when I return I'll tell you every thing relating to him, in the mean time I must advise Mrs. Garrigues not to write to him again, till I send her word how to direct her letters, he being unwilling, for some good reasons, that his present wife should know any thing of his having any connections in America. He expresses great affection for his daughter and grand children. He has but one child here.

1757, BF recorded £10 8*s.* 9½*d.* on November 11 "for sundry disbursements in my Sickness." "Account of Expences," p. 6; *PMHB,* LV (1931), 105.

9. None found.

1. See above, p. 238 n.

2. Not identified, but perhaps one of the merchant firm of Scott & McMichael.

3. See above, I, 58–9 n, for BF's old friend, James Ralph, now seen again for the first time in over thirty years. Mrs. Mary Garrigues (1724–1788), Ralph's daughter by a wife he had abandoned to go to England in 1724, had by this time ten children of her own, one of whom, Isaac (b. 1746), later wrote BF about his grandfather. Ralph had a daughter (1744–1762) by his English wife, who was dead by 1762. W. W. Hinshaw, *Encyclopedia of American Quaker Genealogy,* II (Ann Arbor, 1938), 365, 529; Thomas Faulkner, *The History and Antiquities of Brentford, Ealing, and Chiswick* (London, 1845), pp. 354–5.

I have found David Edwards,[4] and send you some of his letters, with one for his father. I am glad to hear that our friends at] Newark[5] got well thro' the Small Pox.

The above Particulars are in Answer to Things mentioned in your Letters, and so are what follows.

Governor Shirley's Affairs are still in an uncertain State; he is endeavouring to obtain an Enquiry into his Conduct; but the Confusion of Publick Affairs here, occasions it to be postpon'd.[6] He and I visit frequently.

I make no doubt but Reports will be spread by my Enemies to my Disadvantage, but let none of them trouble you. If I find I can do my Country no Good, I will take care, at least, not to do it any Harm. I will neither seek nor accept of any thing for my self; and though I may perhaps not be able to obtain for the People what they wish and expect, no Interest shall induce me to betray the Trust they have repos'd in me: So make yourself quite easy with regard to such Reports.

Mr. Hunter[7] is better than he has been for a long time. He and his Sister desire to be remembred to you.

I believe I left the Seal with Mr. Parker.[8]

I am glad to hear that Mr. Budinot has so seasonable a Supply; and hope he will not go to mining again.[9]

4. David Edwards (d. 1760), of Bury St. Edmonds, later helped BF find information about his Folger ancestors. David Edwards, Pa. Assembly doorkeeper and clerk for the provincial commissioners, may have been his father.

5. BF had visited in Newark, N.J., shortly before leaving for England; see above, p. 174. The friends there probably included the Anglican minister, Isaac Browne; the Archibald Kennedy family, whose son sailed for England on BF's packet; and Col. John Schuyler, whose estate was near Newark.

6. Former Gov. William Shirley had submitted papers to Lord Barrington early in 1757 to refute charges of his misconduct as commander-in-chief in North America. No formal action had been taken when Shirley left England in 1759 to become governor of the Bahamas. John A. Schutz, *William Shirley King's Governor of Massachusetts* (Chapel Hill, 1961), pp. 242–50.

7. William Hunter, BF's post office colleague.

8. Probably a post office seal; see above, pp. 191–4, for James Parker's commission as comptroller from BF and Hunter.

9. Elias Boudinot (1706–1770), silversmith, postmaster, and tavernkeeper in Princeton, N.J., and former neighbor of BF's in Philadelphia, owned a share in some copper mines near New Brunswick which he advertised for sale in 1761. G. A. Boyd, *Elias Boudinot, Patriot and Statesman, 1740–1821* (Princeton, 1952), pp. 6–16.

I am oblig'd to all my Friends that visit you in my Absence. My Love to them.

[Mr. Ralph[1] delivered me your letters very obligingly; he is well respected by people of value here.

I thank you for sending me brother Johnny's journal;[2] I hope he is well, and sister Read and the children.

I am sorry to hear of Mr. Burt's death.[3] He] came to me at New York with a Proposal that I did not approve of; but it show'd his Good Will and Respect for me: When I return, I'll tell you what it was.

I shall entertain Mr. Collinson and Dr. Fothergill with your Account of Tedyuskung's Visit.[4]

I should have read Sally's French Letter with more Pleasure, but that I thought the French rather too good to be all her own Composing. I suppose her Master must have corrected it. But I am glad she is improving in that and her Music. I send her a French Pamela.[5]

1. Not James Ralph; BF probably wrote Relph or Relfe. John Relfe, a merchant on Water St., Philadelphia, advertised in *Pa. Jour.*, Jan. 6, 1757, that he "designs soon for England," and in *Pa. Gaz.*, May 25, 1758, he advertised goods for sale just imported from London and Liverpool. Since BF mentions letters carried to America by a Mr. Relph in January and February 1758 (below, pp. 360, 379), it is probable that Relfe went to London on a buying trip and carried letters for the Franklins in both directions.

2. Probably a wagonmaster's journal, or accounts, of DF's brother, John Read; see above, VI, 221–2.

3. Not identified.

4. Teedyuscung had visited Philadelphia, August 29–September 3, and again a month later, when, among other things, he embarrassed Denny by inquiring after the health of his wife, from whom, as everybody in Philadelphia knew, he was estranged. *Pa. Col. Recs.*, VII, 725–31, 756; Anthony F. C. Wallace, *King of the Delawares: Teedyuscung, 1700–1763* (Phila., 1949), pp. 183–5.

5. Fourteen-year-old Sally Franklin's French lessons probably were a project planned by her and her father; DF had written earlier that "I had no desire of her larning that Language but shee desired it her selef," and she had been studying it for four weeks. To Susanna Wright, July 14, 1757; Yale Univ. Lib. Sally's French letter has not been found. In the Memorandum Book which DF kept (after a fashion) during BF's absence, are several entries of payments to Sally's French and music masters (see above, pp. 167–8). The reference is to a French translation of Samuel Richardson's *Pamela, or Virtue Rewarded.*

You were very lucky in not Insuring the Rum. We are oblig'd to Mr. Booth for his Care in that Remittance. I suppose you have wrote to acknowledge the Receipt of it. I have not yet seen Mr. Birkett.[6]

I am not much surpriz'd at Green's Behaviour. He has not an honest Principle, I fear. I have not yet seen Mr. Wolstenholme, but he is arrived.[7]

I am glad you went to Eliz. Town, and that Ben. has got that good Girl.[8] I hope they will do well. When you write remember my Love to her.

Dec. 3. I write by little and little, as I can find Time. I have now gone thro' all your agreable letters, which give me fresh Pleasure every time I read them. Last Night I received another, dated October 16.[9] which brings me the good news that you and Salley were got safe home, your last of the 9th being from Eliz. Town. Budden's [ship is not yet come up to London, but is daily expected, having been some time at Cowes. Mr. Hall has sent me a Bill, as you mention.[1] Mr. Walsteinholme is come to town and I expect to see him to day. When I have enquired how things are with Green, I shall write some directions to you what to do in the affair.

I am glad to hear that Miss Ray is well, and that you correspond. It is not convenient to be forward in giving advice in such cases. She has prudence enough to judge for herself, and I hope she will judge and act for the best.[2]

6. James Birkett (Birket) and Nathanial Booth were Quaker merchants of Antigua; see above, v, 500. Letters from them to the Pembertons show they had extensive business connections in Philadelphia. Pemberton Papers, Hist. Soc. Pa.

7. See above, III, 153–4 n, for Jonas Green, postmaster at Annapolis, later displaced by BF for not furnishing proper accounts. James Parker to Jared Ingersoll, Feb. 19, 1769, *Papers of the New Haven Colony Hist. Soc.*, IX (1918), 398. Daniel Wolstenholme, Annapolis merchant, had come to England in October 1757 to seek government contracts through John Hanbury. *Md. Arch.*, IX, *passim*, esp. 39, 88–9.

8. For Benjamin Mecom's marriage, see above, p. 216.

9. Not found.

1. See above, p. 270.

2. Catharine Ray married William Greene on April 30, 1758; perhaps she had sought DF's advice about the marriage.

I hear there is a miniature painter gone over to Philadephia, a relation to John Reynolds.[3] If Sally's picture is not done to your mind, by the] young Man, and the other Gentleman is a good hand and follows that Business, suppose you get Sally's done by him and send it me with your small Picture, that I may here get all our little Family drawn in one Conversation Piece.[4]

I am sorry to hear of the general Sickness. I hope it is over before this Time, and that little Franky[5] is recover'd.

I was as much disappointed in my Intention of Writing by that Pacquet, as you were in not receiving Letters by her; and it has since given me a great deal of Vexation. I wrote to you by way of New York, the Day after my Arrival in London, which I do not find you have receiv'd.[6]

I do not use to be a backward Correspondent though my Sickness has brought me behind hand with my Friends in that Respect.

Had I been well, I intended to have gone round among the Shops, and bought some [pretty things for you and my dear good Sally, (whose little hands you say eased your headache) to send by this ship,[7] but I must now defer it to the next, having only got a crimson satin cloak for you, the newest fashion, and the black-silk for Sally; but Billy sends her a scarlet feather, muff, and tippet, and a box of fashionable linen for her dress; in the box is a thermometer for Mr. Taylor and one for Mr. Schlatter, which you will carefully deliver; as also, a watch for Mr. Schlatter. I shall

3. A merchant on Front St., Phila.; the artist is unidentified.

4. Benjamin West (1728–1820) had made a picture of Sally, which BF apparently took with him to England though he did not care much for it. John Hesselius (above, p. 180 n) was about to paint a new portrait of the girl. BF again discussed the proposed composite family portrait in a letter to DF, June 10, 1758. Charles C. Sellers, *Benjamin Franklin in Portraiture* (New Haven, 1962), pp. 47, 52–3.

5. William Dunlap's son, Francis.

6. See above, p. 245; DF received the letter in December.

7. Vessels increasingly left British ports under convoy; BF's letter probably was on board a ship in a convoy which left Deal about December 8. *London Chron.*, Dec. 10, 1757. BF paid £10 12*s.* on December 5 for "things to send to America," and DF acknowledged receipt of the presents the following spring. "Account of Expences," p. 7; *PMHB*, LV (1931), 105.

write to them; the black silk was sent to Mr. Neates, who undertook to forward it in some package of his.[8]

It is now twelve days since I began to write this letter, and I still continue well, but have not yet quite recovered my strength, flesh or spirits. I every day drink a glass of infusion of bark in wine,] by way of Prevention, and hope my Fever will no more return. On fair Days, which are but few, I venture out about noon.

The agreable Conversation I meet with among Men of Learning, and the Notice taken of me by Persons of Distinction, are the principal Things that sooth me for the present under this painful Absence from my Family and Friends; yet those would not detain me here another Week, if I had not other Inducements, Duty to my Country and Hopes of being able to do it Service.

Pray remember me kindly to all that love us, and to all that we love. 'Tis endless to name Names. I am, my dear Child, Your ever loving Husband B FRANKLIN

From Ferdinand John Paris

Copy and draft: Historical Society of Pennsylvania

On November 14 Franklin had sufficiently recovered from his serious autumn illness to confer with Thomas Penn, who for once paid heed and wrote immediately to Denny: "Mr. Franklin was with me this Morning and complains that the Companys intended for Rangers, have been kept in the Forts to the great injury of the Country, the Indians having made several inroads, which in all probability might have been prevented, had they been kept ranging on the Frontiers. I recommend to you to give peremptory orders, that they may be employed in such manners as will best answer the intent of raising them." At the same time Penn probably told Franklin that he had laid the Heads of Complaint before the attorney general and solicitor general who were in town after four months' vacation, an interruption Penn thought was of little consequence since Lord Halifax had "been ill with gout 3 weeks," and Franklin had been too sick for two months to "have attended to

8. BF paid 2*s.* 6*d.* on August 28 "for mending Mr. Schlatter's Watch," and on December 5 noted that Mr. Taylor was debtor 18*s.* for a thermometer. "Account of Expences," pp. 4, 9; *PMHB,* LV (1931), 103, 106. This was probably Abraham Taylor of Philadelphia (above, III, 428 n); William and Samuel Neate were merchants of London and Philadelphia respectively; see above, IV, 115 n.

Business."[9] The following letter is further evidence that business had resumed in London.

[November 23, 1757][1]

As the Proprietaries of Pensilvania think it highly probable, that the House of Representatives, on sending over their Agent, may have charged him with some Applications to the Crown, for Aid or Assistance; Their Concern, for the Safety of the Inhabitants, obliges them to inform the Agent, that they are ready and very desirous, (notwithstanding any Difference in Opinion, in some Matters, which, it's hoped, will soon be adjusted) to use their utmost Endeavours to promote any such Application.

Dated this 23d. Day of November 1757. FERD JOHN PARIS
Agent to the said Proprietaries

To Benjamin Franklin Esqr., Agent to the House of Representatives of Pensilvania.

23d. November 1757. Left an exact Copy of the above (which Copy was signed by Mr. Paris and was enclosed in a Blank sealed Cover, and directed, To Benjamin Franklin Esqr.) at Mr. Franklin's Lodgings, in Craven Street, at the House of Mrs. Stephens,[2] with one Mrs. Sparrow, who say'd she was a Relation of the said Mrs. Stephens and lived there, and would take particular Care to let Mr. Franklin have it, as soon as he came Home (Neither Mr. Franklin, or his Son, being, as she sayd, within)

JNO TOWSE[3]

9. Penn to Denny, Nov. 14, 1757; to Richard Hockley, Nov. 9, 1757; and to Richard Peters, Nov. 14, 1757; Penn Papers, Hist. Soc. Pa. See above, pp. 248–52, for the Heads of Complaint and earlier conversations between BF and Penn.

1. Paris wrote on the draft, "Altered 22. Novr. 1757 according to Mr. Penns Direction (Draft?)." Besides many verbal changes, the final version omitted reference to a possible appeal by BF to Parliament, and to "Information" received that any appeals were planned.

2. Mrs. Margaret Stevenson. Mrs. Sparrow has not been identified.

3. Not identified. The draft was endorsed by Paris: "Demand on Mr. Franklin, whether the prop[rieta]ry can any way assist such Applications, as he may be charged with, for Ayd, to the province?" The care Paris took to see that this letter was properly delivered and attested, together with its curious connection with Penn's letter of the 25th (see below, p. 285) suggests that Paris expected to make use of it at some later stage of the hearings attending BF's agency.

From Isaac Norris

Letterbook copy: Historical Society of Pennsylvania

Benja Franklin Novr 24th 1757

The above is a Copy of my last.[4] I have Since received two letters of the 23d (a Copy, the Original not Come To Hand) and 30th August.[5] We are all extreamly well pleas'd With your Safe arrival there and the Continuence of your Health. Your Conduct I never doubted, but if it is necessary To Say any thing upon it I think you have acted With great Judgment in the Interviews with the Proprietors and the Exclusion of JFP[6] from your Consultations and pray remember me To Billy. I have his manly performance in the Citizen.[7] The Manner of appearing is extreamly well Judged. I have returned him my Thanks, for his Books in a letter to RP,[8] and would write To him, if that becomes necessary, He knows I have a great regard for him: and I know he will be

4. See above, pp. 264–70.

5. Neither letter has been found. Many of the letters BF wrote describing his work as Assembly agent in England, 1757–62 and 1764–75, have been lost. Soon after he reached London in 1757 he apparently began the practice of composing rough drafts in a series of letterbooks and by 1775 he had filled "eight or ten" of these, but only one survived the sacking of the country house near Philadelphia where he stored them on his departure for France in October 1776 (see above, I, xxi). Some of his correspondents, of course, carefully preserved the letters he sent them and many have been located, but other individuals did not. The papers of Isaac Norris, for example, contain surprisingly few letters from BF. While forty-one letters have been located from Norris to BF written during the first English mission, mostly Norris' own letterbook copies, only eight of the many BF wrote him in the same period seem to have survived in any form. Since Norris, as speaker of the Assembly, was the one to whom BF would naturally have written most fully about his activities as agent, the loss is a particular handicap to an understanding of his work.

6. Ferdinand John Paris, the Proprietors' agent.

7. See above, pp. 255–63.

8. Norris wrote Richard Partridge November 24 praising WF for signing the letter to the *Citizen* in order to "drag . . . the Annonimous Scriblers . . . out, if possible, from their lurking Insidious manner of venting their Amazing Absurdities" against the Pa. Assembly and the Quakers. The publications WF sent to Norris were William Smith, *The History of the Province of New York* (London, 1757); John Mitchell, *The Contest in America between Great Britain and France* (London, 1757); and an August magazine, perhaps *Gentleman's*. Norris to Partridge, Nov. 24, 1757, Hist. Soc. Pa.

acquainted With all I have To Say on account of the Province under your Address.

But the little Time I have, ought To make me very laconick. J. Hughs is at Wyoming, Endeavouring to Effect the Engagements of the Government to the Indians, Tho Cloggd in his Commission with Two Companions not very agreeable; but the third of his own chusing; we hear very little from him as he is out of the Post road; but he went with So hearty an Inclination that we are well Assured, He will do every thing in his power. I hope J Galloway, or Some body Else may have wrote of the Difficulties he met with in his Commission for I dare not begin upon them.[9] The N Castle Assembly, have met, made a Speech—continued their Militia law—Struck 20,000 Out of the Interest—of which I am informed they gave £4,000—and adjourned: I am told by the Author, there is an answer to that Speech To appear in This days paper, but I have not Seen it.[1] The Same Gentleman informs me, That he has it from Good hands, That the Governor is inclined to Agree with the Assembly, if they Shew the least inclination, which no doubt they will Chearfully Comply with, in every thing Consistant With their Trust; I Should not be Surprisd at this Conduct, for he is not well used (To Say the least) by those he has Confided in, but what he may think he has in his power I Cannot

9. In response to a request made by Teedyuscung at the Easton Treaty (see above, p. 264 n), Pennsylvania agreed to assist settlement of the Delawares in the Wyoming Valley near present-day Wilkes-Barre. Upon Conrad Weiser's refusal of the task, Denny reluctantly commissioned John Hughes to go to Wyoming to build houses for the Indians, but at the same time made Edward Shippen and James Galbreath, friends of the proprietary interest, joint commissioners. Hughes was refused sole command, but was allowed to have Rev. Charles Beatty (above, VI, 358 n) also commissioned, and the work party left for the valley. By mid-November eight houses were building but Teedyuscung decided to winter in Bethlehem and the work was suspended until spring. *Pa. Col. Recs.*, VII, 727–30, 734–6, 754–6, 770; 1 *Pa. Arch.*, III, 288–9, 297–8, 316–19. No letter about the expedition from Joseph Galloway has been found, though BF later acknowledged one of December 5 which may have reported on the affair.

1. The Delaware Assembly address, which included a spirited denial of Pa. Assembly aspersions on it, appeared in *Pa. Gaz.*, Nov. 10, 1757, and was reprinted in *London Chron.*, Jan. 21–24, 1758. A response by "Philo Patriae" (probably Joseph Galloway, BF's successor as Assembly spokesman) appeared in *Pa. Gaz.*, Nov. 24, 1757.

tell.[2] The Instructions are very particular we have Too much occasion To know, and if besides what we do know, there Should be the Same Instruction (as To Sir W. Keith)[3] That where they had not particularly provided, He Should be guided by the Opinion of the Council, or prehaps by particular members of it; in what Can he do: I Pitty his Situation, on many accounts, which you will hear from others, but for what relates To the Publick; I will assist him in every Honourable Inclination To render himself and the People under his Government Easy and Safe. Our Hundred Thousand Pound is Expended; about £8000 of which is laid out in Barracks, near finished, at the Upper End of the Town;[4] After being driven off, the lot you once tho't of for the Hospital; where they had dug the Cellers, and begun to lay the foundation, at the Expence of about £150, what will become of this poor lot at last?[5] Our Indian Trade Bill has been repeatedly refused, tho' we had made Concessions, which we aprehended would have Secured its passage. However the Governor has agreed To take a £1000 Stock Out of the £100,000, and with that Sum the Commissioners have Sent up Goods To Shamokin, under the Care of John Carson, Towards Supplying the imediate

2. Norris seems to hint here that Denny has agreed to violate his instructions and approve an Assembly measure (probably to tax the proprietary estates) out of disgust with his advisers (principally Richard Peters) and in response to Assembly offers to favor him (with his salary?). The Pa. Assembly was in adjournment and did not meet again until Jan. 2, 1758.

3. Sir William Keith (1680–1749), Governor of Pennsylvania, 1717–26, but dismissed by the Proprietors for taking the Assembly side in a dispute. *DAB*. See also above, I, 53 n, 126 n.

4. On the south side of Mulberry (Arch) St. between Ninth and Tenth Sts., a lot which the Proprietors had refused to give to the Pa. Hospital; see above, V, 294, 301–2.

5. Barracks for 5000 of the King's troops expected to quarter in Philadelphia for the winter were finally built in the Northern Liberties on Third Street under the supervision of Joseph Fox and Benjamin Loxley. Denny was as puzzled as Norris at the change in plans, apparently caused when Richard Hockley threatened suit unless the lot first proposed was properly purchased from the Proprietors. Lord Loudoun also suggested a new site for the barracks. *Pa. Col. Recs.*, VII, 737, 756; *Votes*, 1757–58, pp. 120–1; 1 *Pa. Arch.*, III, 278; Watson, *Annals*, I, 415–16; [Thomas Balch], *Letters and Papers Relating Chiefly to the Provincial History of Pennsylvania* (Phila., 1855), p. 98.

necessities of our Indian Allies;[6] you will find very few Incursions of the Indians for Some time past; if we would by any means Consolidate the Easton Peace; the Indians at Wyoming; would be a very natural Barrier, and all who were at that Treaty were Witnesses, that never any people, did or Could Come with more hearty dispositions to Confirm a lasting Peace, Than Those Savages, as they are calld: but from the different Conduct of the Managers of that Conferance, in behalf of this Government and of the Indians, I fear, the Name is, as the lawyers Call it: Ambu[s]catory; I am writing very late, and must Send in the Morning, So that I will only desire you, to Take the trouble of getting me a Telescopial Telescope; of 24 feet, my Friend R. Charles will pay;[7] and I will be obliged if W F would Collate a list of the Names, of the City lots, with Names, in the letter from W Penn to the Society, in the American library given by W. Kennet p: 140, which may be of use here, and not much Trouble.[8] He may remember, I mentiond it to him at fair hill, but I give him this further memorandum. I am Dear Friend Your Affectionate friend

I N

6. John Carson's store, opened on December 8, seems to have been a success; so he reported to Denny, and its operation pleased Capt. Joseph Shippen. *Pa. Col. Recs.*, VII, 773; *PMHB*, XXXVI (1912), 448–9, 455.

7. Norris wanted a telescope "for the night" to replace a 14 ft. one he had purchased in 1735; Norris to Robert Charles, Dec. 4, 1757, Hist. Soc. Pa. Norris' account with BF and Charles shows that on Sept. 15, 1758, BF bought from John Cuff of London for Norris a 24 ft. refracting telescope, which, with its packing case, cost £17 7*s.* 6*d.* Lib. Co. Phila.

8. Apparently Norris wanted WF to compare a list of the (supposed) present owners of lots in Philadelphia with the list of purchasers in *A Letter from William Penn . . . To The Committee of the Free Society of Traders . . . To which is added an Account of the City of Philadelphia . . . with a Portraiture or Plat-form thereof, Wherein the Purchasers Lots are distinguished . . .* (London, 1683). *PMHB*, LXIII (1939), 148–50; LXVIII (1944), 406. Norris referred WF to White Kennett, *Bibliothecae Americanae Primordia. An Attempt Towards laying the Foundation of an American Library* (London, 1713), which, on p. 140, recorded the full title of Penn's letter. Norris may have sought to question proprietary ownership of the Mulberry St. lot mentioned above; if so, the 1683 list did not help since no purchaser is listed for it there.

From Thomas Penn

Letterbook copy: Historical Society of Pennsylvania

Sir Spring Garden, Novr. 25: 1757.

As I find by what you told me and by my Letters from Pennsylvania that Admiral Holborne[9] had not Station'd a Ship in Delaware Bay in pursuance of the Resolution of the Lords of the Admiralty on our application communicated to me in January last, by Mr. Cleveland's[1] Letter, that I shewed you, I have applied again to that Board, and they yesterday, informed me they had ordered his Majesty's Frigate the Beaver commanded by Capt. Gascoigne now bound to New York, for that Service. This I desire you will inform the House of Representatives of, and heartily wishing it may be found a great protection to the Trade,[2] remain Your affectionate Friend T:P:

Benjamin Franklin Esqr.

From William Hunter

ALS: American Philosophical Society

Dear Sir, Wednesday Morne [Nov. 30, 1757][3]

If convenient, I should be oblig'd to you for three or four

9. Adm. Francis Holburne (1704–1771), commander of the British fleet sent to support Loudoun's proposed assault on Louisbourg in the summer of 1757. *DNB.*

1. John Cleveland (d. 1763), secretary of the Admiralty and M.P. for Plymouth; "a hard-working, hungry Scot who acquired unrivalled knowledge of Admiralty matters, and thereby rose to a position of considerable importance." Lewis B. Namier, *The Structure of Politics at the Accession of George III* (2d edit., London, 1957), p. 39.

2. Capt. Edward Gascoigne left Deal with the *Beaver* and a convoy of ships for North America by December 10, with orders "to see the Virginia Ships to the Capes, and then proceed to New York" before taking her station. *London Chron.*, Dec. 3 and 10, 1757; Penn to Richard Peters, Dec. 1, 1757, Penn Papers, Hist. Soc. Pa. News that the *Beaver* was to be in Delaware Bay appeared in *Pa. Gaz.*, March 16, 1758.

3. On Dec. 1, 1757, BF noted payments of £400 and £20 in accordance with Hunter's request below. "Account of Expences," p. 7; *PMHB*, LV (1931), 105.

Hundred Pound Draughts on your Banker. My Sister wants one of Twenty Pound; for Marketting. Yours, WM. HUNTER

Addressed: To / Mr. Franklin[4]

To William Coleman[5]

MS not found; abstract: Minute-Book of the Academy Trustees, Trustees of the University of Pennsylvania

At a Meeting of the Trustees at the Academy March 14th 1758

Present

Richard Peters	Thomas White
William Coleman	Alexander Stedman

Mr. Franklin having by a Letter to Mr. Coleman dated from London Dec. 8th 1757 requested him to inform the Trustees that he had on their Account discharged a Bill of Articles for an Apparatus in Experimental Philosophy, amounting to £69 11*s.* Sterling and that he had further undertaken to pay Mr. Collinson a Ballance of £138 4*s.* 2*d.* Sterling due to him on the same Account and having in the same Letter likewise requested that the Trustees would remit him the Sum of £207 15*s.* 2*d.* Sterling to reimburse him; the Trustees present taking this Affair into Consideration are of Opinion that the above Sum of £207 15*s.* 2*d.* Sterling should forthwith be remited to Mr. Franklin by the Treasurer, and desire the President to issue an Order for that Purpose.[6]

4. On another part of the cover sheet BF wrote "Latin Drinking Song." Diligent research reveals no connection between Hunter's letter and such an (unidentified) song.

5. See above, II, 406 n.

6. BF had paid £69 11*s.* to Jonathan Sisson (an instrument maker, see above, IV, 448 n) on Nov. 2, 1757. He sent an account to Coleman, Sept. 12, 1758, showing that the Academy still owed him £132 14*s.* 5*d.*, and only on March 4, 1759, did he record final settlement of this account. "Account of Expences," pp. 6, 23, 24; *PMHB,* LV (1931), 104, 113, 116. The balance due to Collinson represented books and instruments the latter had bought for the Academy before BF's arrival in England. See above, VI, 171–2, 228; and this volume pp. 49–50.

To David Hall

ALS: American Philosophical Society

Dear Mr. Hall London, Dec. 9. 1757

I have yours of June 23. July 4. and 31. Sept. 14. and 30. and Oct. 19. and have receiv'd of you since I left Philadelphia, four Bills of One hundred Pounds Sterling each. I thank you for your Care in sending them, and your full Accounts of News, &c.[7]

I have been long ill. But I thank God am now pretty well recover'd, and hope to be a better Correspondent for the future. I have bespoke the Letter of Caslon, but find him very dilatory.[8] I doubt I shall not be able to get you a Hand that is good for any thing.

You mention sending me two Copies of the last Treaty at Eastown, but they proved to be of that at Harris's Ferry.[9] I wish you had sent me a Poor Richard's Almanack.[1] It is impossible to form any Judgment yet when I shall return; but hope it may be early in the Summer.

I am oblig'd to Dr. Evans[2] for the Journal. Lord Anson heard I had such a Thing, and sent for it to day.[3] Say nothing of this.

7. The first, third, and fifth of the letters acknowledged by BF have not been found; the others are printed above. See above, p. 236, for a summary of the payments to BF. The "Accounts of News" BF acknowledged may have been in the missing letters, or may refer to newspapers.

8. See above, VI, 476, for William Caslon and an earlier order of type from him. BF recorded payment of £31 2*s*. to Caslon on Sept. 29, 1758, for "letters sent to my office, under D. Hall, 311 lbs. Bourgeois." "Account of Expences," p. 41; *PMHB*, LV (1931), 114.

9. See above, p. 264 n, for the "last" Easton Treaty, July–August 1757, advertised in *Pa. Gaz.*, Oct. 13, 1757. *Minutes of Conferences Held with the Indians, at Harris's Ferry, and at Lancaster, in March, April, and May 1757*, printed by Franklin and Hall (Phila., 1757), had been advertised on July 7, 1757.

1. *Poor Richard* for 1758 (see below, pp. 326–55), was advertised as in press, *Pa. Gaz.*, Sept. 15, 1757, and as "just published," October 6.

2. Probably Dr. Cadwalader Evans (*c.* 1716–1773), a Philadelphia physician who had lived in Haiti and Jamaica, 1746–48; he was appointed to the staff of the Pa. Hospital, 1759. Frequent letters between him and BF, 1765–73, show they shared political views as well as scientific and philanthropic interests. *Pa. Gaz.*, July 7, 1773; Thomas G. Morton and Frank Woodbury, *The History of the Pennsylvania Hospital, 1751–1895* (Phila., 1895), p. 489.

3. No "Journal" by Evans has been found or identified; Lord Anson, F.R.S., First Lord of the Admiralty, may have been interested in something Evans had written following his capture by the Spanish which had led to his residence in the West Indies.

This Nation has been almost in Despair, on Account of their bad Success everywhere during this Year; but the King of Prussia's late good Fortune begins to revive them again. He will have a great Sum granted him by Parliament.[4] Just now we have the News, that Prince Bevern has gain'd a compleat Victory over the Austrians in Silesia. They were double his Number, tis said, and attack'd him in his Camp, thinking to force his Intrenchments; but after 4 hours bloody Conflict, they gave over the Attempt; he came out and attack'd them in his turn, the Austrians broke and fled three different Ways; he pursu'd 6 German Miles, came up with one Third, and cut them to pieces; the King, who was marching to his Assistance met another Division, and demolish'd that. How much of this will prove true I know not: But that there has been a Victory is generally believ'd.[5]

My Love to Polly and the Children, Mrs. Leacock,[6] &c. in which Billy joins. I have only time to add, that I am, Dear Friend Yours affectionately B FRANKLIN

Mr. Strahan and Family are well

Addressed: To / Mr David Hall / Philada.

Endorsed: B. Franklin Decr. 9. 1757.

William Franklin to Elizabeth Graeme

ALS:[7] Harvard College Library (Sparks)

Dear Madam Craven Street, London Decr. 9, 1757

No Doubt you must be much surpriz'd at so many Vessels arriving at different Parts of America from England, without so

4. This sentence and the preceding one were printed with only slight verbal changes in *Pa. Gaz.*, March 16, 1758.

5. *London Chron.*, Nov. 15–17, 1757, had reported Frederick II's victory over the French at Rossbach; and on December 8 falsely reported that Prince Bevern had defeated the Austrians at Breslau, where, in fact, the Austrians were victorious. *Ibid.*, Dec. 10, 1757. Frederick II did defeat them at Leuthen on December 5, news of which was in the *Chronicle* on the 20th.

6. Probably Hall's mother-in-law; his wife was the former Mary Lacock. *PMHB*, x (1886), 86–7.

7. The first part of this letter, while irrelevant to the activities of the writer's father, is included here for its own interest as showing the reactions of a

much as a single Line from the Man who has so often, and so warmly professed himself your Friend and Admirer. The Thoughts, the Suspicions, that must naturally arise in your Breast on this Occasion, my Imagination pictures in such strong Colours as gives me sensible Pain. But, believe me, my dearest Betsey, notwithstanding Appearances make against me, I am not wholly without Excuse. For some Time after my Arrival at this great Metropolis, the infinite Variety of new Objects; the continued Noise and Bustle in the Streets; and the Viewing such Things as were esteem'd most curious, engross'd all my Attention. Since then, frequent Engagements amongst Politicians, Philosophers, and Men of Business; making Acquaintances with such Men as have it in their Power to be of Service in settling our unhappy Provincial Disputes; and now and then partaking of the publick Diversions and Entertainments of this bewitching Country, have found full Employment for almost every Hour. Even the present Hour is stolen from Sleep; the Watchman's hoarse Voice calling, Past two aClock and a Cloudy Morning. Such is now my Hurry, and such is it like to be; rather increasing than diminishing. Ought not then some Allowance to be made for my past, nay for my future, Silence, when so circumstanced? Be that as it will, I shall write to you as often as possibly I can, and trust to your Friendship for an Apology, if it should not be so often as we both could desire.

It may seem strange, but it is not the less true, that one great Reason why I from time to time delay'd writing, was the Multiplicity of Things I had to tell you. I knew not to which to give the Preference, and all my Liesure would not permit me to mention. How have I long'd to inform you of the Pleasure I enjoy'd in visiting Windsor, its Castle, and its shady Retreats! Places you yourself recommended to me, and which I have often heard you rapturously speak of, tho' your Knowlege of them was purely Ideal. The enchanting Scenes at Vauxhall, is another Theme on which I could dwell for Hours together. What would I not have given for a Power of instantaneously transporting you to that delightful Spot! The many agreeable Walks amidst Rows of

---

young colonial upon his first visit to the British metropolis. Later portions relate more directly to BF's mission.

beauteous Trees lighted with Lamps; the elegant Paintings and Sculpture with which the Boxes, the grand Hall, and Orchestra, are adorn'd; the curious artificial Fall of Water; the ravishing Musick, vocal and instrumental; and the Gaiety and Brilliancy of the Company; would have made you conceive yourself in a Situation beyond even the Elysium of the Ancients. The several pleasant Excursions I have had, during the Summer, to different little Villages in the Country about London, would also fill some Sheets in the Description. But the high Entertainment which that inimitable Imitator of Nature, Garrick,[8] has afforded me, is a Topick unbounded and inexhaustible! Your Participation of these Pleasures, with sundry others of the like Nature, was what I earnestly wish'd at the Time; and was what only could have heighthen'd the Enjoyment of them.

As Politicks is a Subject you have no great Relish for, I shall only mention in general, that as yet I see no Prospect of a Termination of the Affairs my Father has undertaken for the Province. The little Knowledge of (or indeed Inclination to know) American Affairs, among most of those concerned in the Administration; their Prejudices against the Colonies in general, and ours in particular; the many weighty Matters they have before them relative to their own Affairs in Europe; join'd with the Obstinacy and Wickedness of the Proprietors render his Task very uphill and difficult. You will think me justifiable in speaking thus of the Proprietors when you consider that during the Time they express'd themselves strongly inclind to settle Matters amicably with my Father,[9] they were repeatedly publishing scandalous and malicious Falshoods against the Assembly and People of Pennsylvania, with a View of continuing and increasing the Prejudices he and his Party had raised. They trusted that as my Father was obliged to a friendly Negotiation with them (which they could easily contrive to continue till the Sitting of the Parliament) that he would not take any Notice of nameless Aspersions in a News Paper. In the Advantages they expected from this Piece of poor low Cunning

8. David Garrick (1717–1779), the great actor, performed a variety of plays at the Drury Lane Theatre in 1757, including his own farce, *The Modern Fine Gentleman*, revived, six days before this letter was written, under the title *The Male Coquette. DNB.*

9. See above, pp. 248–51.

they have, however, been egregiously disappointed (as you will have seen before this reaches you) by a Paper I published in the Citizen.[1] For altho' it might not be so proper for my Father to take Notice of those Aspersions, while the Negotiation was on foot there could be no Reason why I, as an Inhabitant of Pennsylvania, now on my Travels in England, no ways concerned in conducting the Negotiation, should not vindicate the Honour and Reputation of my Country when I saw it so injuriously attacked. My putting my Name to the Paper, and the Place where I was to be found, was judg'd necessary, as it would be the most effectual Means of putting a Stop to further anonymous Attacks, and as otherwise the Publick could have no Reason for giving greater Credit to one Representation than the other. It has had all the good Effects I could have wish'd; but I am told the Proprietor is much incens'd against me on that Account, tho' he don't venture to complain as he is sensible that he was the Aggressor. As this Paper I make no Doubt will be pretty much canvass'd on your Side the Water, I shall take it extremely kind if you would inform me of a few of the Pros and Cons which it may fall to your Share to hear on the Occasion.[2] It is only for my own private Satisfaction I ask this Favour, and you may depend no other Use will be made of it.

My Father has had several Interviews with the Proprietors at T. Penn's House, and they have always treated him with great Civility. I have not seen Richard, but Thos. Penn I have met with several Times at Court, tho' I believe he does not yet know me by Sight. John Penn I am told is just come to Town, having been sick in the Country almost ever since his Arrival from America.

1. See above, pp. 255–63. WF may have guessed that his letter to *The Citizen* would be reprinted in *Pa. Gaz.*, as it was on Dec. 8, 1757.

2. WF heard later of reaction in Philadelphia to the article: "It gives great Pleasure to all who can bear to hear Truth. But there are some whose Actions will not bear the Light and there are others who are devoted to these, in short there are a contemptible few who swear at the Piece but can't contradict the Truths it contains." Charles Thomson to WF, Jan. 2, 1758; APS. "Betsy" Graeme's response was less favorable; writing on May 7, 1758, she viewed the article with "much Displeasure," called it "a collection of Party Malice," and was incensed at WF's "Attachment to a Party." Her letter is lost, but its tone and some of its contents are apparent in WF's letter of Oct. 24, 1758, printed in *PMHB*, XXXIX (1915), 263–7.

Govr. Morris is arriv'd here and I suppose will join Forces with the Proprietors at least I hope so, and that they will intrust him with the whole Conduct of the Dispute on their Side. His natural Propensity to tell—something *more* than the Truth, cannot fail of giving considerable Advantage to his Opponents.[3]

My Eyes begin to draw Straws, and my Candle is almost burnt down. I must therefore haste to tell you that I have taken the Liberty to send you by this Opportunity, one of the newest fashion'd Muffs and Tippets worn by the gayest Ladies of Quality at this End of the Town, also a Basket for Counters which is the Workmanship of a poor reduc'd Lady of Family who has now no other Way of getting her Livelihood, your Acceptance of which will greatly enhance the Obligations you have laid me under. Mr. Davis,[4] who has been so kind as to take Charge of these Things, is a young Irish Gentleman strongly recommended to my Father by an eminent Scotch Physician of this City, and intends to settle in Philadelphia. He seems to be of a goodnatur'd obliging Temper from what little I have seen of him. I expect him to call early in the Morning for this Letter, the Vessel in which he goes being already gone down to Gravesend. There's another Vessel, called the London, Capt. Finglass, sails at the same time for Philadelphia otherwise I should have sent a Copy of this by her. I have hardly Room to acknowlege the Receipt of yours of Octr. 1, inclosing another dated June 19. The Reason why I wrote not from Sandy hook, was because I was in daily Expectation of sailing, and as I thought it could be no great Pleasure for you to hear how disagreeably we were detain'd.

Farewell, God bless and preserve you, is the sincere Prayer of, Dear Betsy, your truely affectionate Wm: Franklin

3. See above, VI, *passim,* for former Gov. Robert Hunter Morris' disputes in Pa. Though the Proprietors sought without success to secure Morris' appointment as governor of New Jersey, they do not seem to have depended much on him in the contentions with BF. Penn Letterbooks, *passim,* and esp. Thomas Penn to Richard Peters, Jan. 14, 1758; Hist. Soc. Pa.

4. Possibly John Davis (d. 1816), later apothecary at the Pa. Hospital and physician in the Pa. line during the Revolution. *PMHB,* XLI (1917), 258; Thomas G. Morton and Frank Woodbury, *The History of the Pennsylvania Hospital, 1751–1895* (Phila., 1895), p. 528.

To ———

Draft: Library of Congress; also copy: Yale University Library; and French translation: The Rosenbach Foundation

Both the date and the addressee of this letter have been subjects of much difference of opinion. Each of the three surviving manuscript versions bears a different date line. That on the draft, in Franklin's hand, has been heavily scratched out, probably long after the letter was written, by someone other than Franklin. Sparks (*Works*, x, 281), Bigelow (*Works*, ix, 296), and Smyth (*Writings*, ix, 520) all read the obliterated line "Phila. July 3, 1786." Though this is a plausible reading, it is far from certain; the place could be Passy, the day perhaps the 13th; the year is illegible, but could possibly be 1751, 1757, 1761, 1767, 1781, or 1787. The original date line also seems to have been written over and changed before it was finally crossed out. The copy in Temple Franklin's hand which his grandfather sent to Ezra Stiles in 1790 has the date line "London, May 7, 1758," in what appears to be Franklin's hand in old age. The figure "8" also seems to have been written over and changed at some time. Finally, the French copy, in the hand of a clerk Franklin employed frequently during his years in France (1776–1785), bears the date line printed here. Though these contradictions cannot be resolved satisfactorily, the editors have used the French date line since it is the least ambiguous and is on the earliest known manuscript other than the draft, where it is not certainly decipherable.

Though Thomas Paine has often been designated the recipient of this letter (e.g., by Sparks and Bigelow), this is most unlikely if the present editors are correct in the date assigned here; Paine was then a youth of twenty, doubtless unknown to Franklin. The copy sent to Ezra Stiles in 1790 is marked "To Mr. J.H.," probably in Franklin's hand, suggesting Joseph Huey (above, iv, 503–6) as the recipient. But the religious position of the person now addressed and that of Huey, as reflected in Franklin's earlier letter, seem strongly opposed. Franklin could have written the initials "J.H." on the copy of this letter by mistake instead of on that of the Huey letter he sent Stiles in 1790. The editors have not been able to identify any particular "infidel" who might have sent Franklin a manuscript in 1757, nor have they located any particular tract which might be evidence that his advice against publication was disregarded.[5]

5. For an account of official attitudes toward "infidel" publications, and the hazards of offering such tracts to the public at this time, see Ernest C. Mossner, *The Life of David Hume* (Austin, 1954), pp. 319–32.

Dear Sir [Cravenstreet, Dec. 13. 1757]

I have read your Manuscrit with some Attention. By the Arguments it contains against the Doctrine of a particular Providence, tho' you allow a general Providence, you strike at the Foundation of all Religion: For without the Belief of a Providence that takes Cognizance of, guards and guides and may favour particular Persons, there is no Motive to Worship a Deity, to fear its Displeasure, or to pray for its Protection. I will not enter into any Discussion of your Principles, tho' you seem to desire it; At present I shall only give you my Opinion that tho' your Reasonings are subtle, and may prevail with some Readers, you will not succeed so as to change the general Sentiments of Mankind on that Subject, and the Consequence of printing this Piece will be a great deal of Odium drawn upon your self, Mischief to you and no Benefit to others. He that spits against the Wind, spits in his own Face. But were you to succeed, do you imagine any Good would be done by it? You yourself may find it easy to live a virtuous Life without the Assistance afforded by Religion; you having a clear Perception of the Advantages of Virtue and the Disadvantages of Vice, and possessing a Strength of Resolution sufficient to enable you to resist common Temptations. But think how great a Proportion of Mankind consists of weak and ignorant Men and Women, and of inexperienc'd and inconsiderate Youth of both Sexes, who have need of the Motives of Religion to restrain them from Vice, to support their Virtue, and retain them in the Practice of it till it becomes *habitual,* which is the great Point for its Security; And perhaps you are indebted to her originally that is to your Religious Education, for the Habits of Virtue upon which you now justly value yourself. You might easily display your excellent Talents of reasoning on a less hazardous Subject, and thereby obtain Rank with our most distinguish'd Authors. For among us, it is not necessary, as among the Hottentots that a Youth to be receiv'd into the Company of Men, should prove his Manhood by beating his Mother.[6] I would advise you therefore not to attempt

6. BF at first intended to insert here but then crossed out: "If you had a Constitution of Body capable of resisting all the Inclemencies of the Air, and that received no Damage by sleeping under the Hedges, would you therefore burn all our Houses?" BF had used the Hottentot illustration before; see above, IV, 484.

unchaining the Tyger, but to burn this Piece before it is seen by any other Person, whereby you will save yourself a great deal of Mortification from the Enemies it may raise against you, and perhaps a good deal of Regret and Repentance.[7] If Men are so wicked as we now see them *with Religion* what would they be if *without it?* I intend this Letter itself as a *Proof* of my Friendship and therefore add no *Professions* of it, but subscribe simply Yours

B.F.

Endorsed: Rough of Letter dissuading —— from publishing his Piece

William Strahan to Deborah Franklin

MS not found; reprinted from Duane, *Works*, VI, 25–7.

Dear Madam, London, December 13, 1757.

I will not write to you, for the future, as a stranger whom I never had the happiness of seeing, but as to one with whom I have been for some time acquainted, for having had the pleasure for several months past, to be personally known to what you will readily allow, to be your better half, you'll permit me to fancy, I am by no means ignorant of the essential qualities of the other.

I had for many years, conceived a very high, and now find, a very just opinion of Mr. Franklin; this I was naturally led to by the concurring testimony of every body, who knew him, (for the voice of his enemies, if he had any, never reached me) and by the opportunities I have had of judging for myself, during my correspondence with him for a dozen years. But though the notion I had formed of him, in my own mind, before I had the pleasure of seeing him, was really as far as it went, just enough; I must confess it was very unequal to what I now know his singular merit deserves.

I own it is somewhat odd, to entertain a lady with the character of her husband, who must herself, of all others, be the least ignorant in that particular. But as all who know me, know that I cannot

7. "Talking against Religion is unchaining a Tyger; The Beast let loose may worry his Deliverer." *Poor Richard Improved,* September 1751; above, IV, 96.

help speaking my sentiments freely, on any subject that strikes me in a great degree, so I choose to write my mind in regard to Mr. Franklin, before all others to you, because you are the most unexceptionable judge of the truth and propriety of what I say, and because I am persuaded you will listen to me, not only with patience but with pleasure; and indeed, whatever your own personal qualities may be, however amiable and engaging in my mind, your being the choice of such a man, must add greatly to your honour, to be the wife of one who has so much ability, inclination, and success, if you view him in a public capacity, in being eminently useful to his country, must necessarily confer on you great reputation, and to be the bosom friend of one who is equally fitted to promote any kind of domestic happiness, must as necessarily be the constant spring of the most substantial comfort to you.

For my own part, I never saw a man who was, in every respect, so perfectly agreeable to me. Some are amiable in one view, some in another, he in all. Now madam as I know the ladies here consider him in exactly the same light I do, upon my word I think you should come over, with all convenient speed to look after your interest; not but that I think him as faithful to his Joan, as any man breathing; but who knows what repeated and strong temptation, may in time, and while he is at so great a distance from you, accomplish.[8] Besides, what a delightful expedition would this be to Miss Franklin, and how much must it amuse and improve her, to see and live a while in this great city. I know you will object to the length of the voyage and the danger of the seas, but truly this is more terrible in apprehension than in reality; of all the ways of travelling it is the easiest and most expeditious; and as for the danger, there has not a soul been lost between Philadelphia and this, in my memory; and I believe, not one ship taken by the enemy.[9] Is the trouble and risque then of such a voyage, to be compared in any degree, with the pleasure it will afford you and your best friends. By no means. Instead of being afraid of the sea, we ought to have a particular regard for it, as it is so far from being a bar to the communication and intercourse of

8. See below, pp. 359–60, for BF's comments on this proposal, and above, II, 352–4, for "Joan."

9. See above, p. 238 n, for one ship bound for London from Philadelphia which was captured by the French.

different and far distant countries, that it facilitates their correspondence in a very high degree. Nay more, it conveys in the floating castles of your mother country, that protection and assistance which I trust will soon give peace to your borders. I might urge as an additional inducement for you to come over in the spring, that the important business with which Mr. Franklin is charged, in the service of his country, (which I dare say you would wish above all things may be brought to a happy conclusion) may very probably detain him more than one season, which will exhaust your patience to such a degree, that you may repent, when too late, you did not listen to my advice.

Your son I really think one of the prettiest young gentlemen I ever knew from America. He seems to me [to] have a solidity of judgment, not very often to be met with in one of his years. This with the daily opportunities he has of improving himself in the company of his father, who is at the same time his friend, his brother, his intimate, and easy companion, affords an agreeable prospect, that your husband's virtues and usefulness to his country, may be prolonged beyond the date of his own life.

Your daughter (I wish I could call her mine),[1] I find by the reports of all who know her, is a very amiable girl in all respects; but of her I shall say nothing, till I have the pleasure of seeing her. Only I must observe to you, that being the mistress of such a family, is a degree of happiness perhaps the greatest that falls to the lot of humanity. I sincerely wish you, very long, the unabated enjoyment of them. I leave it to your friend, to write you every thing from this place, you would desire to know. But I cannot take my leave of you without informing you that Mr. F. has the good fortune to lodge with a very discreet good gentlewoman,[2] who is particularly careful of him, who attended him during a very severe cold he was some time ago seized with, with an assiduity, concern, and tenderness, which perhaps, only yourself could equal: so that I don't think you could have a better substitute till you come over, to take him under your own protection. He is now perfectly recovered.

My own family are, I thank God, just now in perfect health.

1. Strahan and BF had long cherished the thought that young William Strahan and Sally Franklin might marry.

2. Margaret Stevenson; see above, p. 273 n.

My wife joins me in kindest compliments to you and dear Miss, not forgetting her honest son David[3] and his fire-side. I wish you a speedy and happy meeting with your friends on this side of the water, which will give great pleasure to, Dear madam, Your most affectionate, Humble servant, WILLIAM STRAHAN.

To John Pringle[4]

ALS: The Royal Society

Sir Dec. 21. 1757[5]

The following is what I can at present recollect, relating to the Effects of Electricity in Paralytic Cases, which have fallen under my Observation.

Some Years since, when the News papers made Mention of great Cures perform'd in Italy or Germany by means of Electricity, a Number of Paralytics were brought to me from different

3. David Hall, formerly Strahan's journeyman, apparently as affectionately regarded by Mrs. Strahan as their correspondence shows he was by his former employer.

4. See above, VI, 178 n, for Pringle. By November 24 BF had recovered sufficiently from his long illness to begin attending the regular weekly meetings of the Royal Society. He appeared for the first time that day, signed the obligation, and was formally admitted as a fellow. On December 15 Pringle read a series of communications about the remarkable cure of a paralytic in Berwickshire, Scotland, by electric-shock treatments similar to those BF had tried in Philadelphia (see above, IV, 197–8, 205, 503 n); *Phil. Trans.*, L (1757), Part I, 383–5, 392–5. Probably prompted by the discussion at this meeting, BF furnished Pringle with the additional information in this letter, which was read at the Society's meeting on Jan. 12, 1758. *Ibid.*, Part II (1758), 481–3. Barbeu Dubourg (*Oeuvres de M. Franklin*.... (Paris, 1773), I, 193–5), followed his French publication of it with "Reflexions du Traducteur," commenting further on the physiological effects of electric-shock treatments.

5. BF probably welcomed scientific diversion on this particular day; on it he appeared, apparently for the first time, before the Board of Trade, Lord Halifax presiding, an event of considerable if nightmarish importance to him. He was obliged to listen to a violent denunciation of his fellow agent, Robert Charles. The Board reprimanded Charles for "improper and indecent behaviour," found his representations "irregular and unprecedented, ... and unbecoming his character as an agent," termed other acts of his arrogant and insolent, and found his requests "groundless and injurious." *Journal of the Commissioners for Trade and Plantations from January 1754 to December 1758* (London, 1933), pp. 356–8. Ironically, Charles's counsel was Alexander Wedderburn, notorious as BF's tormentor at the Cockpit in 1774.

Parts of Pensilvania and the neighbouring Provinces, to be electris'd, which I did for them, at their Request. My Method was, to place the Patient first in a Chair on an electric Stool, and draw a Number of large strong Sparks from all Parts of the affected Limb or Side. Then I fully charg'd two 6 Gallon Glass Jarrs, each of which had about 3 square feet of Surface coated and I sent the united Shock of these thro' the affected Limb or Limbs, repeating the Stroke commonly three Times each Day. The first Thing observ'd was an immediate greater sensible Warmth in the lame Limbs that had receiv'd the Stroke than in the others; and the next Morning the Patients usually related that they had in the Night felt a pricking Sensation in the Flesh of the paralytic Limbs, and would sometimes shew a Number of small red Spots which they suppos'd were occasion'd by those Prickings: The Limbs too were found more capable of voluntary Motion, and seem'd to receive Strength; a Man, for Instance, who could not, the first Day, lift the lame Hand from off his Knee, would the next Day raise it four or five Inches, the third Day higher, and on the fifth Day was able, but with a feeble languid Motion, to take off his Hat. These Appearances gave great Spirits to the Patients, and made them hope a perfect Cure; but I do not remember that I ever saw any Amendment after the fifth Day: Which the Patients perceiving, and finding the Shocks pretty severe, they became discourag'd, went home and in a short time relapsed; so that I never knew any Advantage from Electricity in Palsies that was permanent. And how far the apparent temporary Advantage might arise from the Exercise in the Patients Journey and coming daily to my House, or from the Spirits given by the Hope of Success, enabling them to exert more Strength in moving their Limbs, I will not pretend to say.

Perhaps some permanent Advantage might have been obtained, if the Electric Shocks had been accompanied with proper Medicine and Regimen, under the Direction of a skilful Physician. It may be, too, that a few great Strokes, as given in my Method, may not be so proper as many small ones; since by the Account from Scotland of the Case in which 200 Shocks from a Phial were given daily, seems that a perfect Cure has been made. As to any uncommon Strength supposed to be in the Machine used in that Case, [I] imagine it could have no Share in the Effect produced;

since the Strength of the Shock from charg'd Glass, is in proportion to the Quantity of Surface of the Glass coated; [so] that my Shocks from those large Jarrs must have been much greater than any that could be received from a Phial held in the hand.

I am, with great Respect, Sir, Your most obedient Servant

B FRANKLIN

Dr. Pringle

Read at R.S. LIX. January 12. 1758.
An Acct. of the Effects of Electricity in paralytic Cases. In a letter to John Pringle M.D. F.R.S. from Benjamin Franklin Esqr. F.R.S.

From Giambatista Beccaria[6]

I. MS translation and MS Latin original: The Royal Society. II. MS "Note": The Royal Society[7]

Father Beccaria, the strongest and most active supporter of Franklin's electrical theories on the Continent, addressed this letter to him in Latin soon after learning of his arrival in England. Dr. James Parsons[8] made an English translation which, after some delay, was read at the Royal Society, Feb. 7, 1760. Because Beccaria's terminology differed in some particulars from that which had become familiar to English scientists (in large part through Franklin's writings), Franklin undertook to clear up points of possible misunderstanding in a brief "Note" read at the next meeting of the Society, February 14.[9]

6. On Beccaria, of the teaching order of Piarists and professor of experimental philosophy at Turin, see above, V, 395 n.

7. The Latin letter sent to BF appears to be in the hand of a trained scribe, perhaps a fellow member of Beccaria's religious order; it does not bear the author's personal signature. The translation is in Parsons' hand, and BF's explanatory note is an unsigned autograph. The Latin original and BF's note were printed in *Phil. Trans.*, LI, Part II (1760), 514–26.

8. On Parsons, see above, VI, 85 n. He was one of the sponsors of BF's election to the Royal Society (above, VI, 376).

9. The dates as here given are those endorsed on the translation and the Latin original and on the MS of BF's note, respectively, and as recorded in the Society's Journal Book, but the Latin text printed in *Phil. Trans.* is incorrectly noted as "Read Feb. 14, 1760." The Journal Book, in turn, errs in stating that the letter itself was dated "Turin 24th December 1759," although the original reads "1757," as do Parson's translation and the printed Latin text in *Phil. Trans.*

Parsons' translation is printed here, rather than the Latin original, both in order to make it available to a larger number of present-day readers, and because this was the version actually read to the members of the Royal Society. Parsons, however, was more distinguished as an antiquary than as an "electrician." His translation of Beccaria's Latin (obviously difficult in some places) is stiff and far too literal; in some instances he clearly misses the sense, and in others he seems to give up and simply transliterates a technical term into what looks like, but is not, an English equivalent. The editors have therefore undertaken to substitute their own rendering of certain words and phrases, identifying them either in footnotes, by the use of brackets surrounding their substitutions, by adding the Latin original in italics after their rendering, or by a combination of these devices as seems most appropriate in each instance. In two particularly troublesome passages Parsons' translation is given unchanged in the text but Beccaria's Latin and the editors' suggested freer translation appear in footnotes. Readers interested in the Latin original are referred to that version as printed in the *Philosophical Transactions.*

I

[Turin, December 24, 1757]

John Baptist Beccaria [of the sacred schools, sends greetings] to Benjamin Franklin Esqr. the first in Electrical Knowledge &c.

1. Learned Sir, I am glad you are safe arriv'd in London from America; and send you an hypothesis which I struck out from experiments concerning electrical motions: This I divide into two parts, as the very difference [between] these kind of motions seems to require; In the first part I treat of *attractions,* and in the second of *repulsions;*[1]

2. And I now Comprehend the whole of my consideration of *attraction* in a few words as follows: "when the Electrical Fire, being in greater quantity in One body, throws it self by the power of Expansion into another; towards an Equilibrium, it removes the greater part of the *Interjected,* or *Interstitial* air[2] from its place, according to its own greater [mass *(copia)*]. Whence it follows,

1. Here and elsewhere when Beccaria wrote some form of the words *accedo* (or *accessio*) and *discedo* (or *discessio*), Parsons used "accede" and "discede" or corresponding nouns such as "accessions" and "discessions." In each instance the present editors have silently substituted the appropriate form of "attract" or "approach" and "repel," or some similar words.

2. Beccaria: *partem interjecti aeris.*

that the air which is near the bodies,[3] for want of the resistance of the intermediate air, rushes, towards that middle place: but not by passing round the bodies, which is a longer way, and more interrupted from the flowing out of the fire, but by rushing in, from nearby. It is by this [displacing *(trusione)*] of the air, that bodies unequally electrify'd *approach* [each other]; and while they approach they are accelerated, because the more fire flows in, the greater quantity of intermediate air is thrown out, and therefore the greater the attraction; and thus the *momentum* of the air [displaced] from nearby will be increased.

Experiment 1.

3. That the air is [expelled] by the Electrical fire flowing in, is demonstrated by the experiment of the spark which is excited in the middle of the Tube, hermetically seald at one end, and stop'd with [some liquid] at the Other; for while the spark throws out the [liquid], it is [proved *(testatur)*] the air is thrown out also.

4. Nor indeed can the fire, when it flows in, supply the [support *(fulcrum)*] of the intermediate air now driven out, whereby the air adjacent to bodies may be sustain'd; for it flows out again very freely, and passes into the Other body, wherfore as it is not itself sustaind or resisted, neither can it act as a [support].

Experim: 2.

5. The matter is confirm'd by the following [very] clear experiment: I roll'd up a slip of Gilt paper of about eight inches long and four lines broad, so as to form a little solid cillinder D.[4] I suspend this by a silk thread D.G. under [an opening *(fornice)*] of an air pump I.H.K. thro' the top of which, H. the mettal rod BC. passes, [descending into *(desinens in)*] the mettal ball C. I fix the mettal rod LE. arm'd with [a similar] ball [on top], to the plate IK. [Now] the spheres C and E. are in the same plane with

3. Beccaria: *aer a tergo corporibus adjacens*. Here and elsewhere Parsons, apparently puzzled, included an untranslated *a Tergo* somewhere in his sentence. The present editors have silently substituted "near" or "nearby" where necessary, or omitted the Latin entirely.

4. *Phil. Trans.* inserts at this point "[*Vide Tab.* IXX]," referring to the plate inserted there on the facing page and reproduced here opposite. Beccaria's original drawing does not survive, probably because it was turned over to the engraver of the plate, James Mynde.

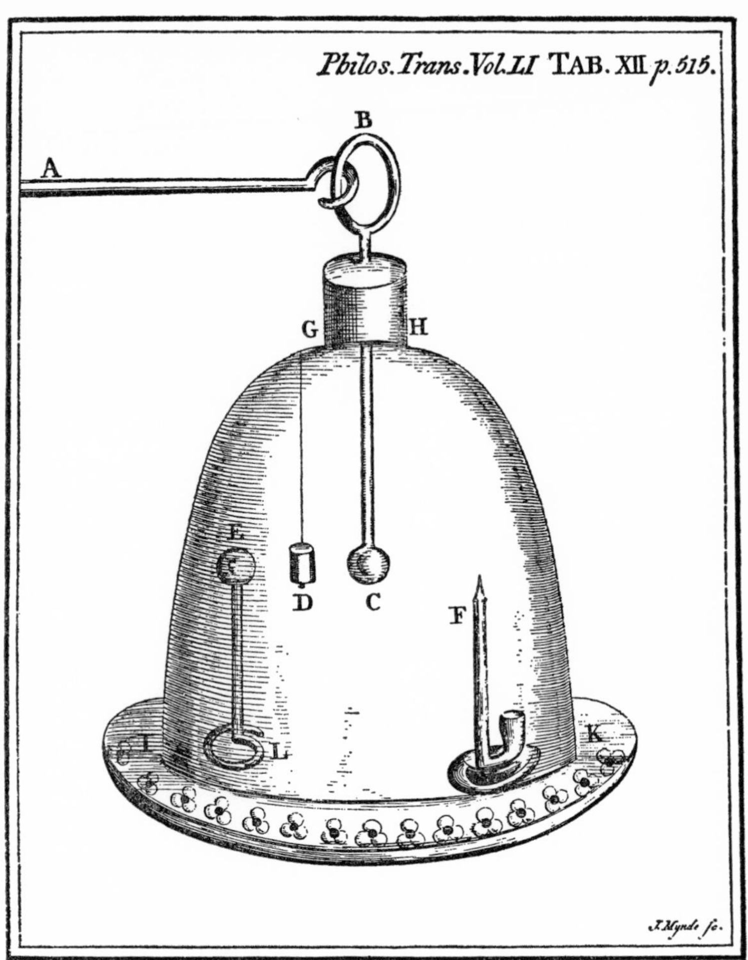
Philos. Trans. Vol. LI TAB. XII p. 515.
A
B
G
H
E
D
C
F
I
L
K
J. Mynde sc.

the cillinder D. and at equal distances from it; then fixing the Chain A. B. which belongs to the electrical Machine [to] the rod B.C. and consequently the electrical fire being sent into the rod B.C. I observe: 1st. that before the air is remov'd, the paper cillinder D. is agitated with the most violent vibrations between the two spheres E.C. 2dly. that while the air is remov'd the agitation is plainly diminished in proportion to the quantity of air removed. 3dly. [when as much air as possible is removed][5] the cillinder D. hardly stirs. When I have observ'd these things, I restore the air again by degrees, and observe that the vibrations increase again in proportion to the restored air, and at length become as violent as before. Which circumstances when I contemplate in particular, and consider them also together, I understand that the quantity or greatness of electrical motions is owing[6] to the air, either intire or in part.

Experiment. III.

6. Because light bodies such as gold leafe, Dust &c. are agitated in rarifyed air with a motion sufficiently sensible, was the reason why I thought, with other [physicists *(physicis)*], from the beginning, that electrical motions, receiv'd in the air, ought not to be attributed to the action of electrical fire. But because, [having now considered the matter more carefully,][7] I see that motions in the residual air bear not a greater proportion to the first motions that are made in the intire atmospherical air, than that which passes between the residual and the first air, I am inclined to acknowledge this error in my self and others, and adopt the contrary Opinion; which experience verifies.

7. I must not omit a part of my Observation, which is very [opportune] towards confirming this matter: Sometimes I used to bring my Experiment from the last [stage] into a dark room; and

5. Beccaria: *Omni, quantus potest, aere subducto;* Parsons: "that all the air being as much as can be taken away."

6. Beccaria's words here are: *intelligo magnitudinem motuum electricorum aeri, vel toti, vel residuo proportione respondere.* Parsons keyed a footnote to "owing," which reads: "Answers to the air: which can mean no more than that the quantity of Electrical motions is as the quantity of air removed."

7. Beccaria: *quod, re nunc accuratius collata;* Parsons: "But because, upon more mature consideration."

then I observed that the fire vibrating the *pendulum,* before the air was remov'd, shined here and there with crackling, light but short sparks near each ball: afterwards this fire in proportion to the removed air, and also the minuteness of the vibrations of the *pendulum,* flow'd out in a more ample, gentle, Continual, tho' not so shining a *Radius.*

8. And this truely demonstrates a reaction of the air, compelling the electrical fire in a certain density; which [corresponds to] the proportion of its Own density; and this reaction of the air [cannot avoid responding] to the action of the electrical fire,[8] endeavoring to throw out the air; and clearly throwing it out, where it can prevail against the fire with a necessary [force *(vi)*].

9. To these I shall add no more towards explaining the attractions of bodies unequally electrify'd, I have brought some arguments in my letters to [Beccari][9] in which however I treated of the mechanical cause of attractions but doubtfully; but a more accurate consideration of the experiments, occasions my discoursing of the cause of attractions with more confidence.

10. Bodies equally electrified repel each other; The cause of which I now proceed to explain:

11. The electrical fire which is in bodies, by what means soever, [sparks in order to balance] the electrical fire[1] which is in the air. (Give me leave to call the one the *proper,* and the Other the *aerial* fire.) If both have an equal proportion to the native capacity of the bodies and of the air, the bodies are attracted, or are at rest in their [original position *(nativa directione)*]; Otherwise if either the *proper* or *aerial* fire is excess, it equally [sets free *(explicat)*] the bodies and compells them to a repulsion.

This is the account:

8. Beccaria: *haec autem aeris reactio non potest actioni non respondere ignis electrici.* Parsons: "this reaction of the air must answer to the action of the electrical fire."

9. Perhaps understandably, Parsons mistranslated *ad Beccarion* as "to Beccaria" thereby confusing the author of this letter, Giambatista Beccaria (1716–1781) of Turin, with Giacomo Bartolomeo Beccari (1682–1766), president of the Institute of Sciences and Arts of Bologna, to whom the former addressed his *Dell' Elettricismo: lettere,* which was in the press when this letter was written. See the next document.

1. Beccaria: *nititur, ut libretur cum igne electrico.* Parsons: "endeavours to be in equilibrio with the electrical fire."

Experiment IV.

12. As often as I proceed to electrifie a Chain several times [for a longer period *(diutius)*], in my Chamber which is a very large One [but closed],[2] I find, that part of its electrical fire is diffus'd into the ambient air; and renders [that air, however much there is in the Chamber,] electrical to excess,[3] whilst it is in a dry State either from the weather or from fire. For I carry into any part of the room two flaxen threads which I suspend either between two fingers, or at the end of a stick, and they repel each other; and whether I keep them in the same place or move them to any Other part of the room, yet they continue to diverge for half an hour, an hour, and sometimes longer.

Experiment. V.

13. If the threads are seperated from the stick or reed, by the assistance of the glass, and in like manner from the ground, they first diverge, and then return to their [original position]. But these things happen after all the sparks are as much as possible drawn out from the Chain, after all the redundant fire[4] is remov'd from it, after the Connexion of the Chain with the ground.

Experiment. VI

14. From a long continued electrification[5] of the Machine I find the Phaenomena in all respects the same:[6] But if the long electrification of the machine continually follows a long electrification of

2. Parsons overlooked Beccaria's "*at clauso.*"

3. Beccaria: *ipsumque etiam, quantuscumque in cubiculo est . . . facere excessu electricum;* Parsons: "and renders it electrical to excess, for so much as there is in the Chamber." As BF explains in his "Remarks," printed with this letter, Beccaria's *facere excessu electricum* would appear in BF's terminology as "electrified positively."

4. In BF's terminology: "all the positive electricity."

5. Here and repeated hereafter Parsons translated Beccaria's *electricitas* as "electricity," even where the sense clearly calls for "electrification"; the correction is made silently wherever necessary.

6. The remainder of this paragraph in the original reads: *At, si diuturna electricitas machinae continuo consequitur diuturnam electricitatem catenae, aut contra, fila, quae arundine suspensa constanter divergere videbam ex alterius electricitate, video principio accedere mutuo incipiente electricitate alterius, tum iterum divergere quemadmodum antea.* Parsons' translation is printed above (except for silent corrections as specified in previous notes), but, in the light

the Chain, or *vice versa,* the threads fix'd to the reed or stick, are constantly observ'd to diverge from the electrification of another body; in the begining I observe that they attract one another, at the begining electrification of another body; and then again to diverge as before.

15. By these experiments, I say, we are in my Opinion taught: I. that while we accumulate several successive fires in the Chain, several successive parts of it passes widely into the ambient air, and adheres to it; and so all the air containd in the chamber becomes electrified to excess.[7] In like manner while we draw out of the machine several successive fires, the machine draws in several successive parts of the fire from the ambient air, and so all the air contain'd in the Chamber becomes deficient of electricity, or electrifyd *in Defect.*[8] II. The threads carry'd in either the fingers or at the end of the stick, repel each other in the air by the electrical excess from the chain, or the electrical defect from the machine,[9] or by the force of the proper native fire overcoming the aerial if they [come together in] the electrical air from the machine; or by the power of the aerial fire overcoming the native proper fire of the threads, if they [come together] in the electrical air from the Chain. III. That these kind of threads diverging by the electrification of the chain, from the consequent electrification of the machine, or the contrary,[1] first attract; because the machine first takes in from the air the excess it had from the chain; or the chain restores to the air, the fire taken from the machine; and so the fire in the air restored to its Native quantity ought to equilibrate with the native fire remaining in the threads. IV. But furthermore from a longer electrification of the machine consequent to the electrification of the chain, or the contrary, the threads diverge

---

of BF's "Note" and of later passages in the letter, the sentence might be freely rendered as follows: "But if a long-continued negative electrification follows a long positive electrification, or vice versa, I see that the threads fixed to the stick, which I saw constantly diverging as a result of the first electrification, now attract one another at the start of the second electrification and then again diverge as before."

7. In BF's terminology: "electrified positively."

8. In BF's terminology: "electrified negatively."

9. That is, repel each other by their positive or negative charge.

1. That is, diverging by the initial positive electrification, from the following negative electrification, or vice versa.

again; because either the machine goes on to take in part of the native fire, or the chain goes on to add more fire to the air than the native quantity. V. that the same threads, when seperated by the glass, diverge in the begining, because they, which have only their Own Native fire, come together in the air which is electric by excess or defect; and then when they are seperated by the glass they at length come to their [original position] because either part of the aerial fire, if the air is electric in excess from the chain, at last pours itself into the threads towards an *equilibrium*, and also flows by the compelling power of the glass, or part of the native fire, or of the proper fire of the threads pours itself into the air, if the air is electric by defect, [because] it may be supply'd from elsewhere by the compulsion of the glass.

16. From hence the following things seem universally to hold: I. that the air contains in itself, its own Native fire. II. that to the native fire of the air, another fire may be added, that part of the native fire may be subtracted from the air, but slowly, and as it were by force. III. that the air lets go the [excess], and takes in the deficient fire, but that in a very slow manner. IV. If the air has, like other bodies, its own native fire, then these are in a native state, if the air, while their native fire remains in bodies, has a greater or less quantity of fire than its native quantity, the bodies repel each other; but every one of these theorems can be illustrated in a surprising manner by other experiments; and be more fully demonstrated.

Experiment 7.

17. Two threads, fastened to the chain, after a few turns of the globe, diverge very much: afterwards from a longer-lasting electrification in the chain they begin to diverge less; and this diverging is diminish'd to a certain degree; so that sometimes the angle of the diverging, after a [longer] continuation of the friction of the globe, becomes double[2] that of the diverging which happen'd from the same electrification when first excited. When I percieve this diverging of the threads diminish enough, then I cease the friction of the globe, but gently apply a very sharp stilus to the chain, wherby I slowly draw forth all the redundant fire from it;

2. Beccaria: *subduplus*, more correctly rendered as "a little less than double," but leaving Beccaria's actual intent somewhat doubtful.

while this is doing the threads approach each other slowly, then gently again diverge to an angle indeed less than the first, tho' great enough, which sometimes scarce amounts to forty five degrees; but then they proceed to diverge for a longer time.

18. That is, the greatest angle from the Electrification first excited, because then a very great quantity of fire is sent in to the chain, and in the threads connected with it, but little or none into the air. Afterwards the angle becomes less, as the fire increases and is consequently sent into the air, the same excess of the fire remaining in the chain. While the fire sent into the chain is slowly diminished by the application of the *Stilus,* the angle is still diminished in proportion as the residual fire in the chain, and the fire, sent in and Joind to the air, approach to an equilibrium; and where both the fires come to an equality the threads resume their [original] direction: when again the fire, yet redundant in the chain, if further diminshd, and the redundant fire in the air not so (for it is Joind to the air, and as we observe is slowly diminished by it,) the threads again repel each other because of the excess of the aerial fire over that in the chain, which aerial fire, in fine, because it is most slowly discharg'd, the threads proceed to diverge [for a very long time *(diutissime)*].

Experiment VIII.

19. If the threads are connected with the Machine, all the same Phaenomena happen in them from a long electrification of the machine, that they had from a long electrification of the chain when connected with it.

20. Wherefore as I have shew'd in general from the begining, if the proper fire of bodies, whatsoever it's quantity be, is in equilibrium with the fire of the ambient air, bodies either remain in their native state or return to it; if one fire exceeds the other bodies repel each other by the power of the fire in excess.

21. And hence if I mistake not learn'd Sir you see the reason why those bodies electrify'd as well from the chain as the Machine repel each other: the proper fire in bodies electrified by the chain[3] overcomes the aerial, and the aerial in like manner overcomes the proper fire in bodies electrified by the Machine.

3. That is, those bodies electrified positively as well as those electrified negatively.

Experiment IX.

22. As often as the threads mutually repel each Other, and diverge from either the increased or diminishd native fire in them, they are attracted to my finger when advanced to them; as often as they repel each other and diverge preserving their native fire, from the native fire of the air either increased or diminish'd, they fly from my finger.

23. And this indeed is very agreable to the Known laws of electrical attraction, and repulsion; for when the native fire in the threads is either increased or diminished, they become as unequally electrified as my finger, which has its own native fire; but when the native fire stands firm in the threads, and they repel each other from the increased or diminished fire in the air; then as they diverge from one another, so they must be repelled by my finger, having also its native fire, by the power of the air, in which the native fire is increasd or diminished. But besides, this very repulsion of the threads from my finger also proves the cause of repulsions which I assert; for both the finger and threads communicate with the ground, and therefore they have not in them any Other fire but the native, by which because they do not repel each other, it remains that they repel by the native fire, either increased or diminish'd, in the air.

24. When I first fell upon this theory of electrical repulsions, I was doubtful whether the aerial fire could not make repulsions in the machine, equal in velocity and greatness to those which the proper fire makes in the chain; thence I again suspected that the quantity of the fire in the machine and chain (universally conveying to all bodies) might be quickly changed; but that the measure of the fire in the ambient air is but slowly increased or diminished: besides another consideration increased my suspicion: that I could never draw as much fire from the air as from the machine, nor could I ever add as much to the air as to the chain; for I could never come to be able to sustain the whole diverging of the threads by the electricity of the air alone, as much as existed from the intire electricity of the machine or chain.

However hence it came to pass, that I communicated these same experiments, and also Others, by Letters to the most learned president of the Bononian Institute,[4] wherin I establish'd this theory of repulsions at large.

But upon considering the matter more maturely I found that the velocity of the repulsions, caused by the aerial fire, ought not to answer to the velocity whereby its quantity is either increased or diminsh'd; but to that velocity whereby its inherent quantity acts; and that the greatness of the repulsions, which come from the same fire, ought not to answer to its absolute, but to its comparative greatness; I have observ'd both these to happen upon occasion.

Experiment X.

25. If in the Sixth experiment, after the diverging of the threads is diminished from a longer electrification of the chain, I draw all the redundant fire, not slowly but immediatly, from the chain (my hand being apply'd to it) the threads indeed begin to come together [as fast as possible] but they suddenly return with equal velocity before they arrive at their [original position]. But this other repulsion, because it happens from the aerial fire overcoming the proper residual fire in the threads, I perceive nevertheless that the very aerial fire (altho' its quantity is slowly changed) causes repulsions of equal velocity with those that are made without the proper fire.

Experiment XI.

26. And that these equally great repulsions happen from the aerial fire I thus understand. After the fire receiv'd into the air, as much as may be, that is round the chain, (all the redundant fire being taken away from the chain, and so the threads now diverging from the aerial fire), I substitute a globe of Sulphur instead of glass, and from the friction of this I observe, the angle of divergence to increase in the begining, which the aerial fire effected, and then continually to diminish.

27. And this is certain that the first frictions of the Sulphureous globe takes away part of the native fire from the chain, and does not in like manner take away the excess of fire of the ambient air (for the air, as we observd before, slowly receives the fire of another body and as slowly parts with it) wherefore the greatness

4. Giacomo Bartolomeo Beccari of Bologna. See above, p. 306 n.

of the divergence is increased which is causd by the aerial fire, not changed by the absolute greatness of the aerial fire, but only by its comparative greatness, the proper fire being therefore diminished, and the proportion of the aerial to the proper [fire] being increased. Therefore because as much of the fire as is collected in the chain, so much is drawn from the machine; the proportion of the aerial fire about the machine, to the residual fire in the machine, will be the same as the proportion of the redundant fire in the chain, to the aerial fire about the chain: wherefore the aerial fire about the machine will make repulsions, not only equally swift, but equally great with those made by the proper fire in the chain.

28. Therefore that I may comprehend in a few words all that seem most likely to explain universally all electrical motions, (for you may easily observe that all suspensions, adhesions, vibrations and an infinite number of Other compositions as so many electrical Ludi [games, demonstrations] are comprehended in the repulsions and attractions). This at length is the Sum of my hypothesis: that the attractions of bodies, unequally electrified, are affected by the electric fire of one body, in which it is more abundant, flowing out into another, thro' the [intermediate] air, and even throwing off that. But that repulsions are caused by the proper fire of bodies expanding it self against the aerial [fire], or by the aerial expanding it self more strongly against the proper fire; which expansion however, of the fire of one body overcoming another, seems to happen without the mutual admixtion of one with the other. For the air contains its own fire whatsoever its quantity be, nor can it discede from it, and drives away the proper fire of conducting bodies that it may not adhere to it.[5]

29. I have I say Learnd Sir, Laid before you this hypothesis, and you will thereby improve it; and if you think it worthy of being laid before the Royal Society, It will be very agreable to me, who, [since] I am not able to add any Ornament, hope my

5. Beccaria: *Aer enim ignem continet suum quantuncumque, ne discedat, arcet proprium deferentium corporum ignem, ne adhaerescat sibi.* Parsons' translation is as printed above, but the editors suggest that this passage might better be somewhat freely rendered as: "For the air retains its own fire sufficiently to keep it from dispersing; it holds off the fire of the conducting bodies so that fire does not cling to the air itself."

dilligence will be acceptable to it. Be careful of your Health, for it is fit you should be long preserv'd for the improvement of Science, and the amplification of what you have so certainly established.

Dated at Turin 24. Xber. 1757.

Endorsed: Translation of a latin Letter from Professor Beccaria of Turin to Mr. Franklin concerning some Electrical experiments. by Dr. Parsons Read at R S. 7 February 1760

II

A Note[6]

December 24, 1757

For the better understanding this Paper, it is necessary to know, that Father Beccaria uses a large Chain, suspended by Silk Lines, for the Purpose of a Prime Conductor; and that his Machine for turning the Glass Globe, is so contriv'd, as that he can on occasion readily isolate it, (i.e. place it on Glass or Wax) together with the Person that works it. When the Communication is thus cut off, between the Earth and the Chain, and also between the Earth and the Machine, he observes, that the Globe being turn'd, both the Chain and the Machine show Signs of Electricity; and as these Signs, when examined, appear to be different in the Chain and in the Machine; and the Globe having, as he supposes, drawn from the Machine Part of its natural or common Quantity of Electricity, and given it to the Chain; he calls the Electricity appearing in the Chain, Electricity *by Excess;* and the Electricity appearing in the Machine, Electricity *by Defect;* which answer to our Terms, of *positive* and *negative* Electricity, or Electricity *plus* and *minus*. And thus his Expressions, *Electrifying by the Chain,* and *Electrifying by the Machine,* are to be understood, Electrifying *positively,* and Electrifying *negatively*.

Endorsed: 14 Feb. 1760. No. 1 Phil. Trans. Vol. LI. part II. p. 525.

6. So captioned by BF in his autograph MS. The Royal Society's clerk struck the words through and substituted: "Remark on the preceeding paper by Benjamin Franklin LL.D." In the adjoining margin he noted: "Read at R.S. 14 Febr. 1760."

From Giambatista Beccaria

Translation of extract (?) in Franklin's hand: Yale University Library; extract (?) in Italian: American Philosophical Society; also copies of extract and translation: Yale University Library[7]

[1757][8]

Father Beccaria thanks Mr. Franklin for his kind Remembrance; should have had a most singular Pleasure in seeing him at Turin, which he had been made to hope by his Letter to Mr. Haldiman:[9] If he had known of his being in Europe, [he would have addressed his 16 Letters on Electricity to him rather than to anyone else].[1] They come out in January, and he shall be very glad to present them to him in Turin, where he would be ready to serve him with all his Attention to the utmost of his Power. In those Letters the Theory of M. Franklin, or rather that of Nature, is more fully demonstrated, and some of them contain some new Discoveries in that Branch [of Natural Philosophy].[2]

7. What appears to be an extract of the original MS is pasted into BF's copy of Beccaria's *Dell' elettricismo: lettere* (Bologna, 1758) in APS. The title page of the book bears the notation in BF's hand "B Franklin's Sent him by the Author 1760." A translation of the pasted note in BF's hand is in the Stiles Papers, Yale Univ. Lib., and in the same collection are also copies in Stiles's hand of both the extract and the translation. BF's English version, corrected as indicated below, rather than the Italian text, is printed here, both to make it understandable to a larger number of prospective readers and also to show what BF thought Beccaria had written him.

8. This letter must have been written in the latter part of 1757 because of Beccaria's statement that his letters would "come out in January." The volume was published in 1758.

9. Probably Jean Abraham Haldimand, a Swiss-born banker in Turin, brother of Lieut. Col. Frederick Haldimand of the Royal American Regiment. No correspondence between BF and either brother has been found.

1. The original Italian of the bracketed words is: "avrebbe diretto a lui 16 sue Lettere intorno l'Elettricità, anzi che ad altri." BF translated this as: "he should have sent his 16 Letters on Electricity to him as well as to others." The correction inserted in brackets above is supplied from Antonio Pace, *Benjamin Franklin and Italy* (Phila., 1958), p. 54. Beccaria addressed the volume to Giacomo Bartolomeo Beccari of Bologna.

2. The Italian text ends with "alcuna scoperta di tal genere." A possible second leaf of the Italian text, not now surviving, may have continued the sentence with the words corresponding to BF's three here bracketed, or BF may simply have added them for clarity.

[Among surviving Franklin papers there are several which cannot be dated even from a specific year but which appear to belong to the time of his English residence as Pennsylvania agent. In some instances they seem to date from the first period of that residence (1757–62), in others from the second (1764–75), and in some they may date from either period. Occasionally there is evidence to show that a document must have been written during a limited part of one of these periods. In accordance with the principles of arrangement stated in the Introduction (above, I, xxxvi), the eleven undatable items which the editors believe belong to the first period of residence in England as agent (or a part of it), or to either period indifferently, are placed here following the more precisely dated documents of 1757. Others will be printed after those dated 1764. For each document the probable inclusive dates are given in brackets at the top.]

To John Canton[3]

AL: The Royal Society

Tuesday [1757–1772][4]

Mr. Franklin's Compliments to Mr. Canton, and requests he would procure for him two more of the long Glass Tubes such as he formerly did him the favour to procure for him.

To John Fothergill

MS Autobiography: Huntington Library

The filthy streets of Philadelphia and London were a persistent challenge to Franklin's civic conscience. He explained in the autobiography that "by talking and writing on the Subject" he had at length done something about the streets of Philadelphia. At an unstated time, perhaps before he retired from business, he "wrote and printed a Paper" (not found) on the advantages of having streets cleaned regularly: "the greater Ease in keeping our Houses clean, so much Dirt not being

3. On John Canton, electrical experimenter, see above, IV, 390 n.

4. This note might have been written at virtually any time before Canton's death, March 22, 1772, except, of course, during one of BF's journeys away from London or during his return to Philadelphia, August 1762–December 1764. Possibly BF's reference to himself as "Mr." places the note before he received his honorary doctorate at the University of St. Andrews, Feb. 12, 1759. His "Account of Expences" contains no entry to help in the dating.

brought in by People's Feet; the Benefit to the Shops by more Custom, as Buyers could more easily get at them, and by not having in windy Weather the Dust blown in upon their Goods, &c. &c." Franklin then "sent one of these Papers to each House, and in a Day or two went round to see who would subscribe an Agreement to pay" sixpence a month per house to a street cleaner. "It was unanimously sign'd, and for a time well executed. All the Inhabitants of the City were delighted with the Cleanliness of the Pavement that surrounded the Market, it being a Convenience to all; and this rais'd a general Desire to have all the Streets paved; and made the People more willing to submit to a Tax for that purpose."[5] Just before departing for England, Franklin drew a bill (not found) for paving the streets, perhaps left with a friend since no such bill is mentioned in the Assembly proceedings for 1757. An act for "regulating, pitching, paving and cleaning" the streets of Philadelphia, perhaps based on Franklin's bill, passed the Assembly on March 26, 1762, during his absence in England, and on Jan. 28, 1763, a committee including Franklin (recently returned home) brought in a supplementary bill which passed the House on February 22.[6]

While John Clifton[7] received credit for first showing Philadelphia the advantages of street lighting, Franklin explained that he himself had devised the four-sided, ventilated lamp which stayed clean much longer than the closed globe used by Clifton and commonly seen in London. Mention of this improvement, Franklin wrote, "puts me in mind of one I propos'd when in London, to Dr. [John] Fothergill, who was among the best men I have known, and a great Promoter of useful Projects."[8] After describing his own amazement at the little effort required to keep Craven Street swept clean and the advantage of having one rather than two gutters in a street, Franklin added: "My Proposal communicated to the good Doctor, was as follows:"

5. Par. Text edit., pp. 312–14.

6. Above, IV, 176 n; *Pa. Stats. at Large*, VI, 196–214, 234–46. The enacted bill contained "an alteration in the Mode of Assessment, which I thought not for the better." Par Text edit., p. 314. It provided for assessment of personal and real estates within the city of Philadelphia based upon returns by ward constables, and a tax of not more than threepence per pound on the assessed valuation; the mode preferred by BF is not known.

7. John Clifton (d. 1759), had placed the first street lamp in Philadelphia in front of his large, two-story brick house at the southeast corner of Clifton's (Drinker's) Alley and Second Street, below Race. Watson, *Annals*, I, 102; W. W. Hinshaw, *Encyclopedia of American Quaker Genealogy*, II (Ann Arbor, 1938), 347.

8. Par. Text edit., p. 316.

[1757–1762][9]

For the more effectual cleaning and keeping clean the Streets of London and Westminster, it is proposed,

That the several Watchmen be contracted with to have the Dust swept up in dry Seasons, and the Mud rak'd up at other Times, each in the several Streets and Lanes of his Round.

That they be furnish'd with Brooms and other proper Instruments for these purposes, to be kept at their respective Stands, ready to furnish the poor People they may employ in the Service.

That in the dry Summer Months the Dust be all swept up into Heaps at proper Distances, before the Shops and Windows of Houses are usually opened: when the Scavengers with close-covered Carts shall also carry it all away.

That the Mud when rak'd up be not left in Heaps to be spread abroad again by the Wheels of Carriages and Trampling of Horses; but that the Scavengers be provided with Bodies of Carts, not plac'd high upon Wheels, but low upon Sliders; with Lattice Bottoms, which being cover'd with Straw, will retain the Mud thrown into them, and permit the Water to drain from it, whereby it will become much lighter, Water making the greatest Part of its Weight. These Bodies of Carts to be plac'd at convenient Distances, and the Mud brought to them in Wheelbarrows, they remaining where plac'd till the Mud is drain'd, and then Horses brought to draw them away.[1]

9. So dated because BF probably made it during his first residence in London, between the years in which he is known to have been interested in street-cleaning measures for Philadelphia.

1. BF excused his attention to "these trifling Matters" by reminding his readers of "the great Number of the Instances in a populous City" when persons are troubled by dirty, dusty streets, thus giving the matter "Weight and Consequence," in the same way teaching "a poor young Man to shave himself and keep his Razor in order . . . may contribute more to the Happiness of his Life than giving him a 1000 Guineas." "Human Felicity," he observed, "is produc'd not so much by great Pieces of good Fortune that seldom happen, as by little Advantages that occur every Day." Par. Text edit., p. 322.

To ———[2]

Draft: American Philosophical Society

Sir [1757–1775]

I have perus'd the Letters and Papers you put into my Hands, and shall, as you desire, say what occurs to me on the considering them.

I do not know Mr. Murdoch personally, but have heard that he is a Person of Credit and some Note in that Country, and esteemed by the People there.

I imagine that little is to be expected from a Suit of Law, to be carried on at such a Distance; it will be expensive, tedious, and the Event uncertain.

By the Letters you have shown me, the Executors Claim of Interest seems indeed to be well founded on his agreeing to the Proposal that he should pay it, &c. But he intimates that he has subsequent Letters from Mr. Sanderson, containing a kind of Discharge of that Agreement *so far as he should be a sufferer by it,* I apprehend the Executors on Sight of such Letters, might think it reasonable to abate so much of their Claim.

If it cannot be settled by Writing, it seems a proper Case to be referr'd to Merchants. It would be best if Mr. Murdoch should agree that it be referr'd to Merchants here, he naming one or two, the Executors one or two others. If it is to be done there, I could name some Persons of Judgment in such Affairs and Men of Integrity, out of whom the Executors might chuse, if they are otherwise unacquainted there.

I suppose that a Factor is not generally accountable for bad Debts. He says there is a considerable Sum of that kind.

It should seem that his ready Agreement to the Paying of 5 per Cent. might be founded on his receiving from the Debtors Six per Cent. as appears by his Letter of Mar. 30. 1745.

2. The draft MS does not indicate the addressee. Apparently he had consulted BF about a debt owed to an estate in England by a resident of one of the colonies, perhaps Maryland. "Mr. Murdoch" may have been William Murdoch, merchant and assemblyman of Prince George's Co., and a commissary official for the British Army in Maryland who did business with John Hanbury and other London military contractors. *Md. Arch.,* LV (1938), *passim;* Pemberton Papers, Hist. Soc. Pa. Mr. Sanderson, mentioned below, has not been identified.

Suppose then that the Executors were to write to him to this Effect; That as they do not (any more than Mr. Sanderson) desire he should be a Sufferer by that Agreement, so they believe he would not desire to be a Gainer by a Noncompliance with it; therefore they propose, that Mr. Murdoch would now state the Account, give Credit for all the Interest he has received on the Outstanding Debts at Six per Cent, and charge those that are bad; which Account if properly vouch'd and supported they would allow, and make a final Settlement with him accordingly.

Specifications for a Dwelling House

Draft: American Philosophical Society

Obviously written in England, this document cannot otherwise be certainly dated. Apparently Franklin contemplated having an English architect prepare plans for a "model home" in Philadelphia suitable for "Tradesmen and People of moderate Circumstances." His description of the land on which it was to be built most nearly fits the lot on the north side of Mulberry (Arch) Street, between that street and Apple Tree Alley, and near Fifth Street, which he had acquired from Christopher and Mary Thompson, Aug. 1, 1741,[3] although the deed shows that lot to have been 140 ft. deep, not 180 ft. as Franklin seems to have remembered it when preparing these specifications. Nothing has been found relating to the actual building of such a "Pattern House." It is clearly not the dwelling he built for himself in 1764–65.

[1757–1775]

Mr. Franklin's Piece of Ground on which he proposes to Build a Dwelling House for a small Family is 22 feet wide, 180 feet deep, fronting to the South at one End on a Street that is 80 feet wide, and at the other to the North on an Alley 20 feet wide.

The Ground is dry, being Loom, Sand and Gravel. We dig about 30 feet before we come to Water, in making Wells; Our Supply of Water is from Wells or Rain Water sav'd in Tubs.

Our Materials for Building are, exceeding good well-burnt red Bricks, Stone Lime that with River Sand makes a very good and hard Mortar, Pine or Oak Boards and Timber; we have a Coarse Stone for Foundations and Cellar Walls; We have Marble for

3. See above, II, 311, and map of Philadelphia at the end of that volume.

Slabs and Chimney Pieces, and two or three kinds of coarser Freestone which are rather hard to work. Iron we have, and People to work it; but our Glass and Lead are from England.

The Plan of a House is desired, to be erected on the South Front of the Ground; to have 3 Stories besides the Offices under the Ground Floor and the Garrets; in which Plan, Regard is to be had chiefly to these Particulars, Convenience, Security against Fire, and Cheapness; so that it may be considered as a kind of Pattern House by future Builders, within the Power of Tradesmen and People of moderate Circumstances to imitate and follow.

From [John] Apthorp[4]

AL: American Philosophical Society

Tuesday morning [1757–1759][5]

Mr. Apthorp's compliments to Mr. Franklyn and desires the favour of his Company to dine with him on Fry-day next ¼ past three.

Addressed: Benjn Franklyn Esqr / Buckingham Street,[6]

From William Deane[7]

AL: American Philosophical Society

Frith Street Tuesday Morning [1757–1759][8]

Coll: Deanes Compliments to Mr. Franklin and Son, Shall be Extreemly glad of the favor of their Company to Dinner tommor-

4. Probably John Apthorp (d. 1772), son of the Charles Apthorp of Boston who was agent for Hanbury & Thomlinson in the northern colonies and involved in supplying specie for British troops in America. John Apthorp became a London partner of Thomlinson and his brother-in-law Barlow Trecothick about 1758. He returned to Boston in 1765 and was lost at sea on a voyage to South Carolina.

5. The terminal date is assigned because of the manner of addressing BF, whom Apthorp would probably have called "Dr." after Feb. 12, 1759.

6. Not BF's address, but only a few blocks from Craven Street; apparently Apthorp did not know exactly where BF lived.

7. Lieut. Col. William Deane (d. 1775) of the British Army, was appointed governor of Upnor Castle before 1758, and was promoted major general in 1770.

8. Certainly not later than 1762 because WF was included in the invitation, and probably not later than Feb. 12, 1759, because BF is called "Mr." not "Dr."

ow to meet Mr. and Mrs. Sargent[9] at half an Hour after three o Clock.

Addressed: To / Mr. Franklin / Craven Street

From Allen and Joseph England[1]

MS memorandum: American Philosophical Society

[1757–1762]

Allen England and his Brother Joseph England are proprietors of certain Tracts of Land scituate upon Christiana Creek in the County of Newcastle, Quantity 1300 Acres their Title to which stands thus—

In 1726 their Father John England advanced £500 to Sir William Keith by way of Mortgage upon the said Lands.

In 1729 the said John England assigned his Right in the Mortgage to his sons Allen and Joseph England.

And soon after the Lands were at a public Auction struck off to them as highest bidders.

They impowered Israel Pemberton[2] of Philadelphia to act as their Attorney for the Management of the said Estate, but have never been able to obtain a satisfactory Account from him, with Respect to the Quality and Value of thereof [*sic*].

They are now determined to revoke their Letter to Israel Pemberton and either send a person from hence, or Impower some other person there, not only for the Management but to sell the Lands.

9. John Sargent (1715–1791), director of the Bank of England, M.P. for Midhurst and later for West Looe. He and his wife were warm friends of Colonel and Mrs. Deane. Sargent and BF struck up a friendship and corresponded at intervals for many years.

1. Sons of John England (d. 1734), a land owner and iron manufacturer of Maryland and Delaware since 1723. He probably had a part in Governor Sir William Keith's plans to promote iron making in Delaware. J. Thomas Scharf, *History of Delaware,* II (Phila., 1888), 916-17; *PMHB,* XI (1887), 67-8, 190–3; XII (1888), 20-1. Nothing is known of the sons except that they seem never to have lived in America.

2. Israel Pemberton (1685–1754) must have acted for the Englands in the 1730s. They apparently did not know, when they made this inquiry, that he had died and that his son, Israel, mentioned frequently in this volume, had succeeded to many of his business enterprises.

And wish their Cousin Wm. Frey[3] would take an Opportunity of asking Benjamin Franklin Esquire what sort of Evidence will be necessary on this Occasion? particularly whether a Certificate of the Execution of Deeds, under the Seal of a Corporation will be Sufficient or is it necessary for the subscribing Witnesses to be Persons who are going into that Country.[4]

Endorsed: For Benjn. Franklin Esqr his Opinion On these Memorandums

From Elizabeth Hubbart ALS: Historical Society of Pennsylvania

Dear Sir [1757–1762][5]

Your tow last Favours gave me a satisfaction better felt then expressed: Indeed I have often longed to Chatt to you in some of those Happy hours you have Blessed me with but feared it was grown Disagreeable or would Interupt Business of Importance pleasing Amusements or more entertaining Conversation, but I most Heartily Accept the Apology you Condesend to make and will not deprive my Self of the satisfaction it gives me by Enquiering into the Merits of it. In return I will Tell you your Severe Morning Lecture tho' it lay dormant so long has at lenght had its desier'd Effect. I have Rose many Times this Summer many Tim[es] before the Sun and in general much Earlier then I Used to do. Now I hope when ever you favour me with your Letters you will remember the Precept of that Blessed Apostle Alixr. Pope which if you dont find in the Bible ought to have been their it Runs thus.

Be niggards of Advice on no Pretence,
For the Worst Averice is that of Sense![6]

You will always find Roome for it in the Mergin.

3. Not identified.

4. There is no evidence how BF may have responded, nor is the result of the intended legal action known.

5. The writer's request (in the second paragraph) that "Cousin Billey" buy her a ticket in the first State Lottery indicates that she wrote this letter during BF's first English residence as agent, when WF was with him. Probably he had already been there long enough so that she felt no need to refer to his voyage in this letter.

6. *Essay on Criticism,* Part III, 578-9.

I know your Generosity will pardon me if I tell you I think you have given me one peice of Advice which to have Succeed'd in must have been a very great Misfortune. It was to lay out the Trifle Mr. Hunter left in your Hands for a Striking Cap to Catch a Ten Thousand Pounder with, the Money I have No Avertion to, the Cap I think a pretty play thing but the Fool that could be catch'd in such a Cobweeb Snare tho' he had Ten times Ten thousand I could Heartily despise.[7] I will once more put my Self in the Way of Providence for that same Ten thousand Pounds, and beg the favour of Cousin Billey to try his Luck in purchasing me a Ticket in the first State Lottery and to be kind enough to send me the No. as soon as possible.

Mr. Bowdoin[8] sends his Compliments and is always enquiring after your Helth and when he may Expect the Happiness of seeing you here. I wish I knew for I have hoped for that Happiness from Spring to Fall and from Fall to Spring I dont know how many Years, and now begin to fear I shall never See you More.

Mama says send my kind Love and tell them I long to See them. All Friends desier their affectionate Regards. That Heaven may Shower its Choisest Blessings on you, and return you soon is the Constant Wish of Dear Sir Your affectionante Neice

E Hubbart

From ——— Knight[9]

AL: American Philosophical Society

Dover-Street [1757–1759][1]

Mr. Knight's compliments to Mr. Franklin and Mr. William Franklin and desires the favor of their company at dinner on tuesday next the 27th.

Addressed: Craven-Street

7. Probably a reference to the story she had told BF about Joseph Hubbard, who, at the age of 80 and with an estate of £10,000, had remarried a month or so after the death of his first wife. See above, p. 69.

8. James Bowdoin; see above, IV, 69 n.

9. Possibly Gowin Knight (1713–1772), F.R.S., whose work on magnetism BF had known and admired before going to England (see above, VI, 103, 177-8). He was appointed principal librarian of the British Museum upon its establishment in 1756. The date line of this note, however, militates against this identification, since from about 1750 to his appointment at the Museum Gowin Knight lived in Crane Court, Fleet Street, and thereafter apparently

From Mrs. Lloyd, Mrs. Morris, and Mr. Lloyd[2]

AL: American Philosophical Society

Thursday Morn: [1757–1759][3]

Mrs. Lloyd Mrs. Morris and Mr. Lloyd present their Compliments to Mrs. Stevenson and Mr. Franklyns, and desire the Favour of their Company this afternoon to meet Miss Gambier.[4]

Visiting and Business Cards

MS and printed cards: American Philosophical Society

[1757–1775]

Among Franklin's surviving papers is a collection of personal visiting cards (or "visiting tickets" as they appear to have been called) and business cards of tradesmen and others. Some of the personal cards are handwritten, as is one of Franklin's own after he received his doctorate; others are printed or engraved, and occasionally decorated with floral borders. They include, among others, the cards of the Earl of Morton, Sir James Jay, the Bishop of St. Asaph, Prince de Masserano, and Thomas Pownall. Among the business cards are those of a limner, a cheesemonger, coal merchants, and the like, and one professional man: "Spence Operator for the Teeth to His Majesty." Because of this appointment the dentist proudly decorated his card with the royal coat of arms. None of these cards can be precisely dated; they are recorded here simply as interesting souvenirs of Franklin's London residence.

---

at the Museum in Montague House, Bloomsbury. *DNB*. Dover Street is off Piccadilly. No correspondence between BF and any other Mr. Knight has been found.

1. Certainly not later than 1762 because WF was included in the invitation, and probably not later than Feb. 12, 1759, because BF is called "Mr.," not "Dr."

2. None of these persons has been identified. They may have been friends of Margaret Stevenson, BF's landlady.

3. Probable terminal date established by the use of "Mr." instead of "Dr." for BF.

4. Possibly one of the daughters of James Gambier (1692–[1740?]) and a sister of John Gambier (1723–1782), acting governor of the Bahamas, 1758–59, and lieutenant governor, 1764–81, and of James Gambier (1725–1789), officer of the Royal Navy, who commanded the *Burford* in the capture of Louisbourg in 1758 and of Guadeloupe in 1759. *DNB*. The three Gambier sisters were Susan, Elizabeth, and Margaret. Sir [John] Bernard Burke, *A Genealogical History of the Dormant, Abeyant, Forfeited, and Extinct Peerages of the British Empire* (new edit., London, 1866), p. 226.

Poor Richard Improved, 1758

Poor Richard improved: Being an Almanack and Ephemeris . . . for the Year of our Lord 1758: . . . By Richard Saunders, Philom. Philadelphia: Printed and Sold by B. Franklin, and D. Hall. (Yale University Library)

This is the twenty-sixth and last almanac in this series which Franklin prepared himself; thereafter David Hall assumed the responsibility.[5] Appropriately, the contents of this almanac make it the best known of all, for it is the direct source of the most widely reprinted of all Franklin's writings, even including the autobiography. Richard Saunders' prefatory address to the "Courteous Reader," which in previous almanacs usually occupies about one page, is in this year expanded to fill not only the usual second page of the pamphlet but also all the available space on the right-hand pages devoted to the twelve months and all but two lines of an additional page after December. In it Franklin created a new *persona,* "a plain clean old Man, with white Locks," called Father Abraham. At a public "vendue" the assembled crowd called on him for comment on "the Times" and for advice on how to meet the "heavy Taxes" now in force.[6]

Father Abraham's speech in response to this call comprises the chief substance of this extended preface. It consists of the selection and careful arrangement in a connected discourse of approximately one hundred of the aphorisms and maxims contained in the earlier *Poor Richard* almanacs. If Franklin had used any one of these aphorisms as a text for Father Abraham's homily (which he did not do) he might well have selected one from April 1744: "Industry, Perseverance, and Frugality, make Fortune yield."[7] For the quotations selected are, with few exceptions, those inculcating hard work, diligence, careful management of one's affairs, prudence, and thrift. Omitting all the other commentary on man and society which the almanacs so extensively provide, Father Abraham focuses attention exclusively upon the prudential wisdom which, in fact, occupies only a relatively small proportion of "the little Spaces that occur'd between the Remarkable Days in the Calendar."

This concentration upon a series of related themes and the wide circulation which has been given to this piece in the course of two

5. There is a considerable possibility that BF also wrote the preface to *Poor Richard Improved* for 1765, which is aimed at the Sugar Act of 1764 and points to instructions found later in the volume for making at home substitutes for West India rum. The matter will be discussed at the appropriate point in a later volume.

6. A possible reference to the levies imposed in Pennsylvania and other colonies to meet the costs of the current war.

7. See above, II, 397.

hundred years have had a profound effect upon the Franklin legend and the public conception of his sense of values. In his own lifetime its homely wisdom contributed heavily to his personal popularity, especially in France during the American Revolution; in more recent years it has been responsible for elevating him to the status of patron saint of American savings banks and for the agreement to make "National Thrift Week" coincide with the week in January which includes his birthday. On the other hand, it has led such a hostile critic as D.H. Lawrence to complain that, having been brought up on "those Poor Richard tags," it had taken him "many years and countless smarts to get out of that barbed wire moral enclosure that Poor Richard rigged up."[8] How little the maxims that Franklin chose to have Father Abraham repeat actually reflect the sum total of the observations on life and behavior he had inserted in the almanacs is apparent from an examination of the entire series as already printed in these volumes; how little they indicate all the values by which he himself lived is revealed in countless other passages in this edition.[9]

The quotations are drawn with considerable impartiality from all the preceding almanacs. No almanac is ignored and only three are represented just once each. On the other hand, the *Poor Richards* for 1737, 1743, and 1754, supply six aphorisms apiece for Father Abraham's speech, and the almanac for 1746 provides eight.[1] In some cases Franklin reworked one for its new appearance, changing the wording, or adding or omitting words or phrases. A few apparent quotations from *Poor Richard* are also included, which, in fact, are not found in any of the earlier almanacs but which, because of their appearance here, have come to be regarded as part of the *Poor Richard* canon.

This preface is dated July 7, 1757, indicating that Franklin wrote it —or at least finished it—while at sea on his way to England. He may have begun the writing while in New York or Woodbridge during the long wait before setting sail, and probably all the material for the almanac except the preface was in Hall's hands before Franklin's ship had weighed anchor at Sandy Hook. The *Gazette* announced, September 15, that *Poor Richard improved* for 1758 was "now in the Press and speedily will be published," and advertised it as "just published"

8. D. H. Lawrence, *Studies in Classic American Literature* (N.Y., 1923), p. 21.

9. For a highly perceptive and well-balanced discussion of this matter, see Harold A. Larrabee, "Poor Richard in an Age of Plenty," *Harper's Magazine*, CCXII, No. 1268 (Jan. 1956), 64–8.

1. The count includes duplications, where a particular aphorism which Father Abraham used appears in identical or very similar form more than once in the series of almanacs. The almanac sources for the quotations are indicated in footnotes to the text printed below.

in the issue of October 6. Franklin probably sent back the copy for the preface by the *Earl of Leicester* packet, Captain Morris, which reached New York on September 10 after a fast passage of thirty-three days from Falmouth.[2]

The bibliographical history of this famous preface is long and complicated. It has never been worked out in full, and perhaps never will be. The present editors have pursued extended inquiry only to the end of the eighteenth century and their investigations still leave several questions unanswered; some appear to be unanswerable.

The preface to *Poor Richard improved* for 1758 has appeared in print hundreds of times in English or in translation, in full or abridged. It has also served as the source for a number of lesser pieces incorporating its central ideas and preachments or imitating its method, but bearing very little direct relation to its actual words. In its original form, or only moderately condensed or modified, it has been variously titled "Preliminary Address prefixed to the Pennsylvania Almanack for 1758," "Father Abraham's Speech . . . ," "The Way to Wealth," "La Science du Bonhomme Richard," or either of the last two as translated into various European languages. In its most familiar and somewhat abbreviated form, the one which has made its contents most widely known to readers of English, it has usually been called "The Way to Wealth." A very short homily based on its ideas, but not representing at all the original text, has become widely known as "The Art of Making Money Plenty in Every Man's Pocket." In one or another version the preface has appeared as a separate pamphlet, a chapbook, or a broadside, in editions of Franklin's collected works, in anthologies of literature or of didactic pieces, in school readers, and in other almanacs. Translations survive in at least fifteen foreign languages.[3]

The present editors have located copies or found listings of 145 reprintings before the end of the eighteenth century.[4] English-language

2. *London Chron.*, Aug. 9, 1757; *N.-Y. Mercury*, Sept. 12, 1757; *Pa. Gaz.*, Sept. 15, 1757. BF landed at Falmouth about three weeks before this packet sailed.

3. The Franklin Collection in Yale Univ. Lib. contains translations into Catalan, Chinese, Danish, Dutch, French, Gaelic, German, Greek, Hungarian, Italian, Norwegian, Polish, Spanish, Swedish, and Welsh. Translations into other languages, including Russian, have been reported but have not been located by the present editors.

4. Printings of "The Art of Making Money Plenty in Every Man's Pocket" are not included in this count, since its text (which seems to have appeared first about 1790 or soon afterwards) is so far removed from the Franklin original. The rebus versions of this little piece apparently were first printed early in the nineteenth century.

reprints include 36 in the colonies or the United States, 51 in England, 7 in Scotland, and 6 in Ireland. Eighteenth-century translations include 28 into French (including one each printed in London, Brussels, and Utrecht and four in Lausanne), 11 into Italian, 3 into German, and one each into Dutch, Gaelic, and Swedish. These 144 eighteenth-century reprintings of a single piece by one American writer are evidence of the extraordinary appeal of Father Abraham's discourse. It is not surprising that the Franklin legend came very early to include the idea that he was the apostle of industry and thrift.[5]

The first known reprinting of the preface was in Boston, issued by Franklin's nephew Benjamin Mecom. The *Boston News-Letter* for March 30, 1758, carried his advertisement that "Father Abraham's Speech" was "This Day Published." This is a 24-page pamphlet, with a very long title which begins: *Father Abraham's Speech To a great Number of People, at a Vendue of Merchant Goods; Introduced to The Publick By Poor Richard, (A famous Pennsylvanian Conjurer and Almanack-Maker) In Answer to the Following Questions.*[6] In addition to the title-piece Mecom printed "Seven curious Pieces of Writing," one of which, interestingly enough, is the full nine stanzas of his uncle's song "I sing my Plain Country Joan," which Mecom headed "Poor Richard's Description of his Country Wife Joan A Song—Tune, The

5. This count is chiefly based on a check of the major bibliographical lists, such as those of Evans, Sabin, and Ford; published lists of the imprints of several American colonies and states; the printed catalogues of the British Museum, Bibliothèque Nationale, and Library of Congress; and the actual holdings of the American Philosophical Society and the Yale University Library. Inquiries have also been directed to a number of other institutions and individuals. Messrs. John Alden of the Boston Public Library, Jack C. Barnes of the University of Maryland, Roger P. Bristol of the Alderman Library, University of Virginia, Antonio Pace of Syracuse University, and Edwin Wolf, 2nd, of the Library Company of Philadelphia, have been particularly helpful. Probable "ghosts" found in some of the bibliographical lists have been eliminated from the count. Copies of about 80 percent of the printings included are in the Yale University Library and have been personally examined by the editors. If a more extended direct search of libraries in the Unites States and abroad had been possible, the total number of printings, and especially of translations into other languages, might have been somewhat extended. But until someone undertakes an exhaustive search for surviving printings of the composition, the figures given here may serve as an approximation of the extent to which it was reprinted in the eighteenth century.

6. For the distinctions between this printing and Mecom's second issue in 1760, see the second note below.

Hounds are all out."[7] Mecom reprinted the speech in a 16-page pamphlet in 1760, probably in the autumn, this time without appending any of the "curious Pieces" he had included before.[8]

Timothy Green of New London, Conn., reprinted the speech from Mecom's 1758 issue in an undated 24-page pamphlet, probably soon after it appeared in Boston.[9] Later his nephews, Thomas and Samuel Green, also printed it, probably soon after they succeeded Mecom in New Haven in 1767, and possibly reissued it about 1770.[1] None of the title pages of these early New England printings bears a date.

The first English reprinting—published only a day or two after Mecom's 1758 Boston issue—was in London in *The Grand Magazine of Universal Intelligence* for March 1758.[2] It carried the heading "Curious preliminary Address prefixed to the Pennsylvania Almanac, entitled Poor Richard improved: For the Year 1758. Printed at Philadelphia."

7. See above, II, 352–4. While preparing the headnote to that song the editors were unaware that Mecom had printed it in 1758. His doing so and especially the heading he gave to it (though the song does not in fact appear in any of the *Poor Richard* almanacs) is further evidence of BF's authorship of the song from a member of his family and of the proper inclusion of the next-to-last stanza as a part of the original.

8. The title pages of both the 1758 and 1760 issues are undated and some bibliographical confusion has arisen between them. The full titles are the same except that the 1758 issue adds: "To which are added, Seven curious Pieces of Writing." The imprint reads: "Boston, New-England, Printed and Sold by Benjamin Mecom, The New Printing-Office, Opposite to the Old-Brick Meeting, near the Court-House." Below this appears: "Note, Very good Allowance to those to take them by the Hundred or Dozen, to sell again." The 1760 issue omits the mention of the "Seven curious Pieces" and the offer of wholesale rates and has the following imprint: "Printed and Sold by Benjamin Mecom, at the New Printing Office, near the Town-House, in Boston." Evans 8131 is clearly a listing of copies of the 1760 issue, though it is incorrectly placed among publications of 1758. Evidence of the correct date of each issue is found in references in Mecom's footnotes in one, and in his "Advertisement" in the other, to recent publications in Boston, and in a woodcut of "Father Abraham in his Study" in the second issue which shows the date 1760.

9. Not in Evans. The copy in Yale Univ. Lib. reprints two of the "curious Pieces" Mecom had included in his 1758 issue.

1. Evans 10619 and 11929. Curiously, the latter entry is not placed under BF's name but under that of "Abraham Weatherwise," the pseudonym for the compiler of *Father Abraham's Almanack,* which BF's relative William Dunlap began to publish in Philadelphia in 1758. No copy of a 1770 New Haven issue of the speech has been located. It may be a "ghost."

2. I, 123–7; announced as "This Day" published in *Lond. Chron.*, March 30–April 1.

FATHER
Abraham's
SPEECH

To a great Number of People, at a *Vendue* of Merchant-Goods;

Introduced to the PUBLICK by

Poor Richard,

A famous PENNSYLVANIA Conjurer, and Almanack-Maker,

In Anſwer to the following QUESTIONS.

Pray, Father Abraham, *what think you of the Times? Won't theſe heavy Taxes quite ruin the Country? How ſhall we be ever able to pay them? What would you adviſe us to?*

To which are added,

SEVEN *curious* PIECES of WRITING.

BOSTON, NEW-ENGLAND,

Printed and Sold by Benjamin Mecom, *at* The NEW PRINTING-OFFICE,

Oppoſite to the Old-Brick Meeting, near the Court-Houſe.

NOTE, Very good Allowance to thoſe who take them by the Hundred or Dozen, to ſell again.

Except for some minor changes, such as in capitalization, spelling, and punctuation, the text is the same as in the original almanac. Almost at once *The London Chronicle* reprinted the piece in the issue of April 1–4, using the same title (except for the omission of the word "Curious") and the same text, and citing the *Grand Magazine* as its source. No further printing in England has been located until 1770 when Mrs. Ann (Fisher) Slack included it in a new edition of her anthology *The Pleasing Instructor or Entertaining Moralist.* She called it "Preliminary Address prefixed to the Pennsylvania Almanac for 1758: On Oeconomy and Frugality."[3] Again the full original text appears, although Mrs. Slack somewhat primly changed such conversational expressions as "won't" and "you'd" to the more literary "will not" and "you would." These are the only early reprintings in England of the full text which the editors have found.

Thus far the various reprintings, both in England and the colonies, followed exactly, or virtually so, the full text as contained in *Poor Richard improved* for 1758. But an important alteration took place in 1771. *The Gentleman's Magazine* for February of that year printed what it called "Substance of a Preliminary Address prefixed to an old Pennsylvania Almanack, intitled Poor Richard Improved.[4] The text was shortened by about one-sixth. All the first two paragraphs after the opening sentence were omitted as were a few of Father Abraham's own comments at various points. The editor dropped out nine of the quoted aphorisms and eliminated a great many of the repetitions of "as Poor Richard says" and parallel expressions. As Mrs. Slack had done the year before, he expanded many of the conversational contractions such as "won't," "you'd," and "they'll." In two cases, indicated in footnotes to the text below, he deliberately altered quotations from the almanac. The whole effect is to tighten as well as to shorten the piece and to reduce somewhat the personal involvement both of Father Abraham and of Richard Saunders himself. Whether "Sylvanus Urban," the pseudonymous editor of *The Gentleman's Magazine*, or someone else was responsible for these changes is not known. Their nature suggests strongly that Franklin was not himself responsible.

3. *The Pleasing Instructor or Entertaining Moralist consisting of Select Essays, Relations, Visions, and Allegories collected from The most Eminent English Authors to which are prefixed New Thoughts on Education.* A New Edition. London. Published Octr. 1, 1770 as the Act directs by Robinson & Roberts in Paternoster Row, and T. Slack in Newcastle. Pp. 82–92. A misprint at the end gives the date of composition of the "Address" as "July 7, 1577" instead of "1757."

4. *Gent. Mag.*, XLI (1771), 59–63.

This version seems never to have been exactly reprinted in England, and only once in America.[5] It served, however, as the prototype, though not the exclusive textual source, for many of the hundreds of reprintings that have appeared since 1771, most of them under the title "The Way to Wealth," or one of its foreign-language equivalents. The normal "Way to Wealth" version repeats all the major omissions and changes of the magazine text, but has numerous minor differences from it. Whoever prepared this new form appears to have had both the earlier full preface and *The Gentleman's Magazine's* shortened version before him. Most notably, he restored some, though not all, of the uses of "as Poor Richard says," and, apparently liking the expression, added it or similar words several times when they are not found in the original. The differences from the magazine text are numerous enough to make clear that it was this text which was used in most of the later English-language printings or translations. The new title was obviously suggested by two sentences near the end of Franklin's "Advice to a young Tradesman" (1748): "In short, the Way to Wealth, if you desire it, is as plain as the Way to Market. It depends chiefly on two Words, INDUSTRY and FRUGALITY."[6]

No edition in this form and entitled "The Way to Wealth" has been found with an imprint date earlier than 1774, but at least one issue with this title and the corresponding textual differences from the *Gentleman's Magazine's* "Substance of a Preliminary Address" must have appeared at least as early as 1773, for Barbeu Dubourg published his French translation of Franklin's works in that year and included in it "Le Moyen de s'enricher" drawn immediately from the new English version.[7]

The strongest candidate for the honor of being the first printed text under the new title is a 16-page pamphlet, the title page of which bears, between two rows of printer's ornaments, only the words *The Way to Wealth, as Clearly Shewn in the Preface of An old Pennsylvania Almanack, intitled Poor Richard Improved.* This pamphlet appears in three undated issues which differ from each other in several typographical details.[8] Probably all three issues were published in Lon-

5. *Pennsylvania Magazine: or, American Monthly Museum,* I (Sept. 1775), 419–22.

6. See above, III, 308.

7. Dubourg's and other French translations are discussed below.

8. Some of these differences are described in L.S.L. [Luther S. Livingston], "News for Bibliophiles," *The Nation,* XCVI, No. 2498 (May 15, 1913), 494–6. Livingston's article, while far from complete, is the most useful summary of the bibliographical history of Father Abraham's speech which the editors have found.

don.[9] Two other printings with the same, or nearly the same, full title have a London 1774 imprint date and three more, undated, are believed to have been published in that or the next year. When Benjamin Vaughan compiled his edition of Franklin's *Political, Miscellaneous, and Philosophical Pieces* (London, 1779), he included this shortened version of the almanac preface, using the same title as the separate printings just mentioned.[1] At the same time Vaughan's London publisher, J. Johnson of St. Paul's Church Yard, issued "The Way to Wealth" in a broadside, which was helpfully mentioned in a note at the end of the text in the volume.[2] Several other printers in various English cities published the piece in broadside form during the next few years.

During the 1780s and 1790s printings in England, Scotland, and Ireland were too numerous to warrant individual mention here. They appeared as separate pamphlets, in magazines, and in anthologies of various sorts.[3] Some of these printings used the title beginning "Preliminary Address" essentially as it had appeared in *The London Chron-*

9. Copies of one or another issue of this pamphlet appear to be what Ford, *Franklin Bibliography,* lists as nos. 110 and 111. Among copies in Yale Univ. Lib. is one which is inscribed at the top of the title page (partly trimmed off): "Lady Juliana P[enn] J: Gunn[ing]." At the bottom, below the lower row of type ornaments, is written in the same hand: "Printed at Pennsylvania 1773." A later inscription on the third page records the transmission of the pamphlet by John Gunning to two other members of his family. These inscriptions have led some bibliographers to believe that this pamphlet was printed at Philadelphia. Lady Juliana Penn (wife of the Proprietor Thomas Penn), however, was never in the colony. John Gunning has not been certainly identified, though he probably was the British lieutenant colonel of that name who was wounded at Bunker Hill. If anyone in Pennsylvania had added the statement about the place of printing, he or she would probably have written more specifically "in Philadelphia" rather than "at Pennsylvania." Furthermore, the editors concur in Livingston's comment that this pamphlet "bears every appearance of being from an English press."

1. Pp. 24–36.

2. "This piece has been printed on a single sheet of paper, of a small size fit for framing, and may be had of the publisher of this work, price twopence. E." The sheet measures approximately 15 3/4 by 12 1/2 inches. BF refers to this broadside, "to be stuck up in Houses," in Par. Text edit., p. 244.

3. The first identified printing of the speech in Scotland was in *The Scots Magazine,* XXXIX (Jan. 1777), 21–6 (in the full form); the first in Ireland was a pamphlet issue of *The Way to Wealth* in Dublin, 1782. Perhaps the most noteworthy anthology appearance is in a collection derived in part from Lord Chesterfield's *Letters to His Son,* entitled *Lord Chesterfield's Advice to his Son on Men and Manners,* 5th edit. (London, 1788), pp. 191–201. The piece was repeated in the 1793 edition.

icle in 1758 and included the full text reprinted there from *The Grand Magazine*. More often, the title "The Way to Wealth" indicates that the text is the shortened version which first appeared about 1773. That the publishers were indebted to the Vaughan 1779 edition of Franklin's works was sometimes shown by their including in the title Franklin's name and some phrase such as "From his Political Works." Title pages which identify publications in twenty cities and towns in the British Isles attest to the widespread interest in this work.

"The Way to Wealth" as a title, and the shortened form which the title indicates, seem not to have appeared in America until 1780 when John Carter, a Providence printer who had served his apprenticeship with Franklin and Hall, used it in the different editions of his *New England Almanack* for 1781.[4] Other printings, in newspapers, magazines, or almanacs, as pamphlets or broadsides, or in anthologies, followed in America during the next two decades.[5] Title-page imprints represent eighteen cities and towns, scattered from Maine to Pennsylvania; only the printers in the southern colonies and states appear as a group to have been indifferent to this highly popular composition.

Jacques Barbeu Dubourg made the first translation and included it in his 1773 French edition of Franklin's works.[6] "The Way to Wealth" in his rendering became "Le Moyen de s'enricher," and "Poor Richard Improved" was transformed, curiously enough, into "Le Pauvre Henri à son aise." In a footnote comment on this change attached to the title of the piece in his own 1779 edition of Franklin's works, Benjamin

4. Carter appears to have published this work first with the title *The New-England Almanack, or, Lady's and Gentleman's Diary* and as "By Benjamin West, A.M."; then, with the same title, as "By Isaac Bickerstaff, Esq; Philom."; and third with the title *Bickerstaff's New-England Almanack, or, Lady's and Gentleman's Diary,* and as "By Isaac Bickerstaff, Esq; Philom." The last appears in two states, with differences in the calendar. John E. Alden, ed., *Rhode Island Imprints 1727–1800* (N.Y., 1949), nos. 812, 813, 810.

5. The most notable American anthology of the eighteenth century to include "The Way to Wealth" is Noah Webster, *A Selection of Lessons in Reading and Speaking . . . being The Third Part of a Grammatical Institute of the English Language,* 3d edit. (Phila., 1787), pp. 85–93. Webster was in Philadelphia during his preparation of this revised and enlarged edition and conferred with BF about some of the pieces he proposed to include, but the surviving correspondence between them does not indicate whether they specifically discussed "The Way to Wealth."

6. [Jacques] Barbeu Dubourg, *Œuvres de M. Franklin, Docteur és Loix* (Paris, 1773), II, 171–81.

Vaughan explained that Dubourg had altered the title "to avoid the *jeu de mots,* in case he had written *Pauvre Richard.*"[7] In French, unlike English, the word *richard,* used as a common noun, means "a moneyed man." Dubourg's text is a rather literal translation of the shortened version which had recently appeared in England. This first translation of Father Abraham's speech attracted little attention in France.

Apparently the next publication in French appeared in the spring of 1777, but in a journal actually published in London. A semi-weekly, *Courier de l'Europe, Gazette Anglo-Françoise,* was subsidized by the French government and served as a vehicle for propaganda, circulating both in the British Isles and on the Continent. A Scottish reader wrote the editor from Edinburgh, March 7, 1777, sending him a copy of Franklin's composition (probably taken from *The Scots Magazine* where it had appeared in the January issue of that year) and urged that both the original piece and his own letter be translated and printed. The editor of the *Courier* complied and, in translating the canny Scot's letter, quoted him as declaring that he regarded Franklin's proverbs as "la quintessence de la sagesse accumulée de tous les siècles." Since the version which came from Edinburgh was the full "Preliminary Address" that had appeared in 1758 in *The Grand Magazine* and *The London Chronicle,* the French translation, which was printed in six installments in *Courier de l'Europe* from March 21 through May 30, 1777, was also essentially a translation of what Franklin had originally written, rather than the shortened form Dubourg had used.[8]

In the same year a third translation, made by Antoine-François Quétant, possibly with the assistance of Jean-Baptiste Lécuy (Lesqui), appeared in Paris. The title page indicates that the pamphlet was issued "à Philadelphie Et se trouve à Paris, chez Ruault, Libraire rue de la Harpe," but the mention of the American city was doubtless only a dodge to escape the requirement of a royal license. The work received a new title, one which was destined to become as familiar in France (and in American naval history through the name of John Paul Jones's ship) as "The Way to Wealth" was becoming in England: *La Science du Bonhomme Richard, ou moyen facile de payer les impôts.* The text was taken, as that in the *Courier de l'Europe* had been, from the full

7. [Benjamin Vaughan, ed.], *Political, Miscellaneous, and Philosophical Pieces* (London, 1779), p. 24.

8. *The Scots Magazine,* XXXIX (Jan. 1777), 21–6; *Courier de l'Europe,* I, 345–6, 369–70, 382, 427, 515–16, 524 (Mar. 21, 28, 31, April 18, May 27, 30, 1777). Franklin's composition was headed: "Preface d'un Almanach de Pensylvanie, intitulé *Almanach du Pauvre Richard* (Poor Richard's Almanack)."

original version but the translation was in somewhat more idiomatic French than either of its predecessors had been.[9]

Franklin's presence in France and his great popularity led to almost instant acceptance of *La Science du Bonhomme Richard* and to its widespread popularity. There were four new editions in 1778 in Paris and one in Avignon the next year. Enthusiasm spread to the French-speaking parts of Switzerland and editions appeared in Lausanne in 1778 and 1779. Then, the market apparently being saturated for the time being, there was a lull, but in 1786 two more printings of the Quétant translation were issued in Paris. An anthology in French containing the piece from *Poor Richard* was published in 1789 in both Brussels and Utrecht editions.

The French Revolution and Franklin's death apparently joined to bring renewed interest in his life and writings, for the last decade of the century saw eleven issues of this work in Paris and two in Lausanne, either alone or in combination with some of his other pieces. One of the Paris editions contained a new translation by J. Castéra.[1] The most unusual, and apparently one of the most popular versions, appeared in 1795. It has a title page in English: *The Way to Wealth or Poor Richard Improved by Benj. Franklin*, followed by a brief preface and the text of the piece in English; then a French title page: *La Science du Bonhomme*

9. For example, where Father Abraham quotes Poor Richard as saying "God helps them that help themselves," these first three French translations have the following renderings: Dubourg: "Dieu aide ceux qui s'aident eux-mêmes." *Courier de l'Europe:* "Dieu aide ceux qui s'aident eux-mêmme." Quétant: "Dieu dit à l'homme: aide-toi, je t'aiderai." Alfred Owen Aldridge, who first used this comparison between Dubourg and Quétant, points out that the latter's version is very similar to the form of the proverb which had appeared in La Fontaine. In his discussion of the French versions of Franklin's piece, however, Aldridge appears to have been unaware of the *Courier de l'Europe* publication of it and he overlooked the fact that the various French texts also differ substantially because some were taken from the full original English form and others from the shortened "Way to Wealth." *Franklin and his French Contemporaries* (N.Y., 1957), pp. 38–59. The 1777 printing of Quétant's translation also included, in the same pamphlet, translations of BF's examination before the House of Commons, 1766; the Constitution of Pennsylvania, 1776; and the examination of Richard Penn before the House of Lords, 1776.

1. J. Castéra, *Vie de Benjamin Franklin, écrite par lui-même, suive de ses oeuvres morales, politiques et littéraires* (Paris, [1798]), II, 413–34. Castéra entitled this piece "Le Chemin de la fortune, ou la science du Bonhomme Richard." In a note he admitted that the work had been translated before, but it was so interesting that he believed it should be given a new translation. In it he followed the shortened "Way to Wealth" version.

Richard, ou moyen facile de payer les impôts. Par Benj. Franklin, followed by a longer preface and the text in French. These in turn are followed by several of Franklin's other short pieces translated into French, for two of which the English originals are also provided. The most curious feature of this publication is that the English text of the Poor Richard composition is the shortened "Way to Wealth" version, while the French text is the full original in the Quétant translation. This composite work appeared in six distinct issues in a single year—one of them a particularly handsome example of the bookmaker's art, of which six copies were printed on large paper and eight on vellum.

The first known Italian translation appeared in a periodical *Scelta di opuscoli interessanti* published in Milan in 1775, with another publication in Turin in the same year and a new Milan edition in 1781. The next printing is a 22-page pamphlet licensed for publication in 1776 but with no place of issue indicated. Seven more Italian printings during the eighteenth century are evidence of the widespread interest in Franklin in the peninsula which he wished to visit but never did.[2] Eighteenth-century translations into other languages may have been considerably fewer, though some examples have been found, as noted earlier, in Dutch, Gaelic, German, and Swedish.

This account of the most important piece in *Poor Richard improved* for 1758 and of its widespread reprintings makes no attempt to pursue its history for the years since 1800. It is perhaps enough to say that the popularity of Father Abraham's speech during the author's own lifetime and the following decade has continued and has spread to many other lands. Although most of the proverbs and maxims it contains may already have been familiar in one form or another in several languages, Franklin's method of bringing them together into a single related series gave them added force and impact and created what is undoubtedly the world's best-known homily on industry, financial prudence, and thrift. As to following Father Abraham's advice and profiting from it, probably most of the millions of readers of this piece—like the people at the vendue—have enjoyed it enormously, have applauded it loudly and long, and then have reverted to their usual practices. One thing, however, is certain: they have bought and read Father Abraham's speech in all its different forms in unknown thousands of copies—and the publishers, at least, have profited from their enthusiasm.

As to the speech itself, one may agree with D. H. Lawrence that Poor Richard's "tags" are detestable, or with Franklin's Scottish admirer that these proverbs are "the quintessence of the wisdom accumulated in all

2. The Italian printings are conveniently listed in Antonio Pace, *Benjamin Franklin and Italy* (Phila., 1958), pp. 416–21 *passim.*

the ages," or one may take a position somewhere in between. In any case, one can recognize the skill with which Franklin wove his maxims together into a connected discourse, and appreciate the fun he had doing it while on his long voyage to England.

Courteous Reader,

I have heard that nothing gives an Author so great Pleasure, as to find his Works respectfully quoted by other learned Authors. This Pleasure I have seldom enjoyed; for tho' I have been, if I may say it without Vanity, an *eminent Author* of Almanacks annually now a full Quarter of a Century, my Brother Authors in the same Way, for what Reason I know not, have ever been very sparing in their Applauses; and no other Author has taken the least Notice of me, so that did not my Writings produce me some solid *Pudding,* the great Deficiency of *Praise* would have quite discouraged me.

I concluded at length, that the People were the best Judges of my Merit; for they buy my Works; and besides, in my Rambles, where I am not personally known, I have frequently heard one or other of my Adages repeated, with, *as Poor Richard says,* at the End on't; this gave me some Satisfaction, as it showed not only that my Instructions were regarded, but discovered likewise some Respect for my Authority; and I own, that to encourage the Practice of remembering and repeating those wise Sentences, I have sometimes *quoted myself* with great Gravity.

Judge then how much I must have been gratified by an Incident I am going to relate to you. I stopt my Horse lately where a great Number of People were collected at a Vendue of Merchant Goods. The Hour of Sale not being come, they were conversing on the Badness of the Times, and one of the Company call'd to a plain clean old Man, with white Locks, *Pray, Father Abraham, what think you of the Times? Won't these heavy Taxes quite ruin the Country? How shall we be ever able to pay them? What would you advise us to?* ——Father Abraham stood up, and reply'd, If you'd have my Advice, I'll give it you in short, for a *Word to the Wise is enough,* and *many Words won't fill a Bushel,* as *Poor Richard says.*[3] They join'd in desiring him to speak his Mind, and gathering round him, he proceeded as follows;

3. Neither of these aphorisms is in an earlier *Poor Richard* in these words.

"Friends, says he, and Neighbours, the Taxes are indeed very heavy, and if those laid on by the Government were the only Ones we had to pay, we might more easily discharge them; but we have many others, and much more grievous to some of us. We are taxed twice as much by our *Idleness,* three times as much by our *Pride,* and four times as much by our *Folly,* and from these Taxes the Commissioners cannot ease or deliver us by allowing an Abatement. However let us hearken to good Advice, and something may be done for us; *God helps them that help themselves,* as Poor Richard says, in his Almanack of 1733.[4]

It would be thought a hard Government that should tax its People one tenth Part of their *Time,* to be employed in its Service. But *Idleness* taxes many of us much more, if we reckon all that is spent in absolute *Sloth,* or doing of nothing, with that which is spent in idle Employments or Amusements, that amount to nothing. *Sloth,* by bringing on Diseases, absolutely shortens Life. *Sloth, like Rust, consumes faster than Labour wears, while the used Key is always bright,*[5] as Poor Richard says. But *dost thou love Life, then do not squander Time, for that's the Stuff Life is made of,*[6] as Poor Richard says. How much more than is necessary do we spend in Sleep! forgetting that *The sleeping Fox catches no Poultry,*[7] and that *there will be sleeping enough in the Grave,*[8] as Poor Richard says. If Time be of all Things the most precious, *wasting Time* must be, as Poor Richard says, *the greatest Prodigality,*[9] since, as he elsewhere tells us, *Lost Time is never found again;*[10] and what we call *Time-enough, always proves little enough:*[11] Let us then be up and be doing, and doing to the Purpose; so by Diligence shall we do more with less Perplexity. *Sloth makes all Things difficult, but Industry all easy,*[12] as Poor Richard says; and *He that riseth late, must trot all*

4. *Poor Richard,* June 1736, not in 1733. Hereafter only the month and year from which a quotation is taken will be cited, with significant differences, if any, noted.

5. July 1744.

6. June 1746.

7. Sept. 1743, adding "Up! up!"

8. Sept. 1741, word order differing.

9. June 1745, "Idleness," not "wasting Time."

10. Jan. 1748.

11. Nov. 1747.

12. April 1734, wording differs.

Day, and shall scarce overtake his Business at Night.[13] While *Laziness travels so slowly, that Poverty soon overtakes him,*[14] as we read in Poor Richard, who adds, *Drive thy Business, let not that drive thee;*[15] and *Early to Bed, and early to rise, makes a Man healthy, wealthy and wise.*[16]

So what signifies *wishing* and *hoping* for better Times. We may make these Times better if we bestir ourselves. *Industry need not wish,*[17] as Poor Richard says, and *He that lives upon Hope will die fasting.*[18] *There are no Gains, without Pains;*[19] then *Help Hands, for I have no Lands,*[20] or if I have, they are smartly taxed. And, as Poor Richard likewise observes, *He that hath a Trade hath an Estate,*[1] and *He that hath a Calling hath an Office of Profit and Honour;*[2] but then the *Trade* must be worked at, and the *Calling* well followed, or neither the *Estate,* nor the *Office,* will enable us to pay our Taxes. If we are industrious we shall never starve; for, as Poor Richard says, *At the working Man's House Hunger looks in, but dares not enter.*[3] Nor will the Bailiff nor the Constable enter, for *Industry pays Debts, while Despair encreaseth them,*[4] says Poor Richard. What though you have found no Treasure, nor has any rich Relation left you a Legacy, *Diligence is the Mother of Good luck,*[5] as Poor Richard says, and *God gives all Things to Industry.*[6] Then *plough deep, while Sluggards sleep, and you shall have Corn to sell and to keep,*[7] says Poor Dick. Work while it is called To-day, for you know not how much you may be hindered To-morrow, which makes Poor Richard say, *One To-day is worth two To-morrows;*[8] and farther, *Have you somewhat to do To-morrow, do it To-day.*[9] If you were a Servant, would you not be ashamed that a

13. Aug. 1742.
14. Sept. 1756.
15. Nov. 1738.
16. Oct. 1735.
17. Oct. 1739.
18. Feb. 1736, with a difference which may have been a printer's error in the original. Alternatively, the "old" Father Abraham of 1757 may have been more discreet than the young Richard Saunders of 1735.
19. April 1745.
20. Jan. 1745.
1. Jan. 1742.
2. March 1756, but "Trade," not "Calling."
3. June 1737.
4. Nov. 1742.
5. Feb. 1736.
6. Oct. 1755.
7. Aug. 1756.
8. April 1757.
9. Jan. 1742; changed in *Gent. Mag.* and "The Way to Wealth" to "Never leave that till tomorrow which you can do today."

good Master should catch you idle? Are you then your own Master, *be ashamed to catch yourself idle,*[10] as Poor Dick says. When there is so much to be done for yourself, your Family, your Country, and your gracious King, be up by Peep of Day; *Let not the Sun look down and say, Inglorious here he lies.*[11] Handle your Tools without Mittens; remember that *the Cat in Gloves catches no Mice,*[12] as Poor Richard says. 'Tis true there is much to be done, and perhaps you are weak handed, but stick to it steadily, and you will see great Effects, for *constant Dropping wears away Stones,*[13] and by *Diligence and Patience the Mouse ate in two the Cable;*[14] and *little Strokes fell great Oaks,*[15] as Poor Richard says in his Almanack, the Year I cannot just now remember.

Methinks I hear some of you say, *Must a Man afford himself no Leisure?* I will tell thee, my Friend, what Poor Richard says, *Employ thy Time well if thou meanest to gain Leisure;* and, *since thou art not sure of a Minute,*[16] *throw not away an Hour.*[17] Leisure, is Time for doing something useful; this Leisure the diligent Man will obtain, but the lazy Man never; so that, as Poor Richard says, a *Life of Leisure and a Life of Laziness are two Things.*[18] Do you imagine that Sloth will afford you more Comfort than Labour? No, for as Poor Richard says, *Trouble springs from Idleness, and grievous Toil from needless Ease.*[19] *Many without Labour, would live by their* WITS *only, but they break for want of Stock.*[20] Whereas Industry gives Comfort, and Plenty, and Respect: *Fly Pleasures, and they'll follow you.*[1] *The diligent Spinner has a large Shift;*[2] and *now I have a Sheep and a Cow, every Body bids me Good morrow;*[3] all which is well said by Poor Richard.

10. May 1741, adding "always" after "be."
11. Not in any earlier *Poor Richard.*
12. March 1754.
13. Not in any earlier *Poor Richard.*
14. Jan. 1735; "bit" instead of "ate."
15. Aug. 1750.
16. Dec. 1740.
17. July 1738.
18. Sept. 1746.
19. May 1756, but omitting "grievous" and "needless."
20. Sept. 1750, but omitting "without Labour," "only," and "they."
1. March 1738.
2. June 1756, and April 1742, which substitutes "good" for "diligent."
3. June 1736.

But with our Industry, we must likewise be *steady, settled* and *careful,* and oversee our own Affairs *with our own Eyes,* and not trust too much to others; for, as Poor Richard says,

I never saw an oft removed Tree,
Nor yet an oft removed Family,
That throve so well as those that settled be.[4]

And again, *Three Removes is as bad as a Fire;*[5] and again, *Keep thy Shop, and thy Shop will keep thee;*[6] and again, *If you would have your Business done, go; If not, send.*[7] And again,

He that by the Plough would thrive,
Himself must either hold or drive.[8]

And again, *The Eye of a Master will do more Work than both his Hands;*[9] and again, *Want of Care does us more Damage than Want of Knowledge;*[10] and again, *Not to oversee Workmen, is to leave them your Purse open.*[11] Trusting too much to others Care is the Ruin of many; for, as the Almanack says, *In the Affairs of this World, Men are saved, not by Faith, but by the Want of it;*[12] but a Man's own Care is profitable; for, saith Poor Dick, *Learning is to the Studious,* and *Riches to the Careful,* as well as *Power to the Bold,* and *Heaven to the Virtuous.*[13] And farther, *If you would have a faithful Servant, and one that you like, serve yourself.*[14] And again, he adviseth to Circumspection and Care, even in the smallest Matters, because sometimes *a little Neglect may breed great Mischief;*[15] adding, *For want of a Nail the Shoe was lost; for want of a Shoe the Horse was lost; and for want of a Horse the Rider was lost,*[16] being overtaken and slain by the Enemy, all for want of Care about a Horse-shoe Nail.

So much for Industry, my Friends, and Attention to one's own Business; but to these we must add *Frugality,* if we would make our *Industry* more certainly successful. A Man may, if he knows not how to save as he gets, *keep his Nose all his Life to the Grindstone,*[17]

4. Aug. 1737, but in first line "transplanted" instead of "removed."
5. Not in any earlier *Poor Richard.*
6. June 1735.
7. Nov. 1743, but "it," not "your Business."
8. Dec. 1747.
9. Sept. 1755.
10. July 1746.
11. Nov. 1751.
12. June 1754.
13. Dec. 1754.
14. Oct. 1737, "a faithful Servant and one that you like."
15. Not in any earlier *Poor Richard.*
16. Feb. 1752.
17. No similar expression in any earlier *Poor Richard.*

and die not worth a *Groat* at last. *A fat Kitchen makes a lean Will,*[18] as Poor Richard says; and,

Many Estates are spent in the Getting,
Since Women for Tea forsook Spinning and Knitting,
And Men for Punch forsook Hewing and Splitting.[19]

If you would be wealthy, says he, in another Almanack, *think of Saving as well as of Getting: The Indies have not made Spain rich, because her* Outgoes *are greater than her* Incomes.[20] Away then with your expensive Follies, and you will not have so much Cause to complain of hard Times, heavy Taxes, and chargeable Families; for, as Poor Dick says,

Women and Wine, Game and Deceit,
Make the Wealth small, and the Wants great.[1]

And farther, *What maintains one Vice, would bring up two Children.*[2] You may think perhaps, That a *little* Tea, or a *little* Punch now and then, Diet a *little* more costly, Clothes a *little* finer, and a *little* Entertainment now and then, can be no *great* Matter; but remember what Poor Richard says, *Many* a Little *makes a Mickle;*[3] and farther, *Beware of* little *Expences; a small Leak will sink a great Ship;*[4] and again, *Who Dainties love, shall Beggars prove;*[5] and moreover, *Fools make Feasts, and wise Men eat them.*[6]

Here you are all got together at this Vendue of *Fineries* and *Knicknacks*. You call them *Goods,* but if you do not take Care, they will prove *Evils* to some of you. You expect they will be sold *cheap,* and perhaps they may for less than they cost; but if you have no Occasion for them, they must be *dear* to you. Remember what Poor Richard says, *Buy what thou hast no Need of, and ere long thou shalt sell thy Necessaries.*[7] And again, *At a great Pennyworth pause a while:*[8] He means, that perhaps the Cheapness is *apparent* only, and not *real;* or the Bargain, by straitning thee in thy Busi-

18. July 1733, omitting "makes."
19. July 1733, omitting last line.
20. Oct. 1743, but "of saving, more than of getting."
1. April 1746.
2. Sept. 1747.
3. "Hints for those that would be Rich," *Poor Richard* 1737.
4. Jan. 1745.
5. May 1749.
6. May 1733.
7. April 1738.
8. Jan. 1739.

ness, may do thee more Harm than Good. For in another Place he says, *Many have been ruined by buying good Pennyworths.*[9] Again, Poor Richard says, *'Tis foolish to lay out Money in a Purchase of Repentance;*[10] and yet this Folly is practised every Day at Vendues, for want of minding the Almanack. *Wise Men,* as Poor Dick says, *learn by others Harms, Fools scarcely by their own;*[11] but, *Felix quem faciunt aliena Pericula cautum.*[12] Many a one, for the Sake of Finery on the Back, have gone with a hungry Belly, and half starved their Families; *Silks and Sattins, Scarlet and Velvets,* as Poor Richard says, *put out the Kitchen Fire.*[13] These are not the *Necessaries* of Life; they can scarcely be called the *Conveniencies,* and yet only because they look pretty, how many *want* to *have* them. The *artificial* Wants of Mankind thus become more numerous than the *natural;* and, as Poor Dick says, *For one* poor *Person, there are an hundred* indigent.[14] By these, and other Extravagancies, the Genteel are reduced to Poverty, and forced to borrow of those whom they formerly despised, but who through *Industry* and *Frugality* have maintained their Standing; in which Case it appears plainly, that a *Ploughman on his Legs is higher than a Gentleman on his Knees,*[15] as Poor Richard says. Perhaps they have had a small Estate left them, which they knew not the Getting of; they think *'tis Day, and will never be Night;* that a little to be spent out of *so much,* is not worth minding; *(a Child and a Fool,* as Poor Richard says, *imagine Twenty Shillings and Twenty Years can never be spent)*[16] but, *always taking out of the Meal-tub, and never putting in, soon comes to the Bottom;*[17] then, as Poor Dick says, *When the Well's dry, they know the Worth of Water.*[18] But this they might have known before,

9. Sept. 1747.

10. Oct. 1740, but differs: ". . . He is the greatest fool that lays it [money] out in a purchase of repentence."

11. Jan. 1749, omitting "scarcely."

12. 1734, p. [21], and December 1743, both complete; Feb. 1737, "Felix quem, &c." only.

13. March 1746, omitting "Scarlet and Velvets"; March 1757: "Scarlet, Silk and Velvet, have put out the Kitchen Fire."

14. May 1746.

15. May 1746.

16. July 1754, omitting "and a Fool."

17. Not in any earlier *Poor Richard.*

18. Jan. 1746.

if they had taken his Advice; *If you would know the Value of Money, go and try to borrow some;*[19] for, *he that goes a borrowing goes a sorrowing;*[20] and indeed so does he that lends to such People, when he goes *to get it in again.* Poor Dick farther advises, and says,

Fond Pride of Dress, *is sure a very Curse;*
E'er Fancy *you consult, consult your Purse.*[1]

And again, *Pride is as loud a Beggar as Want, and a great deal more saucy.*[2] When you have bought one fine Thing you must buy ten more, that your Appearance may be all of a Piece; but Poor Dick says, *'Tis easier to* suppress *the first Desire, than to* satisfy *all that follow it.*[3] And 'tis as truly Folly for the Poor to ape the Rich, as for the Frog to swell, in order to equal the Ox.

Great Estates may venture more,
But little Boats should keep near Shore.[4]

'Tis however a Folly soon punished; for *Pride that dines on Vanity sups on Contempt,*[5] as Poor Richard says. And in another Place, *Pride breakfasted with Plenty, dined with Poverty, and supped with Infamy.*[6] And after all, of what Use is this *Pride of Appearance,* for which so much is risked, so much is suffered? It cannot promote Health, or ease Pain; it makes no Increase of Merit in the Person, it creates Envy, it hastens Misfortune.

What is a Butterfly? At best
He's but a Caterpillar drest.
The gaudy Fop's his Picture just,[7]

as Poor Richard says.

But what Madness must it be to *run in Debt* for these Superfluities! We are offered, by the Terms of this Vendue, *Six Months Credit;* and that perhaps has induced some of us to attend it, because we cannot spare the ready Money, and hope now to be fine without it. But, ah, think what you do when you run in Debt; *You give to*

19. April 1754.
20. July 1743, in German version.
1. May 1751, but "an empty Curse" in first line.
2. March 1750.
3. June 1751.
4. Oct. 1751; the first two words are changed in *Gent. Mag.* and "The Way to Wealth" to "Vessels large."
5. July 1752.
6. June 1757.
7. Feb. 1740.

another Power over your Liberty.[8] If you cannot pay at the Time, you will be ashamed to see your Creditor; you will be in Fear when you speak to him; you will make poor pitiful sneaking Excuses, and by Degrees come to lose your Veracity, and sink into base downright lying; for, as Poor Richard says, *The second Vice is Lying, the first is running in Debt.*[9] And again, to the same Purpose, *Lying rides upon Debt's Back.*[10] Whereas a freeborn Englishman ought not to be ashamed or afraid to see or speak to any Man living. But Poverty often deprives a Man of all Spirit and Virtue: *'Tis hard for an empty Bag to stand upright,*[11] as Poor Richard truly says. What would you think of that Prince, or that Government, who should issue an Edict forbidding you to dress like a Gentleman or a Gentlewoman, on Pain of Imprisonment or Servitude? Would you not say, that you are free, have a Right to dress as you please, and that such an Edict would be a Breach of your Privileges, and such a Government tyrannical? And yet you are about to put yourself under that Tyranny when you run in Debt for such Dress! Your Creditor has Authority at his Pleasure to deprive you of your Liberty, by confining you in Goal for Life, or to sell you for a Servant, if you should not be able to pay him! When you have got your Bargain, you may, perhaps, think little of Payment; but *Creditors,* Poor Richard tells us, *have better Memories than Debtors;*[12] and in another Place says, *Creditors are a superstitious Sect, great Observers of set Days and Times.*[13] The Day comes round before you are aware, and the Demand is made before you are prepared to satisfy it. Or if you bear your Debt in Mind, the Term which at first seemed so long, will, as it lessens, appear extreamly short. *Time* will seem to have added Wings to his Heels as well as Shoulders. *Those have a short Lent,* saith Poor Richard, *who owe Money to be paid at Easter.*[14] Then since, as he says, *The*

8. Not in any earlier *Poor Richard.*

9. Aug. 1748.

10. July 1741.

11. Jan. 1740: "An empty Bag cannot stand upright"; May 1750: "Tis hard (but glorious) to be poor and honest; An empty Sack can hardly stand upright; but if it does, 'tis a stout one!"

12. Sept. 1736.

13. Dec. 1737.

14. March 1738: "He that would have a short Lent, let him borrow Money to be repaid at Easter."

Borrower is a Slave to the Lender, and the Debtor to the Creditor,[15] disdain the Chain, preserve your Freedom; and maintain your Independency: Be *industrious* and *free;* be *frugal* and *free.* At present, perhaps, you may think yourself in thriving Circumstances, and that you can bear a little Extravagance without Injury; but,

For Age and Want, save while you may;
No Morning Sun lasts a whole Day,[16]

as Poor Richard says. Gain may be temporary and uncertain, but ever while you live, Expence is constant and certain; and *'tis easier to build two Chimnies than to keep one in Fuel,*[17] as Poor Richard says. So *rather go to Bed supperless than rise in Debt.*[18]

Get what you can, and what you get hold;
'Tis the Stone that will turn all your Lead into Gold,[19]

as Poor Richard says. And when you have got the Philosopher's Stone, sure you will no longer complain of bad Times, or the Difficulty of paying Taxes.

This Doctrine, my Friends, is *Reason* and *Wisdom;* but after all, do not depend too much upon your own *Industry,* and *Frugality,* and *Prudence,* though excellent Things, for they may all be blasted without the Blessing of Heaven; and therefore ask that Blessing humbly, and be not uncharitable to those that at present seem to want it, but comfort and help them. Remember Job suffered, and was afterwards prosperous.

And now to conclude, *Experience keeps a dear School, but Fools will learn in no other, and scarce in that;*[20] for it is true, *we may give Advice, but we cannot give Conduct,*[1] as Poor Richard says: However, remember this, *They that won't be counselled, can't be helped,*[2] as Poor Richard says: And farther, That *if you will not hear Reason, she'll surely rap your Knuckles.*[3]

15. Oct. 1757, but "the *Security* to *both,*" instead of "and the Debtor to the Creditor."

16. Nov. 1754.

17. Feb. 1757, but "maintain" instead of "keep."

18. May 1739: ". . . than run in debt for a Breakfast"; see also Dec. 1757: "Sleep without Supping, and you'll rise without owing for it."

19. Nov. 1756.

20. Dec. 1743, but omitting "and scarce in that."

1. Feb. 1751.

2. Aug. 1747.

3. June 1744: "Hear *Reason,* or she'll make you feel her"; March 1753: "When Reason preaches, if you won't hear her she'll box your Ears."

Thus the old Gentleman ended his Harangue. The People heard it, and approved the Doctrine, and immediately practised the contrary, just as if it had been a common Sermon; for the Vendue opened, and they began to buy extravagantly, notwithstanding all his Cautions, and their own Fear of Taxes. I found the good Man had thoroughly studied my Almanacks, and digested all I had dropt on those Topicks during the Course of Five-and-twenty Years. The frequent Mention he made of me must have tired any one else, but my Vanity was wonderfully delighted with it, though I was conscious that not a tenth Part of the Wisdom was my own which he ascribed to me, but rather the *Gleanings* I had made of the Sense of all Ages and Nations. However, I resolved to be the better for the Echo of it; and though I had at first determined to buy Stuff for a new Coat, I went away resolved to wear my old One a little longer. *Reader,* if thou wilt do the same, thy Profit will be as great as mine. I am, as ever, Thine to serve thee, RICHARD SAUNDERS.

July 7, 1757.

A good Receipt for the Fever and Ague.[4]

Take two Ounces of Jesuits Bark, one Ounce of Snakeroot, one Ounce of Salt of Tartar, and Half an Ounce of Camomile Flowers; put them into a Half Gallon Bottle, filled with Jamaica Spirit, and set it into a Kettle of Water, over a moderate Fire, and let the Ingredients infuse three Days, the Water being kept rather warmer than Blood warm. Dose for a grown Person Half a Jill, three or four times between the Fits; for a Child of a Year old a Tea Spoonful, mixed with Balm Tea; the Quantity to be increased according to the Age of the Person. The Ingredients, by adding more Spirit to them, make a good preventing Bitter.

JANUARY. *I Month.*

On AMBITION.[5]

I know, young Friend, *Ambition* fills your Mind,
And in Life's Voyage is th'impelling Wind;

4. David Hall printed this recipe in *Pa. Gaz.*, Sept. 8, 1757, and used it again here as a filler in the almanac.

5. Not identified.

But at the Helm let sober Reason stand,
And steer the Bark with Heav'n-directed Hand:
So shall you safe *Ambition's* Gales receive,
And ride securely, tho' the Billows heave;
So shall you shun the giddy Hero's Fate,
And by her Influence be both good and great.

One Nestor is worth two Ajaxes.

When you're an Anvil, hold you still;
When you're a Hammer, strike your Fill.

FEBRUARY. *II Month.*

She bids you first, in Life's soft vernal Hours,
With active Industry wake Nature's Powers;
With rising Years, still rising Arts display,
With new-born Graces mark each new-born Day.
'Tis now the Time young Passion to command,
While yet the pliant Stem obeys the Hand;
Guide now the Courser with a steady Rein,
E'er yet he bounds o'er Pleasure's flow'ry Plain;
In Passion's Strife, no Medium you can have;
You rule a Master, or submit a Slave.

When Knaves betray each other, one can scarce be blamed, or the other pitied.

He that carries a small Crime easily, will carry it on when it comes to be an Ox.

MARCH. *III Month.*

"For whom these Toils, you may perhaps enquire";
First for *yourself.* Next Nature will inspire,
The filial Thought, fond Wish, and Kindred Tear,
Which make the Parent and the Sister dear:
To these, in closest Bands of Love, ally'd,
Their Joy or Grief you live, their Shame or Pride;
Hence timely learn to make their Bliss your own,
And scorn to think or act for Self *alone;*

Happy Tom Crump, ne'er sees his own Hump.

Fools need Advice most, but wise Men only are the better for it.

APRIL. *IV Month.*

Hence bravely strive upon your own to raise
Their Honour, Grandeur, Dignity and Praise.
  But wider far, beyond the narrow Bound
Of Family, *Ambition* searches round;
Searches to find the Friend's delightful Face,
The Friend at least demands the second Place.
And yet beware; for most desire a Friend
From meaner Motives, not for Virtue's End.
There are, who with fond Favour's fickle Gale
Now sudden swell, and now contract their Sail;

Silence in not always a Sign of Wisdom, but Babbling is ever a Mark of Folly.

Great Modesty often hides great Merit.

You may delay, but *Time* will not.

MAY. *V Month.*

This Week devour, the next with sickening Eye
Avoid, and cast the sully'd Play-thing by;
There are, who tossing in the Bed of Vice,
For Flattery's Opiate give the highest Price;
Yet from the saving Hand of Friendship turn,
Her Med'cines dread, her generous Offers spurn.
Deserted Greatness! who but pities thee?
By Crowds encompass'd, thou no Friend canst see:

Virtue may not always make a Face handsome, but *Vice* will certainly make it ugly.

Prodigality of *Time* produces Poverty of Mind as well as of Estate.

JUNE. *VI Month.*

Or should kind Truth invade thy tender Ear,
We pity still; for thou no Truth can'st hear.
Ne'er grudg'd thy Wealth to swell an useless State,
Yet, frugal, deems th'Expence of Friends too great;
For Friends ne'er mixing in ambitious Strife,
For Friends, the richest Furniture of Life!
  Be yours, my Son, a nobler, higher Aim,
Your Pride to burn with Friendship's sacred Flame;

Content is the Philosopher's Stone, that turns all it touches into Gold.

He that's content, hath enough; He that complains, has too much.

Pride gets into the Coach, and *Shame* mounts behind.

JULY. *VII Month.*

By Virtue kindled, by like Manners fed,
By mutual Wishes, mutual Favours spread,
Increas'd with Years, by candid Truth refin'd,
Pour all its boundless Ardours thro' your Mind.
Be yours the Care a chosen Band to gain;
With them to Glory's radiant Summit strain,
Aiding and aided each, while all contend,
Who best, who bravest, shall assist his Friend.

The first Mistake in publick Business, is the going into it.

Half the Truth is often a great Lie.

The Way to see by *Faith,* is to shut the Eye of *Reason:* The Morning Daylight appears plainer when you put out your Candle.

AUGUST. *VIII Month.*

Thus still should private Friendships spread around,
Till in their joint Embrace the Publick's found,
The common Friend! Then all her Good explore;
Explor'd, pursue with each unbiass'd Power.

But chief the greatest should her Laws revere,
Ennobling Honours, which she bids them wear.
Ambition fills with Charity the Mind,
And pants to be the Friend of all Mankind.

A full Belly makes a dull Brain: The Muses starve in a Cook's Shop.

Spare and have is better than *spend and crave.*

Good-Will, like the Wind, floweth where it listeth.

SEPTEMBER. *IX Month.*

Her Country all beneath one ambient Sky:
Whoe'er beholds yon radiant Orbs on high,
To whom one Sun impartial gives the Day,
To whom the Silver Moon her milder Ray,
Whom the same Water, Earth, and Air sustain,
O'er whom one Parent-King extends his Reign
Are her Compatriots all, by her belov'd,
In Nature near, tho' far by Space remov'd;
On common Earth, no Foreigner she knows;
No Foe can find, or none but Virtue's Foes;

The Honey is sweet, but the Bee has a Sting.

In a corrupt Age, the putting the World in order would breed Confusion; then e'en mind your own Business.

OCTOBER. *X Month.*

Ready she stands her chearful Aid to lend;
To Want and Woe an undemanded Friend.
Nor thus advances others Bliss alone;
But in the Way to theirs, still finds her own.
Their's is her own. What, should your Taper light
Ten Thousand, burns it to yourself less bright?
"Men are ungrateful." Be they so that dare!
Is that the Giver's, or Receiver's Care?

To serve the Publick faithfully, and at the same time please it entirely, is impracticable.

Proud Modern Learning despises the antient: *Schoolmen* are now laught at by *Schoolboys*.

NOVEMBER. *XI Month.*

Oh! blind to Joys, that from true Bounty flow,
To think those e'er repent whose *Hearts* bestow!
Man to his Maker thus best Homage pays,
Thus peaceful walks thro' Virtue's pleasing Ways:
Her gentle Image on the Soul imprest,
Bids each tempestuous Passion leave the Breast:
Thence with her livid Self-devouring Snakes
Pale Envy flies; her Quiver Slander breaks:
Thus falls (dire Scourge of a distracted Age!)
The Knave-led, one-ey'd Monster, Party Rage.

Men often *mistake* themselves, seldom *forget* themselves.

The idle Man is the Devil's Hireling; whose Livery is Rags, whose Diet and Wages are Famine and Diseases.

DECEMBER. *XII Month.*

Ambition jostles with her Friends no more;
Nor thirsts Revenge to drink a Brother's Gore;
Fiery Remorse no stinging Scorpions rears:
O'er trembling Guilt no falling Sword appears.
Hence Conscience, void of Blame, her Front erects,
Her God she fears, all other Fear rejects.
Hence just Ambition boundless Splendors crown,
And hence she calls Eternity her own.

Rob not God, nor the Poor, lest thou ruin thyself; the Eagle snatcht a Coal from the Altar, but it fired her Nest.

With bounteous Cheer,
Conclude the Year. *Vale*

To John Waring[6]

ALS: American Philosophical Society

Revd. Sir, Cravenstreet, Jan. 3. 58.

I send you herewith the Extract of Mr. Sturgeon's Letter,[7] which I mentioned to you. He is, among us, esteemed a good Man, one that makes a Conscience of the Duties of his Office, in which he is very diligent; and has behaved with so much Discretion, as to gain the general Respect and Good-will of the People. If the Associates of Dr. Bray should think fit to make Tryal of a School for Negro Children in Philadelphia, I know no Person under whose Care it would be more likely to succeed. At present few or none give their Negro Children any Schooling, partly from a Prejudice that Reading and Knowledge in a Slave are both useless and dangerous; and partly from an Unwillingness in the Masters and Mistresses of common Schools to take black Scholars, lest the Parents of the white Children should be disgusted and take them away, not chusing to have their Children mix'd with Slaves in Education, Play, &c. But a separate School for Blacks, under the Care of One, of whom People should have an Opinion that he would be careful to imbue the Minds of their young Slaves with good Principles, might probably have a Number of Blacks sent to it; and if on Experience it should be found useful, and not attended with the ill Consequences commonly apprehended, the Example might be followed in the other Colonies, and encouraged by the Inhabitants in general.[8] I am, Sir, Your most humble Servant

B Franklin

Mr. Waring

Endorsed: Mr. Franklin Feb: 17: 1758

6. See above, pp. 98–101, for Waring's earlier inquiries on behalf of Bray's Associates.

7. See above, p. 252.

8. Waring reported the substance of this letter at a meeting of Bray's Associates, April 5, 1758, whereupon it was resolved that a school for Negro children be opened in Philadelphia under Sturgeon's care. Minutes of The Associates of the late Rev. Dr. Bray (S.P.C.K. House, London), p. 113. See below, p. 377, for BF's next letter about the school.

To John Pringle

MS not found; reprinted from Benjamin Franklin, *Experiments and Observations on Electricity* (London, 1769), p. 362.

Sir, Craven-street, Jan. 6, 1758.

I return Mr. Mitchell's paper on the strata of the earth[9] with thanks. The reading of it, and perusal of the draft that accompanies it, have reconciled me to those convulsions which all naturalists agree this globe has suffered. Had the different strata of clay, gravel, marble, coals, lime-stone, sand, minerals, &c. continued to lie level, one under the other, as they may be supposed to have done before those convulsions, we should have had the use only of a few of the uppermost of the strata, the others lying too deep and too difficult to be come at; but the shell of the earth being broke, and the fragments thrown into this oblique position, the disjointed ends of a great number of strata of different kinds are brought up to day, and a great variety of useful materials put into our power, which would otherwise have remained eternally concealed from us. So that what has been usually looked upon as a *ruin* suffered by this part of the universe, was, in reality, only a preparation, or means of rendering the earth more fit for use, more capable of being to mankind a convenient and comfortable habitation. I am, Sir, with great esteem, yours, &c. B.F.

From David Hall Letterbook copy: American Philosophical Society

Sir Philadelphia, 6th Jany. 1758

My last to you was by the Mercury, Capt. Robinson,[1] in which I promised to remit you by the next Vessel; and accordingly, you

9. John Michell (1724–1793), astronomer and geologist, held various appointments at Cambridge, 1749–67, and served as rector at Thornhill, Yorkshire, for the last 26 years of his life. *DNB*. The paper here mentioned was probably "Conjectures concerning the Cause, and Observations upon the Phaenomena of Earthquakes; particularly of that great Earthquake of the First of November, 1755, which proved so fatal to the City of Lisbon . . .," read before the Royal Society, Feb. 28, March 6, 13, 20, and 27, 1760. *Phil. Trans.*, LI, Pt. II (1760), 566–634. John Michell is not to be confused with the Virginian Dr. John Mitchell (above, II, 415 n).

1. The ship *Mercury*, Capt. Thomas Robinson, cleared Philadelphia for

have inclosed the first Copy of a Bill of Exchange for One Hundred pounds Sterling, (the second Copy of which I have sent by Capt. Troy Via Dublin) the Exchange as you will see by the Bill 64,[2] The Receipt of which you will please to advise me of. This Makes Six Hundred Pounds Sterling, I have remitted you since you left Philadelphia, and I shall continue remitting, as I get the Cash, till near the Time of your leaving England. I am &c.

D HALL

To Benjamin Franklin Esqr. per the Speedwell Capt. Robinson

Copy per via Dublin Capt Troy

To John Bartram

Extract:[3] The Royal Society

London, Jan. 11. 1758.

I thank you for your Account of the Aurora.[4] A very considerable one appear'd here the same Evening, being Saturday, Nov. 12. I did not see it, but have heard of it from several. If it was the same that you saw; it must have been very high, or very extensive, as the two Places are 1000 Leagues asunder.

To John Nourse[5]

Reprinted from Stan V. Henkels, Catalogue No. 965 (June 7–8, 1907), p. 15.[6]

Sir Craven Street, Jan. 13, 1758

Please to send by the Bearer, Pere Charlevoix's History of the French Settlement in America.[7] Yours &c. B FRANKLIN

London before Jan. 12, 1758; it was taken by the French, but then retaken. The snow *Hibernia,* Capt. John Troy, cleared for Dublin, before January 5. *Pa. Gaz.,* Jan. 5 and 12, 1758; *Pa. Jour.,* May 4, 1758. The record of Hall's remittances shows that the copies of the bill here mentioned were dated January 6. See above, p. 236.

2. See above, p. 270 n, for exchange rates between Pa. currency and sterling.

3. In BF's hand. Read before the Royal Society, Feb. 25, 1762, and printed in *Phil. Trans.,* LII (1762), 474.

4. See above, p. 271.

5. John Nourse (d. 1780), dealer in French and scientific books, and "for

To Deborah Franklin

MS not found; reprinted from Duane, *Works*, VI, 28–9.

Dear Debby, London, January 14, 1758.

I wrote a very long letter to you lately, two whole sheets full, containing answers to all yours received during my sickness.[8] I have since received your kind favours of November 13 and November 16th. It has given me great concern that you should be so disappointed in having no letters by captain Luthwycke; you know by this time how it happened;[9] but I wonder you should expect letters from me, by the way of Ireland; it being quite out of my knowledge, when vessels are to sail from thence.

I am thankful to God for sparing my little family in that time of general sickness, and hope to find them all well, at my return. The New York paper you sent me was the latest that came, and of use to our friend, Strahan.[1] He has offered to lay me a considerable wager, that a letter he has wrote to you will bring you immediately over hither;[2] but I tell him I will not pick his pocket; for I am sure there is no inducement strong enough to prevail with

---

many years bookseller to his Majesty." H. R. Plomer, G. H. Bushnell, E. R. McDix, *A Dictionary of Printers and Booksellers Who Were at Work in England, Scotland and Ireland from 1726 to 1775* (Oxford, 1932), p. 183; *Gent. Mag.*, L (1780), 203.

6. The ALS was again offered for sale in *The Month at Goodspeed's*, XXXIV, No. 3 (Dec. 1962), 66, with a facsimile reproduction (p. 68) confirming the text as quoted in the Henkels catalogue. Another letter from BF to Nourse, March 18, 1758, not found, was offered for sale by Maggs Bros., Catalogue No. 220 (June 1906), p. 60.

7. On June 28, 1758, BF paid Nourse £4 18*s*. "for books," perhaps including Père Pierre François Xavier de Charlevoix's *Histoire et description générale de la Nouvelle France . . .* (3 vols., Paris, 1744), also published in a six-volume edition, but not translated into English until 1761. "Account of Expences," p. 33; *PMHB*, LV (1931), 112.

8. Probably that of Nov. 22–Dec. 3, 1757; see above, pp. 272–9.

9. Capt. Walter Lutwidge of the packet *General Wall*, on which BF had sailed to England, left Falmouth on Sept. 2, 1757, and reached New York on October 15. *N.-Y. Mercury*, Oct. 17, 1757. See above, pp. 243, 245, for BF's first letters to his wife after reaching England.

1. William Strahan's paper, *The London Chronicle*, Jan. 10, 1758, published nearly two columns of news from America, much the same as had appeared in the *N.-Y. Mercury* on Nov. 14, 1757.

2. See above, pp. 295–8.

you to cross the seas. I would be glad if I could tell you when I expected to be at home, but that is still in the dark; it is possible I may not be able to get away this summer; but I hope, if I stay another winter, it will be more agreeable than the greatest part of the time I have hitherto spent in England. But however I must bring my business to some conclusion.

I received Sally's letter of November 12th,[3] but cannot now write to her. I wrote to my friends generally by last packet,[4] and shall write to them again by a ship of Mr. Ralph's,[5] to sail from here in about a fortnight. I am not yet quite so hearty as before my illness; but I think I am daily stronger and better, so I hope I have had my seasoning; but much writing still disorders me.

My duty to mother, and love to Sally, Debby, Mr. Dunlap,[6] and all friends that inquire after me. I am, my dear child, Your ever loving husband, B. FRANKLIN.

Billy presents his duty to you and mother, and love to his sister.

To [Isaac Norris][7]

Extract:[8] Historical Society of Pennsylvania

Dated Janry: 14. 1758.

Extract from Mr. Franklin's Letter.

Benjamin Franklin[9] insisted in a Conference with the Proprietaries,[1] that if, when Commissioners were named in a Bill,[2] the

3. Not found.

4. The packet *Halifax* left Falmouth about Dec. 12, 1757, and arrived in New York on Jan. 19, 1758. *N.-Y. Mercury*, Jan. 23, 1758. Of such letters only an abstract of one to William Coleman, December 8, and one to David Hall, December 9, have been found.

5. Or Relfe; see above, p. 276 n. The ship in question may have been part of the large convoy which gathered in the Downs in late January and sailed for America on Feb. 25, 1758. *London Chron.*, Jan. 31 and Feb. 28, 1758.

6. I.e., DF's mother Sarah Read, Sally Franklin, DF's niece Deborah Croker Dunlap, and William Dunlap, now Philadelphia postmaster.

7. Later references by BF and others make it clear that Norris received this letter, even though his name does not appear on the copied extract. It may, however, have been addressed to the Pa. Assembly Committee of Correspondence of which Thomas Leech, Joseph Galloway, Joseph Fox, John Hughes, William Masters, and Thomas Yorke, as well as Norris, were members. Leech had replaced Norris as speaker on Jan. 2, 1758.

8. No full text has been found; this copy in an unknown hand probably

Governor might not strike out or change them at his Pleasure, as none but his own Creatures might be admitted, and the Assembly might as well trust him with the whole, and that it was an undoubted Right of the House of Commons to name Commissioners in Bills in all Cases where they thought it necessary and proper, and to have such Commissioners so named stand without Alteration and Amendment and therefore our Assembly claimed the said Privileges; To which He[3] answered that in such Cases, that before the House of Commons inserted the Names of Commissioners in Bills, the List was privately settled with the Ministry by the Committees; but tho' it might be a Privilege of the House of Commons, it did not follow that it was the Privilege of a Pennsylvania Assembly. That We were only a kind of Corporation acting by a Charter from the Crown and could have no Privileges or Rights but what was granted by that Charter, in which no such Privilege as We now claim was any where mentioned. *But says I*[4] Your Father's Charter expressly says that the Assembly of Pennsylvania shall have all the Power and Privileges of an Assembly according

---

was made without Norris' permission, when the original was laid before the Assembly committee sometime before March 18, 1758. A proprietary assemblyman, possibly William Allen or William Plumsted, may have copied it for partisan reasons, after which Richard Peters sent a copy to Thomas Penn that he received before July 5, 1758. Thomas Balch printed the extract, perhaps from the copy used here, in *Letters and Papers Relating Chiefly to the Provincial History of Pennsylvania* (Phila., 1855), pp. 110–11. William Allen to F. J. Paris, March 18, 1758; Penn to Peters, July 5, 1758; Penn Papers, Hist. Soc. Pa.

9. In paraphrasing the opening lines of this letter, the copyist failed to make the meaning entirely clear. BF apparently insisted that when commissioners were named in the bill the governor ought not to have the power to strike or name them at his pleasure; otherwise only his creatures would be admitted.

1. Held one or two days before BF wrote this letter; see the final note to this document.

2. Specifically the Indian trade bill which, since November 1755, had been passed repeatedly by the Assembly and as often rejected by the governor. See above, VI, 451.

3. Thomas Penn; apparently from this point BF's letter was copied verbatim.

4. BF. These words and the next group in italics are also italicized in Balch, *Letters and Papers*, pp. 110–11, but there are no other italics in that version. BF's usage in the original is not known.

to the Rights of the Freeborn Subjects of England, and as is usual in any of the British Plantations in America.[5] *Yes says he* but, if my Father granted Privileges he was not by the Royal Charter impowered to grant, Nothing can be claim'd by such Grant. *I said,* If then your Father had no Right to grant the Privileges He pretended to grant, and published all over Europe as granted those who came to settle in the Province upon the Faith of that Grant and in Expectation of enjoying the Privileges contained in it, were deceived, cheated and betrayed. *He answered* they should have themselves looked to that. That the Royal Charter was no Secret; they who came into the Province on my Father's Offer of Privileges, if, they were deceiv'd, it was their own Fault; and that He said with a Kind of triumphing laughing Insolence, such as a low Jockey might do when a Purchaser complained that He had cheated him in a Horse. I was astonished to see him thus meanly give up his Father's Character and conceived that Moment a more cordial and thorough Contempt for him than I ever before felt for any Man living—A Contempt that I cannot express in Words, but I believe my Countenance expressed it strongly. And that his Brother was looking at me, must have observed it; however finding myself grow warm I made no other Answer to this than that the poor People were no Lawyers themselves and confiding in his Father did not think it necessary to consult any.[6]

5. A direct quotation from William Penn's Charter of Privileges, 1701, section II.

6. This conference and BF's letter about it significantly affected his relations with the Proprietors. For that reason the following four letters are quoted (all from Penn Papers, Hist. Soc. Pa.):

Thomas Penn to William Allen, Jan. 12, 1758: "Mr. Franklin was with me this Day chiefly on a Bill for regulating the Indian Trade, in which the House will not allow the Governor to join in the nomination of the Persons appointed to reside among the Indians, which I think very necessary. Mr. Franklin told me the Bill was on the Plan of the Boston Act, but on examination I found the general Court made all the appointments, and superintended the whole Affair, which was the method I thought most proper, when I told him of the mistake he would have put it off, as mistaking the General Court for the House of Representatives." Actually the Massachusetts "Great and General Court" consisted of the two legislative houses, the Council and the House of Representatives, both elective, and was not a judicial body as Penn may have thought.

Thomas Penn to Richard Peters, Jan. 14, 1758: "We have received the

To Deborah Franklin

MS not found; reprinted from Duane, *Works*, VI, 29–30.

My Dear Child, London, January 21, 1758.

Mr. Lorimer,[7] a friend who is going over to General Abercromby, to assist him as a secretary, called on me just now, to

7. Not identified, but possibly a misprint for Joshua Loring (1716–1781), a native of Boston, Mass., who went from England to America at about this time to superintend naval construction on the lakes of the New York frontier. *DAB; Gertrude S. Kimball, ed., *Correspondence of William Pitt* (N.Y., 1906), I, 145, 153, 159. Gen. James Abercromby (above, VI, 459 n) had recently been appointed to succeed Lord Loudoun as commander in North America.

Indian Trade Bill, and yesterday had a Conference with Mr. Franklin upon it, on hearing a second of the same sort, except with regard to the Commissioners, had been presented he claimed an absolute Power in the House to name the Commissioners and that they ought not to be altered, this point I could not allow as we were to use our discretion in passing Laws, but left it however to be considered after we receive our Council's opinion on the Case. . . . I shall write you soon more at large about this Bill when we receive the opinions about our Right to alter Bills, that may be called Money Bills, and to alter Commissioners names in Bills—if the two Commissioners were not really improper People that might have been dispensed with. Mr. Franklin at this time suggested the impropriety of Persons concerned in the Indian Trade being in Office, which made it necessary for them to negotiate Publick Business with those People and mentioned you as such. I joined with him in opinion of the impropriety of it, but told him I was very fully assured you had no such concerns."

William Allen to Ferdinand J. Paris, March 18, 1758, apparently after reading a copy of BF's letter: "[Franklin] is a very artful, insinuating fellow, and very ready, at expedients; I wish he may not, by the concil of Dr. Fothergil, or otherwise - - - - - - - be able to infuse wrong notions, of things, into Mr. Penn's breast, and deceive him, by false accounts. I am informed, notwithstanding his smooth behaviour, that *he gives our people*, here, the most *disadvantageous impressions*, of Mr. Penn, who, he says, is *determined to deprive them* of *all* the priviledges they derive, from his father; upon the whole, suggests every thing, that a very bad heart is capable of doing, in order to inflame them, still more, again[st] the proprietary family."

Thomas Penn to Richard Peters, July 5, 1758, after reading a copy of BF's letter: "The Extract of Mr. Franklin's Letter to Mr. Norris is a most impudent Paper, and vile misrepresentation of what passed. In it [the conference] I represented to him that it was as unsafe for the People, as it was for us, to claim Priviledges by my Father's Charter, that could not be warranted by the King's Charter to him, and did not exult at all on the occasion, but spoke it out of concern for the Safety of the People, and not in any manner as my

acquaint me that he is on the point of setting out. I seize a minute or two just to let you know we are well, that is, I am well, compared to what I have been during a great part of the time since my arrival, and I hope with the spring to recover my full strength. Billy is quite hearty and presents his duty, love, &c.

I have wrote to you by several opportunities, lately, and particularly one long letter of two sheets, which I hope will come to hand, as it contained, a full answer to a number of yours, received during my illness, and I have no copy of it.[8]

I begin to think I shall hardly be able to return before this time twelve months. I am for doing effectually what I came about; and I find it requires both time and patience. You may think perhaps, that I can find many amusements here to pass the time agreeable. 'Tis true, the regard and friendship I meet with from persons of worth, and the conversation of ingenious men, give me no small pleasure;[9] but at this time of life, domestic comforts afford the

8. See above, pp. 272, 359, for the only surviving letters from BF to his wife since his illness.

9. Rumors circulating in America at this time exaggerated BF's influence in England. Jane Mecom wrote DF, Jan. 29, 1758, excusing herself for not knowing how to address "Governers and Baronets Ladys," and Benjamin Mecom wrote DF a day later of "A Report in Town of Uncle Franklin's further Promotion." APS.

Brother tells me that could give any cause of offence, and how Mr. Franklin looked I cannot tell, my Brother says like a malicious V. as he always does, however from this time I will not have any conversation with him on any pretence. I have shewn it to my Lord Hallifax and some other People, to shew how well disposed this Man is to settle differences—I think what he pretends to have said has no meaning, the present Charter was not a means of settling the Province which was settled before, and I believe the Dutch, were invited to go over from the general good account of the Country, and never read over the Charter or thought of it."

Isaac Norris acknowledged BF's letter, April 29, 1758, and noted the "Effrontery" of the Proprietors and their agents. After BF learned that Peters had sent a copy to Penn he wrote Joseph Galloway, Sept. 16, 1758, and April 7, 1759, and Isaac Norris, March 19, 1759, expostulating vigorously against allowing his confidential letters to get into the hands of the proprietary supporters in the colony. He acknowledged that he might have refrained from comparing Thomas Penn to "a low Jockey," but did not "much repent of it." On July 31, 1759, Norris denied that he had been in any way personally responsible for the leak. These letters from and to BF will be printed in full at the appropriate places in this edition.

most solid satisfaction, and my uneasiness at being absent from my family, and longing desire to be with them, make me often sigh in the midst of cheerful company.

My love to my dear Sally. I confide in you the care of her and her education; I promise myself the pleasure of finding her much improved at my return.

While I am writing, three letters came in, one from Mr. Hall, one from Rhoads, another from Dr. Bond,[1] but none from you: they are by way of Bristol. I must send this away immediately, lest Mr. Lorimer should be gone. My respects to those gentlemen, to whom I shall write, and to my other friends by Mr. Ralph's vessel,[2] which sails next week. I am, Your ever loving husband,

B. FRANKLIN.

PS. When you write to Boston, give my love to sister Jenney—as I have not often time to write to her. If you please you may send her the inclosed little picture.[3] B.F.

From Robert Charles: Receipt

ADS: Historical Society of Pennsylvania

London 26th January 1758

Received from Benjamin Franklin Esqr. Twenty Six Guineas, on Account of the Province of Pensylvania for which Sum I hereby promise to be accountable.[4] R CHARLES

£27 6s. 0d.

Endorsed: No. 56 Jany. 26—1758 Robt. Charles £27 6. 0[5]

1. The letter from David Hall may have been that of Nov. 20, 1757 (above, p. 272); none from Samuel Rhoads (above, II, 406 n), or Drs. Thomas or Phineas Bond (above, II, 240 n), at this time have been found.

2. John Relfe; see above, p. 276 n.

3. Reproduced as the frontispiece of this volume. See the note in the List of Illustrations (above, p. xv) for information about it.

4. BF recorded this payment in his accounts, but Charles did not mention it in the accounting for his agency submitted on Aug. 10, 1762; he was paid for copying documents, buying the journals of the House of Commons, and other routine expenses during 1758. "Account of Expences," p. 12; *PMHB*, LV (1931), 108; Mabel P. Wolff, *The Colonial Agency of Pennsylvania, 1712–1757* (Phila., 1933), p. 209.

5. The document also bears the initials "I.N." probably indicating that at some time Isaac Norris approved the payment.

From Thomas and Richard Penn

Letterbook copy: Historical Society of Pennsylvania

Sir London January 28th: 1758.

We have considered the proposal you yesterday made to us, that as Supplys will very soon be wanted for the defence of the Province, and other Publick Services, for the Current year, and as the points in difference between us, and the Representatives of the Province of Pennsylvania, now under the consideration of His Majesty's Attorney, and Sollicitor General,[6] cannot be settled in time for Acts to be passed for this purpose, we would consent, for the present, that, the Lieutenant Governor may give his assent to an Act for raising such a Sum of Money as shall be thought proper, for the Service of the present year, of the same Tenor, and with the same exception, with the Act intituled, a Supplement to the Act intituled an Act for granting the Sum of Sixty thousand Pounds to the King's use, and for striking fifty five thousand Pounds thereof in Bills of Credit, and to provide a fund for sinking the same, and for granting to His Majesty the additional Sum of One hundred thousand Pounds.[7]

We being desirous on our parts to remove every obstacle that may impede the general Service, or prevent such measures being taken as shall be thought necessary for the Security of the Province, tho' we have many objections to the said Act, shall, in consideration of the present necessity, signify our consent to the Governor that he may give his assent to such a Law.[8] We are Your very affectionate Friends

T:P:
R:P:

Benjamin Franklin Esqr.

6. See above, pp. 248–52, for the "points in difference." Solicitor General Charles Yorke had given his opinion on them, favorable to the Proprietors, on Jan. 13, 1758 (MS copy in Penn Papers, Hist. Soc. Pa.), but Attorney General Charles Pratt's delay prevented the Penns from responding to the "points in difference" until Nov. 27–28, 1758; see *Pa. Col. Recs.*, VIII, 276–81, and the next volume of this edition.

7. See above, pp. 152–3 n, for the passage of this act.

8. See below, pp. 370, 372, for the renewal of the dispute between BF and the Proprietors over the supply bill.

To Deborah Franklin

ALS (fragments):[9] American Philosophical Society

[*First half page missing*] [January? 1758][1]

good Order. I receiv'd also his Letter relating to the Aurora Borealis,[2] it was seen here at the same time, and I shall endeavour to procure him a particular Account of it.

It was an unlucky Mistake, that of putting your Letter under Cover to Mr. Colden, as it occasion'd a Week's Delay in your receiving it. I do not find you have receiv'd a Letter I wrote you the Day after I arriv'd in London, which Mr. Collinson at whose House I wrote it, put on board a New York Vessel for me. Your Letter per Lyon never came to hand.[3]

I have long since wrote to Mr. Hall[4] that I had receiv'd his Bills, in all, since I left Philadelphia five Hundred Pounds sterling. So I hope his Anger is over. I know not whether I can write to him per this Oppor[tunity].

[*One half page missing*]

sending it. I am glad he escap'd with his Life from those Cannibals. My Love to him and Patty and their Children; and to Cousins Dunlap.[5]

I find Marble Work in great Vogue here, and done in great Perfection at present. I think it would much improve Cousin Josey,[6] if he was to come over and work in some of the best Shops for a Year or two. If he can be spar'd without Prejudice to Cousin Wilkinson,[7] to whom my Love, send him to me by the first Ships,

9. This letter appears to have been written on all four pages of a folio sheet, only the bottom halves of which have been found. Missing portions have been indicated.

1. Though the dateline is missing, the contents require the placing of this letter between BF's letters to DF of Jan. 21 and Feb. 19, 1758.

2. From John Bartram; see above, p. 271.

3. For BF's letter of July 27 to DF, see above, p. 245, and for the loss of Captain Lyon's ship carrying her letter to him, see above, p. 238 n.

4. See above, p. 287.

5. The lucky refugee from "Cannibals" (Indians?) was probably DF's brother John Read; see above, VI, 221 n. His wife's name was Martha (Patty). See above, V, 199 n, for William Dunlap.

6. Joseph Croker; see above, p. 218 n.

7. Not identified, but relatives of DF's mother of that name were woodworkers in Philadelphia; e.g., an Anthony Wilkinson carved figure-heads for

and I will get him into Employ here: As he seems an ingenious sober Lad, it must certainly be a great Advantage to him in his Business hereafter, when he returns to follow it in America.

I am sorry to hear of any Disturbance in the Academy, the rather as by my mistaken Zeal for its Welfare in introducing that imprudent Man,[8] I think myself in some Degree the Cause of those Misfortunes.

[*One half page missing*]

Stephens to Mr. Dicker, and he tells me he has order'd [some]thing for her, and endeavour'd to prevail with Mrs. Grant to send her something handsome, but doubts the Success. Mrs. Grant was here a few Days since on a Visit to my Landlady, but I was abroad and did not see her. I have not been at Bristol, so could not see Mrs. Estwick's Friends; but shall go thither in the Spring.[9]

I should have been proud of a Letter from Goodey Smith[1] tho' it was to be a Letter of Reproof.

As you desire to know several Particulars about me, I now let you know that I lodge in Craven Street near Charing Cross,

---

ships in 1729 and 1742. *PMHB,* LVI (1932), 162; LVIII (1934), 140, 144–5. Presumably young Croker, a promising craftsman, was apprentice or journeyman to an artisan relative.

8. William Smith; see above, IV, 467–9, 475, for BF's earlier and higher opinion of him. The "Disturbance" was probably the same incident referred to somewhat obliquely by Joseph Shippen on Jan. 12, 1758: "I am sorry for the unfortunate accident in the academy, between Mr. Smith and Mr. Allen's son. I hope the consequence of the quarrel will teach that gentleman to practice more philosophy in his discipline for the future." [Thomas Balch,] *Letters and Papers Relating Chiefly to the Provincial History of Pennsylvania* (Phila., 1855), p. 105. The furor created by Smith's imprisonment, Jan. 6, 1758, could not have been known to BF at this time.

9. The persons mentioned in this paragraph and their relationships are but vaguely known, but the central figure was probably Sir Alexander Grant (d. 1772), a London merchant who made a fortune in the West Indies, later acquired lands in Scotland, and served as M.P. for Inverness burghs, 1761–68. G. E. Cokayne, *Complete Baronage* (Exeter, 1904), IV, 358. BF frequently sent bills of exchange drawn on him by Mrs. Stevens (above, V and VI *passim*). Mr. Dicker was probably Samuel Dicker, a Jamaica merchant, perhaps also the same who was M.P. for Plymouth and died in 1760. *PMHB,* LVI (1932), 168; *Gent. Mag.,* XXX (1760), 46. Nothing is known of Mrs. Estwick nor of the connection between Mrs. Grant and BF's landlady, Mrs. Margaret Stevenson. BF does not appear to have visited Bristol until 1760.

1. DF's old friend Mary Smith.

Westminster; We have four Rooms furnished, and every thing about us pretty genteel, but Living here is in every respect very expensive.[2] Billy is with me, and very serviceable. Peter has behav'd very well. Goodeys I now and then get a few; but roasting Apples seldom, I wish you had sent me some; and I wonder how you, that us'd to think of every thing, came to forget it. Newton Pippins would have been the most acceptable

[*One half page missing*]

made them tight they hurt me, and if slack they slipt down, she knit and presented me with a Pair, of a Sort I never saw before, but find I can wear them very well, for their roughness makes them keep up without being drawn tight. Saying just now that I wish'd I had another Pair to send to you, that you might show them to Mrs. Smith and to Mrs. Holwell, my Madam fetch'd a new Pair her Daughter had knit for her, but coarser than mine, and desires you would do her the favour of accepting them. I shall send them per Budden, with some things I have bought for you; for I have receiv'd your £100 and am going about with Mrs. Stephenson to pick up something agreable to send you, intending to lay it all out.[3] I shall not go to Holland, as I intend to see great Part of England as soon as the Weather will permit Travelling. I wrote to you by a Man of War lately sailing for New York, and sent you my Picture in Miniature.[4] My Love to Dr. and Mrs. Redman, Mr. Hughes, Mr. and Mrs. Duffield,[5] and to all enquiring [Friends.[6] Mr. Hunter is returni]ng in April. Polley[7] is well, gives her Respects, and has [sent some things to Sally. My Respects to]

2. See above, pp. 245 n, 273 n, for the Franklin lodgings in London.

3. See below, pp. 381–3, for BF's shopping and the knitted garters. Mrs. Smith was probably "Goodey" Smith, previously mentioned. Mrs. Holwell has not been identified but presumably was a neighbor or friend of DF.

4. See above, pp. 363–5.

5. See above, V, 356 n, for Dr. John Redman; VI, 284–5 n, for John Hughes; and this volume, p. 211 n, for Edward Duffield.

6. Beginning with this word, BF finished his letter with four lines written vertically along the left-hand margin of the page, so the first half of each line is missing. Though too much has been lost to permit certain reconstruction of the text, the editors have supplied plausible words in brackets to complete the sense of what remains of BF's letter, though other conjectures might be equally valid.

7. See below, p. 381, for the plans of William Hunter and his sister Polly to return to America.

Miss Polley Morris,[8] and tell her I thank her for her Favour in the [last Packet. I have seen some of my] old Acquaintance here but not many; the Nun must be dead,[9] but [her garret remains as it was. Time will only] allow me to add that I am as ever my dear Child Your loving Husband B FRANKLIN

From Thomas and Richard Penn

Letterbook copy: Historical Society of Pennsylvania

Sir London February 2d: 1758.

Our Letter to you of the 28th. of January was a direct and explicit answer to your own proposal made to us the Day before.[1] Yesterday your Letter of the 31st: was left at Spring Garden, wherein you write that you had mentioned some other Matters to us; whatever might be said before the proposal last resolved upon was made, it is not in the least necessary to repeat, and we believe you could not yourself hope we should entertain a proposition of that sort, so as to comply with it.

We greatly dislike many parts of the Bill, which you proposed should be re-enacted, but yet rather than the Publick Interest and His Majesty's Service should suffer we consented to that Bill for the present year at your request, as much the lesser evil, and have given our Lieutenant Governor directions accordingly, as we acquainted you on the 28th. past.[2] We are Your affectionate Friends

T: P:

R: P:

Benjamin Franklin Esqr.

8. Perhaps Mary Morris (1738–1765), who married Joseph Potts in 1764; "Mary" was a common name in the numerous Morris family, however. Robert C. Moon, *The Morris Family of Philadelphia* (Phila., 1898), I, 427.

9. In his autobiography, BF remembered an old nun who had lived in the garret of his Duke Street lodgings, 1725–26. Par. Text edit., pp. 120–2.

1. See above, p. 366, for the letter of the 28th; BF's of the 31st mentioned below has not been found. See below, p. 372, for a final letter in this dispute.

2. On February 2 the Penns also wrote Richard Peters that they had consented to the passage of a new supply bill on the same terms as that of 1757. They then continued: "Mr. Franklin at first proposed to withdraw Instructions for the present, or at least to give a more general power to the Governor to agree with the House if they should desire to amend the Bill, in any particular, the first we could by no means agree to, and we did not think the

From David Hall

Letterbook copy: American Philosophical Society

Sir Philadelphia, 6th. February 1758

My two last to you by the Speedwell Captain Robinson to London and Capt. Troy to Dublin;[3] contained the first and second Copies of a Bill of Exchange for £100. Sterling, which I hope are come safe to hand, and paid long before this Reaches; but in Case of both Copies miscarrying have sent you the third.

Inclosed you have also the first Copy of another Bill of Exchange for £100. Sterling more (which makes the Seventh Hundred remitted you since you left Philadelphia) which you will please to advise me; when it comes to hand. Yours D H

By the Packet, Capt. Morris Via New-York[4]

To Benjamin Franklin Esqr.

2d Copy via Belfast Capt. Nichols[5]

---

last at all advisable, as we could not but believe some undue advantage might be taken, by the House of such a liberty. We have therefore made our Licence to the Governor absolute, but as Mr. Franklin informs us the Members are not satisfied with the method of valuing Estates, and some others had been proposed, one of which might probably be agreed to in the next Bill, we thought it proper to signify to you and desire you will to the Members of Council or such of them as you shall think proper privately, that if a more just and equal assessment shall be fixed upon or any alteration, more constitutional, in favour of Government or conformable to our Instructions, is proposed, that you will advise the Governor to pass the Bill which we shall certainly approve of, provided such an exception, as before mentioned of our Estate is incerted. If the Governor should be unwilling to deviate from our Letter, you will shew this to him, otherwise it is not necessary.

"We do not agree to this exception with any desire to make an undue advantage of it or to contribute less to the necessary Defence of our Country in time of War, in proportion to our Incomes than other People in it; but if it shall appear after we shall have agreed to a just method of Taxation, and the other Points in difference with the House, on an examination of this Affair, that what we have contributed is not as much in proportion to our Income as what has been given by the People in general is to theirs, we shall very willingly make up the deficiency, if it is more, no doubt it will be returned to us, this you may occasionally say for us." Yale Univ. Lib.

3. See above, p. 357.

4. Morris' packet, *Earl of Leicester,* left N.Y., Feb. 18, 1758 (*Pa. Gaz.,* Feb. 23, 1758), and reached England late in March.

5. *Pa. Gaz.,* Feb. 16, 1758, recorded clearance of the brig *Gregg,* Capt. William Nickells, for Belfast.

From Thomas and Richard Penn

Letterbook copy: Historical Society of Pennsylvania

Sir February 9th: 1758.

We acknowledge that your proposal, which we assented to, was not the first, or only one, you made; but those others, were such, as we thought very unreasonable for you to expect, or for us to come into, considering the Circumstances in which, the Affair stands, at present.[6]

We have not, on the present, or any former occasion, prohibited, or restrained, just and equitable Measures, for the valuation of Estates, being pursued; Our present Orders are not, in their Nature, restrictive, or prohibitory, but are permissive; You well know that, by our former Orders, we, on our parts, laboured and contended for Justice and Equality, as well, towards the Inhabitants, as ourselves; We are glad to hear from you, that the Assembly dislike their own former Bills, and are disposed to come into just measures; In doing whereof, they will not meet with opposition, but ready concurrence from Us.[7] We are Your affectionate Friends

T: P:
R: P:

Benjn: Franklin Esqr.

Endorsed: I delivered, this Day, a Letter to Mr. Franklin, of which the above is a Copy. J Aiskell.[8]

6. See above, pp. 366, 370, for earlier letters from the Penns on this controversy. BF may have answered their letter of February 2, in a communication not found, asking again for consideration of the "other Matters" he had mentioned on January 31. Apparently the Proprietors thought that on January 27 he had agreed on behalf of the Assembly to a renewal of the supply act of the previous year without change (see above, pp. 145–52) but was now making further demands. Lack of minutes or of BF's own letters makes it impossible to tell whether the Proprietors misconstrued his meaning or whether there had in fact been such an agreement. In either case, by January 31 BF had decided either to explain the misunderstanding to them, or perhaps to seek even better terms than the mere renewal of the 1757 act. If he had received Isaac Norris' letter of Nov. 24, 1757 (see above, p. 282), he may also have decided that Governor Denny could be brought to concede more than his instructions permitted. BF appears to have wanted new proprietary instructions permitting some changes in the method of assessing estates.

7. See above, p. 370 n, for the Proprietors' secret direction to Peters to

To Joseph Galloway

ALS: Yale University Library

Dear Sir, London, Feb. 17. 1758

I received your Favour of December 5th. by Mr. Hunt;[9] but the Papers refer'd to are not yet come to hand, being in his Chest that is still at Bristol.

The Affair of obtaining a Permission to export Grain, &c. from the Colonies to the European neutral Ports, meets with Difficulty while the Parliament have the Regulating the Corn Market in England under Consideration.[1] But if this Vessel does not leave

---

facilitate a change in the method of assessing estates. On February 10 Thomas Penn commented to Peters: "what has passed between us and Mr. Franklin you will see by the Copys of Letters enclosed. Since the last we have not heard from him, but as he was not content with what he agreed we should at first do, wanting to gain his great point, I expect he has not done writing yet. It is some satisfaction to see that this just and equitable Tax is now allowed not just and equitable, and that when we agree to their Measures, they quarrel with their own proceedings." Penn Papers, Hist. Soc. Pa. Penn's resolve to reject Assembly protests against his instructions to the governors had doubtless been strengthened by the solicitor general's favorable opinion of them given on Jan. 13, 1758: "I am of Opinion that most of the Restrictions, layd upon the Governor, by the Instructions of the Proprietarys, are expedient, and even necessary for the Good of the Colony, and the Mother Country; and *all of them* are just, lawful, and agreeable to the Spirit of the Charter, granted by the Crown." MS copy, Penn Papers, Hist. Soc. Pa.

8. Not identified.

9. Galloway's letter has not been found. John Hunt (1712–1778), was a London Quaker merchant who had been in Pennsylvania advising the Friends and was now returning to lay Quaker proposals on Indian affairs before British ministers. Amelia M. Gummere, ed., *The Journal and Essays of John Woolman* (N.Y., 1922), p. 512.

1. The Board of Trade had ordered, Oct. 9, 1756, that provisions from the North American colonies be sent to other British possessions only. Directed principally against exports to Dutch islands in the West Indies which were immediately reshipped to French possessions, the embargo was a great blow to Philadelphia merchants and stimulated a lively illegal trade in the city. They particularly wanted to re-open trade with Portugal and the Wine Islands, which, they asserted, would furnish a market for at least one-third of Pennsylvania's surplus, and would in no way benefit France. *Pa. Col. Recs.*, VII, 386–7; Victor L. Johnson, "Fair Traders and Smugglers in Philadelphia, 1754–1763," *PMHB,* LXXXIII (1959), 141–5. Galloway wrote approvingly, June 15, 1758, of BF's attention to this matter, which, however, was not adjusted as the Philadelphia merchants wished.

Portsmouth before the End of this Month, I hope to write you something more certain on that head.[2]

My Patience with the Proprietors is almost tho' not quite spent. They continue to profess a sincere Desire of settling everything with the Assembly amicably on reasonable Terms, but that they may act safely they would have the Attorney and Solicitor General's Opinion on some Points that relate to the Prerogative of the Crown; this Opinion they say they press for with all Earnestness, but have not yet been able to obtain; and the principal Men among your Friends here, who have Influence at Court, and whose Assistance I am advis'd to secure, will have me to believe the Proprietors are sincere, and that the Difficulties alledged by them of obtaining that Opinion are real and not affected; so I am oblig'd to wait from time to time, or take upon myself the Blame of Rashness, if I should come to open War with People suppos'd to be so well-disposed, who, it will be said, might have been brought to very reasonable Terms by an Agent of more Temper. I think, however, that Matters will not continue in this Situation much longer.[3] The Publication of the Defence of the Province, mention'd in mine of Sept. 2.[4] will probably be one of the first Acts of Hostility on our Side, as being necessary to prepare the Minds of the Publick; in which the Proprietors will be gibbeted up as they deserve, to rot and stink in the Nostrils of Posterity.

As the extraordinary Lower County Speech and Address has been published here, where never appeared before any Proceedings of that Government, it is plainly done by the Proprietary Tools to continue the Prejudices against the Province. Billy will therefore get the Remarks on it, now come to hand, printed also, and in the same Paper.[5]

2. BF's letter was probably carried by one of the ships that left Spithead under convoy on March 11 and reached Philadelphia in mid-May. *Pa. Gaz.*, May 18, 1758.

3. See the preceding document for BF's latest negotiations with the Proprietors.

4. BF probably meant December 2, not September, which seems too early a date for plans about Richard Jackson's *An Historical Review of the Constitution and Government of Pennsylvania*, finally published under BF's guidance in June 1759.

5. See above, p. 282, for the Delaware address and the reply to it. The reply apparently was not printed in *London Chron.*

A great Force is now going to America, where, it is said, very vigorous Measures are to be pursu'd this ensuing Campaign. If it should prove such another as the last, the Nation would be quite dispirited. It knows and feels itself so universally corrupt and rotten from Head to Foot, that is has little Confidence in any publick Men or publick Measures; and the Want of that Confidence turns, thro' Disunion, all their Strength into Weakness. Mr. Pitt's Abilities, and hitherto steady and disinterested Conduct, indeed seems at present their principal Foundation of Hope. They have reason therefore to pray for some Success this Year to strengthen his Hands and his Interests, as well as for his Life or Health; for if he should fall through, it is thought by many that his Place could scarcely be supplied, and that everything would go into Confusion. His universal Character of Integrity is what gave him his present Power, rather than the Favour of the King which he had not, or Party Interest which was little more than popular Esteem and Opinion. Men of Abilities were in the Ministry before, but one of that kind seem'd to be wanting for a Center of Union, who was, or at least was generally believ'd to be, an HONEST MAN. Measures proposed by a Man of Abilities without Honesty, are always suspected, and he becomes weak thro' the Diffidence of those that should concur with and help him; but the Man of moderate Talents who is believ'd to mean well, and to act uprightly for the common Good, has everyone's ready Assistance, and thereby is able to do more than the other of superior Parts: But when Ability and Integrity meet in the same Person, his Power of doing Good must be greater, as he can himself plan right Measures, will receive all necessary Advice, can distinguish what is good, and can have all the necessary Assistance in the Execution. It is thought, however, by some, that Mr. Pitt fail'd of the last Particular at Rochfort;[6] for that Envy, and an Apprehension lest Success in that Attempt might establish his Power, influenc'd the Inaction now so much complain'd of. But as he seems more

6. Pitt organized an amphibious expedition against Rochefort near the mouth of the Charente River, Bay of Biscay, for the summer of 1757. Owing to the contractors' mismanagement the ships did not reach their destination until nearly the end of September and after one minor success the expedition withdrew, largely on the score of the lateness of the season. Gipson, *British Empire*, VII, 122–3.

confirm'd in his Station, it is hop'd the Commanders for the ensuing Year, will be more solicitous of recommending themselves to his Favour.[7] They cannot indeed wish for a finer Opportunity of recommending themselves to the publick Favour, and gaining infinite Applause; for a long Series of ill Success has created such an Appetite for good News, that a small Victory obtain'd would be magnify'd to a great one, and the Man who procures us a Bonfire and a Holiday, would be almost ador'd as a Hero.

The Indian Treaty under the Great Seal,[8] Mr. Hunt thinks is also in his Chest; it is not, however, yet come to hand. But Mr. Thomson's Piece on the Causes of the Indians Uneasiness he has just receiv'd, and I am to have a Sight of it.[9] Their Complaints are

7. William Strahan wrote of a different reason for Americans to applaud Pitt: "The defence of our Colonies in America is so much at heart with Mr. Pitt, that those who are not sufficiently sensible of their Importance say he is America mad." To David Hall, Feb. 22, 1758, APS; printed with slight alteration in *Pa. Gaz.*, June 15, 1758.

8. Of July–August 1757; see above, p. 264 n.

9. Though this suggests John Hunt cooperated with BF, in fact his activities undercut BF's agency. Hunt and his companion, Christopher Wilson, left Philadelphia carrying Charles Thomson's *An Enquiry into the Causes of the Alienation of the Delaware and Shawanese Indians*, and under admonitions reflected in Israel Pemberton's comment to Dr. John Fothergill, Jan. 6, 1758: "I desire B Franklin may soon see [*An Enquiry*... and supporting documents], but hope neither he nor his Son will make any Public use of them: but what thou and R. Partridge and J. Hunt" and other Friends approve. Hunt and Wilson reached London on January 21, and on the 26th conferred amicably with the Penns for three hours. They told the Proprietors that Richard Peters and others had sent misleading reports about leading Pennsylvania Quakers, who in fact were friends of the Penn family and interests. The Penns promptly agreed to seek an accord with the Quakers on Indian policy. Two days later Hunt and Wilson talked to Lord Granville who was also receptive to their proposals to settle disputes with the Indians. Hunt and Dr. Fothergill drew a plan for regulating the Indian trade according to Quaker views, which they gave to Granville who in turn agreed to show it to the King. Only Pitt's serious illness prevented Granville from bringing the emissaries and their plan before him immediately. On February 18, Hunt and another Quaker, Richard How, talked again with Granville. Dr. Fothergill was "the principal person on whom [Hunt] depend[ed] for Assistance." Hunt sent his only copy of Thomson's *Enquiry* to Granville on February 20, and talked to him about it on the 25th, "after which we intend to send [the *Enquiry*] to B. Franklin," who, Hunt assured Pemberton, would not be allowed to make any public use of it without Quaker consent. BF apparently had not yet seen the *Enquiry* on May

now in the Hands of the Ministry,[1] but when they will have Leisure to consider them, God only knows. For tho' Securing the Affections of the Indians, by doing them Justice, be a Matter of great Consequence, they have other Affairs at present on their Hands that seem to them of more immediate Importance.[2]

Billy writes, and will send you some Pamphlets. I am, my dear Friend, with great Esteem, Yours affectionately B FRANKLIN

Jos. Galloway Esqr.

Endorsed: Benja. Franklin's Letter Feby. 17. 1758.

To John Waring

ALS: American Philosophical Society

Reverend Sir Craven Street, Feb. 17. 1758

I beg Pardon for not answering sooner your Favour of the 16th past.[3] I unluckily mislaid it just after it came to hand, and was in daily Expectation of finding it. It is now before me; and I am of Opinion that for £30 a Year, Sterling, a good Master might be

26, 1758, when Hunt wrote James Pemberton that it was "in the hands of some of our great Men who appear to be much pleas'd with it." At the same time London Quakers depreciated BF's activity: Thomas Crosby wrote James Pemberton on Feb. 10, 1758, that BF "has [not] done much as yet." All the above letters in the Pemberton Papers, Hist. Soc. Pa. These comments, set beside Hunt's failure to consult BF about his conferences with the Penns and Granville, make it apparent that the Quakers hoped to persuade British ministers *on their own* of the correctness of their Indian policy. They deliberately kept BF in the dark about their plans lest he somehow receive credit the Quakers very clearly wanted reserved for themselves as a religious society. See above, p. 173, for earlier Quaker coolness toward BF's agency.

1. Complaints about Indian affairs in Pennsylvania had been before the Board of Trade for over a year. Records of the Easton Treaty of 1757, laid before it on Dec. 16, 1757, contained complaints by the Indians of unfair treatment by proprietary agents. *Journal of the Commissioners for Trade and Plantations, 1754–1758* (London, 1933), pp. 277–8, 346, 353, 357. BF, however, did not present a formal petition on behalf of Teedyuscung until Feb. 2, 1759.

2. The Quakers reported, on the other hand, that the attention of the ministers was fixed on Indian affairs. Christopher Wilson to Rachel Pemberton, Feb. 7, 1758; Pemberton Papers, Hist. Soc. Pa.

3. Not found; see above, p. 356, for BF's letter to which Waring's was a reply, and for references to earlier letters about the Bray's Associates' plan for Negro schools in America.

procur'd that would teach 40 Negro Children to read; I think he could scarce do his Duty to a greater Number without an Assistant. But as the School may not probably be so large for some time, and if they were taught some useful Thing besides Reading it might be an Encouragement to Masters and Mistresses to send them. I think a Mistress might be best to begin with, who could teach both Boys and Girls to read, and the Girls to knit, sew and mark; a good One might be had, I believe, for about £20 Sterling, that would well instruct in this Way about 30 Scholars. And when the School becomes so numerous as to make a Division necessary, then a Master may be procured for the Boys, and the Mistress retained for the Girls; the whole Charge not exceeding £50 Sterling per Annum for 60 or 70 Children.

This whole Charge, however, it is not necessary that the Associates should pay. If they set the School on foot and engage for the Salaries, it will be sufficient. Most of the Owners of Negro Children are able to pay for their Schooling, and will be willing if they like the Design, see it well manag'd, and find it useful. The Persons you intrust as Visitors of the School (suppose the Minister, with the Assistance of the Church Wardens and Vestry) may appoint the School-master or Mistress, agree with and pay them, receive what can be obtain'd for the Schooling, and draw on the Associates only for the Deficiency. The Accounts should be fairly stated and laid before you from time to time, perhaps quarterly: A Year or two's Trial will show you what is to be expected from this Undertaking, and I hope it may, at a small Expence, afford you much Satisfaction.

I find by the enclosed, which I lately receiv'd from Philadelphia, that your Letter to me, concerning Mr. Wheatly's Will, being receiv'd in my Absence, was communicated by my Wife to James and Mary Hunter.[4] I do not think it prudent to deliver the Money to the Parents for the Use of the Children, having no Opinion of their Management; but shall apply Part of it to the Binding the Boys Apprentices to Trades, and the Remainder, with the Interest in the mean time arising, towards purchasing Tools and Stock when they come to act for themselves. I believe the eldest Boy may be now fit to go Apprentice, and shall by the next Ship write

4. See above, p. 99, for Wheatley's legacy to the Hunter children. The enclosure, perhaps an extract from a missing letter of DF's, has not been found.

to a discreet Friend to get him a good Place, and take some Care of the other's Schooling. With great Respect, I am, Revd. Sir, Your most obedient and most humble Servant B FRANKLIN

P.S. Whenever it is convenient to you, the Legacy may be paid into the Hands of my Banker, Mr. Henton Brown in Lombard Street,[5] and I will give you the proper Discharge.

Addressed: To / The Reverend Mr J. Waring / in Woodstreet / Spital Fields

To Deborah Franklin

AL (incomplete): American Philosophical Society[6]

My dear Child, London, Feb. 19. 1758.

I have wrote you several long Letters lately; the last was by Mr. Relphe,[7] and at the same time I wrote to my dear Sally.

Last Night I receiv'd yours of the 1st and 6th of January, which gave me the great Pleasure of hearing that you and my little Family were well. I hope you continue so, and that I shall have

5. Henton Brown (*c.* 1698–1775), London banker and zealous Quaker, handled many of BF's financial affairs during his years in London. *London Chron.*, Sept. 26, 1775; *PMHB*, LV (1931), 100–32.

6. This letter is a good illustration of some of Jared Sparks's editorial practices. He printed it from this MS in 1838 in *Works*, VII, 163–7, but with numerous unnoted excisions and "corrections." He omitted, for example, the whole of the seventh paragraph which begins "Peter behaves very well," possibly because he deplored the reference to BF's Negro slave, almost certainly, too, because the description of BF's sleeping garments offended his sense of delicacy. At the end of the tenth paragraph mention of Goody Smith's "fat Knees" was likewise too much for Sparks's sensibilities; he allowed her to make a pair of garters for BF but none for herself. In the middle of the next paragraph he changed "There is also 56 Yards of Cotton" to "There are also," etc., and made similar revisions elsewhere. The beer jug that reminded BF of his "fat jolly Dame" had the coffee cups "in it," not "in its Belly," and the descriptions of the contents of case no. 2 and of BF's intended purchase of table china and silverware are entirely omitted. Did the editor think Poor Richard had become too extravagant? The original MS still shows Sparks's penciled deletions and emendations throughout. Bigelow (*Works*, III, 5–9) copied from Sparks, but Smyth (*Writings*, III, 430–5) followed the MS faithfully.

7. John Relfe; see above, p. 276 n.

the Happiness to find you so. The Letter you mention to have sent me per Capt. Robinson is not come to hand; but that per Mr. Hunt I received and answered.[8]

I regret the Loss of my Friend Parsons.[9] Death begins to make Breaches in the little Junto of old Friends that he had long forborne, and it must be expected he will now soon pick us all off one after another.

Your kind Advice about getting a Chariot, I had taken some time before;[1] for I found that every time I walk'd out, I got fresh Cold; and the Hackney Coaches at this End of the Town, where most People keep their own, are the worst in the whole City, miserable dirty broken shabby Things, unfit to go into when dress'd clean, and such as one would be asham'd to get out of at any Gentleman's Door.

As to burning Wood, it would answer no End, unless one could furnish all one's Neighbours and the whole City with the same. The whole Town is one great smoaky House, and every Street a Chimney, the Air full of floating Sea Coal Soot, and you never get a sweet Breath of what is pure, without riding some Miles for it into the Country.

I am sorry to hear that a storm has damag'd a House of my good Friend's Mr. Bartram's.[2] Acquaint him that I have receiv'd the Seeds, and shall write to him shortly. I hope the Speaker is recovered of the Illness you mention.[3]

Peter[4] behaves very well to me in general, and begins to know the Town so as to go anywhere of Errands. My Shirts are always well air'd as you directed. Mrs. Stevenson takes Care of that. I am much more tender than I us'd to be, and sleep in a short Callico Bedgown with close Sleeves, and Flannel close-footed Trowsers;

8. None of DF's letters have been found; see above, p. 000 n, for Robinson's clearance from Philadelphia, and p. 000 n, for John Hunt. William Strahan reported to David Hall, Feb. 22, 1758, that he had received a letter of Jan. 6, 1758, via Capt. Robinson by that date. APS.

9. William Parsons had died on Dec. 17, 1757.

1. BF had hired a private coach for which he recorded payments of £12 12*s.* per month to one T. Bowman, beginning on Dec. 23, 1757. "Account of Expences," p. 12; *PMHB,* LV (1931), 107, 109.

2. John Bartram.

3. See below, p. 386, for Isaac Norris' illness.

4. BF's Negro servant; see above, p. 203.

for without them I get no Warmth all Night, so it seems I grow older apace. But otherwise at present I am pretty well.

Give my Thanks to Dr. Bond for the Care he takes of you. I have wrote to him by this Vessel.[5]

Mr. Hunter and Polly talk of returning this Spring.[6] He is wonderfully recruited. They both desire to be remembred to you. She receiv'd your Letter and answer'd it. Her Answer I enclos'd in one of mine to you. Her Daughter Rachel, who plays on the Harpsichord and sings prettily, sends Sally one of her Songs, that I fancy'd.

I send you by Capt. Budden, a large Case mark'd D.F. No. 1. and a small Box DF No. 2. In the large Case is another small Box, containing some English China; viz. Melons and Leaves for a Desert of Fruit and Cream, or the like; a Bowl remarkable for the Neatness of the Figures, made at Bow, near this City;[7] some Coffee Cups of the same; a Worcester Bowl, ordinary. To show the Difference of Workmanship there is something from all the China Works in England; and one old true China Bason mended, of an odd Colour. The same Box contains 4 Silver Salt Ladles, newest, but ugliest, Fashion; a little Instrument to Core Apples; another to make little Turnips out of great ones; Six coarse diaper Breakfast Cloths; they are to spread on the Tea Table, for no body breakfasts here on the naked Table, but on the Cloth set a large Tea Board with the Cups; there is also a little Basket, a Present from Mrs. Stephenson to Sally, and a Pair of Garters for you which were knit by the young Lady her Daughter, who favour'd me with a Pair of the same kind, the only ones I have been able to

5. No letter to Thomas or Phineas Bond has been found.

6. William Hunter and his sister Mary returned to America in the spring of 1759; none of the letters mentioned in this paragraph has been found.

7. Among BF's possessions exhibited at the Metropolitan Museum of Art, in 1936, was a "Dish, Porcelain. English (Bow), about 1755. Bought in England by Franklin. *Lent by* Franklin Bache." *Benjamin Franklin and His Circle* (N.Y., 1936), p. 140. BF recorded payment of £19 3*s.* 6*d.* on February 16 for "sundry goods sent to Mrs. Franklin with insurance as per Mr. Collinson's account" (probably shipping expenses), and £10 5*s.* on the 25th to Mrs. Stevenson for "goods bought . . . to go to Philadelphia." Further payments to Mrs. Stevenson and to various tradesmen and merchants are doubtless also chargeable to the items described in this and the following paragraph. "Account of Expences," pp. 30, 12; *PMHB,* LV (1931), 108–9.

wear; as they need not be bound tight, the Ridges in them preventing their Slipping. We send them therefore as a Curiosity for the Form, more than for the Value. Goody Smith may, if she pleases, make such for me hereafter, and they will suit her own fat Knees. My Love to her.

In the great Case, besides the little Box, is contain'd some Carpeting for a best Room Floor. There is enough for one large or two small ones; it is to be sow'd together, the Edges being first fell'd down, and Care taken to make the Figures meet exactly: there is Bordering for the same. This was my Fancy. Also two large fine Flanders Bed Ticks, and two pair large superfine Blankets, 2 fine Damask Table Cloths and Napkins, and 43 Ells of Ghentish Sheeting Holland; these you ordered. There is also 56 Yards of Cotton printed curiously from Copper Plates, a new Invention, to make Bed and Window Curtains; and 7 Yards Chair Bottoms printed in the same Way, very neat; these were my Fancy; but Mrs. Stevenson tells me I did wrong not to buy both of the same Colour. Also 7 Yards of printed Cotton, blue Ground, to make you a Gown; I bought it by Candlelight, and lik'd it then, but not so well afterwards: if you do not fancy it, send it as a Present from me to Sister Jenny. There is a better Gown for you of flower'd Tissue, 16 Yards, of Mrs. Stevenson's Fancy, cost 9 Guineas; and I think it a great Beauty; there was no more of the Sort, or you should have had enough for a Negligée or Suit. There is also a Snuffers, Snuff Stand and Extinguisher, of Steel, which I send for the Beauty of the Work; the Extinguisher is for Sperma Ceti Candles only, and is of a new Contrivance to preserve the Snuff upon the Candle. There is also some Musick Billy bought for his Sister, and some Pamphlets for the Speaker and for Susy Wright.[8] A Mahogany and a little Shagrin Box with Microscopes and other Optical Instruments loose, are for Mr. Allison if he likes them; if not, put them in my Room 'till I return. I send the Invoice of them, and wrote to him formerly the Reason of my exceeding his Orders.[9] There are also two Sets of Books a Present

8. BF sent pamphlets, not identified, to both Isaac Norris and the Wright family living on the Susquehanna River; see above, VI, 101 n, 112 n.

9. See above, p. 286, for BF's purchases for the Academy. No letter to Francis Alison (see above, IV, 222–3 n), vice-provost and professor there, has been found.

from me to Sally, *the World* and *the Connoisseur*;[1] my Love to her. I forgot to mention another of my Fancyings, viz. a Pair of Silk Blankets, very fine. They are of a new kind, were just taken in a French Prize, and such were never seen in England before: they are called Blankets; but I think will be very neat to cover a Summer Bed instead of a Quilt or Counterpain. I had no Choice, so you will excuse the Soil on some of the Folds; your Neighbour Forster[2] can get it off. I also forgot, among the China, to mention a large fine Jugg for Beer, to stand in the Cooler. I fell in Love with it at first Sight; for I thought it look'd like a fat jolly Dame, clean and tidy, with a neat blue and white Calico Gown on, good natur'd and lovely, and put me in mind of—Somebody. It has the Coffee Cups in its Belly, pack'd in best Chrystal Salt, of a peculiar nice Flavour, for the Table, not to be powder'd. No. 2 contains cut Table Glass of several Sorts. I am about buying a compleat Set of Table China, 2 Cases of silver handled Knives and Forks, and 2 pair Silver Candlesticks; but these shall keep to use here till my Return, as I am obliged sometimes to entertain polite Company.

I wrote you per former Letters everything relating to Mr. Ralph[3] and other Friends Affairs, which I hope you have received.

I hope Sally applys herself closely to her French and Musick, and that I shall find she has made great Proficiency. The Harpsichord I was about, and which was to have cost me 40 Guineas, Mr. Stanley[4] advises me not to buy, and we are looking out for another, one that has been some time in use, and is a try'd good

1. *The World*, a weekly magazine published from Jan. 4, 1753, to Dec. 30, 1756, London, printed for R. and J. Dodsley, appeared in two folio volumes, 1757; and *The Connoisseur, by Mr. Town, Critic, and Censor-General*, a weekly magazine published from Jan. 31, 1754, to Sept. 30, 1756, London, for R. Baldwin, appeared in two folio volumes in 1756. Lord Chesterfield and Horace Walpole were frequent contributors to *The World* as was William Cowper to *The Connoisseur*, and both magazines, reprinted frequently during the eighteenth century, were of the fashionable, literary variety thought useful to amuse and "improve" young people.

2. Not identified, but perhaps Moses or Thomas Forster, both of whom signed articles of agreement for the Association Library, 1758; *PMHB*, XLII (1918), 201–2.

3. Probably James Ralph; see above, p. 274.

4. John Stanley (1714–1786) was a blind musician, for nearly sixty years one of England's leading organists. *DNB*.

one, there being not so much Dependance on a new One, tho' made by the best Hands.[5] Sally's last Letter to her Brother is the best wrote that of late I have seen of hers. I only wish she was a little more careful of her Spelling. I hope she continues to love going to Church, and would have her read over and over again the whole Duty of Man and the Lady's Library.[6]

Look at the Figures on the China Bowl and Coffee Cups, with your Spectacles on; they will bear Examining.

I have made your Compliments to Mrs. Stevenson. She is indeed very obliging, takes great Care of my Health, and is very diligent when I am any way indispos'd; but yet I have a thousand times wish'd you with me, and my little Sally with her ready Hands and Feet to do, and go, and come, and get what I wanted. There is a great Difference in Sickness between being nurs'd with that tender Attention which proceeds from sincere Love; and [*remainder missing*].

From David Hall   Letterbook copy: American Philosophical Society

Sir. Philadelphia, 20th Febry. 1758

My Letter to you of the Sixth Instant,[7] by the Packet Capt. Morris via New York contained the third Copy of a Bill of Exchange for £100. Sterling and the first Copy of another Bill for £100. Sterling more; that per Capt. Nicholl via Belfast the second Copy of the last mention'd Bill; and now you have the third Copy of the same Bill, in Case of Miscarriage.

To Benjamin Franklin per the London Derry Capt. McDonnell[8]

Copie

5. BF paid £42 for a harpsichord in 1759; probably the same instrument which Francis Hopkinson reported, Dec. 13, 1765, was so complex and hard to play as to be "entirely ruined."

6. *The Ladies Library*, by Mary, Lady Wray, was first published in 1714 with an introduction by Sir Richard Steele; and *The Whole Duty of Man*, of uncertain authorship, first appeared in 1658 as *The Practice of Christian Graces*. Both works were reprinted frequently in the eighteenth century; see above, II, 206, 211, for BF's sale of *The Ladies Library* in 1738.

7. See above, p. 371.

8. *Pa. Gaz.*, Feb. 23, 1758, reported clearance of the ship *Willey*, Capt. John M'Connell, for Londonderry.

From Isaac Norris

Letterbook copy: Historical Society of Pennsylvania

My Good Frd B Franklin Febry. 21 1758

Our old Inviterate Scribler has at length wrote himself into a Jail.[9] How far this was good Policy to do him that Honour, I will not undertake to say; I know the Comittee have wrote largely upon this head,[1] and it has cost the House a Great deal of Time in going Thro' a formal Trial for Libelling, which is, for any thing I know, the first Instance of the kind, as, I think, the House of Commons make very short work with such as give them occasion To exercise their Powers in vindicating their rights and Priveledges Generally or the Rights of Particular members. A short but severe Indisposition renderd it impossable for me to attend the House at the Beginning of this Session and I am Convinced it will not be Prudent in me to resume the Chair, at least 'till the Parson's Accusation and acquital are at an end. The Present Speaker[2] Complains Much To me of the fatigues of his Honorable Seat, but he stands so much fairer in his Charrecter as a Good Churchman (and in some sort a Spiritual Father in the Vestry) than the Scribling

9. William Smith had been taken into custody, Jan. 6, 1758, upon order of the Assembly, for causing a libelous attack on that body by William Moore to be translated and published in the *Philadelphische Zeitung*. Following a "trial" before the House and a defiant speech, he was recommitted on January 25 and remained in jail, conducting his college classes from there, until about April 11, 1758. See above, VI, 246–7 n, for the background of Moore's quarrel with the Assembly, and VI, 420–22 n, 456–7, for Smith's earlier "scribling." The case dominated Pennsylvania politics during 1758, and required BF's attention in London during April 1758 and for over a year following. A lengthy but unreliable account of the case is in William R. Riddell, "Libel on the Assembly: a Prerevolutionary Episode," *PMHB*, LII (1928), 176–92, 249–79, 342–60. Theodore Thayer, *Pennsylvania Politics and the Growth of Democracy, 1740–1776* (Harrisburg, 1953), pp. 68–70; Joseph H. Smith, *Appeals to the Privy Council from the American Plantations* (N.Y., 1950), pp. 646–9; and Albert E. Gegenheimer, *William Smith Educator and Churchman 1727–1803* (Phila., 1943), pp. 139–48, recount the episode from varying points of view. *Votes*, 1757–58, esp. pp. 11–40, and *Pa. Col. Recs.*, VII and VIII, contain voluminous records.

1. No letter at this time from the Pa. Assembly Committee of Correspondence to BF has been found.

2. Thomas Leech, long a pillar of the Anglican Church in Philadelphia, and one of BF's political allies. See above, VI, 456 n.

Priest ever did or ever will, whilst he pursue's his present Schemes, in which he is evidently made a Tool to narrow Presbyterian Politicks,[3] That I Consider it as a favourable interposition of Providence that I was not in the Chair And That the Dispute is carried on by Members of the Same Church, whose Names and Principles are So well known and established.[4] There is a Visible Difference and Disgust between the Governor and his Council, these speak of him with great freedom and Disrespect, whilst he on the Other Side, plainly sees it, and is supposed to be trying To emancipate himself from the Shackles imposed upon him by his Instructions. It is generally Said and believed here that our late Governor makes it a Principle part of his Voyage to supplant this Gentleman, and distroy the Most Essential Parts of our Charters.[5] But as he is yet detained at New York, tis not improbable The first point may be decided before his Arrival in England, and in the other we have all great Confidence in the Justice of our Cause, and the known Abilities to defend it. By the Accounts and Estimates laid before us, the Hundred Thousand Pound is Expended, and the Province between £20 and £30,000 indebted which has necessitated the House to reduce their Provincial Forces To 700 Men for the Ensuing year,[6] for which we are now endeavouring

3. The formal reunion of New Light and Old Light Presbyterians in 1758 strengthened both the personal power of William Allen and that of the proprietary party he supported; Anglicans such as William Smith found the Presbyterians unruly but indispensable allies, while Norris' reference to "Presbyterian Politicks" reflects the increased challenge the reunited denomination presented to the Quaker party. Dietmar Rothermund, *The Layman's Progress, Religious and Political Experience in Colonial Pennsylvania, 1740–1770* (Phila., 1961), pp. 98–108.

4. Proprietary leaders held Quaker trickery, not Providence, responsible for Norris' "illness"—faked in their view to permit an Anglican to preside over Smith's "persecution." Thomas Penn to William Smith, May 26, 1758, Penn Papers, Hist. Soc. Pa.

5. Peters' letters to Penn were full of complaints about Denny; the Proprietors had long since determined to replace his as soon as possible. Former Governor James Hamilton had left N.Y. on Feb. 19, 1758, and returned again as governor of Pennsylvania in November 1759.

6. According to the commissioners' accounts, their funds had been exhausted by Nov. 10, 1757, and payments under the new £100,000 supply act of April 22, 1758, indicate accumulated debts of well over £30,000. The Assembly had resolved the reduction in forces on Feb. 15, 1758. *Votes*, 1757–58, pp. 122, 41; *ibid.*, 1758–59, p. 107.

To raise the Supplies, Tho' the Cry is almost Universal against the Useless Burden Those forces were to the Province all the last year either for want of Proper orders, or some other Neglect in the executive Part of the Government into which an enquiry will probably be tho't necessary, but notwithstanding this load of Debt and the want we have been in for mony, the free gift lies yet unpaid. The Commissioners in their repeated applications to the Governor have requested him to interpose his Good offices with the Reciever-General By which means I am told they have Squeezed out six Hundred Pounds since I last mention'd this Proprietary Free Gift, which seems To be pressed out of their Treasury by peicemeal, and with great reluctance.[7] I will not enter into the Reasons of this Conduct, Our Frontiers having been a Considerable time, in a great degree, quiet we have more leisure To Consider the Internal Interest of the Province, and we have accordingly Sent up a Bill, for Regulating the Indian Trade, a Second time, in which the House have made such Concessions on their Part, as will fully evince their great desire To obtain that Bill on any Terms Consistent with the good purposes it is designd To answer, but I Cannot give much hopes of Success, after Seeing the proposed amendments which Come so intirely from the Council, that some of the most Essential alterations were posted up at the Coffee-house before the Bill was sent down the first Time, but I hope to be able to give a further Account of it, before I am obliged to Close this letter for which end I have orderd the Bill and the Amendments to be copied so far as they have been already proceeded in.[8] We were told in the house a few days ago, by W. A.[9] (a worthy Member) that Lord Loudon had wrote to our Governor Complaining That Some of the People of this Province (as he was inform'd by Sir Wm. Johnson) had without the knowledg or consent of the Government Sent a Messenger to the

7. See above, VI, 480, for earlier efforts to collect the balance of the Proprietors' gift of £5000, pledged in the autumn of 1755.

8. A revised version of the often proposed bill to regulate the Indian trade had passed the House on February 11, was returned by Denny with amendments on the 16th, and, after approving some changes, the House sent it to Denny again on the 18th. *Votes*, 1757–58, pp. 40–2. The various changes proposed by Denny and the Assembly are in *Pa. Col. Recs.*, VIII, 19–25. The bill became law on April 8, 1758.

9. William Allen.

Seneka's; as I apprehended by the Manner in which it was mention'd, by our Said member, that he pointed at the Quakers, out of his great Affection to That People,[1] I made it my Bussiness to enquire of them, whether they had been concern'd in any message of the kind, *which they Utterly deny; so That it may be depended upon, they have no hand in it,* if any such Message has been Sent To those Indians, Tho' I think the Goverment engaged to do somthing of that Sort at their late Conferences at Easton, and which Teedyscung has Since Solicited, and Complain'd of, as not yet Comply'd with, this Armistice (if I may use the Word) with the Indians, seems to discompose a Set of Political Schemes Carried on here, by some of our Men in Power, for which Reason all possible Obstructions were necessary to oppose it at Easton, and the Same Reasons Continue for breaking it, as soon as that can be conveniently accomplished, but in this I think the Governor has no hand, for the Publick Affairs appear to be Transacted by Other Powers, Than Those regularly Constituted by our Charters. I propose to Send an anecdote on This head, if I Can get it Transcribed in time, upon which You may form your Own Judgment.[2]

1. Norris intends sarcasm here; Allen in fact vilified the Quakers: "I am . . . perfectly acquainted with them and their actions. I can assure you, they are *the bitterest enemys* [Thomas Penn] has . . . there *is hardly one in a thousand* . . . but is full of *bitterness*." To F. J. Paris, March 18, 1758; Penn Papers, Hist. Soc. Pa. Loudoun's letter to Denny, Jan. 21, 1758, reporting Johnson's complaint about "Private Societies" (Quakers) interfering in Indian affairs, is in 1 *Pa. Arch.*, III, 338.

2. The "anecdote," probably not sent to BF, was recounted to Robert Charles who Norris knew would pass it on to BF. Norris quoted a portion of a memorandum book he had kept at the Albany Conference, July 6, 1754: "After Delivering our Presents, The Commissioners of Maryland withdrew, and John Penn and Richard Peters, Agents for the Proprietarys Proceeded with the Six Nations in the Purchase of Land, which was Compleated, and the Deed, after much Hissitation on the Part of Some of the Indians, was Signed at Our Lodging; the bounds of This new Purchase are as follows—Consideration A Thousand Pieces of eight, and an Indorsment on the Counterpart for as much More, when demanded at Philadelphia whenever the lands beyond the ALLEGANY HILLS begin to be Settled." Norris then commented: "Now this Second Purchase Mony was never demanded, nor Paid, nor does this Appear at all upon the Proprietarys Deed as it is recorded, So that the Proprietarys offer of releasing the lands beyond the Allegany Hills is only offering to reconvey what I am well assurd was never paid for—and Govr. Morris's Generous offer of Lands There was likewise premature. Tho' Govr.

Febry 22. The Governor has not yet given any Answer to our Indian Trade Bill so that I must send it in the Condition it first came down to the House with the Assembly's Answer, which, tho' the Lines differ a little from the Original Bill will be intelligible enough by the Numbers and Marks in the Margine.[3] I am &c.

P S Upon a Requisition of Lord Loudoun we have just now Resolved to augment our Provincials to a Thousand Men 700 of whom to be ready for his Lordship by the beg[inning] of April.[4]

See my Letter to B.F: of April. 5. 1759 postea pag. 103.

Endorsed on first page: recd by BF see his Letter 10 June 1758.

Morris might be ignorant of this Circumstance, it ill became his Secretary [Richard Peters], if he did not inform him better." Norris to Charles, February 1758; Norris letterbook, Hist. Soc. Pa.

Norris' insinuation to BF about "Obstructions" probably confuses a number of different moves in the complicated Indian negotiations. Clearly Norris thought the Indians expected more money for lands sold at Albany in 1754, and that the proprietary agents intended to cheat them out of it. Furthermore, it is quite probable that the Quakers had sent messages to the Senecas and other western Indians calling for a peace conference in the early spring; Sir William Johnson, Lord Loudoun, and other officials certainly thought so, and Israel Pemberton himself wrote of the importance of bringing the Senecas into the peace plans. On the other hand, a reputed Quaker message to the Iroquois offering to give them guns to kill English soldiers and other non-Pennsylvanians was almost surely part of a plot by some enemies of the Quakers to discredit them. These enemies perhaps included the proprietary agents, as Norris suspected, or George Croghan who had come to despise Quaker manipulation of the Indians at Easton in August 1757, but surely not John Hughes as Croghan himself later charged. In any event, Norris' insinuations show that partisan politics dominated nearly every motive and move in forest diplomacy. *The Papers of Sir William Johnson*, II (Albany, 1922), 769–71, 774–7; IX (Albany, 1939), 824–5, 868–9; Theodore Thayer, *Israel Pemberton King of the Quakers* (Phila., 1943), p. 150; Nicholas B. Wainwright, *George Croghan: Wilderness Diplomat* (Chapel Hill, 1959), p. 139; Julian P. Boyd, ed., *The Susquehannah Company Papers*, II (Wilkes-Barré, 1930), iv-v n.

3. The copy has not been found, but the bill can be reconstructed from the amendments cited in *Votes*, 1757–58, pp. 40–2, and *Pa. Col. Recs.*, VIII, 19–25, and its form as finally passed, in *The Statutes at Large of Pennsylvania* V (Harrisburg, 1898), 320–30.

4. Loudoun's letter to Denny of Feb. 13, 1758, demanding the troops was laid before the Assembly on the 20th and the resolve passed two days later. *Votes*, 1757–58, pp. 42–4.

To David Hall   ALS: Salem County [New Jersey] Historical Society

Dear Mr. Hall   Pensa. Coffee house Feb. 22. 58

I have wrote you a long Letter by this Vessel,[5] and only add this Line to inform you, that I have receiv'd of your Papers but twice since my Arrival here; and when I want to know what they contain am oblig'd to borrow them of Mr. Neate,[6] who has them regularly. The Reason of this I do not know. I am Yours affectionately   B FRANKLIN

Addressed: To / Mr David Hall / Printer / Philadelphia / Per the Myrtilla / Capt. Budden[7]

Endorsed: Mr. Franklin Feb. 22. 1758.

Additional Instruction to the Deputy Postmasters of North America[8]   Printed in *The Pennsylvania Gazette,* April 20, 1758.[9]

General Post-Office, March 10. 1758

Whereas the News-papers of the several Colonies on this Continent, heretofore permitted to be sent by Post free of Charge, are of late Years so much increased as to become extremely burthensome to the Riders, who demand additional Salaries or Allowances from the Post-Office on that Account; and it is not reasonable, that the Office, which receives no Benefit from the Carriage of News-papers, should be at any Expence for such Carriage: And Whereas the Printers of News-papers complain, that they frequently receive Orders for News-papers from distant

5. Not found, but in it BF may have mentioned that he, WF, and William Strahan had attended the premier performance of the play *Agis,* by John Home, on the 21st. Strahan to Hall, Feb. 22, 1758, APS. The play, full of patriotic zeal, produced "not a clap only, but sometimes a shout of applause," from the audience. *Gent. Mag.,* XXVIII (1758), 117–19.

6. William Neate (d. 1775), of the Philadelphia-London firm of Neate & Neave; see above, IV, 115 n; *Gent. Mag.,* XLV (1775), 254.

7. The *Myrtilla,* Capt. Richard Budden, left Spithead under convoy on March 11, and reached Philadelphia before May 18. *Pa. Gaz.,* May 18, 1758.

8. See above, pp. 194–8, for earlier instructions about the post office.

9. Reprinted in *Pa. Gaz.,* July 6, 1758, and in other colonial newspapers; e.g., *Pa. Jour.,* Apr. 27, 1758, *N.-Y. Mercury,* May 1, 1758, and *The Boston News-Letter,* May 11, 1758.

Post-Offices, which they comply with by sending the Papers, tho' they know not the Persons to whom the Papers are to be directed, and have no convenient Means of collecting the Money, so that much of it is lost; and that for Want of due Notice when distant Subscribers die, become Bankrupt, or remove out of the Country, they continue to send Papers some Years directed to such Persons, whereby the Posts are loaded with many Papers to no Purpose, and the Loss so great to the Printers, as that they cannot afford to make any Allowance to the Riders for carrying the Papers: And whereas some of the Riders do, and others may, demand exorbitant Rates of Persons living on the Roads, for carrying and delivering the Papers that do not go into any Office, but are delivered by the Riders themselves:[1]

To remedy these Inconveniencies, and yet not to discourage the Spreading of News-papers, which are on many Occasions useful to Government, and advantageous to Commerce, and to the Publick; You are, after the first Day of June next, to deliver no News-papers at your Office (except the single Papers exchang'd between Printer and Printer) but to such Persons only as do agree to pay you, for the Use of the Rider which brings such Papers, a small additional Consideration *per Annum,* for each Paper, over and above the Price of the Papers; *that is to say,* For any Distance not exceeding Fifty Miles such Paper is carried, the Sum of Nine pence Sterling *per Annum,* or an Equivalent in Currency: For any Distance exceeding Fifty Miles, and not exceeding One Hundred Miles, the Sum of One Shilling and Six pence Sterling *per Annum;* and in the same Proportion for every other Fifty Miles such Paper shall be carried; which Money for the Rider or Riders, together with the Price of the Papers for the Printers, you are to receive and pay respectively, once a Year at least, deducting for your Care and Trouble therein, a Commission of Twenty per Cent. And you are to send no Orders to any Printer for Papers, except the Persons for whom the Papers are to be sent, are in your Opinion responsible, and such as you will be accountable for. And you are to suffer no Riders, employ'd or paid by you, to receive more than the Rates above mentioned, for carrying any Papers by them delivered on their respective Roads; nor to carry and deliver any Papers but

1. See above, p. 238, for complaints about newspaper deliveries by post riders.

such as they will be accountable for to the Printers, in Consideration of an Allowance of the same Commissions as aforesaid for collecting and paying the Money.

And as some of the Papers pass thro' the Hands of several Riders between the Place where they are printed and the Place of Delivery; you are to pay the Carriage-Money you collect for the Riders, to the several Riders who have carried such Papers, in Proportion, as near as conveniently may be, to the Distances they have been carried by each Rider respectively.[2]

FRANKLIN and HUNTER.

From Alexander Gordon[3]

ALS: American Philosophical Society

Sir. Portsmouth 15 March 1758.

Leaving London the 5th. Instant I was taken ill of a Fever on the Road, which has gather'd strength and Confined me to my Bed ever since, so that I am Brought quite low and am at this time scarce able to sit up to write. How dismall Alass is my Situation; in a Strange place, without Money, without Freinds, and in a Sick and very Weak Condition. I know nobody here, the Captain and all the Officers of the Vulture[4] (of which I was some time Clerk) being seperated, some gone one way and some another. But Good God, how bitter is the Reflection that if it should please him of his Mercy that I should recover, a Jail must be my hard Lott, for what less may I, can I expect. The Physician and Apothecary as well as the Landlord, calling on me Repeatedly for

2. Though these new instructions seem to be of fundamental importance for newspaper circulation, nothing has been discovered about their impact except that BF defended them in a letter to David Hall, April 8, 1759.

3. Son of Thomas Gordon (1712?–1772), a Scots merchant of Philadelphia, promoter of St. Peter's Church, signer of the anti-Quaker petition of October 1755, and known to BF as an advertiser in *Pa. Gaz.* Of Alexander, little is known except that he died in Lisbon, probably before his father wrote BF, Feb. 5, 1769, recalling BF's kindness to Alexander and seeking aid for his stepson, Henry Benbridge, the painter. *PMHB,* XL (1916), 191; XLVIII (1924), 54; Ledger "D"; *DAB:* Benbridge; MS copy of petition, N.Y. Pub. Lib.

4. The sloop *Vulture* of the Royal Navy, Capt. Scrafe, had been in New York, April–June 1757, waiting to sail in Lord Loudoun's Louisbourg expedition, and in February 1758 was at Portsmouth. *Pa. Jour.,* April 21 and Aug. 11, 1757; *London Chron.,* Feb. 28–March 1, 1758.

Money, and if I have not wherwith to satisfie their Clamours, that will certainly be my Portion.

Now Sir having no Acquaintance with any Gentlemen in London, and my Father having no Dealings there, I know not who to apply to, to Advance me such a Sum as will Enable me to pay off my Doctor, Apothecary and Landlord, (which I believe will Amount to about £7) except Sir unto you, who was once well Acquainted with my Father Mr. Thomas Gordon of Philadelphia. And now Sir I make it my Earnest Request that you would please to Advance me a small Sum and take my Bill upon my Father (upon whom I never before drew, tho' not for want, of his Liberty) as I know the Circumstance's of the Case Considered he will pay it with the greatest pleasure. Please Sir let me have an Answer by return of Post,[5] and in the Interim, I am, with the greatest Respect Sir Your most Obedient humble Servant

ALEXANDER GORDON

P.S. please direct for me at the Haunch and Vine on Portsmouth Common

I am now Entirely out of Business, had it not been for this Fever should have Sailed with Admiral Brodrick,[6] but please God I recover shall I hope soon get a Birth. A G

From Ezra Stiles

Draft:[7] Yale University Library

Dear Sir Newport 30 Mar 1758

Just before you sailed from New York, you was so kind as to inclose me a Copy of your philosophic Letter to Dr. Lining. I re-

5. BF sent Gordon £10 on March 22, 1758, for which the young man furnished drafts on his father. "Account of Expences," p. 13; *PMHB*, LV (1931), 109.

6. Gordon's fever probably was a blessing in disguise; Rear Admiral Thomas Brodrick's ship, the *Prince George*, burned off Ushant on April 13, 1758, with nearly 800 men on board. Only 250 were saved, including Brodrick, who was rescued "stark naked" after being in the water for an hour. *DNB*. *London Chron.*, May 13, 16, 18, 1758, and *Gent. Mag.*, XXVIII (April, 1758), 228–30, printed dramatic eye-witness accounts of the disaster.

7. This retained draft seems to be in part an outline; the letter actually sent to BF may have been somewhat longer.

turned you Thanks and Reflexions upon it in a Letter July last[8] too long to copy, by the Brig *Prince of Orange* Edward Jackson Captain taken on Passage from hence to London and carried into Bayonne.

It is thot that Air is absolutely necessary to Fire: a Candle is extinguished in an exhausted Receiver &c. The solar Rays or that fluid which by the solar Action is put in Motion and thence becomes *luminous,* is also hot. This Fluid subsists in *Vacuo,* may there be in Motion or accumulated, and I believe would burn in *vacuo*. If a Piece of dry Wood or combustible Matter was fixt under an exhausted Receiver, on which the Focus of a Beam of solar Rays collected by a Lens was injected: should the Wood take Fire, it would shew that the Air is not absolutely necessary. I do not know how the Experiment might suceed—perhaps it has been often made. But the Fire may be excited in some Matter (tho' not in all) without Air, yet I question whether it can be propagated and continued without it. Air may be very necessary to imbibe, receive and carry off the Smoke and dissipable Matter; as fast as by the Action of Fire it is separated—for if this be not removed and carried off, it will soon entangle, obstruct the Action of common elementary Fire, which is a different Element from Electricity.

If the Globe (I write unconnected) was stript of Atmosphere nor Smoke, nor Flame, nor Vapor, nor Vegetables would ascend. May not the constant Ascent of the subtle Tails of Comets in Opposition from the Sun, imply an universal etherial Fluid surrounding the Sun like an Atmosphere to beyond the planetary Regions, even beyond the longest Tract of the Comets of our System? or is the universal Expanse of material Creation permeated by it? Yet as each Planet may be presumed furnished with its Atmosphere for Exhalation and Circulation of Vapor, animal Respiration &c: Analogy would lead us to think the same of every Sun or Center of each System.

A Morning without Dew, and the Pot's boiling dry, are said to prognosticate Rain; and perhaps both may confirm Mr. new Theory of Dew, that it is a nocturnal Exsudation of the whole

8. See above, pp. 184–90, for BF's letter to Lining, and pp. 239–43, for Stiles's letter to BF. Both letters deal with the nature and effects of heat, as do Stiles's next three paragraphs here.

Globe thro' Vegetables &c.[9] Perhaps if we had the curious Glass mentioned in Hermippus[1] we shou'd see the Earth, at least Vegetables, in a Morning surrounded with a fine Fog, like that said to be visible by it around human and all animal Bodies from Perspiration. It may be objected to this nocturnal Perspiration of the Earth, that Mornings are clear, Morning Air is clear, not impregnated with Fog or any gross Vapor. To this—Perhaps tho' it may rise to considerable Height in warm Evenings; yet the Chill induced by Morning, may condense and confine the Earth, while the superior purified Air receives its Morning Sweetness. When the Air is dry, like a Sponge, it may absorb all the transpiring rising Dew, and leave the Earth, and Vegetables dry: as the Water is plentifully absorbed from a boiling Pot. If the Dew arises from the Earth to no considerable Height—perhaps an Experiment on the Top of St. Pauls or some high Steeple might determine the Question. Near the Earth the upper and under Surfaces of Things, will be wet, unless by Accident, but at a given Distance, objects may remain dry, while Grass &c. is wet.

I feel impatient to see the Acts of the Council AD 304 found last Summer in the Stone Chest dug up at Granada in Spain. Tho' I am no strong Believer in Councils. Would gladly know the Success in delineating, and defining the Alphabet of the Sinai Inscriptions.[2]

Pardon my using the Freedom to cover herewith a Letter to Mr. Samuel Chandler the Author of the History of Persecution and Translation of Limborch's Inquistion.[3] Let me beg the Favour

9. This theory appeared in an article dated Sept. 26, 1757, and signed "A.B." in *Gent. Mag.*, XXVII (1757), 450–2.

1. A German physician, Johann Heinrich Cohausen, printed an ingenious parody in Latin, *Hermippus Redivivus* (Frankfurt, 1742), which told of a microscope that made a variety of minute particles visible to the eye. John Campbell translated it into English in 1743, with the subtitle "The Sage's Triumph over Old Age and the Grave." In a Dublin edition of 1760, the microscope is described on pp. 55–7.

2. Stiles's interest in the Granada excavations and the Sinai inscriptions probably arose from *Gent. Mag.* notices; the excavations were reported in July 1757 (XXVII, 300); in 1753 (XXIII, 203), an account of Robert Clayton's translation of *A Journal from Grand Cairo to Mount Sinai,* had told of a £500 reward for further exploration of the ancient Hebrew inscriptions said to be there.

3. Rev. Samuel Chandler of London (1693–1766; see above, V, 204), author

you'll be kind eno' to deliver it. Should you happen in Acquaintance with any young Minister of the Independents of a generous and liberal Turn, forgive my Vanity in asking you to do me the Kindness to introduce me to his Correspondence. Mr. Chauncy Whittelsey Mar. 1, was ordained Colleague with Mr. Noyes, &c.[4]

I find the Lunar Eclipse 30th. July 1757 was observd at London, the End 31 D. I h. 5′ 42″ app. Time. It ended here by my Watch set by a Meridian the preceeding Noon 30 D. VIII h. 23′. Whence Difference of Meridian 4 h. 42¾′; which is 8 or 10 Minutes less than we used to allow. Lunar Eclipse 23d January last, Beginning observed about XI. 25′ P.M. I have compared several Obs[ervations] of the same Eclipses at London and here, and find they give different Numbers. Perhaps this is to be attributd to the inaccurate Measures of Time, and Want of Niceness in Observation. I reckon if we could ascertain the Longitude of Places to a Minute or so of Time, it would sufficiently answer the common uses of Geography and Navigation.[5]

I find an Account of the magnetism of erect Iron Rods I mean upper Ends, I formerly wrote you, mentioned in the philos.

---

of *History of Persecution* (London, 1736) and translator (London, 1731) of Philipp van Limborch's *Historia Inquisitionis*, published in 1692.

4. Whittelsey (above, IV, 213 n) had been chosen co-minister of the First Church of New Haven, joining another friend of Stiles and BF, Rev. Joseph Noyes (above, III, 108 n), thus making the First Church an even firmer Old Light stronghold, a welcome circumstance to Stiles. Edmund S. Morgan, *The Gentle Puritan: A Life of Ezra Stiles, 1727–1795* (New Haven, 1962), p. 198; Franklin B. Dexter, ed., *Extracts from the Itineraries and Other Miscellanies of Ezra Stiles . . .* (New Haven, 1916), pp. 571–3. Stiles's letter sent to BF doubtless recounted the ordination at some length.

5. Stiles could have read about the eclipses of June 30, 1757 and Jan. 23, 1758 in *Gent. Mag.*, XXVII (1757), 352, and XXVIII (1758), 17. He was attempting to calculate the longitude of Newport by measuring the difference between the time of an observation of a celestial event (in this case the end of a lunar eclipse) in London and its observation at Newport, on clocks both set to Greenwich time. His difference, four hours, 42¾ minutes, converts to approximately 70°41′; ten minutes of time more than that would be 73°11′. The actual longitude of Newport is approximately 71°20′; thus Stiles's new calculation was considerably more accurate than that formerly accepted. See above, pp. 208–10, on the determination of shipboard longitude in the eighteenth century.

Transactions.[6] I think the Comet of September last past unobserved in New England, its Course being direct and from a Northern Lat. to the Ecliptic, shew it not that of 1682.[7] I am told there are antient Inscriptions engraved on Stone 150 or 200 Miles up Isequibe River, or away back from Surinam. An Acquaintance of mine here told me he was informed of them by one, who said he had seen them. Whether this is like Dr. Cotton Mather's Inscription at Taunton?[8] or any Thing more of Reality? With great Esteem and Respect, I am, Dear Sir, Your Obliged Friend And Obedient Servant EZRA STILES

To Benja. Franklin Esqr. Birchin Lane[9] London.

This, with a Letter to Mr. Saml. Chandler London, sent by Capt. Galatly, who saild in the   from this Port for London Apr 1758

Capt. Gallatly was taken by the French.[1]

6. Stiles's letter is lost, but see above, VI, 103, 177–8, for his interest in magnetism, several accounts of which had appeared in *Phil. Trans.* during the 1740s.

7. The comet of September–October 1757, described in *Gent. Mag.*, XXVII (1757), 392–3, 479, and in *Phil. Trans.*, LI (1757), 408–15, was not a reappearance of Halley's comet of 1682, which did not pass through its perihelion until March 1759, though predicted for 1757.

8. Stiles maintained a life-long interest in mysterious inscriptions on stones, especially those that might be evidence of pre-Columbian discoveries of America. He may have inquired of his friend Capt. Simon Newton of Newport about the South American inscriptions. Those in Taunton, Mass. (the Dighton Rock) still puzzle scholars. Cotton Mather had written of them to the Royal Society in 1712. Morgan, *Stiles*, pp. 132, 137–8, 436–7; *Phil. Trans.*, XXIX (1714–16), 70–1.

9. At the Pennsylvania Coffee House, BF's address for many of his American correspondents.

1. *Gent. Mag.*, XXVIII (October, 1758), 503, records that "The Diligence, Gately, from Rhode-Island for London, is taken" by a French privateer.

Index

Compiled by Helene H. Fineman